Favored Flowers

FAVORED FLOWERS
Culture and Economy in a Global System

Catherine Ziegler

DUKE UNIVERSITY PRESS

DURHAM & LONDON 2007

© 2007 Duke University Press
All rights reserved
Printed in the United States of America on acid-free paper ∞
Designed by Jennifer Hill
Typeset in Adobe Garamond Pro by Keystone Typesetting, Inc.
Library of Congress Cataloging-in-Publication Data
appear on the last printed page of this book.

Contents

Acknowledgments

I am indebted to many people for their help and support with the research and writing of this book. Deborah Poole convinced me in difficult times that I could complete the project. Her early critical readings sharpened my analysis and invigorated my perception. At the New School for Social Research, William Milberg stepped in with ideas, encouragement, and support at key moments. At the City University of New York Michael Blim, Jane Schneider, and Marc Edelman were unfailingly generous with their time, ideas, and encouragement. Thanks also to Nancy Foner, who supported my anthropological research and writing from the beginning. I owe huge thanks to Richard Wells, Liz Fitting, and Erin Koch for their help with my early drafts, and to two anonymous reviewers for comments on a later one.

Within the flower industry I have many more debts. Gary Page has helped me repeatedly. He and Jaap Kras opened many doors in distant places. My thanks go also to Jaap and Cindy Long for their illuminating conversations. Henri van der Borg, John Ackell, and Mike Thomas have been tirelessly patient with my questions, year after year. Paul Daum has my eternal thanks for permitting me access to his archive of flower industry documents, which enabled me to include critical pieces of information and ideas in this study. I would also like to thank Paul Poelstra, Simon Zwarts, and Remko v. d. Marel in the Netherlands for giving me time out of their very busy lives. I am grateful for everything I learned from Ramiro Penaherrera, Miguel Mascaro, and Hanspeter Hug in Ecuador. My thanks also go to the many flower buyers, flower sellers, flower growers, and flower traders who contributed so much to this project and who are not named in this book.

I owe much to my husband Bill Ziegler and my daughters, Nancy and Susan, for their help with the manuscript, for keeping everything going during my absences, and for their unflagging support. Finally, it is thanks to William Roseberry's enthusiasm and encouragement that I started this project years ago. His memory inspired its completion.

Introduction

Imagine two hundred million roses—mostly red—blooming simultaneously. Every year flower growers around the globe prune, nurture, and tend these flowers to ensure that each one reaches perfection on the same day—February 14. On that day millions of Americans and countless other people around the world collectively express love with gifts of red roses. Thirty years ago far fewer Americans imagined that roses were needed to express their love—this luxury was not yet a necessity.

Last Valentine's Day Peter Webster gave his wife Megan a dozen roses.[1] The roses were a mixture of colors and shapes. Some were bright red with folded-back petals, six were a deep maroon with petals tinted pale beige on their underside, and the rest were a dark crimson red. Three of the roses in the arrangement were named 'Charlotte.' Several days earlier these same 'Charlotte' roses grew in Tabacundo in the Ecuadorian Andes under the care of Liliana Ortega. Liliana was responsible for hundreds of rose shrubs including many 'Charlotte' plants. She pruned, cleaned their beds, trimmed and watched them carefully until the buds reached the perfect moment for cutting.

Liliana's supervisor was pressing her to meet her quota of cut blooms. They were all urgently needed for a holiday when roses yielded much higher prices for their growers. Liliana was working overtime cutting roses from all her plants. But she was troubled by the late yield of her 'Charlotte' plants. January had been unusually cold in this part of Ecuador. The plants were sheltered in plastic-covered greenhouses, but their growth was slowed by the chilly weather and some blooms would not develop until after Valentine's Day. Finally she snipped three fat-budded 'Charlotte' roses from adjacent plants. She felt confident they would open soon after reaching their final destination in the United States.

Liliana's three 'Charlotte' roses sat for hours in a conditioning solution that prepared them for a long journey without water. Then a skilled packer carefully bundled them in a paper wrapper with other 'Charlotte' roses and added them to similar bunches in a long cardboard box labeled Far View Farms. After brief chilling, the box of roses made the seventy-kilometer journey to Quito airport where it was loaded onto a plane for Miami. Far View Farms' box of roses was one of sixty thousand arriving in Miami that February 9. Like all the others it passed through an X-ray machine (smugglers hide drugs in flowers occasionally) and health inspection (for unwanted insects) before moving a few blocks from the airport. The 'Charlotte' roses went to Vogler Brothers' refrigerated warehouse for rechilling. John Vogler, a partner in this flower-importing firm, carefully checked the box label against his computer printouts and immediately assigned it to a truck heading for New Jersey and New York.

At mid-day on February 11 the box of 'Charlotte' roses from Far View Farms arrived with many others outside Peacock's wholesale florists in New Jersey, about twenty miles west of Manhattan. Still chilly from their journey in the refrigerated truck, the roses were moved into a cool warehouse. Albert Peacock's efficient warehouse crew unpacked the box. Then they repacked two hundred 'Charlotte' roses, including Liliana's, into a second box with other kinds of roses for delivery to Maple's Florists in lower Manhattan. On the morning of February 12 Benny Maple unpacked Liliana's 'Charlotte' roses. He cut the bottoms of the stems so the roses would drink quickly and placed them in a bucket of hydrating solution before adding them to hundreds of blooms in his cooler.

Benny had always been pleased with Albert Peacock's roses, but they were basic varieties. Earlier that day, at about six o'clock in the morning, he had gone to the Wholesale Flower Market on 28th Street "looking for something special." He selected several bundles of flowers from Holland and France. Then Benny noticed some old-fashioned 'Forever Young' roses from a local Connecticut grower. They were fragrant and very fresh. Benny took one bunch along with another of the newer 'Black Beauty'—a maroon rose with a pale underside to each velvet petal. 'Ambiance' was another appealing rose, yellow with a pink-orange veining suffusing the tips of the petals. Joe, the salesman who had given him reliable advice for years, reminded Benny this popular fragrant variety had a long vase life, so Benny took two bunches.

Benny, his wife Alice, their two designers Jennifer and Paul, their assistant José, and two temporary helpers, Miguel and Felipe, worked all day to remove thorns and excess foliage and trim the stems of thousands of blooms before putting them into fresh buckets of hydrating solutions in the coolers.

Then Alice, Jennifer, and Paul began making arrangements to fill the orders they had already received. Alice also began making arrangements to keep in their glass-fronted display coolers for "walk-ins." She was concerned that the bad weather forecast for Valentine's Day would limit their "walk-in" customers who provided a substantial part of the store's profit from this important holiday. Tired from working fourteen hours for several consecutive days, still Alice was very pleased with the quality of her roses today. She especially liked her 'Ambiance' and her 'Forever Young.' They were opening nicely, as were some of the 'Charlotte' roses. She loved the way 'Forever Young' flattened its darker outer petals before unswirling its center to reveal a delicate fuzz of lemon stamens. Its four-inch blooms exhaled a faint fragrance. They would all be beautiful for some days after Valentine's. After looking them over, Alice made several small arrangements using 'Ambiance.' Others used only 'Charlotte.' Finally she took a small, square clear glass vase and made an arrangement that combined her three remaining 'Charlotte' with six 'Black Beauty,' three 'Forever Young,' and some burgundy alstroemerias. She was pleased with the juxtaposition of the different shades of red and different sizes and shapes of the rose blooms. It was a pricey arrangement at one hundred dollars, but she felt sure someone would want it.

Peter Webster, like many gift buyers on Valentine's Day, left his shopping until late in the day. Rain and sleet discouraged him from leaving his Wall Street office at lunchtime. But on his way home he took a slight detour past Maple's Florists. Some days earlier he had decided that this would be the place to buy Valentine flowers for Megan. He focused on the arrangements in the glass-fronted cooler. He looked at the 'Ambiance' roses for a long time, captivated by their warm blush. But somehow he felt they were not quite right to express the love he felt for his wife of six months. Then Jennifer drew his attention to the arrangement of mixed red roses. Peter sniffed the flowers briefly, catching a light fragrance that he knew would please Megan. Immediately he felt that this arrangement with its complex, subtle differences in tints and forms—some fully open and velvety, others still hesitating to open their buds—would appeal to Megan's romantic nature. It was a little unusual, but not too much. They had known each other for a long time, there had been differences and separations, but now they were married and very happy. Peter felt Megan would understand that these flowers represented the complexity and depth of their relationship and his love for her. It was more than he had intended to pay, but he felt the arrangement was perfect, so he handed over his credit card and took Megan's flowers home.

Introduction

Flowers are one of many gifts Peter might have chosen for Valentine's Day; chocolates and jewelry are also frequently chosen gifts. Consuming—choosing, purchasing, and using things like roses and chocolates—is a complicated cultural and social process. Consuming communicates social information about status, taste, gender, and the nature of relationships and community, among other things. Its communicative quality distinguishes between classes and sectors and helps identify groups with shared values. Furthermore, when consumers select and use certain commodities to satisfy specific cultural needs and desires, they also confirm that these goods have special value in relation to particular cultural understandings—that they offer channels for the circulation and confirmation of meaning. And because certain commodities have cultural significance that is widely shared, people use them deliberately as tools to shape roles, identity, status, and relationships.

Production and distribution are critical to these expressions of meaning since "human needs themselves, evolve and take shape through the kinds of things available" (Slater 1997, 103). Fresh flowers are now available in staggering quantities. Billions of fresh blooms are flown to the United States each year, allowing Americans to choose from an endless array without concern for season. In the depths of the northern winter, millions of summer roses are delivered fresh—so Americans can express their cultural understandings. These roses grow primarily in Colombia, Ecuador, California, and Holland. Other summer flowers, including carnations, lilies, sunflowers, peonies, and hundreds more, also grow far from those who consume them. Some travel from places as distant as New Zealand, Chile, and South Africa. All these flowers are grown, delivered, offered, and acquired through markets and other processes that make consumption both an economic and cultural activity.[2]

This study describes the changing fresh-cut flower trade. I follow flower production, distribution, and final consumption in the New York Metropolitan Area (NYMA). I begin with the history of flower provisioning and consumption in the region since 1870 and then focus on the last three decades of the twentieth century to explain why suddenly so many flowers are desired, traded, and consumed.[3] It is a story populated by energetic and assertive individuals, including plant hunters, impassioned collectors and cultivators, Gilded Age hostesses, migrating growers, and globe-trotting wholesalers.

Global Commodity Chains

Global commodity chain theory provides the framework for this investigation. Current interest in global chains of production and distribution developed from concern with the history of world trading (Wallerstein 1974; Braudel 1984; Wolf 1990) and the relationship between processes that occurred in *peripheral,* usually developing regions and processes that occurred in *core,* usually industrialized regions. These relationships frequently involved exchanges that tended to favor "those involved in core-like production processes" (Wallerstein 2004, 17), or in other words, industrialized regions benefited more than developing regions. Subsequent research into global systems of trade and provision employed terms with slight differences of emphasis. These included "systems of provision" (Fine and Leopold 1993; Fine 2002), "global commodity chains" (Gereffi and Korzeniewicz 1994), and "filières" and "global value chains" (Gereffi, Humphrey et al. 2001; Sturgeon 2001).

The commodity chain framework offers three analytic advantages that are critical to this study. First, it permits nuanced analysis of the organization of global and international systems of production and distribution. Second, commodity chain analysis explores the nature of power and governance within the chain—specifically which firms, institutions, or other entities coordinate and integrate the functioning of the chain and determine who participates in it. It also incorporates the notion that firms are networked into dependent relationships nationally and internationally and acknowledges the importance of cooperation, organization, management, and competition. Finally, the commodity chain approach allows exploration of the social fields within which interconnected individual producers, traders, and consumers operate, innovate, and adjust their behavior (González 1998; Stanford 2000a).

Gereffi clarified the organization and governance of commodity chains associated with large-scale manufacturing systems when he divided them into two types: producer-driven or buyer-driven (1994b).[4] However, this conception also contributed to a bipolar framework. Chains driven by alternative governance such as middlemen enterprises or systems with multiple forms of governance received little attention.[5] Subsequently Humphrey and Schmitz (2000) described four different forms of chain organization and governance: market relations, network relations, quasi-hierarchy, and hierarchy.[6] Gereffi's recent work (2001) also acknowledged that older and newer forms of governance may coexist in a given industry, and some recent research has documented this alternative form of structure and governance. For example, Freidberg compared the different systems delivering French beans to United Kingdom consumers and to French markets (2004). Tewari's work on the Indian garment industry (1999) also showed multiple forms of governance in the same commodity chain.

This present study contributes to commodity chain research by describing in detail a multi-stranded chain governed by middlemen rather than big producers or big buyers. By following the entire commodity chain and its evolution over a century from a local to a global industry, I show how governance of the system altered over the twentieth century. First consumers, then growers, and eventually certain middlemen directly influenced the types of flowers produced. In this period, the chain diversified along two lines that I define as the specialty chain and the abundant chain. Power and influence in the chain also altered in correspondence with changes among consumers and in the larger economic and social systems. My study also reveals that this is a networked, somewhat hierarchical market system. To some extent individual participants in the U.S. flower system always depended on networks of relationships; however, as global production and trade increased, so did competition, risk, and uncertainty. As change accelerated, networks of cooperation, trust, and reciprocity became essential to many participants. Social relationships increasingly conferred advantage on those within the global commodity chain able to establish and sustain them.

My principal ethnographic focus is the complex middle sector of this chain: exporters, importers, wholesalers, and retailers. I follow their activities as they employ a range of strategies to respond to activity among their competitors, shifts in supply, and changes in consumer behavior. Their actions, I suggest, have helped to determine the forms of governance that dominate the strands of this chain today. This ethnography also reveals the dynamic nature of the chain as middlemen respond to uncontrollable structural changes and to alterations in growing and consuming practices. Their actions send social, cultural, and economic waves back and forth along the chain and constantly alter this system of provision.

This book also addresses another limitation of much commodity chain and value chain research—neglect of the consumer. Not all theorists have ignored consumers. Fine's systems of provision framework added a social dimension to chain analysis in two ways: it included consumers and acknowledged that different systems of provision evolve in part as a "consequence of distinct relationships between the various material and cultural practices comprising the production, distribution, circulation and consumption of the goods concerned" (Fine and Leopold 1993, 5). Furthermore, Fine argued later that "each system of provision is attached to a cultural system that conditions the meanings taken by consumption" (Fine 2002, 7). Although Fine and some of the global commodity chain literature recognize a role for consumers and consumer culture in shaping commodity chains, there has been little empirical research (Friedland 1994, 2001; Goldfrank 1994; Korzeniewicz and Martin 1994; Taplin 1994; Collins 2000). Only a handful of scholars have examined consumers' impact in depth (Mintz 1985; Schneider 1994; Roseberry 1996; Tranberg Hansen 2000). Instead, the majority of case studies focus on production processes, with little attempt to explore fully the social and cultural interactions of the entire chain.

A second objective of this study, therefore, is the role of the consumer in the function of the fresh-cut flower global commodity chain. Fine and Leopold suggest that "production adjusts as forms of distribution alter and when the cultural meaning of the good changes. Each sector of the chain changes the others" (Fine and Leopold 1993, 15). This study reveals how Fine and Leopold's interactive process works by describing the precise ways in which changing consumer interests and preferences are communicated in a market system and how they influence what is produced.

Fresh-cut flowers are an apt commodity for tracing the interactions of culture and economy in a global value chain. Flowers are unlike other frequently studied commodities such as food and clothing, because they are not necessary to life: they have no utilitarian function. For those who consume them, the function of fresh-cut flowers is always to express cultural or social meaning. Fresh flowers laid on a grave, for example, demonstrate the cultural importance of honoring the dead. When people decorate spaces—whether church or ballroom—with extravagant displays of flowers, they signal aspects of identity and social status.

I focus principally on the New York Metropolitan Area to show that, for the most part, detailed knowledge and information about consumer preferences is trapped and unused in large parts of this particular commodity chain system. When massive numbers of consumers adopt a practice—giving red roses on Valentine's Day, for example—unambiguous signals reach rose growers, who respond by tailoring a year's production to satisfy this desire. In this case consumers agree on a meaning for red roses. Their choice influences the activities of people in the flower commodity chain and what is produced. More generally, however, the less-obvious, everyday preferences of the mass of flower consumers are poorly understood and even ignored. Instead, the desires of small groups of elite consumers animate the chain. A social network of traders and growers analyzes these elite preferences and then communicates and acts on this information. The choices of a few influence which flowers are grown and eventually offered to different sectors of consumers in the United States.

I also argue that today's flower consumption practices responded to organizational change when the flower trade expanded from a local to a global industry in the years between 1970 and 2004. Increased competition among producers and distributors helped to generate highly segmented and differentiated markets. Related changes included a dramatic increase in the quantities of flowers produced and consumed, the development of many new types of flowers, and, in some markets, swift obsolescence of passé flower colors and varieties. At the same time, in the NYMA, new kinds of distribution and retailing gave greater visibility to fresh-cut flowers, dramatically reduced prices, and removed several barriers to purchase that existed under older systems of provision. All these changes together presented consumers in metropolitan areas with a great bounty of new, varied, and inexpensive flowers. Consumers put them to use in new floral holidays and other practices.

New, intensified, and extended floral practices arise in part from easier access to fresh flowers. However, they are also a consequence of changes in consumer culture. In recent decades, a host of new and detailed needs, desires, and relationships has invaded consumer consciousness, especially in the dynamic, fluid societies that constitute urban metropolitan areas like New York.[7] Some of these needs relate to conceptions of the self and the way consumer goods are employed in identity-creation.

Reflecting on consumers' changing cultural concerns and their interest in expressing identity and cultural meaning with things such as flowers leads to another interest of this study. To what degree do consumers themselves shape the personal meanings of things like flowers by their uses of them and to what extent are meanings imprinted on these things by structural forces such as the media industries?[8] I explore the interplay between these two levels of meaning —meaning shaped by media industries and meaning shaped or reshaped by consumers of flowers in daily practice. Consequently this analysis illuminates some of the effects of structural *cultural* forces—in this case the magazine industry—on this particular commodity chain. It also illustrates the effects of outside *economic* forces such as government policies, tariffs, and trade treaties. I show how both forces influence—but do not determine—the eventual outcome for all participants in the fresh-cut flower global commodity chain.

Methodology

This is an ethnography of a dynamic system. Traditional ethnographic methods rely on daily, face-to-face observation of a single group or community over the long term. Observation of a complex global system, in contrast, requires ethnographic research in multiple locations. Recent examples of multi-sited ethnography attest to the value of this method for studying global systems of provision (Alarcón González 2000; Tranberg Hansen 2000; Bestor 2001; Freidberg 2004).

The implicit methodological problems of mobile ethnography include variable accessibility and uneven research quality at different sites (Marcus 1995). I countered these possible limitations by staging shorter periods of fieldwork over several years.

Ethnography is a reflexive activity, constantly changed by what one learns.[9] On return visits to the Netherlands, I benefited from fresh insights gained during intervening periods spent in Ecuador or Miami or observing changing practices among wholesalers in the New York area. The total time invested in multi-sited fieldwork and other research—about seven years—deepened my understanding of the speed of change in the global system and the importance of continuous systemic adjustment to that change. The dynamism of the system and the consequences for its participants are clear to me in ways that would not have been possible if I had observed this system from one location. I am also aware that as I write this, the flower system will already have changed. Some relationships will have strengthened, others weakened, and alliances will have shifted. New flowers will have appeared; others will have fallen out of favor. The account I give here describes the flower provisioning system between 1998 and 2005.

My own identity as a middle-aged white woman familiar with flowers and with the economic and class characteristics of the typical flower buyer in the United States was an asset in this project. In many, although not all, sites my obvious interest in flowers seemed to encourage people to share their experiences and views. Some clearly hoped I would be able to document their personal experiences and transmit their particular view of the flower industry to an interested public. In other cases—especially in the informal flower-trading sectors—my appearance seemed to suggest unwelcome official intrusion or an educational and economic divide that precluded communication.

This multi-sited research began with supermarkets, florist shops, designer studios, and other retailing sites in neighborhoods and communities in the New York Metropolitan Area. It extended to growers and traders in southern New Jersey, Connecticut, upstate New York, Florida, and California. Following the global flow of New Yorkers' flowers finally took me to Colombia, Ecuador, Costa Rica, and the Netherlands. My visits varied in length and season. I explored rows of flowers in open fields, in glass greenhouses, in plastic houses, and under textile shade coverings. I attended early morning auctions and observed different ways of packing flowers in globally dispersed rooms and sheds. In Miami I watched U.S. Department of Agriculture inspectors X-ray and disturb some of this same careful packaging while checking for bugs and drugs. Visiting refrigerated shipment and trans-shipment warehouses, trucking centers and flower-testing laboratories in Aalsmeer and Miami also absorbed some of my time. In Ecuador, Holland, and Miami, I watched bouquetmakers deftly arranging flowers in bunches designed to appeal to distant consumers.

My primary research method was the formal interview; I conducted some two hundred and fifty in all segments of the chain. I quote from these interviews throughout the text. I also tried to engage in what Bestor refers to as "inquisitive observation" (2004), especially in flower markets and other retailing spaces. Interviews with consumers were often informal. I was mindful of the discrepancy between what people say they do and how they actually behave.

The seasonal cycles of the flower industry determined the interview schedule. In New York, January and much of July and August are quiet periods when retailers are willing to chat. For Latin American growers, July and August are also quiet. November, December, and January are the months when Dutch flower growers can spare a few hours to describe their work and lives. Exporters, importers, and wholesalers are busy at all times of the year.

I also attended trade shows. These shows nurture local and global social relations and are occasions to transmit information and ideas. Most major shows aim to display new technology and new flowers to an international audience of breeders, growers, distributors, and retailers. Many are held each year, all around the globe, and I attended major shows in Bogotá, Quito, Aalsmeer, Miami, and New York City. Smaller shows such as one held in Philadelphia in March 2001 allowed foreign and domestic growers to show their finest flowers to retailers. At shows and trade meetings I made new connections, strengthened older ties, and observed the personal nature of some transnational relationships in the chain.

I followed connections and relationships up and down the chain. I tracked links between retailers in different parts of the New York area to one or two of their favored wholesalers. From these same wholesalers I traveled to their favorite importers in Miami, exporters in Aalsmeer, and eventually to growers in Holland, Ecuador, Colombia, Costa Rica, and California. Many growers, I found, have only a vague idea where their flowers eventually end up. Once they have delivered their flowers to the Aalsmeer auction or the Miami consignment market, growers lose sight of their progress along the global commodity chain.

Several factors guided my selection of flower retailers for interviews. I was interested in gauging the influence of ethnicity, income, and urban or suburban location on floral practices and tastes. I chose a number of florists for their location in New York neighborhoods with particular demographic characteristics, especially ethnicity and income range. I also distributed interviews among different types of retailers: supermarkets, traditional florists, freelance floral designers, and corner convenience stores.[10] Interviews with convenience store retailers were the least rewarding because of language difficulties. Many spoke only Korean and most were reluctant to talk and offer information or opinion. Throughout these years of multi-sited fieldwork I repeatedly encountered certain key growers, wholesalers, and retailers and enjoyed continuing conversations about the intricacies of the flower business and the incessant change that characterizes it.

Filling in the gaps around my informants' views and clarifying their sometimes vague statements about the trends they were witnessing required continuous investigation through secondary sources. These included newspapers, magazines, and journals produced by growing, trading, and retailing institutions and organizations as well as independent magazines aimed at growers, traders, retailers, and consumers. I extracted statistical information from U.S. government sources such as the Census Bureau and U.S. Department of Agriculture. Reports published by U.S. flower-industry institutions such as the Society of American Florists, by quasi-governmental organizations such as

Vereniging van Bloemenveilingen in the Netherlands, and by government institutions such as the U.S. International Trade Commission were a valuable resource.

Finally, the lives of certain flowers are essential to this study. I focused on roses because they are the most popular flower in the United States. Lilies, orchids, and gerberas also merited attention because they are important in the international trade and are sold widely in the New York area. I also followed a fifth flower, lisianthus. When I began this study, lisianthus was a new bloom in the global cut flower chain. Today it is readily available on New York streets and grows in Ecuador, the Netherlands, Colombia, California, Florida, and many other regions.

Overview of Chapters

Chapter 1 focuses first on the nineteenth-century popularity of flower growing, gardening, and collecting among English and American upper and middle classes. These practices influenced the commercial production of particular flowers and the tastes for those flowers. A second section describes the cultural activities associated with cut flowers between 1870 and 1970. In New York, flowers for funerals, weddings, and domestic decoration were important during the entire century, while flower consumption for collective and religious celebrations declined. Fresh flower use spread gradually from the small social and economic elite to the middle sectors. By the mid-twentieth century, broadly favored flower practices reflected the interests and values of the expanding middle classes.

Chapter 2 describes changing production and trade in the same period. I show how power in the cut flower commodity chain shifted from consumers to growers. Popular flower types also changed. In the late nineteenth and early twentieth centuries small fragrant blooms were popular. Great quantities were grown for the winter season in New York. But after the 1920s, sturdy roses, carnations, chrysanthemums, and gladioli gradually replaced delicate flowers. As mass production expanded in the southern and western United States, these four flowers eventually dominated the choices of most flower consumers.

After 1970 flower production and consumption changed dramatically. Chapters 3, 4, and 5 focus on flower production. Chapter 3 outlines the development of a global trade in fresh-cut flowers, made possible by jet transportation, new cultivation and communication technology, international financial arrangements, and other factors. Flower growing declined in the United States as more and more flowers were imported. Faced with competition from cheap imported carnations, roses, and chrysanthemums, remaining flower growers in the United States concentrated on diversity, eventually offering a great range of unusual blooms.

In the 1980s and 1990s Colombia and Ecuador began to send more fresh flowers to the United States. Chapter 4 explores some of the structural factors that influence flower growing for the international trade in Ecuador and the Netherlands. It reveals how political, institutional, and economic conditions in each nation contribute to distinct positions in the global flower market for flowers from—and flower growers within—these two countries. These factors strongly influence the types of flowers produced, how they are grown, and the way they are marketed by growers in each nation.

In chapter 5 I turn to the daily experiences of flower growers in the Netherlands and Ecuador. I explain how they connect with two of the world's most important flower markets: Aalsmeer and Miami. I also explore accelerating cycles of new flower innovation and the declining power of global flower growers. I focus particularly on growers' needs for certain types of knowledge, about new flowers, new technology, competition, and changes in consumer tastes. Networks of social relationships help some Dutch and Ecuadorian growers to acquire that knowledge and, in some cases, ease the marketing of flowers.

Chapters 6 and 7 together explore changes in the middle sector of the fresh-cut flower global commodity chain. Chapter 6 describes new structures and processes in the middle sector and their effects. The expansion of global flower trade and subsequent increases in flower imports encouraged the formation of two distinct chains of provision in the United States. The specialty chain serves a higher-end market, and the abundant chain delivers flowers to a lower-priced, mass market. Within these two chains, smaller chains serve different groups of consumers. I focus on chains leading to the New York Metropolitan Area, where new wholesale and retail forms appeared after 1980, destabilizing the traditional florists' century-long dominance of retail flower services.

Chapter 7 analyzes the way middlemen began to govern the flower chains as they adopted new communication and logistical technology and developed strong social networks. Cooperation and risksharing are important factors in this skillful governance as is specialized knowledge about new flowers, changing tastes, and, most importantly, sources of flower supply. This chapter also shows the way changing consumer tastes are communicated along the commodity chain to growers and influence what is produced. Finally, chapter 7 describes changing flower retail. It reveals how competition among new flower retailers generated new flower consumers. It also explores the failure of large-scale corporate restructuring in the cut flower industry and briefly describes a new entrant, Dole Fresh Flowers. This powerful corporation grows and trades flowers and may eventually alter the structure and governance of the cut flower commodity chain once again.

In Chapter 8 I focus on the people at the end of the global commodity chain—consumers of fresh flowers. I describe popular new flower uses and the persistence of old ones. I argue that some flower practices expanding in the New York Metropolitan Area, developed as a result of changes in production and retail. I follow several representative consumers as they buy flowers for home decoration, gifts, and rituals like weddings, to illustrate how their practices induce pleasure, restore memories, and substantiate conceptions of self and community. But new practices are also a consequence of increasing emphasis in the media industries on individual identity. In this chapter, therefore, I consider the influence of the consumer magazine industry on flower consumption. With floral metaphors and images of flower-saturated existences and celebrity lives, magazines—and other media—inspire participation in the world of flowers.

My conclusion summarizes the themes, arguments, and findings of this study. I also offer suggestions for additional areas of research within the global commodity chain framework.

14

One

Tastes, Traditions, and Trade, 1870–1970

In *Old New York New Year's Day*—Edith Wharton's story about the tastes, manners, and morals of elite New York society in the 1870s— a prosperous New York woman named Lizzie Hazeldean "paused before a Broadway florist's window and looked appreciatively at the jars of roses and forced lilac, the compact bunches of lilies-of-the-valley and violets, the first pots of close-budded azaleas. Finally she opened the shop-door, and after examining the Jacqueminots and Marshal Niels, selected with care two perfect specimens of a new silvery-pink rose" (Wharton 1924, 25).

In her appreciation of flowers and her attraction to the new, Lizzie Hazeldean was typical of her class and time. She is the appropriate starting point for an examination of floral cultural practices, favored flowers and the means of growing and delivering them to generations of flower buyers over the succeeding century. In this period dominant segments of the cut flower commodity chain altered in response to the expansion of the chain and to incremental adjustments in relationship between its component growers, traders, and consumers. These adjustments were themselves conditioned by broad economic, social, and technological changes. In the earliest period (1870–1920) the needs and desires of New York "society" and upper-middle-class consumers dominated the types of flowers produced and when and how they were grown. Between 1920 and 1970, growers' interests ultimately structured what was produced for and consumed by a growing middle class. In the third period (1970–2005), described in detail in succeeding chapters, middlemen came to orchestrate an expanding system that linked globally dispersed growers to U.S. flower consumers.

This chapter identifies the historical flower consuming practices that survived to flourish in the contemporary period. These practices carry meanings that resonate with contemporary New York Metropolitan Area consumers today. Persisting floral customs reveal something of the values that have been accepted—or rejected—in the continuous process of negotiating social and cultural transformation. Certain floral holidays—Mother's Day, Valentine's Day, and Secretary's Day—increased in popularity because they were relevant to the values of new middle-class consumers, while other holidays and practices—such as wearing fresh flowers—declined or disappeared because they were irrelevant. Yet, at the same time, these changing floral tastes and practices hinged on the types of blooms growers decided to produce and retailers chose to offer to consumers.

New Classes and the Culture of Flowers

Fresh flowers have long had a role in supporting cultural meanings and expressing certain social and cultural values. Goody's useful term the "culture of flowers" incorporates some of the complexity of this role. It implies simultaneously the cultivation and growing of plants and flowers, the meanings assigned to flowers, and the spread of "knowledge, the enjoyment and richness of flowers" (1993, 27). The term also encompasses "the complex social and cultural organization of production" and the sense that flower growing accompanies rising standards of living, a certain level of luxury, and "civilization" (25–26).

Few people participated in the culture of flowers before the nineteenth century. Kings, nobles, and wealthy merchants were among those who had the leisure and resources for such activities. Its spread was criticized—generally by the Christian church—for being part of "cultures of luxury" and wasteful expenditures and for its role in the diversion of limited resources to the production of luxuries for the rich (Goody 1993, 65).

During the later nineteenth century, however, economic and social transformations helped to spread interest in plants and flowers in England and in parts of Europe and the United States. In Britain the Industrial Revolution began a movement of rural labor to cities. It also created industrial wealth, new businesses, and new kinds of employment that eventually assisted the formation of new class sectors. This was a slow process. Even in 1867, when most people lived in cities and towns, three quarters of the population was in the manual laboring class while the "genuine middle class" of merchants, doctors, architects, engineers, and so on numbered about 200,000. A broader definition of middle class that included all those who could afford domestic servants, expanded the middle classes to 1.4 million in 1871. By 1901 the middle and lower middle classes constituted about 30 percent of the British population—or about twelve million people—with about five and a half million of them living reasonably or comfortably (Ohmann 1996; Hobsbawm [1968] 1999, 132–45).

In the United States these transformations proceeded more slowly still. In 1850, six out of ten people in the United States worked on farms, but by 1900 six in ten worked for wages in shops, homes, and factories. The value of manufactured goods rose from $1.9 billion in 1859 to $13 billion in 1899, expanding at more than twice the rate of population growth. Capital—"wealth capable of producing more wealth"—had an especially dramatic rate of increase in the last fifteen years of the nineteenth century (Ohmann 1996, 50). A great deal of this capital was invested in manufacturing while railroad construction and development of government land also helped, as Ohmann puts it, in "transferring wealth upwards" (1996, 52).

Regular crises of overproduction and declining prices contributed to a high rate of business failure and severe depressions marked each decade after the 1860s. Nevertheless this era of industrial capitalism in the United States produced the most rapid capital formation in history. Much of the resulting wealth concentrated in a small, enormously rich upper class. Some of it, however, spilled onto the swelling upper middle and middle classes that increasingly shaped their values and identity through material consumption encouraged by mass production, new department stores, domestic advice books, magazines, and advertising (Miller 1981; Dudden 1983; Ohmann 1996; Norton et al. 2001).

Ideas about Puritan thrift, Christian virtue, and an earlier nineteenth-century ideology of domestication and morality linked to the "cult of true womanhood" were adjusted to accommodate displays of luxury and consumption. New employers such as department stores, banks, railroads, and insurance companies aided the evolution of a new kind of middle-class person as well as a new type of worker. Previously the expansion of the middle class had been associated with becoming the proprietor of a small business. Now the employee in a bureaucratized, impersonal, hierarchical working structure identified with the bourgeois culture and aspired to its lifestyle. New and aspiring members of the middle classes could shape their identity through consumption guided by new institutions like department stores including Wanamaker in Philadelphia and Lord and Taylor in New York.[1]

Magazines and newspapers were an important part of this reconfiguration of the middle classes. In New York, editors and publishers "scanned the culture of the city, and played a balancing act between their own interests and the *perceived* interests of an urban audience" (Wells 1999, 21; emphasis in original).

Tastes, Traditions, and Trade

Wells suggests that even as early as 1836 the penny papers contributed to the definition of the middle class, including the married woman's role in that class. By printing approving accounts of the daily provisioning activities of a young, middle-class wife—her class clearly signaled by her accompanying maid— papers like the *New York Herald* engaged in shaping "the cultural boundaries of respectable behavior [providing] a more confident feel for what it did and did not mean to be in a social order, rather than outside it" (45).

Amid these social transitions the culture of flowers became a component of the expression, elaboration, and stabilization of a developing middle-class culture. These expressions took different forms in different settings. One form was the cultural phenomenon known as the "language of flowers" and the idea that flowers could carry secret messages or the arrangement of a bouquet could conceal complicated codes. Nineteenth-century middle classes on both sides of the Atlantic embraced this faddish notion. Traditional meanings of flowers were organized and elaborated. White orange blossoms, for example, meant virginity, the carnation signified "lively and pure love," the red rose deep passion, and the white rose carried "a message of innocence and virginity" (Goody 1993, 249).[2] Remnants of this idea persist today in little guidebooks and a widespread but vague sense among flower buyers that certain flowers have particular meanings of which they are ignorant.

In Britain two other enthusiasms spread a culture of flowers—the rise of domestic flower gardening and a passion for plant collecting. Flower gardening and plant collecting are complex, costly activities and their wider adoption depended on the spread of new wealth to growing upper middle classes and leisure for hobbies and interests. An emerging gardening literature was also important. It provided new conceptions of smaller-scaled gardens and information about new plants to an increasingly receptive public. Another factor was a widespread fascination with the science of botany. This new discipline developed as global exploration and an enlarging colonial empire presented appreciative Victorians with thousands of exotic new plants. Wealthy owners of greenhouses or "hot-houses" were among the first to grow and propagate the new plants. Gradually, however, new plants and flowers reached a broad, eager public.

NEW GARDENS

The new garden designs that appeared in the mid-nineteenth century represented a complete rethinking of earlier garden practices. Under the previously dominant English Landscape Gardening School, the wealthy employed imaginative landscape gardeners to reshape the rural landscape into "great natural curves, crowned . . . with clumps of trees, natural forest and boundary screens" (Fleming and Gore 1979, 119). To create an idealized view, a hundred thousand trees might be planted, entire villages moved, and thousands of laborers employed.[3] A later variation, the "picturesque" garden improved the landscape near the country house with winding gravel walks, neatly cut lawns, and circular beds filled with flowers. This picturesque style provided the foundation for the new style of garden design (Hyams 1966; Plumptre 1993).

Three imaginative garden designers—John Claudius Loudon, Joseph Paxton, and William Robinson—turned their attention from contouring estates to designing gardens for the small urban and suburban villas, the homes of the middle classes.[4] Their new garden designs drew heavily on the paths, lawns, and flower beds of "picturesque" gardens. However, densely planted, productive, rural "cottage" gardens also provided an important inspiration and eventually gave a name to the emerging style.[5]

All three designers helped establish an important gardening literature that spread ideas about the new style of gardening and knowledge about the plants and flowers available.[6] One of Loudon's major contributions was his novel placement of flowers and plants. His garden and landscape ideas were adapted and promoted in the American setting by Andrew Jackson Downing.[7] Robinson is credited with reintroducing wild nature into gardening style. His ideal was a cottage garden filled with native English flowers and the finest exotics flooding in from abroad, all blooming abundantly together.[8] Robinson's particular planting style was later elaborated by Gertrude Jekyll, one of its best-known exponents. Her books and ideas are still influential in flower gardening in Europe and North America.[9] As enthusiasm for the new garden styles spread, garden owners, on both sides of the Atlantic, sometimes spent lavishly to acquire new and unusual roses and other kinds of flowers. By the later part of the nineteenth century, flower gardening as an adjunct to homemaking was an accepted pastime for middle- and upper-class women in Britain and the United States (Fleming and Gore 1979; Plumptre 1993).

These changing garden styles reflected the ethos of their respective times. The eighteenth-century English Landscape Gardening School demonstrated the concentration of wealth and power in land-owning classes and resonated with the age's concern for reason, the achievements of civilization, and the control of nature. Wild and cottage garden styles, in contrast, evolved at a time of Victorian enthusiasm for exploration and a fascination with natural science and the beauty and astonishing profusion of the forms provided by wild nature. This enthusiasm for natural science and botany paved the way for a third factor in new garden design and in the diffusion of the culture of flowers: hothouse gardening.

Hothouse gardening—in heated glass structures later known as greenhouses—allowed the cultivation and propagation of flowers and fruits from tropical regions. More importantly for this study, roses, camellias, lilies, violets, and many other types of flowers could be forced to bloom outside their natural seasons. Previously a luxury of kings and wealthy aristocrats, by the early nineteenth century this complex form of gardening was popular among the growing classes of wealthy industrialists and merchants. The repeal of the British glass tax in 1845 meant that the passion and practice of hothouse gardening could be adopted further down the social ladder. Improved sheet-glass-making technology and manufacturing processes further reduced the price of glass by 1860.[10] Cast iron construction allowed for larger panes and more light in the greenhouse. In England and America, prosperous middle-class homeowners began to display their plant collections in glass conservatories attached to their houses (McGuire 1989). These larger, stronger, cheaper, light-filled greenhouses made out-of-season commercial cut flower growing feasible.

Impassioned plant collectors and gardeners depended for satisfaction both on the developing plant nursery industry and on an extraordinary Victorian profession: plant hunters. These men engaged in a highly competitive business as they traveled around the globe seeking new plants. Orchid hunting in remote places was a particularly dangerous form. Susan Orlean (2000) refers to it as "a mortal occupation" and describes one expedition to the Philippines in 1901 in which seven of the eight hunters died.[11] The surviving hunter eventually emerged from the jungle with almost fifty thousand *Phalaenopsis* plants. A century earlier few of these captured plants survived the journey back to Europe; one plant in a thousand lived through the voyage from China to England. The discovery of the terrarium principle in 1829 and the consequent invention of the Wardian case—a glass-topped wooden case that could be stored on deck to protect plants during long sea voyages—eventually reduced the hazards of global travel for plants.[12] By the 1870s plant hunters were safely sending hundreds of thousands of plants back to England in these cases (Hyams 1966; Plumptre 1993; Orlean 2000).

Plant hunting was funded by collectors, nurseries, and by two powerful new scientific institutions, the Royal Botanic Society of London and the Horticultural Society. Both were important in feeding Victorian appetites for exotic plants and flowers and both influenced the types of cut flowers we buy today (Hyams 1966; Brockway 1979; Nichols [1902] 2003). The Royal Horticultural Society concentrated on spreading knowledge about plants and gardening and training gardeners and designers, while the Royal Botanic Society's research center at Kew Gardens focused on botanical science and developing economic crops.[13] Kew administrators and botanists tested, developed, and transported tea, rubber, and sisal plants around the world to new profitable homes on British colonial plantations. However, many of the plants shipped back to Kew by hunters had no large-scale economic applications. Instead, they joined the thousands of plants brought to England by private collectors decorating new public parks and gardens, sustaining a growing nursery trade and fueling enthusiasm for domestic flower gardening and the culture of flowers. By mid-century the bursting flower beds and vast plant collections at Kew and the Royal Horticultural Society's gardens at Chiswick drew hundreds of thousands of visitors annually.

NEW FLOWERS

Among the flowers collected by plant hunters were the parents of several of those most important in today's global commercial cut flower trade. The forebears of modern oriental and Asian hybrid lilies and chrysanthemums made the trip to Europe from China and Japan around the 1860s (Fleming and Gore 1979; Mabberley 1993). Alstroemeria (Peruvian lily) arrived from Peru in the 1830s and soon found a permanent place in the cottage garden. Its hybrid descendants eventually returned to the Andes to become one of Colombia's important cut flower exports. Four roses from China landed in France during the first decades of the nineteenth century. French breeders eventually transformed their descendants into the hybrid tea roses that provide most fresh cut roses today.[14] Their creations included the 'General Jaqueminot' and 'Maréchal Niel' roses that captured Lizzie Hazeldean's attention. These roses, however, enjoyed very brief lives. "The day they are cut they are at their best," wrote Gertude Jekyll of these and other roses, "the next day they will do, but the third day they lose colour, scent, and texture" (Jekyll and Mawley [1902] 1983, 73). Even so, by the end of the nineteenth century, these ephemeral roses were a favorite of the commercial cut flower trade.[15]

Orchids did not immediately become popular among plant enthusiasts. A

Tastes, Traditions, and Trade

tropical orchid native to the Bahamas bloomed in England in 1731, but propagation problems and ignorance of their cultivation requirements slowed their adoption for another century even though commercial orchid growing was established near London by 1812.[16] In 1833 the Duke of Devonshire became enamored of *Oncidium* orchids after seeing one at an exhibition. He instructed the aforementioned Joseph Paxton—his head gardener at the time—to begin a collection. "Vogues are usually set by persons of influence and renown," notes Reinikka, and "thus it was that orchids became fashionable in the glasshouses and conservatories of the British upper classes" ([1972] 1995, 136). As Orlean explains, "the Duke's obsession ignited the fashion for orchids in English high society that continued for decades. Orchids were seen as the badge of wealth and refinement and worldliness; they implied mastery of the wilderness and of alien places; their preciousness made them the beautiful franchise of the upper class. So many new varieties were being found every day that no collector could ever rest—orchids were an endless preoccupation. Once the vogue for orchids began, the prices paid for the plants, the measures taken to obtain them, and the importance attached to them took on an air of madness. This Victorian obsession, this 'orchidelirium,' was a rapacious desire" (Orlean 2000, 73–74).[17]

Around 1838, James Boott, a Londoner, sent an orchid to his brother John in Boston. Orchid fever infected Americans and by mid-century "orchids . . . had become widespread in popularity. They continued, however, as symbols of the wealthy classes" (Reinikka [1972] 1995, 31).

Orchids' costliness, exacting cultural requirements, and difficulties in hybridizing ensured that orchid owning would remain a mark of wealth, refinement, and status for another century. In fact, orchid ownership did not spread until the late twentieth century, when propagating, hybridizing, transportation, and retailing innovations made orchid plants and cut flowers readily available. Prices dropped substantially and millions of Americans bought orchids (see chapter 8).

Changing Consumption and Changing Flowers

In the second half of the nineteenth century, emigrating English and German nurserymen and gardeners brought new horticultural techniques and new plants and flowers to the United States. Middle-class Americans moving to new suburbs followed the British styles and installed lawns, flower-filled beds, and wild or "informal" gardens (Seaton 1988; McGuire 1989; Plumptre 1993).

Middle-class women satisfied their seasonal cut flower needs—for gifts, dinner table, and church decorations—from their own flower gardens.

Demand for out-of-season flowers was growing, however. A small commercial cut flower industry developed around New York after 1870, and over succeeding decades the growing numbers of florists worked hard to satisfy the needs of a thriving New York "society," which included the elite "Four Hundred" who could comfortably fit into Mrs. Astor's private ballroom (Epstein 2002, 33), as well as members of the upper middle class like Lizzie Hazeldean. The desires and activities of this white Protestant establishment determined the types of flowers grown, the timing of harvesting and production, and therefore, the work of the city's traditional florists. Particular social customs and cultural understandings underpinned the floral practices popular among these upper classes. One group of practices helped establish class identity and social status through elaborate displays of flowers, especially in the decoration and presentation of the home. A second category of floral work involved customs related to female identity and sexuality, particularly the practice of women wearing or carrying fresh flowers—often the gifts of male admirers. Rituals and religious practices dominated another economically important group of floral activities connected with birth, death, marriage, and motherhood.

SOCIAL STATUS AND CLASS IDENTITY

Demand for fresh flowers in New York exploded in the last decades of the nineteenth century and the early part of the twentieth during what contemporaries described as a "Floral Age" (Dunlop 2000, 29). In 1899 a New York florist claimed that floral expenditures (in terms of flower stems sold) had increased one hundred times over the previous five years along with growing numbers of debutante balls, cotillions, marriages, and other society celebrations.[18] "Flowers, chiefly raised in hot-houses, have an enormous sale in New York, and fetch preposterous prices," a visitor reported in 1904. Fresh flowers, he noted, were produced for the "vast demands of society," consequently making "winter, in the Metropolis, the great season of floral activity."[19]

Floral practices marking social status developed in concert with expanding wealth and the desire to shape class identity and distinctions between the upper and emerging middle classes. Expensive flowers were among the goods conspicuously consumed as part of a complex of behaviors documented by Thorstein Veblen in *The Theory of the Leisure Class*. The fashion required wives, menials, and dependents of wealthy men to involve themselves in tasteful and pleasing domestic adornments that were not substantially useful.[20] Retail florists accommodated the trend by inventing extravagant and expensive presentations of floral gifts. Bunches of violets, for example, were fastened with "heavy silk cords with tassels" and scented "violet-colored lace paper put around them."[21]

As more flowers were bought, given as gifts, and used up by more and more people, distinguishing tastes for particular flowers and their presentations also emerged. Shortages were common. Scarcity or abundance predicted desire or disinterest by high-status groups, as did price.[22] Costliness implied beauty until, as Veblen observed, "some beautiful flowers pass conventionally for offensive weeds; others that can be cultivated with relative ease are accepted and admired by the lower middle class, who can afford no more expensive luxuries of this kind; but these are rejected as vulgar by those people who are better able to pay for expensive flowers and who are educated to a higher schedule of pecuniary beauty in the florist's products; while still other flowers, of no greater intrinsic beauty than these, are cultivated at great cost and call out much admiration from flower-lovers whose tastes have been matured under the critical guidance of a polite environment" ([1899] 1994, 133).

Thus pampas grass plumes—much favored in the previous year—had, by 1878, become "too common to be fashionable" and their prices declined accordingly.[23] By 1880 primroses and pansies were classed among "the common brood of flowers" and florists neglected them except in times of flower shortages. Greater production and lower prices reduced the popularity of fragrant sweet peas among the upper-class sectors responsible for the majority of flower buying. Novelty was a considerable factor in floral demand, just as it would be a century later. Dwarf flowering cherries were imported from Japan, for example, then coaxed into bloom and their flowers sold to those who demanded something new and were prepared to pay for it. Thus rarity and scarcity, while generally deplored by florists, could afford them substantially higher prices.

DECORATING THE HOME

By the end of the century, suburban communities separated the middle classes from their inferiors and the vices of the masses. A million people lived in the suburbs of New York by 1900, with one hundred thousand traveling by train into the city daily (Ohmann 1996, 125). The suburban house and garden exemplified a new way of life for the upper middle class to which the lower middle classes aspired. In their new villas designed for privacy they focused on luxury and comfort (Ohmann 1996; Cross 2000). By 1910 the population of Manhattan had reached 2.3 million. About three quarters of the population lived in tenements, but new townhouses, apartment buildings, and suburban houses were being constructed for the prosperous classes (Foner 2000, 43). The home was the locus of social and cultural ideals and expressed the taste, personality, and quality of the bourgeois woman. As representative of her family and class she demonstrated the value of devoting time and effort to establishing a domestic space expressive of the self (Auslander 1996, 96–97). Domestic flower arrangements came to signify middle- and upper-middle-class status. Flower arranging for the house was a daily duty. Writing in 1901, Mabel Osgood Wright described how "I spent [sic] several hours every day now in arranging my flowers, for outdoor roses are blooms of a day that need frequent renewal."[24] Replacing these fast-fading cut roses added pleasure to a wife's daily tasks, suggested Gertrude Jekyll, since this was "a household duty of that pleasant class that is all delight and no drudgery" (Jekyll and Mawley [1902] 1983, 73).

As in Europe, social codes prescribed fresh flowers in the house for celebrations, dinner parties, and for receiving callers (Dudden 1983; Donzel 1997). Such displays—and time for pleasure and delight—were probably rare in rural American households, but in urban settings even the poorest working-class wife might show her taste with "a potted plant at the window" (Gordon and McArthur 1988). Indeed, in Donzel's account of floral use in France and England, "every welcoming household had a little bouquet in the middle of the family table." A bouquet symbolized a certain idea of domestic happiness, and above all, "it was no longer an extravagance" since improvements in horticulture and new prosperity had put "cut flowers within the reach of almost every pocketbook" (Donzel 1997, 129).

In the United States such symbols of middle-class domestic happiness were rarely within reach of the poor majority. As noted earlier, floral purchasing was the privilege of what Ruth Cowan refers to as "the comfortable classes," that is, those people "who could, in any given time or place, afford to live decently or comfortably" (1983, 153). In the succeeding decades the "comfortable" and "less comfortable" classes began to merge. Suburban populations expanded in the 1920s as the house and garden—those marks of middle-class respectability —extended to the white-collar and skilled working classes including immigrant families (Cross 2000, 60). Garden clubs flourished and the popularity of some garden flowers followed "crazes." In 1925 the head gardener at the New York Botanical Gardens, speaking of newly popular peonies, explained: "A new flower will rise to celebrity but only persons blessed with a big estate and a professional gardener can grow it. Then suddenly comes its development as a home plant and it is brought within the reach of all—like the mass production of Paris fashions."[25] By 1930, 18 percent of the total population could enjoy suburban houses and gardens; in the years after World War II the proportion rose, reaching 38 percent by 1970.

In the affluent 1950s, women's identification with the home re-emerged with renewed emphasis (Noland 1997; Woloch [1996] 2002). A fresh ideal of full-time housewifery and motherhood developed and was supported in television programs and magazines. In reality more women spent a great deal of time working outside the home (Cowan 1983; Stole 2003). Nevertheless, late-nineteenth-century ideas about status, taste, and creativity as expressed in the house persisted. Home decorating—including flowers—and buying new domestic goods helped women to "create a public image to present to neighbors and the wider community" (Cross 2000, 109).

WEARING FRESH FLOWERS

In the late nineteenth century, young upper-class women signaled celebrations and holidays by wearing or carrying large quantities of highly fragrant and perishable blooms, often the gifts of male admirers. Details such as appropriate hours for wearing flowers varied locally but the custom was widespread. Weddings and balls were accepted occasions for well-bred women to cover themselves in scented blooms.[26] At the upper levels of Paris, London, and New York society, female dress for balls involved low necklines and voluminous skirts adorned with fragrant fresh flowers (Donzel 1997).

Fragrance was an important floral quality. Flower growers provided great quantities of scented blooms such as double primroses, stocks, carnations, violets, roses, tuberoses, and Cape jasmine. Men bought four-fifths of the flowers sold in New York City, giving most as gifts to women to signal love, desire, or respect, among other things. They threw enormous quantities of blooms onto stages as gifts for actresses and dancers. Well-dressed men also wore fragrant flowers themselves in their buttonholes.[27] Fragrance added to the pleasure, but more prosaically, in a crowded city with poor sanitation, malodorous streets, and infrequent bathing for the majority, scented blooms also fulfilled a masking function.

As noted earlier, fragrant flowers of the time were highly perishable. Fragrance in all flowers evaporated within a day and the blooms themselves lived scarcely two days after picking.[28] They could not be grown far from their intended consumers. Winter-blooming fragrant violet, *Viola odorata,* was one of the most popular flowers for wearing and for domestic decoration between 1890 and 1910. In the last decade of the nineteenth century most violets came from the Rhinebeck region, about one hundred miles north of New York City. William Saltford, an immigrant English gardener, established violet cultivation in this Hudson River town around 1886.[29] By 1916 over a hundred violet growers flourished in Rhinebeck. Acres of reflecting glasshouses caused the town to be popularly named "Crystal City" (Verrilli 1997, 1). Typically, a million violets were shipped by rail from Rhinebeck in the week before Easter, in response to a demand that resembled the contemporary craze for red roses on February 14.[30] Popular young women reportedly suspended huge clusters of violets from their waists or carried bouquets of thousands.

Less extravagant but common personal flower decorations may be presumed from an 1893 *New York Times* article about the Union Square market, describing "a very pretty young girl who had wandered about in the crisp air until her cheeks were the color of the roses she wore in her coat."[31]

The practice of carrying and wearing flowers slowly faded after World War I. The reasons for the decline are not clear, but changing clothing styles are often mentioned. By the 1920s, dresses were straight, lightweight, and shorter. There were fewer defined waistlines from which to suspend sheaves of violets. In the 1930s Eleanor Roosevelt wore violets at an inauguration and Mrs. Vincent Astor was "photographed in a violet house" while entertaining the editor of *Harper's Bazaar* magazine (Verrilli 1997, 12). These celebrity associations prompted a brief sales surge, making violet corsages popular Valentine's Day gifts in the 1930s. In the long term, however, violet production was doomed by changes in consumer tastes, styles, and fashions.[32] The decline was gradual. As late as the 1950s, violets were popular Easter gifts for women and large quantities still grew in the Rhinebeck region. Today not a single violet house remains, although the one remaining flower grower in the region still produces a few bunches along with his specialized anemones.

New clothing fashions were part of larger changes in a society influenced by the Progressive movement and World War I. Many more women became wage workers in factories or offices while others followed more traditional employment as waitresses, domestic servants, and shopgirls. By 1920, one fifth

Tastes, Traditions, and Trade

1 Palmolive Soap advertisement, 1927.

2 Dermetics Ageless Beauty advertisement, 1944.

of workers were women and during the 1920s the number of married women workers increased by 25 percent (Cowan 1983; Norton et al. 2001; Woloch [1996] 2002). These new women workers probably had little direct influence on changing flower consumption. As members of the "hard-pressed" classes that Cowan describes in her study of the changing conditions of women's household work, they purchased few luxuries (1983, 169).

Cosmetics, however, were one luxury that appealed to many young women, and cosmetics manufacture tripled during the 1920s. Marketers began to employ images of flowers in advertisements for soaps, creams, and cosmetics as a means of coupling their products with cultural ideals such as femininity and the purity of youth. A Palmolive soap advertisement from 1927, for example, employs flowers and bridal imagery to signal youth and the desirability of "naturalness" through cleansing (see figure 1). Particular flowers, such as the expensive orchid corsage featured in a 1948 advertisement for Dermetics skin care, represented class and status (see figure 2).

Corsages remained popular for another forty years and women of all classes continued to wear them at important events. In the 1960s "mother and daughter" corsages were common and "still carefully matched to the new

Easter clothing" (Noland 1997, 224). But by the 1970s, social life and clothing had become less formal. Specifically seasonal clothing purchases like the spring or Easter coat disappeared in the New York Metropolitan Area as new and cheaper forms of casual clothing were presented to consumers. Retailers offered fewer enticements associated with seasons and rituals; instead they encouraged consumers to acquire new clothing continuously. By 1970, corsages were rare. Wearing and carrying fresh flowers was largely limited to brides and their wedding entourages.

WEDDING RITUALS

After the 1870s, flowers—previously discouraged by the clergy—returned to church decoration for worship and for weddings and other rituals.[33] Within a few decades flowers became a status-signifying component of rituals such as funerals, weddings, and New Year's Day observances for wealthy New Yorkers. The April 1893 wedding of Cornelia Martin to the Earl of Craven at Grace Church on Broadway is suggestive of the trend. Arriving wedding guests "walked through a 'vista of great Bermuda lilies' trimming each pew." In the chancel, "palms stacked to a height of forty feet formed a backdrop for banks of daisies, hydrangeas, lilies, roses, azaleas, and rhododendrons reaching to a height of thirty feet. The four chancel columns were festooned with spring flowers, the chancel rail was buried under mounds of lilies of the valley, and the steps leading to the altar were carpeted with loose rosebuds and lilies" (Dunlop 2000, 4).

Miss Martin carried a bouquet of costly white orchids. Probably they came from the orchid growers, Lager and Hurrell in Summit, New Jersey, who were famed for their expensive white orchids (Reinikka [1972] 1995, 67). The bridesmaids clutched "bundles of white lilacs and Mabel Morrison roses" (Dunlop 2000, 5). The bride disdained the wreaths and tiaras of orange blossoms that had been popular with wealthy brides since Queen Victoria wore them for her own wedding in 1840. Orange blossoms, as noted earlier, symbolized virginity and had done so since at least the sixteenth century. Their use intensified—perhaps through association with the "language of flowers"—along with the taste for a white gown, among French and English upper classes during the nineteenth century (Goody 1993; Donzel 1997; Money-Collins 1997). In Paris a horticulturalist grew orange blossoms all year round after 1860 to satisfy the desires of wealthy brides (Donzel 1997). Middle-class brides settled for cheaper orange blossoms from Nice, while the poorest brides contented themselves

3 Nineteenth-century bride.
Library of Congress, Prints
and Photographs Division,
LC-USZ62-38598.

with "an artificial bouquet that was kept as a souvenir under a glass globe" (Goody 1993, 227). Orange blossoms were soon popular in America for bridal wreaths, bouquets, and also as decorations on the bridal gown, to symbolize fertility and happiness (Money-Collins 1997).

The bouquet as signifier of the bride's role has multiple origins but one lay in a codified ritual of floral gifts from the upper-class groom to his bride. Donzel explains that these gifts began "on the first day of the engagement, [when] the arrival of the prospective husband was preceded by a fine basket of flowers." Prescribed types of flowers—possibly laden with hidden messages—were delivered daily until the wedding. This "litany of roses, guelder roses, violets, and white lilacs came to an end only on the day of the ceremony, when the groom made a final present of flowers." French brides were given a basket of flowers, explains Donzel, but the upper-class English bride's final gift was "a bouquet, thereby launching the tradition of walking down the aisle with a profuse, and sometimes vast, bouquet in hand" (1997, 120–23).

Bouquets became more elaborate as the nineteenth century progressed. Wealthy brides often carried a bouquet weighing ten to fifteen pounds and cascading in a "shower" almost to the bride's feet. Small flowers such as lily-of-the-valley, gardenia, orange blossom, stephanotis, and small white rosebuds were

Chapter One

4 Late-twentieth-century bride with cascading bouquet. © Corbis.

suspended on "white ribbons in long bows." Middle-class brides contented themselves with a small nosegay or posy bouquet with a very "slight cascade" (Money-Collins 1997, 145–46). The late-nineteenth-century bride in figure 3 is being shown a sewing machine by her husband who still holds her small bouquet.

Forms of cascading bouquets were popular until the 1950s.[34] They were labor-intensive, requiring careful and costly preparation of a basic form and considerable wiring of tiny delicate blooms and clusters. The invention of floral foam in the 1950s allowed faster and easier assembly of bouquets and other wedding flower presentations. Small delicate flowers still required wiring to wooden picks for insertion into the preshaped foam bouquet holders, but carnations, chrysanthemums, roses, and lilies with strong, stiff stems inserted quickly into floral foam. The resulting reduction in labor and other costs eventually favored small geometric bouquets assembled on floral foam bases. This style persisted for twenty to thirty years until the wedding of Lady Diana Spencer to Prince Charles in 1981 revived the cascading bouquet (Money-Collins 1997). (See figure 4.) They remained fashionable for over ten years until smaller hand-tied bouquets became popular in the 1990s.

Tastes, Traditions, and Trade

For much of the period covered in this chapter, it was the wealthy who enjoyed costly cascading bouquets, orange-blossom tiaras, and other elaborate nuptial flowers. Less prosperous and even poor people, however, also appreciated the beauty of flowers and desired them for themselves. Dunlop recounts how, at the conclusion of Cornelia Martin's wedding ceremony, a "thick and jostling crowd" of ordinary people gathered outside to observe the bridal party. As invited guests departed, the crowd burst into the church and began stripping "the altar of its beauty by tearing down vines, cutting roses, and breaking off entire stems of Easter lilies." The uninvited, Dunlop remarks, "liked flowers too" (2000, 5–6).

In the century between 1870 and 1970, social and economic transformations influenced the popularity of certain flowers and their cultural deployment. However, changes in production and trade were equally important in determining the ways flowers were enjoyed and by whom. The following chapter describes the changing fortunes of American flower growers and the evolution of the wholesalers and florists who mediated between the growers' widening world and the narrow sphere of local New York consumers.

Two

Favored Flowers: Growers and Traders, 1870–1970

Lizzie Hazeldean might have found her roses in any one of the twenty florists' shops established on Broadway in the 1870s.[1] Lizzie would have paid at least sixty or seventy cents for each rose, more than many New Yorkers pay today.[2] Several city florists were also growers. So her roses might have come from a shop supplied by its own hothouses in nearby Harlem, Flushing, or Jersey City. The majority of florists, however, depended on growers in places like Hoboken and Union Hill, New Jersey, and Rhinebeck, New York.

The Rise and Decline of American Flower Growers

Most growers were small establishments usually with only two or three green-houses. Yet a few produced very large quantities of flowers. A Jersey City grower, for example, shipped 100,000 roses a year.[3] His blooms probably included the dark red 'General Jacqueminot' and yellow 'Maréchal Niel' mentioned by Edith Wharton, since these were among the most widely grown of that period's commercially produced rose varieties.[4] Another horticultural-ist cut about half a million blooms a year in his twenty-five greenhouses in Flushing. Most were small fragrant flowers such as stocks, carnations, violets, tuberoses, and jasmines.[5] The choice of blooms was limited by the technology of the time. Plants that flowered in response to warmer temperatures (rather than day length, for example) in coal-heated greenhouses could be coaxed into flowering months in advance of their natural spring flowering dates.

GROWER-FLORISTS

In a reversal of nature's order, more flowers were sold in New York City in winter than in summer. Some, such as camellias, came from far away hothouses in Philadelphia and Baltimore, probably by train.[6] September, December, and January were the months of greatest demand, coinciding with the winter social season of balls, parties, and other entertainments enjoyed by wealthy segments of the population. Lower classes dominated the "financially insignificant" summer demand.[7] They favored the cheaper garden flowers produced by small growers in their natural seasons and sold at street stalls or at the seasonal flower market that opened in Union Square by 1893.[8] In warmer months street vendors peddled flowers arranged in little bouquets, baskets, and buttonholes.[9] All these forms of flower vending exist in New York City today, much as they have in cities for centuries.[10] At this stage the term "florist" still applied equally to growers or sellers or arrangers of flowers. But as intermediary wholesalers gradually appeared, industry segments began to differentiate.[11] By 1916, growers, wholesale florists, and retail florists were distinct trades.[12] The new wholesale florists aided growers by "collecting, sorting, pricing, packing, and delivering product." Soon the wholesaler became "the industry's banker, collecting money on behalf of the grower and extending credit to the retailer," an important function even today (Carbonneau et al. 1997, 44). Retail florists benefited from this dependable source of varied flowers and credit. Yet wholesalers could do little to overcome the problems of persistent cycles of surplus and shortage and correspondingly uneven and unpredictable prices. Wholesale florists were not entirely popular with New York growers. Some growers opened an indoor flower market on West 23rd Street in 1895 in order to bypass the "commission men"—wholesale commission florists—whose "handling of their wares had not been altogether satisfactory."[13]

EARLY EXPANSION

Carnations and gladioli are two of the few flower species suited by nature for distant production. Carnations open slowly and have a post-harvest life of many weeks. Gladioli flowers open serially and slowly along a strong stem and also enjoy a long life. When cut at a very early stage of bud opening, their stiff stems allow them to be shipped standing upright in wooden crates without damage to the heavy blooms. Distant growers slowly began to concentrate on carnations and gladioli and the increasingly popular roses and chrysanthemums. By 1918, carnation growing was established in Colorado (Eskilon 1997), while gladiolus cultivation began in Florida in the late 1920s.[14] Florida dominated gladiolus production by the 1930s and does so today (Waters Prevatt 1983). New railroads and well-developed railway express services delivered these fresh blooms to the populous, prosperous northeastern market. After World War II, flower growers accelerated the geographic relocation of production to southern and western states. Chrysanthemums joined gladioli on Florida flower farms in the early 1950s. Growers and their cuttings suppliers in Ohio and other northern regions saw the advantages of different climates for cheap counter-seasonal production aimed at the northeastern late winter market.[15] Interstate road systems, rail, and increased passenger flights offered new means of rapidly transporting cut flowers. Other flowers—and their growers—moved west to establish new farms with relatively lower production costs. By 1970, 70 percent of carnations were grown in Colorado and California, and one third of all roses and standard chrysanthemums came from California. By that time these five flower crops—roses, carnations, gladioli, pompon chrysanthemums, and standard chrysanthemums—dominated American flower growing and were collectively termed the major cut flowers (see table 1).

Roses also persisted in local production around eastern and midwestern cities for two reasons. Rose shrubs were expensive but could produce excellent flowers for ten or more years—local growers wanted to recover their investment. Roses were also intolerant of long journeys. The global rose, scentless and sturdy enough to endure long travel times, was not developed until decades later.

FADING LOCAL GROWERS

As flower growing moved west and south the total number of U.S. flower farms halved between 1950 and 1970. At the same time the efficiency and productivity of each farm improved, while prices barely increased. The quantities of flowers produced and consumed multiplied. Carnations and pompon chrysanthemum production doubled, while standard chrysanthemums quadrupled (see table 2).[16]

Many local flower growers in the New York metropolitan region disappeared during this period. This trend mirrored a general decline in farm and agricultural employment during the mid-twentieth century. However, three factors specific to flower growing contributed to the decline. One was changing demand for particular species and varieties of flowers. Local growers were unable or unwilling to adopt new flower types to meet new demands. Rising costs of production were a second factor. Intensifying competition from the cheaper flowers of distant mass-production growers prevented many local growers from increasing their prices and passing on their rising costs. Third, new suburbs began to absorb established flower farms and greenhouses sur-

1 Geographic shift in production of major flower crops, 1949–1970

CARNATIONS IN 1000 UNITS BUNCHES/BLOOMS

	1949	1957	1961	1970
California	19,300	102,500	135,000	382,700
Colorado	29,300	58,500	79,000	162,800
Florida	0	0	0	0
Illinois	28,200	20,200	15,700	6,200
New York upstate	n/a	8,400	7,100	5,400
New York Long Island	n/a	20,500	17,100	10,300
Total units from these areas*	76,800	210,100	253,900	567,400

ROSES IN 1000 UNITS BUNCHES/BLOOMS

	1949	1957	1961	1970
California	54,600	67,400	73,600	156,700
Colorado	6,600	3,200	2,400	15,100
Florida	90	n/a	1,700	2,500
Illinois	64,900	45,700	32,500	29,900
New York upstate	n/a	19,100	18,400	14,100
New York Long Island	n/a	14,000	14,500	14,200
Total units from these areas*	126,200	149,500	143,100	232,500

CHRYSANTHEMUM (STANDARD) IN 1000 UNITS BUNCHES/BLOOMS

	1949	1957	1961	1970
California	7,800	25,600	38,700	81,500
Colorado	270	400	400	500
Florida	80	750	3,700	9,300
Illinois	2,800	5,300	5,100	3,400
New York upstate	n/a	2,800	4,300	3,100
New York Long Island	n/a	1,700	2,500	1,800
Total units from these areas*	10,900	36,500	54,800	99,600

CHRYSANTHEMUM (POMPON) IN 1000 UNITS BUNCHES/BLOOMS

	1949	1957	1961	1970
California	1,800	2,900	3,300	10,000
Colorado	150	200	100	160
Florida	30	7,500	8,400	11,800
Illinois	900	1,200	1,000	600
New York upstate	n/a	800	900	900
New York Long Island	n/a	700	700	600
Total units from these areas*	2,900	13,200	14,500	24,000

*Figures do not sum due to rounding

Source: Fossum (1973)

2 Number of United States flower growers, productivity, and prices, 1950–1970

	CARNATIONS			CHRYSANTHEMUM (POMPON)			CHRYSANTHEMUM (STANDARD)			ROSES		
	1950	1959	1970	1950	1959	1970	1950	1959	1970	1950	1959	1970
Growing establishments	3,536	3,275	1,875	n/a	4,694	2,598	n/a	4,135	2,462	595	583	464
Quantity in millions of stems or bunches	251	429	640	14	24	36	40	90	171	390	360	469
Productivity per establishment in 1000 stems or bunches	71	131	341	n/a	5	14	n/a	22	70	656	618	1011
Average price per unit in cents	8.0	7.2	7.8	71.4	79.2	86.1	17.5	17.8	19.9	7.9	8.6	12.8

Source: Fossum (1973)

rounding major urban areas. As land values appreciated, some northeastern growers sold their properties to real estate developers and moved to other parts of the country, establishing new farms with lower production costs. Others simply closed up.

THE RISE OF THE MAJOR CUT FLOWERS

Between 1950 and 1970 the five major cut flowers increased their share of the total value of flower production from 43 percent to 86 percent. Specialty cut flowers declined correspondingly from about 57 percent to 14 percent (see figure 5). New cultivation technology—such as "improved" insecticides and cooling systems for greenhouses—was partly responsible for increased productivity in major flowers.[17] Larger growers were more apt than smaller ones to adopt new technology and therefore increase productivity. Breeders had also begun to develop roses and chrysanthemums with new "profitable characteristics" including disease resistance and longer post-harvest life (Haley 1972). Such benefits were not necessarily passed on to the consumer in the form of longer vase life. Instead they encouraged flower farms to spring up further and further away from the final marketplace. High volume and cheaper production sustained low prices for middlemen but not necessarily for consumers since retail was still dominated by traditional florists.[18]

Carnations, chrysanthemums, roses, and gladioli now dominated most consumers' flowers choices. Why they tolerated such limited choice is unclear. General acceptance of mass-produced and uniform commodities may have been one of them. Piore and Sabel argue that relatively homogenous consumer tastes in the United States allowed greater success for mass-produced products. Consumer tastes in parts of Europe, in contrast, were more likely to be educated, defined, and differentiated by producers or retailers (1984, 41). Yet even undemanding consumers eventually lost interest in these standardized blooms. An American Florists Marketing Council study suggested that during the 1970s fewer people than previously were buying flowers. Most purchased only for obligatory occasions such as funerals and as gifts for special occasions such as birthdays. Few people bought flowers for themselves.[19]

Consumers didn't complain and growers didn't change. They successfully resisted significant innovation for almost two decades probably because, as Piore and Sabel put it, "the costs of innovation are easier to calculate than the potential benefits, it is easy to err on the side of caution and avoid change. Once caution has become a habit, new products are designed to fit the existing

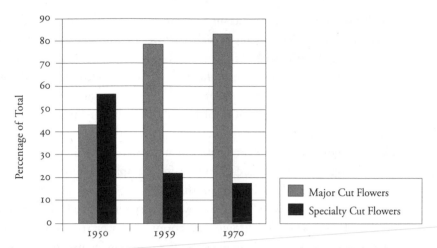

5 The major cut flowers and specialty cut flowers as a percentage of value of all cut flowers and greens, 1950–1970. Adapted from Fossum (1973).

setup—instead of the setup being refitted to suit the new product" (1984, 264). Undoubtedly locally grown seasonal specialty cut flowers with short seasons, such as peonies, stocks, and anemones, were offered in small quantities. But, as I discuss further along in this chapter, the wholesale and retail florists who governed over 90 percent of retail flower sales preferred the major cut flowers. It is likely they offered specialty flowers to the consuming public infrequently.[20] When they did, the low prices, improved quality, and perceived value of the major flower types made other flowers relatively expensive and therefore unappealing to the enlarging postwar middle classes.

NEW TRADING RELATIONSHIPS

The predictable quality of these uniform blooms, arriving from new growing areas, began to change the nature of middlemen services. It hastened the decline of the local consignment system and encouraged the emergence of additional levels of middlemen.

Under the consignment or commission system first established in New York in the late nineteenth century, the wholesale florist promised to act for the grower and to obtain the best possible price consistent with flower quality, market competition, and the ever-present need to sell flowers while fresh. For that service he retained a portion of the sale price as a commission.[21] The system had persisted in part because of the unevenness of flower quality and supply. Wholesalers were reluctant to promise a particular price in advance when important pricing qualities such as flower freshness, bloom size, color, and stem length varied with each bundle of blooms (Goodrich 1972). Disputes were common since wholesalers, rather than growers, graded and priced flowers and few uniform grading standards existed (Carbonneau et al. 1997, 45).

The consignment system was tolerated because it benefited both wholesaler and grower. When blooms were abundant and market prices low, the wholesale florist could accept consignment flowers without personal risk. When blooms were scarce and expensive, for example in holiday periods, he could usually depend on his relationship with the consignment grower to ensure a supply of flowers. For the grower the system offered advantages in periods of abundance and strong competition, when he trusted the wholesaler, with whom he had a long relationship, to give preference to his flowers. Growers were rarely knowledgeable about urban customers or current market conditions and prices. So this system spared them the daily business of price negotiation and marketing for which they were ill-prepared. The consignment system is still widely used in the U.S. international flower trade and will be discussed further in chapter 5. But the consignment system did not satisfy the needs of new large-scale growers. Large technology-intensive farms required substantial capital investment and their owners demanded more certainty about the market prospects for the enlarged crop. Fortunately, the uniform quality, predictable volumes, and low prices of mass-produced flowers soon allowed sellers and buyers to agree on prices prior to delivery and dispense with the consignment process.

High volumes of production, however, presented another problem for this new breed of growers. They depended on distant urban markets to absorb large quantities of flowers yet few had connections with wholesalers in the major markets in the Midwest and Northeast or with the supermarket chains that began retailing flowers in the 1970s. These difficulties were resolved for some growers by the emergence of another intermediary, the local grower-shipper, who advised neighboring growers, located the best customers, and traded cut flowers between the two for prices fixed in advance of delivery (Haley 1972).[22]

Thus, by the 1970s, growers and middlemen were operating in a dual marketing system: consignment for smaller growers and direct sales for larger ones.[23] Dana Goodrich's study of this system led him to suspect that it would eventually favor the larger, distant grower who sold his flowers at a fixed, agreed price. Wholesalers, he suggested, would give sales preference to the flowers in which they had already invested, rather than those they were handling on consignment. Eventually, this understandable attitude would confer advantage on the distant grower over the local grower. The distant grower could expect prompt payment at an agreed price while the local grower's consigned flowers might not be sold at any price (1972, 94–95). Over time, the consignment relationship between wholesalers and U.S. growers shifted in favor of direct payments as Goodrich predicted.[24] These relationships had little time to settle before the system was destabilized by the appearance of growers who were even more geographically distant from their principal markets.

NEW GROWERS

American growers had pushed the limits of seasonal constraints with the winter production of flowers in Florida, Colorado, and California. Climate and poor cultivation technology, however, were still limiting factors. Seasonality was still the general rule in mass flower production—standard chrysanthemums appeared mostly in fall and winter, roses and carnations were available from late spring to late fall. The revolutionary notion of growing and supplying massive quantities of the same flower in all seasons had occurred to only a handful of growers.[25]

At a colloquium on the future of domestic floriculture in the early 1970s, one of the speakers presciently predicted that flower growing was about to change. Future growers, he said, would need to invest millions of dollars in large farms with sophisticated management teams, efficient marketing, and production tailored to demand. Growers could no longer "afford to put millions of dollars in production of a crop and not know where it's being marketed and for what price." Instead flowers would be "grown for a specific market and . . . packaged or bunched by the grower for final sale to the public." The new "mass" market segment, he predicted, would buy from one source and expect to save on their quantity purchases. While his prediction was correct, the speaker did not foresee that most of these new growers would emerge in Colombia, Ecuador, and other Latin American countries rather than the United States (Haley 1972, 83–84).

The carnation again pioneered dramatic changes with important consequences for U.S. domestic flower growing. In the mid- to late 1960s a handful of Colombians began growing carnations near the Colombian capital, Santa Fe de Bogotá. At the time, the entire U.S. demand was met by domestic flower growers with the exception of small quantities of flowers imported from Canada, Netherlands, and Mexico. The very idea of growing perishable cut flowers in Colombia for sale in North America required considerable vision. Edgar Wells, a Colombian of British descent, was that visionary. Apparently, on a visit to New York City, Wells was impressed by the prices being paid for summer flowers at the Wholesale Flower Market on 28th Street.[26] Newly established regular jet flights between Bogotá and Miami may have been another factor in his decision to explore flower farming.[27] After consulting a Florida agronomist, Wells elected to grow carnations on the savannah of Bogotá. The region is suitable for many flower crops but he chose carnations for the same reasons they had appealed to Colorado and California growers: their sturdiness and long post-harvest life ensured tolerance of the long journey to northeastern U.S. markets. His firm, Flores Colombianas, imported carnation cuttings and other essentials from the United States and exported its first shipments of cut flowers to Miami in 1965.[28]

Future flowers raised in Colombia would flourish with technological innovations but these early plantings depended almost entirely on natural advantages. The high savannah area near the capital has rich soil and an ideal climate for flower growing. At 8,600 feet (2,650 meters) temperatures are even and moderate. Costly heating or cooling is needed only occasionally. Uniform twelve-hour days seduce many flowering plants into contented reproduction that ensures several crops a year. The seasonal and climatic challenges that limit U.S. growing areas do not apply here. Furthermore, wages for agricultural workers were, and are, significantly lower.[29] With these advantages, even allowing for the cost of air transportation, flowers destined for the high-paying U.S. markets could be grown and exported very profitably all year round.[30] From these imaginative beginnings Colombian flower growers eventually formed the world's second-largest cut flower exporting industry.

In the mid-1980s a fledgling Ecuadorian flower exporting industry also began rapid expansion. Several Ecuadorian farms were established by flower growers with previous experience in Colombia and Costa Rica.[31] But here the carnation played no part. By concentrating on large-headed, hybrid tea roses and growing them very well, Ecuadorian growers quickly claimed a share of the U.S. import market.

Total flower imports into the United States grew from $4 million in 1970 to $700 million in 2004. These new growing regions were responsible for much of the increase but not for all. After the mid-1980s, existing exporters to the

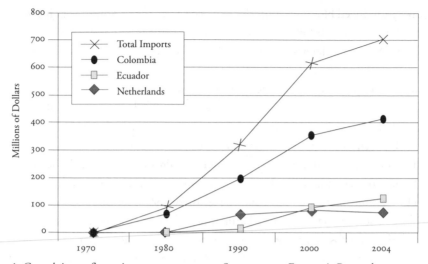

6 Growth in cut flower imports, 1970–2004. Source: USDA Economic Research Service. Trade Data Services.

United States such as Holland, Italy, and France expanded their production and began competing more actively in the international markets. After 1994 and the passage of NAFTA, Mexican and Canadian imports also expanded.

Figure 6 illustrates the rise of total U.S. imports of cut flowers between 1970 and 2003 as the United States developed into the world's largest market for imported fresh-cut flowers, principally from Colombia, Ecuador, and the Netherlands. Colombia's exports to the United States rose to $360 million during these three decades. Ecuador's export expansion occurred primarily in the 1990s while the Netherlands' exports expanded rapidly in the 1980s, then declined as a revaluation of the Dutch guilder made Dutch flowers suddenly expensive for Americans. The value of the Netherlands' exports to the United States increased slightly in the 1990s as the dollar appreciated (see chapter 3).

RESISTANCE TO IMPORTS

Throughout the twentieth century, growers with one or another system of production periodically attempted to exclude other cheaper flowers from a highly competitive market. Combatants generally claimed fairness and defense of free trade. As early as 1925, New York hothouse growers attempted to exclude from the wholesale market flowers produced by small seasonal growers. They insisted they needed to protect their capital investment and expensively produced blooms against the reduced prices for all flowers that inevitably followed the seasonal flood of cheaper field- or garden-grown flowers.[32] In comparison with later growers' attempts to protect their markets this was a modest effort. In the early 1970s, U.S. growers became openly concerned about the quantities of cheaper flowers coming from Colombia. California growers and shippers, who were responsible for a third of the nation's flowers, claimed they had lost 70 percent of their eastern sales to Colombian flowers.[33]

Regional and national associations were formed or activated to restrain flower imports, including the Bay Area Flower Promotion Council, the Floral Trade Council, and Roses Inc., an association of American rose growers.[34] Throughout the 1970s, 1980s, and 1990s, these and other trade organizations pursued legal remedies against Latin American flower growers or requested government subsidies for domestic growers.[35] Some actions focused on violations of anti-dumping and subsidies codes, others objected to proposed free trade agreements.[36] Growers claimed that unreliable imports would eventually cause flower shortages leading to price increases and lower demand.[37] These calamities did not occur; as we will see in the following chapters, the opposite proved to be the case.

Middlemen—importers, wholesale florists, and retail florists—benefited from the steady supplies of inexpensive imported blooms. Their lack of cooperation in these efforts to control imports was a persistent concern for growers. The problem was summed up by the Floral Trade Council in its January 1992 newsletter: "United States fresh-cut flower growers are not getting a lot of help from other groups in our efforts to bring about fairness in international trade, so we must do all of this on our own."

FADING U.S. GROWERS

U.S. growers predicted that imports would put them out of business; indeed, as noted earlier, their numbers and total output eroded steadily between 1970 and 2004 (Bonarriva 2003).[38] The greatest losses were in Colorado and Ohio, regions heavily committed to growing the carnations now flooding in from Colombia. Florida and California also lost growers to the competition from foreign flower producers. Failure to innovate was a continuing factor. Domestic growers who invested in new growing technologies and new flower varieties appeared to thrive. Those who specialized in one flower but grew many varieties or sought new markets also flourished. John Van Geest, a member of a transplanted Dutch family, described, in our interview, their crop and technology transitions:

We came here in 1967—thirty years ago—and started growing carnations [and] mums [chrysanthemums]. In early seventies we started looking at different crops for a niche because of the Colombian pressure. Good Dutch flowers were lilies, gerberas [they were] more exotic—not the commodity flowers. Gerberas were not being grown here [in California]. They are a difficult plant to grow. If they can grow them in Holland we should be able to do it here we thought. We use mechanized shading, humidity and feeding. Without them we would have three times the workforce. We also use hydroponics with a rockwool base. All the water is recycled—pumped round and heated up to kill pathogens.

Other trends added to the difficulties for U.S. growers. The oil embargo of the early 1970s created major problems as the price of greenhouse heating oil in the northeastern United States rose from ten cents to more than a dollar a gallon in a year.[39] Once again these costs could not be passed on and many small growers in the cold states simply closed their greenhouses (Haley 1972; Royer 1998). But even in New England some growers survived by adapting their crops. A Hudson Valley anemone grower, Bill Blocker, whose family once specialized in violets, recalled some of the changes he had witnessed:

> The biggest change is in number of greenhouse operations locally—there were six greenhouse flower growing operations [here] and seven in Dutchess and Ulster [counties]. Now only us and one other. They were growing mums [Chrysanthemums] carnations—they couldn't compete with South America. They have been closed and condos built over the land. We have a little niche product that grows in cool climates so we have survived. Generally you can't compete with low labor cost countries even with their big transportation costs. But growing operations have become more efficient. You can operate a place the size of this with one grower and computerized watering [and] feeding. . . . You have to find a niche product and market.

A final problem for domestic growers was uneven demand. From about 1900 to about 1980, most retail flower sales in the United States passed through traditional retail florists for whom profits came from religious and secular holidays such as Easter, Mother's Day, Christmas, or Thanksgiving when demand and prices were high. Small growers could not always tailor their production to meet these dates and there was little steady, weekly demand for flowers to absorb surplus blooms outside these holiday peaks. In missing a key holiday—unseasonably warm or cool weather might produce blooms too early or too late—a grower could miss his year's profit. After the 1980s this difficulty

	ALL U.S. FARMS			FARMS WITH SALES $100,000 OR MORE			FARMS WITH SALES LESS THAN $10,000		
	1987	1992	1997	1987	1992	1997	1987	1992	1997
No. of farms	4,561	6,065	5,381	913	901	818	2,285	3,455	3,035
Sales in millions dollars	595	645	718	542	579	658	7	10	9
Farms as percentage of all U.S. farms				20	15	15	50	57	56
Sales as percentage of all sales				91	90	92	1	2	1
Average farm sales in $1000				593	642	804	3	3	3

Source: *The Changing Floriculture Industry.* SAF 2000. Data taken from the Census of Agriculture and includes farms with at least $1,000 in agricultural sales.

began to diminish for wholesalers and retailers as steady supplies of flowers flowed into supermarkets and consumers began to make regular flower purchases. However, this did not help the small domestic grower who still depended on the holiday calendar because he was unable to supply the large weekly flower quantities demanded by supermarket chains.

Table 3 illustrates recent change in the total number of U.S. flower growers and their sales. Although the number of flower growers increased between 1987 and 1997, it is evident that the eight hundred farms with sales of $100,000 or more, a mere 15 percent of all U.S. farms by 1997, were responsible for 90 percent of the sales. Furthermore, sales for this group increased by 35 percent between 1987 and 1997.[40] By 2003 the number of large-scale growers had declined to less than 550. However, sales per farm continued to increase (Jerardo 2004). In 1997 almost 60 percent of U.S. flower growers were small producers with annual sales averaging $3,000. They supplied local markets with one or two specialized flowers or sometimes with many types of flowers over a growing season. Some sold to wholesalers but many sold directly to the consumer from their farms or from market stands. By 2003 their share had risen to 6 percent of the shrinking national output (Jerardo 2004, 9).

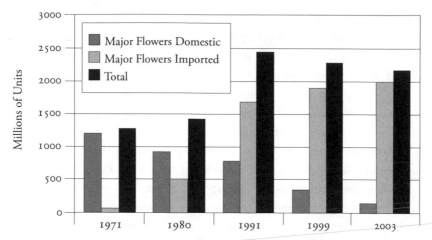

7 Major cut flower imports and domestic production, 1971–2003. Source: *The Changing Floriculture Industry* (SAF 2000) and USDA Economic Research Service Floriculture and Nursery Crops Situation and Outlook Yearbooks 1990/1997/1999/2004.

Over the thirty-year period 1971–2003, the domestic growers' share of total U.S. flower consumption of major cut flowers—roses, carnations, and chrysanthemums but excluding gladioli—shrank dramatically. By 2003 domestic growers supplied only 5 percent of U.S. demand for standard carnations, 25 percent for chrysanthemums, and 20 percent for roses (Jerardo 2004, 60).[41]

Wholesale and Retail Florists Strengthen their Positions

The wholesaling system, as previously explained, evolved during the last decades of the nineteenth century. It was well established in New York, Chicago, and other large cities by the turn of the century.[42] In urban areas wholesale florists located in terminal markets handled growers' cut flowers on consignment and distributed them to local retail florists.[43] The wholesale florist was essential to the retail florist because he divided large quantities of flowers into small bunches of blooms and offered a broad selection gathered from a wide range of growers. Most importantly, the wholesaler extended long-term credit to the retailer (Goodrich 1972).

During the expansive postwar years between 1950 and 1970, the number of wholesale florists in the United States doubled (see table 4). Most, however, were not especially profitable. Wholesale florists' average sales increased by only 38 percent and in the mid-Atlantic region by only 20 percent during that

Favored Flowers

time. In fact, according to Goodrich's study, 55 percent of all wholesalers had the same sales in 1967 as in 1954.[44] Goodrich's 1970 study of the major urban terminal markets suggests that the top 15 percent of wholesale florists produced about 60 percent of sales and were probably doing well. For the majority, however, profits were not keeping pace with inflation. It is possible that in a business often transacted in cash, sales were under-reported. Nevertheless, the average wholesale florist seemed to be struggling.[45]

There were several reasons for this weak performance. First, many more wholesalers were competing for the business of retail florists who were not expanding their numbers at the same rate. Second, few wholesalers were supplying supermarkets and other nontraditional flower retail outlets. Wholesalers were reluctant to alienate their traditional retail florist customers by supplying their retail competitors. Instead, growers and supermarket retailers were either dealing directly with each other or through the new intermediary segment in the chain, the grower-shipper (Goodrich 1972). Finally, extensive reliance on the consignment system was detrimental to wholesalers in the long term. Goodrich suggests that locally grown flowers were accepted on consignment because of personal relationships between growers and wholesalers who felt "a moral obligation to nearby growers after many years of such service" (94–95). By 1970, cheaper, good-quality standard chrysanthemums and carnations were available from California or Colorado.[46] Prices were reasonable even with the transportation costs to northeastern markets (Royer 1998). Retailers were now accustomed to these inexpensive good-quality, long-distance blooms. If not offered them they might turn to other wholesalers (Carpenter 1972, 40). Yet northeastern wholesalers still used the consignment system for as much as 60 percent of their flowers.[47]

While personal relationships and a moral obligation were important, economic and other factors may have influenced these continuing arrangements. Many wholesalers had a large proportion of their liquid assets tied up in accounts receivable because retailers were slow to pay. Distant flowers increasingly required prompt payment while payment through the consignment system was more elastic. Today's growers, for example, complain that under the consignment system they have to wait sixty to ninety days for payment as the consumer's money trickles slowly back down the chain to the grower. Furthermore, personal relationships ensured dependable supplies at holiday times when prices and profits were high. Finally, local flowers were probably fresher and, in their particular varieties, more suitable to the desires

4 Wholesale florist establishments and average annual sales, 1948–1967

	MID-ATLANTIC WHOLESALE FLORISTS			U.S. WHOLESALE FLORISTS		
	Number of wholesale florists	Annual sales millions dollars	Avg. annual sales thousands dollars	Number of wholesale florists	Annual sales millions dollars	Avg. annual sales thousands dollars
1948	179	42	235	636	148	233
1954	252	60	238	966	223	231
1958	218	62	284	903	202	224
1963	268	74	276	1065	297	279
1967	302	85	281	1305	422	323

Source: Adapted from Fossum (1973)

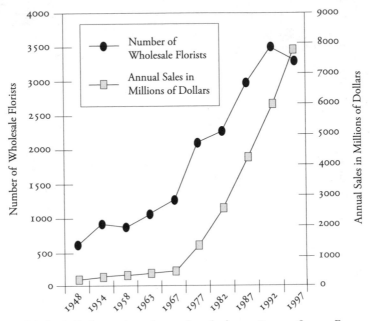

8 Wholesale florists total numbers and total sales, 1948–1997. Source: Fossum (1973): 1948–1967. *The Changing Floriculture Industry* (SAF 2000): 1977–1997.

of some local consumer sectors. But after 1970, as local growers steadily disappeared, wholesalers throughout the New York Metropolitan Area increasingly sought flowers from growers in California and Florida and eventually in Colombia, Ecuador, and the Netherlands. By the 1980s, year-round production of great quantities of the major cut flowers on large Andean farms provided wholesalers and retailers a continuous flow of good-quality standard blooms. Shortages of flowers that had plagued middlemen for a century in periods of peak demand around holidays were at last overcome. As imports expanded in the last three decades of the twentieth century both the number of wholesalers and their total annual sales rose dramatically, far exceeding the rate of growth in the previous twenty-year period 1948–67 (see figure 8).

For decades urban wholesale florists have had a long list of complaints. Their retail florist customers are disappearing. Rising costs, long hours, and city traffic present intractable problems. Even in the early 1970s they recommended against—and still do—entering a business that requires high capital investment for display premises, employees, and delivery services but offers only low returns on that investment. A final affliction is the necessity of supplying long-term credit to slow-paying retail florists, thus freezing large amounts of their capital (Goodrich 1972).[48] Yet these problems were not insurmountable. The new streams of abundant, imported flowers opened channels for innovative freelance wholesale florists who competed with the old established firms. These new wholesalers, appearing in the 1980s, surmounted barriers to entry by combining display and delivery services in the back of a single van, by being the sole employee, and by selling only on a cash basis. Their effect on retail and consumption will be explored in later chapters.

TRADITIONAL RETAIL FLORISTS

In the late nineteenth century, retail florists formed institutional links that shaped a coherent and vocal group, contrasting strongly with the weaker organizations of the less numerous wholesale florists and growers.[49] They offered three principal categories of floral service in response to the consumer demands described in the previous chapter. First, they provided flowers for religious holidays such as Christmas and Easter and rituals such as weddings and funerals. All social classes dependably demanded these services although total expenditures varied. Funerals were particularly important. In fact they were the bedrock of most florist businesses, since each funeral typically required many floral tributes, arrangements, and decorations. A second category involved flowers for celebrations and gifts for women and depended heavily on the social activities of the upper economic sectors. Flowers for domestic decoration constituted an unpredictable third category. Consumer expenditures and therefore retail florists' work in these last two categories waxed and waned with economic, social, and cultural shifts. Both were strongly influenced by periods of prosperity and austerity but generally were a dependable source of income in urban areas.

The number of retail florists grew with the population, rising prosperity, and expanding middle classes.[50] Average sales for New York area florists were double the national average as early as 1935, a trend that persisted through most of the century. In the years 1950–70, retail florists complained often about "poor quality, high prices and unreliable supply" from domestic growers. But they apparently enjoyed greater financial success than their wholesale colleagues. As figure 9 suggests, the number of florists increased in this period by about 50 percent but average florists' sales almost doubled; some of them were doing well.[51]

Until 1970, retail florists sold about 90 percent of all cut flowers. Competi-

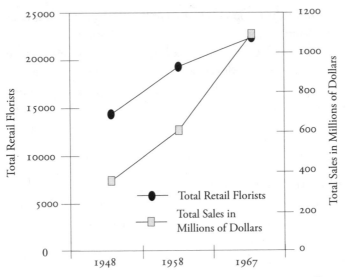

9 Traditional retail florists numbers and sales, 1948–1967. Source: Fossum (1973).

tion came chiefly from other florists and seasonal flower sellers.[52] However, there were signs of growing competition from nontraditional floral retail, especially supermarkets, which had captured about 37 percent of floricultural retail sales. Potted plant sales rather than cut flower sales accounted for most purchases at supermarkets but eventually these "other outlets" would dominate cut flower sales (see chapter 6).

CHANGING FLOWERS

In the century from 1870 to 1970, choice in cut flowers became steadily standardized and limited. The trend intensified after World War II but actually began much earlier. In 1925 the *New York Times* quoted a florist who deplored the market disappearance of charming garden flowers and the dominance of expensive greenhouse blooms.[53] By 1970, delicate garden flowers had dwindled in the commercial cut flower trade. The five major flowers constituted 80 percent of the blooms handled in terminal wholesale markets (Goodrich 1972, 91).

Why did florists allow specialty flowers to decline so much in commercial markets? Growers, as explained earlier, focused on the five major blooms because their cultivation techniques had been improved and mastered and allowed easy and profitable mass production. Retail florists, despite the regret reported by the *New York Times* in 1925, apparently also preferred carnations, chrysanthemums, and roses as their basic flowers (Eskilon 1997). Their popularity with florists rested on their long post-harvest life, their durability, and the long, strong stems that were easy to arrange in newly developed foam core bases. Furthermore, especially by the 1950s, predictable prices for standard blooms aided profitability for efficient retail florists. In effect many retail florists acted as gatekeepers of choice. Because they preferred inexpensive durable flowers that stored well and required less labor in presentation, many of them offered their customers a declining selection.

Consumer tastes were also changing. The postwar economic boom brought prosperity and a greatly improved standard of living to many Americans. Buying power spread gradually from a small upper social group to an enlarging middle class. Between 1950 and 1970 per capita real disposable income in the United States rose by 50 percent, from $6,200 to $9,900 (in 1987 dollars) (McConnell and Brue 1996; Norton et al. 2001). In New York City decades of substantial immigration—during which the foreign-born population sometimes reached 40 percent—altered the city's ethnic composition (Foner 2000). The social power of the proportionally diminishing white, Protestant upper class waned. Its traditions, tastes, and floral demands declined in importance; different values and floral customs surfaced.

The roles and experiences of women also affected flower consumption as the "comfortable" and "less comfortable" classes converged and the average American lived at a "decent" and "healthful" level (Cowan, 1983). A steady increase in the number of working women fueled some of the decent living. By the end of the 1950s, one third of the workforce was female and 55 percent of these women workers were married, rising to 60 percent by 1970 (Norton et al. 2001).[54] They enjoyed material improvements for their families and greater autonomy in purchasing decisions. A wife could buy an electric iron or a vacuum sweeper or flowers for a special occasion without consulting her husband or waiting for him to provide them.

Earlier floral customs had symbolically linked delicate fragrant blooms to an ideal of female sexuality, vulnerability, and dependence. But flowers to wear at balls and parties had little relevance to the values and interests of the middle classes who were economically important as consumers. New Yorkers still observed traditional Easter and Christmas rituals but paid increasing attention to a swelling list of nonreligious observance and gift days. Mother's Day, Valentine's Day, and eventually, Secretary's Day grew in popularity and required different sorts of flowers and presentations. Possibly a persistent ideal of female domestic thrift also contributed to the decline of delicate and perishable flowers. Many of them lost their scent on the first day after cutting and died on the second. Relative to the gradually dominating major blooms, they offered poor value to the growing postwar consuming classes. Finally, a general inclination toward social conformity, alluded to earlier, may also explain a growing preference for standardized fresh flowers.

My own feeling is that the economic power of larger growers and the gatekeeping skills of retail florists were important factors.[55] Specialized growers and some retailers continued to offer small quantities of the delicate garden or specialty flowers. By 1970, however, carnations, chrysanthemums, and roses formed the great majority of the bouquets expressing affection, affirming social roles, and welcoming guests to new middle-class homes in the suburbs.

Over the next thirty years the structure and governance of the fresh-cut flower commodity chain changed far more than during the entire previous century. Its reorganization brought an abundance of cheap blooms to New York Metropolitan Area consumers. The following chapters explore these organizational changes and corresponding changes in the relationships between flower growers, traders, and consumers.

Three

Fresh Flows: Global Flower Growing, 1970–2005

> The more perishable the commodity is and the greater the absolute restriction of its time in circulation as a commodity on account of its physical properties, the less it is suited to be an object of capitalist production.—KARL MARX, *Capital*

Writing in the late nineteenth century, Marx could not anticipate the revolutions in hybridization, packing, chilled storage, and rapid distribution that would transform horticulture over the next century. By the late twentieth century, advances in the control of natural processes made many types of horticulture—especially the production of perishable fruits and vegetables—increasingly attractive to capital investment. Susan Mann refers to this as "the civilization of nature." She argues that large capital investment in agriculture occurs only when the many natural barriers to efficient production are overcome. One of the most important of these is the time between harvests because delays slow reinvestment and the turnover of capital. Until the civilizing process occurs, Mann contends, production is left in the hands of small growers or simple commodity producers (1990).

During the last half of the twentieth century, in some agricultural regions, some horticultural crops like fresh-cut flowers steadily migrated from fields to greenhouses. Their high planting densities, small land requirements, and rapid reproduction suited them to enclosed growing environments. New technologies such as hydroponics, non-soil growing mediums, better propagation techniques, and light manipulation allowed multiple crops a year for some types of flowers such as chrysanthemums and carnations. Fresh-cut flowers quickly became a highly profitable "civilized" crop.

This "civilizing" process was an essential factor in attracting capital to cut flower growing and to the global expansion of the industry. Yet, as this chapter explains, it was not the only factor. Access to markets and technology, tariffs, state involvement, and local cultural characteristics are among a host of other important factors. Together they have stimulated the global growth of flower-growing enterprises ranging from tiny family farms to multinational businesses.[1] All are engaged in providing fresh flowers to North Americans, Europeans, Japanese, and many others.

The global expansion of flower growing and trading that occurred between 1975 and 2005 coincided with a similar trend in other kinds of horticultural production. At the same time, banking, manufacturing, finance, and media also reorganized into global operations (Korzeniewicz 1994; Taplin 1994; Gereffi 1994b; Castells 1996; Hirst and Thompson 1999). Information and goods (new and used) began to circulate more rapidly in a world in which barriers of time, distance, communication, and culture diminished (Harvey 1989; Blim 1992; Castells 1997; Warde 1997; Tranberg Hansen 2000). In that same period easier access to U.S. (as well as European and Russian) markets tempted not only Latin American growers but floriculturalists in more distant nations such as New Zealand, Israel, and Thailand. Braudel describes how the lure of "high prices at the far end of a trading chain" motivated seventeenth-century trade. When "the word got round . . . the whole chain went into motion" (1984, 44). High prices have precisely the same effect today. As new forms of communication speed the circulation of gossip and information about prices and markets, more growers join the global cut flower commodity chain. Increasing competition for markets forced U.S. domestic flower growers and some global growers to innovate and seek new solutions to this problem. They gradually adopted a strategy of continuous innovation and accommodation of change (Piore and Sabel 1984, 17). Over three decades a flexible flower system evolved. Individual sectors adjusted at different rates, but continuous responsive adjustment characterized the overall system. Competition, constant innovation, and cultural distance undermined the growers' previously strong position in the fresh-cut flower commodity chain. Governance of the extended chain gradually passed from growers to middlemen (see chapters 5, 6, and 7). Yet all participants—growers, traders, and consumers—remained tightly connected in a complex global chain (see figure 10).

Three important characteristics distinguished this new epoch of flower production and trade from the earlier period, 1870–1970. First, the majority of flowers for U.S. and New York Metropolitan Area consumers were globally grown rather than domestically produced. Second, a maturing global system generated an explosion of diversity in commercial cut flower varieties. Third, the "civilization of nature" freed flower choice from many of the earlier seasonal constraints while the shortages and related price fluctuations that troubled the pre-1970 flower trade virtually disappeared.

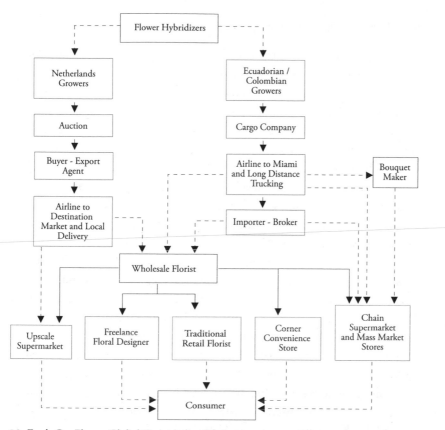

10 Fresh Cut Flower Global Commodity Chain

The first of this chapter's four sections outlines the global expansion of flower growing and the diversification of flower types. It also describes some of the effects of international flower production and trade on the U.S. flower growing industry. The second section analyses production differences between Colombia, California, Ecuador, and the Netherlands—the four primary suppliers of fresh flowers to the U.S. market today. The third section examines trade agreements while the final section describes the technological and financial innovations crucial to the reorganization of U.S. domestic flower production and the rise of a global trade in cut flowers.

New Growers, New Blooms

In 2003 the global trade in fresh-cut flowers amounted to about $4.6 billion. About sixty-five countries today produce flowers for export. The Netherlands, however, dominates the global production and export of fresh flowers, as it has done since the inception of large-scale fresh flower exporting in the late 1960s. The cut flower trade literature and popular press articles often focus on the production in developing countries of flowers intended for consumers in industrialized nations (Maharaj and Dorren 1995; Hughes 2000; Hughes 2004).[2] Yet this can give a misleading sense of global production since such perspectives seldom discuss the fact that most are exported from developed countries. In fact over 70 percent of these global flowers are exported from nations high on the United Nations human development index.[3]

As table 5 shows, six countries export about 90 percent of the world's flowers.[4] Some of the flowers produced by these major exporters find their way to the United States. Table 6 shows the major nations sending flowers to the U.S. market. Flowers from Colombia, Ecuador, Holland, Mexico, Costa Rica, and Canada have been consistently important for over a decade, while other supplying countries have changed their positions from year to year. Ireland, India, and China sent exports to the United States only recently, reflecting their emerging flower-exporting industries. Today, more than 70 percent of the fresh-cut flowers consumed in the United States are imported, primarily from Colombia, Ecuador, and the Netherlands.[5] Most of the remaining 30 percent are grown in California (Jerardo 2004).

In contrast to the 1950–70 trend toward species standardization, the period 1975–2005 was marked by expanding diversity in the species and varieties of flowers grown, traded, and consumed. Especially after 1985, apparent consumption of the four major flower crops declined while specialty flowers quadrupled (see figure 11). Furthermore both domestic and imported supplies of specialty cut flowers increased (see figure 12). California flower growers turned to new flowers in the early 1980s. Ewout Loogman, a grower of Dutch origin living in California, was one who learned to grow new flowers. "We had fifteen acres of chrysanthemums in greenhouses when I first came here," Ewout explained during our interview. "Because of competition from South America we started gerberas, alstroemerias, lilies—new things that grew well here. Over time we had many different products." Ewout acknowledged that diversification was thrust on him by competition from Colombian chry-

5 Principal global cut flower exporting countries, 1998 and 2003

1998 rank	Country	1998 exports mil. US$	% Total	Cumul. %	2003 rank	Country	2003 exports mil. US$	% Total	Cumul. %
1	Netherlands	2,296	56	56	1	Netherlands	2,779	61	61
2	Colombia	600	15	71	2	Colombia	679	15	76
3	Ecuador	202	5	76	3	Ecuador	293	6	82
4	Israel	175	4	80	4	Kenya	175	4	86
5	Kenya	132	3	83	5	Spain	87	2	88
6	Spain	96	2	85	6	Italy	77	2	90
7	Italy	80	2	87	7	Israel	73	2	92
8	Zimbabwe	62	2	89	8	Belgium	55	1	93
9	Thailand	52	1	90	9	Thailand	50	1	94
10	Belgium	32	1	91	10	United States	47	1	95
11	France	30			11	United Kingdom	36		
12	Mexico	29			12	Germany	31		
13	Germany	29			13	Rep. of Korea	29		
14	Costa Rica	28			14	Costa Rica	27		
15	New Zealand	23			15	New Zealand	23		
16	United States	21			16	Canada	21		
17	Turkey	17			17	France	19		
18	Canada	16			18	Mexico	18		
19	Australia	16			19	Singapore	16		
20	South Africa	15			20	South Africa	16		
	All Others	137				All Others	125		
	Total	4,088				Total	4,676		

Source: 1998: International Floriculture Trade Statistics, 1999. 2003: United Nations Statistics Division—Commodity Trade Statistics Database.

6 Major cut flower suppliers to the United States, 1990 and 2004

1990 rank	Country	Imports in $1,000	% Total imports	% Cumul.	2004 rank	Country	Imports in $1,000	% Total imports	% Cumul.
1	Colombia	199,139	61.0	61.0	1	Colombia	414,858	59.3	59.3
2	Netherlands	63,371	19.3	80.3	2	Ecuador	134,215	19.2	78.5
3	Mexico	13,438	4.0	84.3	3	Netherlands	65,599	9.4	87.9
4	Ecuador	9,597	3.1	87.4	4	Canada	21,074	3.0	90.9
5	Costa Rica	9,195	3.0	90.4	5	Costa Rica	18,501	2.6	93.5
6	Thailand	4,017	1.2	91.6	6	Mexico	14,256	2.0	95.6
7	Canada	3,830	1.2	92.8	7	Israel	5,685	0.8	96.4
8	Peru	3,624	1.2	94.0	8	New Zealand	4,257	0.6	97.0
9	Guatemala	3,316	1.2	95.2	9	Guatemala	4,037	0.6	97.6
10	France	2,952	0.9	96.1	10	Thailand	3,240	0.5	98.1
11	Israel	1,967			11	Peru	2,604		
12	Australia	1,549			12	Brazil	2,268		
13	Italy	1,245			13	Chile	1,983		
14	Jamaica	1,230			14	Dominican Rep.	1,171		
15	Taiwan	825			15	Australia	1,157		
16	Dominican Rep.	801			16	Italy	783		
17	New Zealand	696			17	South Africa	688		
18	Chile	558			18	France	667		
19	Swaziland	518			19	Kenya	597		
20	Brazil	468			20	Ireland	429		
	All other countries	3,910				All other countries	1,535		
	Total imports	326,246				Total imports	699,604		

Source: USDA Economic Research Service. Trade Data Services. Figures do not sum to 100 because of rounding.

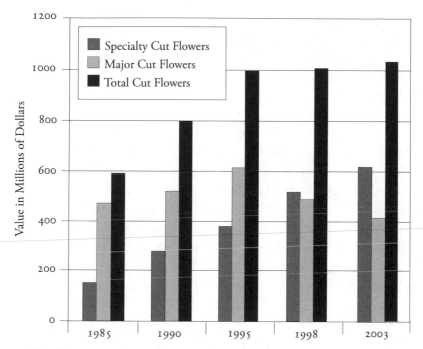

11 United States specialty cut flowers in relation to consumption of all cut flowers, 1985–2003. Sources: USDA Economic Research Service Floriculture and Nursery Crops Situation and Outlook Yearbooks 1990/1997/1999/2004.

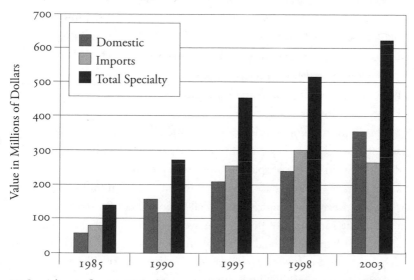

12 Specialty cut flowers: United States domestic production and import increases, 1985–2003. Sources: USDA Economic Research Service Floriculture and Nursery Crops Situation and Outlook Yearbooks 1990/1997/1999/2004.

santhemums.[6] By 2000, he farmed thirty-five acres (about fourteen hectares), growing twelve different flowers all year round as well as several seasonal blooms. He echoed the stories of many other U.S. growers when he said that diversification and expansion were critical to survival.[7]

About 70 percent of current U.S. domestic production comes from California, where cut flower growers now offer more than one hundred different species and many varieties within those different species. They include perishable and fragrant rarities like sweet pea (*Lathyrus*), tuberose (*Polianthes*) and lily-of-the-valley (*Convallaria*) that were popular a century earlier. Colombian growers did not offer them, in part because of their delicacy and preference for cool growing temperatures.[8] New organizations helped California growers develop these crops. The Association of Specialty Cut Flower Growers, established in 1988, focused on educating growers about the production and marketing of specialty flowers.[9] Soon after, the California state government established the California Cut Flower Commission to market California flowers and conduct grower-directed research and educational programs (Carbonneau et al. 1997, 43). In 2000, Roses Inc. became the International Cut Flower Growers Association. The change reflected the altered composition and production of Roses Inc.'s grower members, fewer of whom were growing roses. This grower organization also educates growers and aims to "advance the interests of commercial cut flower growers."[10] Marketing assistance from these organizations probably contributed to expanding consumer interest in unusual blooms. Yet even as early as 1982, a Boston florist observed that once his customers had seen "fancy flowers" like "alstroemerias, brodiaeas, ixieas" they would no longer settle for a bunch of chrysanthemums.[11]

By 1982, however, Colombian flower growers were already experimenting with specialty flowers. They soon exported alstroemerias (the Peruvian lily first hybridized in Europe), oriental and Asiatic lilies, and gerbera along with roses, carnations, and chrysanthemums. By 2004, Colombian exports included almost fifty types of specialty flowers, representing 43 percent of their flower exports.[12] Growers have a financial incentive to aim for specialty flowers. In 2000 the average import price of all imported cut flowers was twenty-two cents but for specialty flowers the average price was eighty-four cents (reflecting perhaps additional costs in production).[13] By the early 1990s, flowers once rare and luxurious such as freesia, alstroemeria, lily, and gerbera, joined carnations, pompon chrysanthemum, gladioli, and many roses in the ranks of commonplace flowers.

7 Comparison of principal United States cut flower suppliers, 2003

Country	Approx. no. growers	Approx. tot. hectares	Approx. exports $mil. (California and Netherlands total production)	Avg. production in $/hectare
Colombia	500	5,600	787	140,000
California+	300	2,100	366	174,000
Ecuador	250	3,200	287	89,000
Netherlands*	6,700	6,000	3,500	583,000

*Four-fifths of California flowers are field grown.
+Total Netherlands floriculture—cut flowers and potted flowers.

Sources: Colombia: Asocolflores and USITC 3580 Feb. 2003. California: California Cut Flower Commission. Ecuador: Expoflores and Floraculture Int'l. April, 2005. Netherlands: Flower Council of Holland.

Flower Suppliers

Four regions supply most U.S. flowers: Colombia, California, Ecuador, and the Netherlands. Each has a distinct mode of production. In Colombia and Ecuador the average farm size is ten to twelve hectares, although a single growing enterprise may own several farms and a few control hundreds of hectares. The typical Dutch farm, in contrast, is less than one hectare. Netherlands flower growers are numbered in the thousands compared with a few hundred each in Colombia, Ecuador, and California.[14] Furthermore, as table 7 suggests, average productivity per hectare is lower in Colombia and Ecuador than in California and the Netherlands. One Dutch hectare produces flowers with an approximate export value six times that of an Ecuadorian hectare and four times that of a Colombian hectare. Variations in productivity, types of flowers grown, mix of flowers, and the market value of each flower type in domestic and global markets contribute to these differences (see chapter 5).[15]

California produces many field-grown flowers while blooms from Colombia, Ecuador, and the Netherlands are more likely to have grown in glasshouses or plastic-covered houses. Furthermore, while all grow roses and chrysanthemums, roses represent close to 80 percent of production for Ecuador but only about 20 percent of the production for the Netherlands and 6 percent for California. California produces large quantities of gerbera (now considered a major cut flower) but also has the greatest proportion of total production in specialty cut flowers (see figure 13).

Fresh Flows

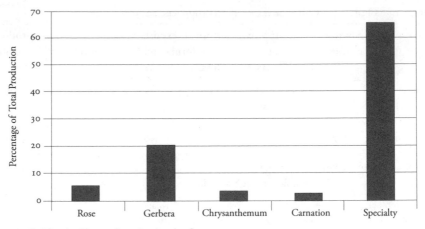

13 California: Share of production by flower type, 1997.
Source: Prince and Prince (1998).

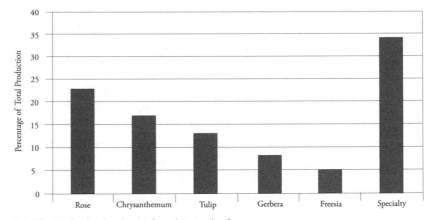

14 The Netherlands: Share of production by flower type, 2000.
Source: VBN Statistiekboek 2000.

The Netherlands specializes in roses, followed by chrysanthemums and tulips. Tulips are suited to the Netherlands' soil and climate and are difficult to grow in the other three regions (although tulip production in the United States and exports from Chile are increasing). The Netherlands' large specialty cut flowers sector has by far the greatest diversity of species as well as enormous volume—as much as three billion blooms annually. As noted earlier, average prices for specialty flowers are higher than average prices for major cut flowers (see figure 14).

Chapter Three

Colombia's production initially concentrated on the three traditional major cut flowers—roses, carnations, and chrysanthemums. However after 1990, disease, global competition, and low market prices in proportion to shipping weight and freight costs prompted a reduction in chrysanthemum and carnation production, while specialty cut flowers expanded. Colombia's specialty segment includes alstroemeria and gerbera (considered major flowers in California) as well as newer specialty flowers such as aster and liatris (see figure 15). Ecuador's dominant crop is roses. Gypsophila, carnation, and chrysanthemum and specialty cut flowers are minor crops whose exports declined between 1995 and 2003 (see figure 16).

Tariffs, Trade Pacts, and Subsidies

Tariffs and subsidies offer valuable protection for national flower industries. As explained in chapter 2, faltering U.S. flower growers faced with global competition tried, but failed, to qualify for domestic subsidies, perhaps because they lacked the political weight of the cotton, soybean, or sugar industries. In the 1980s and late 1990s their attempts to block foreign flower imports through duties and opposition to trade agreements were more successful.[16] Following successful suits in the late 1980s, the International Trade Commission approved various anti-dumping and countervailing duties against Canada, Mexico, Chile, Colombia, Costa Rica, and Ecuador. These duties added to the costs of flowers imported from those countries and created difficulties for their growers.[17] At times, U.S. tariffs on imported flowers from Costa Rica were as high as 19 percent of the market value at port of entry while 10 percent was levied against other Latin American countries. Imports did not decline as a result of anti-dumping duties; instead these duties encouraged some Colombian growers to convert their production to specialty cut flowers that brought higher prices and were less likely than the major flowers to be monitored and subject to anti-dumping duties.[18] Such shifts eventually changed the market for certain species such as gerbera and freesia as Colombians began growing them in large quantities. Dutch and Californian growers reshaped their strategies by introducing new varieties of gerbera and freesia and exploiting other specialty cut flower species.

In the early 1990s, U.S. political concerns also intervened to benefit Latin American flower growers. The first Bush administration was concerned to encourage production of legitimate crops like flowers and discourage coca

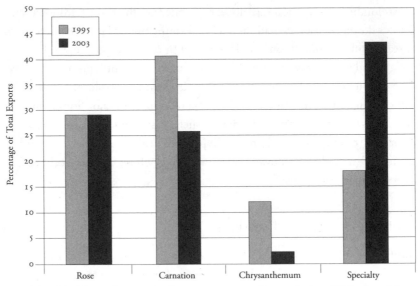

15 Colombia: Share of exports by flower type, 1995 and 2003. Source: White (1997) for 1995 and Asocolflores for 2003.

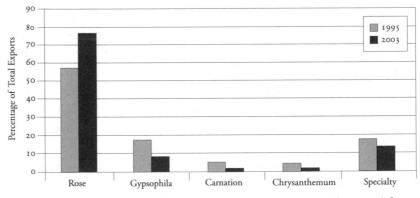

16 Ecuador: Share of exports by flower type, 1995 and 2003. Source: White (1997) for 1995 and Expoflores for 2003.

growing in the Andean region.[19] The Andean Trade Preferences Act was passed in 1991 and eliminated all tariffs on flowers from Colombia, Ecuador, Bolivia, and Peru, substantially improving the flower exporting prospects of these nations.[20] The Caribbean Basin Economic Recovery Act (CBERA) (1984) aided other countries, especially Costa Rica. The Generalized System of Preferences (GSP) aided imports from Chile while Israeli flowers benefited from the United States-Israel Free Trade area. Duty-free flowers from Sub-Saharan African nations benefit from the African Growth and Opportunity Act (AGOA) 2000 although imports have not changed substantially since its passage. However, flower imports from Mexico increased sharply following the passage of 1994 North American Free Trade Agreement—then declined again after 2001. Mexican flower growing may have benefited from increased levels of American investment in Mexico since 1994. At least one large California flower-growing enterprise is now producing some of its flower crops in Mexico. The strength and weakness of the U.S. dollar since 1994 may have been a factor in fluctuating Mexican as well as Canadian flower exports.[21] Freedom from import duties confers definite advantages in the global flower trade—it aids competitiveness and helps to offset rising costs for such things as labor and imported equipment. By 2001, as a result of these various trade agreements, 85 percent of U.S. flower imports entered duty free. The European Union, in contrast has an 8.5 percent to 12 percent tariff on imported cut flowers from many countries (Bonarriva 2003), making it a less attractive market for many Latin American growers. Yet there are other less obvious barriers for exporting countries; phytosanitary regulations are one of the most important. These plant health regulations mandate inspection of incoming flower shipments for insects and diseases that are potential sources of infestation for the receiving country.[22] Phytosanitary regulations severely limit market opportunities for some flower-exporting countries. Japan, for example, has rigorous standards that few exporting countries can satisfy. In some receiving countries enforcement acts as an unevenly applied political tool that protects a domestic flower-growing industry. For example, New Zealand's flower exports to Australia sometimes undergo rigorous inspection and lengthy fumigation but pass easily into the Netherlands and the United States.

After 2003, roses and other cut flowers imported into European Union countries faced stricter phytosanitary regulations that make exporting to European Union countries expensive, bureaucratic, and time consuming. By discouraging and reducing competitors these new requirements may protect

European Union rose growers, including those in the Netherlands who alone produce about two billion rose stems annually.[23]

Innovation

New technologies and other innovations were critical to the geographic expansion of flower growing and trading. Perishability, as we have seen, is a governing characteristic of cut flowers. The majority would still be grown around the cities that consume them were it not for the development of refrigerated trucking and storage in the 1960s. The declining cost of rail, trucking, and eventually jet transportation was another important factor. This permitted growers to establish farms in areas with lower production costs thousands of miles from their prime markets. Recent innovations in flower handling, hybridizing, and propagation improved quality and lengthened post-harvest life, while also vastly expanding the variety of commercial cut flowers. During the last decade, new communication and other technologies smoothed flower trading and marketing. Finally, flexibility in international financial transactions contributed to transnational investment in flower growing. These important factors are briefly examined below.

TRANSPORTATION

Because value depends on freshness, swift transportation from farm to market is fundamental to profitable production and trade in cut flowers. Value may decline as much as 25 to 50 percent with each day that passes after harvest (depending on flower species). Consequently, the fastest forms of transportation were always rapidly adopted; rail in the late nineteenth century, trucking in the mid-twentieth century, and jet transportation in the late twentieth century. Each innovation allowed flower growing to migrate to ever distant and cheaper areas of production.[24] After 1970, international jet passenger and cargo flights encouraged international flower growers to produce for the U.S. and European markets. The declining costs of air freight were a related factor. By 2000, more than 70 percent of the flowers consumed in the United States reached their markets entirely or partly by air. Yet in some ways the air transportation that strengthened global flower growing also proved to be a weakness. One problem with air transportation is a penalizing variation in cost. Growers in Kenya and New Zealand, for example, are many thousands of miles from their nearest markets. New Zealand growers compensate by concentrating on new and unusual flowers such as gentians and long-stemmed calla lilies that command high prices. Colombia and Ecuador are closer to their primary North American market, but they produce similar flowers and Ecuadorian air freight rates to Miami are considerably higher than those of neighboring Colombia despite similar transit times. Ecuadorian growers absorb these costs to remain internationally competitive. By 2005 the rising costs of oil had increased the costs of flying flowers around the world for all global growers. A second problem is service disruption.[25] When service falters or airline companies fail unpredictably, flower growers are left with limited or no alternatives for transporting their flowers to distant markets.[26]

Flower growers located within or adjacent to their major market enjoy a significant transportation advantage because they can use trucks. The Netherlands, for example, exports about 95 percent of its flowers by truck to other European nations. California, Mexico, and Canada also depend heavily on trucking to transport their flowers to U.S. markets. Lower costs, consistently cool temperatures, and regularly scheduled services over the interstate highway system are reasons to favor trucking over air transportation. Consequently, most flower shipments travel by road from California to northern and central regions of the United States and from Florida to the northeastern cities (First Research 1978; Waters and Prevatt 1983).[27]

HYBRIDIZATION

As flower production was gradually severed from the "natural" season of bloom and distant and different climates were utilized for flower growing, new flowers were introduced. Hybridization or breeding evolved rapidly if not quite in tandem with the emergence of new growing regions and climates. Early breeders of commercial cut flowers attempted to develop characteristics such as new tints and shades, more open blooms, and so on to enhance floral appeal to retailers and consumers. Recently breeders have exploited characteristics intended to extend the geographic and climatic range of certain flowers. These new characteristics appeal to the grower rather than to the consumer. They include higher bloom yield per plant, disease resistance, tolerance of a greater range of growing temperatures, tighter buds for uniform packing, longer post-harvest life, and diminutive bloom sizes to fit into ready-made bouquets. Breeding and testing a new rose, carnation, or alstroemeria takes about five to seven years. Breeders bring new flowers to the attention of growers only when they are completely satisfied with their appearance and performance. The search for profitable new flowers tremendously increased the number of hybrid new flowers introduced in the period 1975–2000. (See chapter 5 for more discussion of breeding and genetically modified flowers.)

Tissue culture propagation, another important development of the last twenty years, also helped to spread new flower forms. This laboratory process generates identical, healthy plants from the tissue of a mother plant. Not all flowers lend themselves to this reproductive process; roses, for example, are reproduced by the more laborious process of grafting. But where appropriate, in orchids or chrysanthemums for instance, the tiny tissue-cultured plants are easily multiplied, rooted in a sterile medium, and air-freighted to growers or propagators around the world.

HANDLING AND GRADING

Growers and shippers also developed new cost-saving methods of packing, palletizing, and handling fresh flowers. All contribute to longer post-harvest life and therefore preservation of the flower's quality and value during long-distance trading.[28] Flower shipping boxes, for instance, are standardized for uniform packing and palletizing for air transportation. Specialized forms of packaging and cushioning within the boxes have been developed to protect different flower forms. Packing systems for rose, gerbera, anthurium, gypsophila, and orchid are each quite different.

However, uniform quality grading—an important aspect of most long-distance trade in perishables—is poorly developed in the U.S. cut flower industry. One reason for this problem is the enormous numbers of different types of flowers, each with its own quality characteristics. Grading of the major cut flowers has been standardized to some degree. Roses, for example, are usually graded by variety, stem length, and tightness or openness of bud. Importers, wholesalers, and retailers are reasonably certain of receiving the requested variety, stem length, and bud aperture. Freshness grading and freshness dating (both important components of quality and widely used in Europe) are rarely used among growers supplying the U.S. trade.[29] This lack of dependable, industry-wide quality or freshness grades is a significant factor in the need for long-term personal relationships. In effect, as I show in succeeding chapters, such relationships substitute for industry standards—they provide personal guarantees of freshness and quality.

COMMUNICATION

Flower growers and traders gradually adopted most new forms of communication including telex, fax, and the Internet, when they appeared. However, telephone still remains one of the most important means of communication at this time. Frequent conversations (sometimes with cellular phones) between individuals in the chain are considered essential to gauge quality, discuss availability, and negotiate quantity and price. Sophisticated telephone systems, satellite as well as cellular, have been adopted by some Latin American growers who handle their own marketing. These systems give them a service edge by allowing their customers to reach them anywhere and at all hours. More and more growers also invest in computerized bar-coding technology to track boxes of flowers, reducing casual losses and again offering their customers a higher level of service.

The Internet, widely employed in some industries to create new communication or trading opportunities, is unevenly utilized in the cut flower industry. Among flower traders its chief contribution seems to be in speed rather than innovation. Transactions between growers and sellers with well-established relationships are accelerated through e-mail and websites. Exporters in Holland, for example, continuously update their computerized inventory of available flowers. Their auction flower purchases are immediately listed and available for purchase by their global wholesale florist customers. In theory, Internet communication should allow growers to dispense with trading through the major physical markets in Aalsmeer, Miami, and other places and permit them to arrange direct transactions with wholesalers or even retailers. In practice, however, uncertainties about grade, quality, and transportation restrain adoption of such aspects of Internet trading.[30] A lack of reliable information about market prices and conservatism or skepticism among growers and traders may also be limiting factors (see chapter 6). Some Dutch growers use the Internet to review data on their sales at the auction and employ linked data management programs to shape decisions about new plantings. However, Trip's study (2000) of chrysanthemum growers suggests this fusion of electronically gathered information with data management programs is not yet widespread in the Netherlands. Many traditional retail florist establishments use computers for interflorist orders and other transactions. Internet order gatherers, such as 1-800-FLOWERS and several other types of Internet floral services are a growing but still very small component of floral retailing (see chapter 6).

INTERNATIONAL INVESTMENT

Easier transfer of international funds in the last few decades has almost certainly encouraged the development of new flower farms. In the early days of global flower growing in the 1960s and 1970s, international investment often meant that a grower emigrated with his family to a new location, taking his own and other family members' funds with him to begin a new enterprise. That still happens but funds can now be transferred around the world within days, and in today's cut flower industry money migrates more often than people.

By 2000 the globalization of the flower industry and the dispersal to many growing regions of Dutch people, finance, and expertise, ensured that most flower-producing countries had some foreign (usually individual but occasionally corporate) investors. Colombia appears to lack Dutch influence, but it is evident in Costa Rica, Chile, Zimbabwe, Ecuador, Canada, the United States, and many other major flower-growing regions around the world, both visibly, through growers and expert advisors, and invisibly, through investors.[31] Americans also invest in growing and exporting in Ecuador, Chile, Mexico, and Costa Rica. Dole Fresh Flowers, a privately owned transnational corporation, owns four of the largest farms in Colombia as well as farms in Ecuador and Mexico and is said to produce 25 percent of Colombian flower exports. (See chapter 7 for more on Dole Fresh Flowers.) A few other, non-Colombian individuals occupy special market niches. A Swiss grower near Bogotá sells 70 percent of his small, high-quality production to wholesalers in Switzerland. Although precise figures on these kinds of investments are not available, anecdotal evidence from growers and traders suggests that cross-national investment in growing and trading enterprises is common.

PROSPERITY

Finally, increased, dispersed prosperity in the northern consuming regions was a necessary condition for the expansion of the flower industry. This study is concerned with consumption in the New York Metropolitan Area of the United States but increased wealth and greater demand for cut flowers in Europe and Japan also contributed to the evolution of new flowers and new technologies that aided growing, exporting, and trading around the world after 1970 (Burket and Workman 1977). Between 1970 and 2000 the population of the United States increased by about 38 percent, from 203 to 281 million, and wealth per capita increased more than in previous periods (Norton et al. 2001). During the boom period 1990–2000, median family incomes grew 9.5 percent. Improvement was concentrated in the top quintile of families, with modest increases in the middle sectors while, by some measures, the bottom 40 percent of families had declines in real income (Norton et al.

2001).[32] Yet the absolute numbers of consumers in these various quintiles increased, including those in the middle and upper sectors who are more apt to buy flowers.

Conversely, setbacks in economic prosperity, changes in exchange rates, wars, terrorism, and threats of epidemics are among the many unpredictable and uncontrollable factors that can suddenly reduce demand for flowers or halt their distribution. The Russian economic collapse of 1998, the terrorist attacks in New York and Washington in September 2001, and the SARS epidemic of 2003, for example, were serious setbacks for many growers and traders of flowers.

Today's global growers share unevenly in the effects of tariffs, technology, investment, and the "civilization of nature." The following chapter explores how these factors constrain or encourage growers and the important role of the state in these processes in two different regions, the Netherlands and Ecuador.

Four

State and Structure:
Floriculture in a Global System

Netherlands and Ecuadorian flower growers have successfully supplanted many American domestic growers, yet each has done so by
developing distinctly different flower-growing industries. Three
factors help to structure these differences. One is historical variation in land
availability and distribution. Another is distinct national political and economic conditions. A third is the willingness and ability of state institutions to
nourish, support, or oversee economic development strategies in a national
flower-growing industry.[1] The following sections explore these factors and
provide background for a later examination of the daily choices and decisions
of individual growers in chapter 5.

Floriculture in the Netherlands

In 1728, Daniel Defoe described the Dutch role in worldwide trade in terms
that are strikingly appropriate for the Netherlands' role in the global flower
trade today. The Dutch, he wrote, "really are, the Middle Persons in Trade,
the Factors and Brokers of Europe . . . they buy to sell again, take in to send
out, and the greatest Part of their vast Commerce consists in being supply'd
from All Parts of the World, that they may supply All the World again."[2]

For centuries, agricultural trade has been of great importance in this wet
and grassy land set in the delta of three major rivers, at the edge of the North
Sea in Western Europe. The climate is mild and maritime throughout its
41,500 square kilometers (16,000 square miles). One quarter of the land lies
below sea level and 18 percent is covered by water (Hooker 1999). Population
concentration in the western cities of Amsterdam, Delft, and The Hague
encouraged the early development of horticultural cash crops, including vegetables, fruits, and flower bulbs.[3] By the twentieth century the percentage of
workers employed in agriculture had begun to decline, falling dramatically
from 31 percent in 1899 to less than 2 percent in 1999 (Strijker 1986). At

the same time, improved productivity generated troubling agricultural over-production. Fortunately, the formation of the European Economic Community in 1957 and later the European Community Free Trade Area in 1968 offered a new market for this surplus. Private firms and agricultural cooperatives succeeded in the new European market for three reasons. First, Holland commanded a well-developed agricultural infrastructure, especially in processing and distribution. Second, education and knowledge about various agricultural production techniques were extensive. The state also invested heavily in agricultural research that was closely linked with the needs of the industry. Third, a long tradition of trading rather than manufacturing prepared the Dutch to take advantage of the new situation quite rapidly (Strijker 1986). These factors contributed, in turn, to the current commanding success of Dutch floriculture.

Today, over 50 percent of the nation's income derives from foreign trade. Twenty percent of exports are agricultural and Holland is the world's third largest exporter of agricultural products behind the United States and France.[4] The Netherlands is a prosperous nation. With a population over sixteen million, its Gross Domestic Product per capita in 2003 was over $31,900 ($29,500 at purchasing power parity), while inflation in recent years has averaged 2.9 percent.[5] For some decades Holland has been the world's largest flower exporter. In 2003 exports (excluding potted plants and other forms of flower production) were valued at about US$2.8 billion.[6]

FLOWER GROWING

Large-scale commercial flower growing began around 1900. An expanding market and easy distribution through cooperative auctions established in 1912 allowed each grower to specialize in one or two flowers. Wholesale buyers transported flowers from the growing areas clustered around auction centers to urban consumers. A growing and marketing apparatus evolved that was "delicately adapted to meet the demand for flowers by the different categories of consumers" (Van Stuijvenberg 1961, 288). By 1960, 50 percent of flower production was exported to other European countries, especially to Germany, still the major market for Dutch flowers. Dutch floriculturalists were well positioned to supply an expanding European Community and after the 1970s the Dutch flower industry grew dramatically. By 2003, 6,700 Dutch flower growers occupied 6,000 hectares of greenhouses and were producing cut flowers and flowering potted plants valued at 3.5 billion dollars (farm value).[7]

State and Structure

Flower growing in glass greenhouses (still occasionally referred to as "hot-houses") was common in the first part of the twentieth century but increased substantially after the 1970s. Compared with other forms of Dutch agriculture it is very labor intensive and employs about one third of total Dutch horticultural labor. It is also highly productive. Flower farms occupy only 6 percent of the total horticultural land area but generate almost 50 percent of horticulture's production value (Product Board 2000). The number of individual flower farm holdings has declined since 1970, suggesting concentration, yet the average farm size increased only from .22 to .87 hectares and the small farm still dominates (Statistiek 1999; Product Board 2000).[8] Today's Dutch flower grower is typically a self-employed individual who runs his own small growing enterprise of less than one hectare and is expert in growing one flower species to a very high standard. About a third of flower workers are family members. They are employed in tending and harvesting flowers rather than in organizational, marketing, or management roles (Statistiek 1999). The experiences of these growers are explored in chapter 5.

MARKETING

The economic well-being of Dutch flower growers and wholesale flower buyers depends on the system of cooperative auctions that market most of the millions of blooms produced daily by Dutch growers. The auction system and its benefits to flower growers are described in chapter 5. Here, however, I would like to stress the close spatial relationships that are a key element of auction complexes. These large complexes provide goods and services for the flower farms often tightly clustered around the auction centers. They also arrange transportation, trade, and distribution of the blooms. All these activities are carried out by closely connected groups of households, firms, and institutions working within what is sometimes referred to as a "cluster" (Porter 1990; Humphrey and Schmitz 2000), an "agribusiness complex" (Cardol 1988), or an "industrial district" (Piore and Sabel 1984; Cardol 1988). Within these complexes, intragroup social relations (connections among growers) are far stronger than intergroup social relations (between segments of the commodity chain). This contrasts with the Ecuadorian pattern of growing and distribution, where, as we will see, social relations between commodity chain segments (for example, between growers and importers) are key elements in a grower's economic well-being (see chapters 5 and 6).

The Netherlands has a long tradition of government by consensus among social groups who effectively take part in the state through mechanisms of consultation and compromise (Van Der Horst 1996). Shetter describes Dutch social and economic planning as deriving naturally from the two well-entrenched Dutch habits—careful organization and preparation and consultation at many levels. State agricultural support began as early as the agricultural crisis of the 1880s when cheap cereals grown on American prairies began to impact Dutch trade and agriculture. In response, the state encouraged a shift to high-value nontraditional export crops and provided support in three areas: trade policy, education, and research. Government funds aided the national farmers' society in founding agricultural schools and an agricultural extension advisory service. Research centers were often associated with advanced agricultural schools such as Wageningen University, which today is one of the most important.

After World War II the government introduced vertical oversight organizations known as Product Boards (Productshappen) and horizontal associations of trade workers (Bedrifschappen). Membership in Bedrifschappen is still mandatory for all growers, wholesalers, exporters, and retailers. Contributions are collected through automatic deductions on all sales at the auctions. The Product Board for Horticulture (Productschap Tuinbouw) was among the organizations established soon after World War II and currently oversees the flower industry.[9] It has wide-ranging powers and connections. It orchestrates market and technical research and helps to implement and regulate environmental and energy policy, agricultural financial support, and other matters affecting growers under both Netherlands and European Union jurisdiction. On behalf of the Ministry of Agriculture, Environment, and Fisheries, it has authority to organize new market structures, issue import certificates, and administer export support grants. The Product Board for Horticulture coordinates with so many government and private organizations that it is not easy to distinguish separate roles and areas of interest for different institutions. It collects about five hundred million euros from farmers and traders of horticultural products such as flowers. Recently farmers have begun questioning the size and legality of their contribution in relation to new European Union regulations. Some fear this may jeopardize the legality of the Product Board levy and perhaps the institution itself.[10]

Other state policies supported, improved, or stimulated agriculture. To give one example, small landholdings have long dominated Dutch agriculture, in part because of the Netherlands' inheritance tradition. Eventually, some were too small to be economically viable. In the 1950s the government introduced a program to buy out small farmers unable to keep up with technological change. Over time, the state leased or sold the purchased land to neighbors with more capital and reduced the number of inefficient farming enterprises. This kind of program—and later forms of subsidy including an energy subsidy, recently phased out—clearly helped horticulturalists including flower growers. It is less clear whether the European Union's[11] Common Agricultural Policy (CAP)—which originally was intended to improve agricultural productivity—has helped flower production in the Netherlands.[12] Implementation of CAP has varied from country to country over its forty-year existence. The Netherlands' early interventions seemed to be limited to stabilizing food prices, restricting imports, and supporting exports. Other structural changes that accorded with the CAP included a reduction in the farming population through the buyout schemes mentioned above and offering alternatives to agriculture through education and the creation of urban job opportunities (Zobbe 2001). Possibly, greenhouse vegetable growers with low incomes may have been encouraged to convert to more profitable flower production with the aid of agricultural subsidies. Overall, however, it is difficult to discern direct benefits from CAP for Dutch flower growers.

The Dutch state has certainly encouraged floricultural research and education. Dutch research on flower breeding and growing technology and automation is continuous, innovative, and arguably sets the global standard. Much research is conducted in public institutions linked to the university system.[13] Some is carried out through the vocational education system devoted to training about 12,000 future growers, wholesalers, retailers, and floral designers. The Netherlands also exports its floral education. Floral experts and student interns travel each year to as many as fifty flower-growing nations where they study distant markets and cultures. Many return to those same countries to work. This Dutch floricultural diaspora helps reduce the cultural and knowledge barriers of a long commodity chain as its flower industry responds to changing tastes, helps to shape tastes for new flowers, and opens new markets (see chapter 5). Growers also continue their education through membership in their particular Bedrifschap or growers association. Lily and gerbera growers' study groups, for example, meet several times a year for tours of each other's greenhouses. These tours allow growers to follow the progress of new varieties, exchange gossip, and as Paul van der Heiden, a gerbera grower, put it, to "see how the competition is doing."

The Dutch government's long-term support policies encouraged continuous innovation or "upgrading" in the Dutch flower system in ways that recall the aforementioned "clusters" or "industrial districts" in which firms were sheltered against "paralyzing shocks from the market; by providing access to any skills and knowledge that the firms lacked; and by policing competition" (Piore and Sabel 1984, 32).

Less obviously, the Netherlands government has also assisted flower growers in ways that are not always evident and may be overlooked by the growers themselves. Not least was the state's willingness to support them in critical periods while neighbors such as Belgium failed to attend to the needs of their horticultural growers. Certain technological changes were missed by Belgian growers but adopted and developed by Dutch growers. The construction of the Schipol Airport and the linked highway system adjacent to the Aalsmeer auction complex were extremely beneficial for Dutch flower exports. The effects of this intentional clustering and public-private governance and what Humphrey and Schmitz call the "steering" of the industry (2000) has encouraged the spread of knowledge, speeded the adoption of new flower forms and growing technology, improved quality, and substantially contributed to current Dutch dominance of the global flower trade.

These Dutch institutions and state policies are also suggestive of Peter Evans's model of the developmental state. For Evans the developmental state resembles a Weberian bureaucracy and engenders "corporate coherence" and autonomy. State structures are embedded in social networks that provide information and allow "decentralized private implementation" of policy. The developmental state takes on a sort of midwifery role in encouraging and assisting entrepreneurs (1995, 12). Evans contrasts the developmental state with the predatory state, where individuals pursue their own goals and cohesion depends on personal ties. Personal goals tend to supersede collective ones. The characteristics of the predatory state recall the setting for the flower industry in Ecuador.

Finally, the Dutch society itself supports flower growers through an appreciation of and respect for small agriculturalists. In the Netherlands the horticultural economy and society are sufficiently intertwined that floriculturalists are not simply growing flowers. Instead, as the horticultural educator Piet van der Voort explained during our conversation, they are producing a complete "way of life."

State and Structure

This widespread involuntary ordering of many aspects of social and professional life through licensing and regulation by government bodies or institutions like the Productschappen and the Bedrifschappen involves extensive guidance and control that serve to maintain the institutions themselves as well as perpetuate established traditions and forms of training. Such guidance is resented only occasionally.[14] The debate is not about whether there should be so much regulation but rather what form it should take (van der Horst 1996, 116–18). Group solidarity is highly valued in Dutch society, where group norms shape social conformity (Shetter 1997). This willingness to cooperate and organize into associations, study groups, and chapters and to be legislated, levied, and taxed by a range of different bodies has influenced the prevalence of cooperative marketing structures, information sharing, and other forms of cooperation among growers, contrasting strongly with the competitive grower relationships evident in other flower-producing regions such as Ecuador.

These involuntary institutional structures assist flower growers and exporters to develop information, transparency, and economic security that are valuable to the small entrepreneur and often denied their global competitors. For example, a flower exporter who has received an overture from a New York Metropolitan Area wholesaler can apply to his Bedrifschap for a detailed credit history of that wholesaler. Such information reduces his risk in dealing with an unknown customer. At the same time, a financially pressed New York wholesale florist, anxious to preserve a good credit record in the Netherlands, may give payment preference to his Dutch accounts before his Ecuadorian or Colombian or even California creditors, who are denied credit information and may have to wait longer for payment.

MONETARY POLICY AND CURRENCY EXCHANGE

Currency exchange rates have had important consequences for the flower trade. Among economically equivalent nations, they are as significant a factor in exporting flowers as in exporting cars, clothing, and other commodities. Currency fluctuations introduce volatility to the trade in flowers, creating barriers and opportunities. In the late 1980s, for example, after the guilder was revalued, Dutch flower exports to the United States dropped dramatically. Dutch chrysanthemums became too expensive for the U.S. market and chrysanthemums from Colombia quickly filled the void.[15] By the early 1990s,

Ecuador's flower industry also began to fill gaps in supplies. Between July 1995 and February 2002, the dollar rose 50 percent in value, drawing flowers from around the globe to U.S. markets. High-quality Dutch blooms became financially attractive to U.S. buyers once again, especially in the New York Metropolitan Area (see chapter 6). Supermarkets featured Dutch blooms in their moderately priced bouquets alongside inexpensive "commodity" flowers from Colombia. At the same time, the strength of the dollar affected domestic growers. Prices for flowers from California rose in comparison with previous prices for similar species and varieties from the Netherlands and France. Yet as the euro appreciated against the dollar after 2002, Dutch flowers once again became costly for Americans. The Brazilian real, however, declined against the dollar. Brazilian flowers (and California blooms) became cheaper for Americans and flower imports from Brazil surged (see table 6).

Currency value is in effect "a weather vane, showing the direction [in which] the winds of international capital are blowing."[16] As that weather vane turns in response to the breezes generated by shifting flows of global capital, flower growers can only watch and try to recalibrate over time, perhaps adjusting their global position by growing the open orange blooms favored in the United States rather than the tight pink ones popular in Germany.

Floriculture in Ecuador

Ecuador is a very different setting for flower growing. With thirteen million people and an area of 277,000 square kilometers, (107,000 square miles) the country is mountainous and far larger and less densely populated than the Netherlands. In 2004 per capita Gross Domestic Product had risen to about $2,200 as Ecuador participated in a general improvement in the world economy (ECLAC 2004).[17] Ecuador's pronounced income inequality increased between 1990 and 2002, especially in rural areas (ECLAC 2004). Population is divided between a small upper class, an urban middle class, and a large, mostly rural, impoverished class.[18] In fact, about 80 percent of the population lives below the poverty line with 25 percent living on less than one dollar a day.[19] Poverty is a compelling reason why many Ecuadorians migrate to cities from rural areas or abroad to Europe or North America (ECLAC 2004). The society is 65 percent mestizo, 25 percent indigenous, and 10 percent Spanish, black, and others.

State and Structure

FLOWER GROWING

Flower growing in Ecuador is a young industry that emerged about 1985. The government of Febres Cordero (1984–88) adopted a neoliberal or free-market economic and political model and introduced policies that emphasized the expansion of exports (Krupa 2001, 7). During the late 1980s the state's nontraditional agricultural exports program benefited from various kinds of international support. USAID offered technical advice. Financial assistance came from the International Monetary Fund, the World Bank, and the Inter-American Development Bank (Krupa 2001, 7). Urban and rural elites began looking for new investment opportunities among nontraditional exports. Flower growing was a new way to exploit nature and a fresh choice for Ecuadorian entrepreneurs. Specific state and banking policies and the agricultural economy's past practices encouraged the focus on flowers. The phenomenal growth of cut flower exports in neighboring Colombia over the preceding fifteen years also offered a ready model and a source of expertise.[20] With similarly advantageous climate, an abundance of low-cost labor, and the expectation of a quick return on investment, cut flowers seemed an ideal export commodity for Ecuadorian entrepreneurs (Mena 1999, 36). In fact, exports of cut flowers expanded rapidly. Worth a half million dollars in 1985, they increased to $13 million in 1990 and about $287 million in 2004.[21] From the outset Ecuadorian growers concentrated on roses. Early Ecuadorian growers differentiated themselves in the North American and global market by exploiting subtle differences in new hybrid tea rose varieties and by producing roses of exceptional size and quality. New Ecuadorian growers tended to copy this successful formula partly because knowledge and expertise in flower species other than roses was generally scarce (especially compared with the Netherlands and California) and depended on individual experimentation. Rose-growing complexes developed first around Cayambe and Tabacundo about seventy kilometers north of the capital city of Quito and the international airport. Later Cotopaxi, about eighty kilometers south of Quito, became an important growing area. When Ecuadorian agronomists and growers describe the natural advantages of the Cayambe/Tabacundo region for rose growing, they usually cite its altitude (about 2,800 meters or 9,200 feet), light, temperature, soil, and water conditions.[22]

Unlike the majority of their Dutch counterparts, Ecuadorian flower growers do not tend their own ranges but rather are managers of much larger enterprises, usually family-owned, private companies.[23] Ecuador has no tradition of educated prosperous small holders and the peasant population lacks the economic resources to enter an industry that by 1985 was already capital intensive. Instead flower growers emerged from the wealthy entrepreneurial and land-owning classes, chiefly in the highland or Sierra region. Ecuadorian and Colombian flower-marketing chains mandate a minimum farm size of about six to eight hectares, and enterprises of twenty or more hectares are not uncommon. Many of the larger growing enterprises have several farms and employ production managers, a full-time or part-time agronomist, and salespeople. The Ecuadorian grower is effectively both a manager and an international marketer of his products. He is quite different from the Dutch grower in his talents, education, commodity chain connections, and marketing objectives.

Floriculture makes a steady contribution to the Ecuadorian economy. While other exports faltered, flower exports grew consistently during the 1990s. In 2000, cut flowers were the country's fifth largest export after petroleum and petroleum products (49 percent), bananas (17 percent), shrimp (6 percent), and tinned fish (5 percent) and by 2003 had climbed to fourth place.[24] For the handful of Ecuadorians with access to the requisite capital, flower exporting was a sound investment during the 1990s in contrast to some other products of nature such as bananas, shrimp, and coffee (see figure 17).

In 2000, after years of steady growth, the value of Ecuadorian flower exports declined in relation to volume. Growers' profits slipped as flower prices fell in U.S. markets in response to increased competition from other global growers. Some growers sold their flowers at prices barely exceeding their costs, exacerbating the problem of sliding prices. Ecuadorian growers had other problems too, including dwindling sales in Russia—formerly a spectacular market for big-headed roses—increasing production costs, and high air freight rates to Miami and Europe.[25]

Ecuadorian growers' concentration on roses compounds their vulnerability in the global market despite their reputation for high-quality blooms. In 2003, roses represented about 80 percent of Ecuador's flower exports, and about 70 percent of these roses were sold to the United States and Canada. Such concentration offers little flexibility during declines in North American demand for roses when alternative flower types and markets would be strategically useful. Colombian rose production, in contrast, is limited to about 30 percent of total flower exports. Colombians also grow many of the lower-priced pompon chrysanthemums, asters, and other "short-cycle" flowers that mature in thirteen weeks and are then replanted. This ensures frequent har-

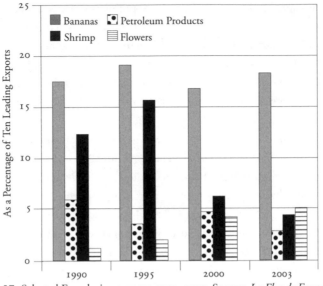

17 Selected Ecuadorian exports, 1992–2003. Source: *La Flor de Ecuador*, May 2001.

vest and rapid turnover of varieties that are part of "the civilizing process." "The short cycle flowers are important" explained Miguel López, a former flower importer in Miami, "because they allow you to [catch] the color holidays" like orange for Thanksgiving more easily than longer cycle flowers like roses. "The Colombians are ahead on that."

Ecuadorians are not alone in the declining value of their flowers. Worldwide the volume of exported roses is increasing, while the total value of global rose exports is declining.[26] Germany, the United States, and France are major rose-consuming countries, together buying half the world's roses.[27] A small decline in demand or a shift in currency exchange in one of these nations can alter the total global market and the prospects of Ecuadorian growers. The demand for large-headed roses has increased and generally they command higher prices than the two other rose forms common in the cut-flower trade—spray roses and "sweetheart" or small-headed roses. These factors—as well as more competition from African growers of spray and small-headed roses—have inspired Colombian, Israeli, and Dutch growers to convert more hectares to large-headed roses. "The Ecuadorians," noted a Dutch commentator recently, "are not alone in their market anymore."[28]

Chapter Four

Marketing flowers from Ecuador is not easy. Each Ecuadorian grower individually absorbs the trouble and costs of creating markets for his flowers and providing a level of service that will satisfy his customers. I examine the problems for individual growers in more detail in chapter 5. Difficulties seem to be rooted in the lack of "clusters" of supporting industries and a profound lack of cooperation and coordination within the industry (Porter 1990; Fairbanks and Lindsay 1997).[29]

Collective marketing groups are a theoretical alternative. Ideally these are composed of farms with different species or varieties of flowers of similar quality. However, this marketing solution is only occasionally successful in Ecuador. Weak cooperation is evident in low membership in Expoflores, the association of Ecuadorian flower exporters.[30] Studies demonstrate the benefits of trade associations in improving marketing, cooperation between businesses, and sharing knowledge within clusters (Humphrey and Schmitz 2000), but few Ecuadorian growers seem convinced. The lack of cooperation has consequences that extend beyond marketing into many areas of flower growing. For instance, there are few collective and systematic ways of improving a grower's knowledge about flower species other than roses. Attempts at species diversification are usually an individual process of trial and disappointment (see chapter 5).

With virtually no domestic market for their flowers, Ecuadorian growers are entirely dependent on distant consumers. Their long commodity chain introduces spatial and cultural barriers between grower and consumer and adds difficulties and costs in gathering market and other kinds of knowledge essential to growing decisions. In other words, successfully marketing flowers from Ecuador (or Colombia, Costa Rica, and many other places) is a complicated business. The majority of growers cannot overcome—or even begin to face—all these difficulties and simply send their blooms on consignment to Miami importers.

Unlike Dutch growers, very few in Ecuador enjoy the flexibility of offering small quantities of specialized blooms for sale. Instead, in order to meet the varied demands of wholesale florists, importers, supermarkets, bouquet makers, and other entities that may constitute a customer base, the Ecuadorian flower grower must produce a wide selection of roses and large volume in each variety. This in turn necessitates high capital investment in a large growing enterprise sometimes with several farms.

State and Structure

Producers of agricultural products from less industrialized, especially tropical, regions, face unstable boom and bust cycles partly because growers in regions with similar climate, economic conditions, and resources can easily compete (Llambi 1994; Coronil 1997). Producers of discretionary consumer products such as flowers are additionally vulnerable to alterations in the economies of their principal markets and unpredictable shifts in consumer demand. Despite these limitations, cut flower growing has been embraced by both less industrialized and more industrialized nations. Indeed, a 1997 study of the world's floriculture industry by the World Trade Center in Geneva was designed to "help developing countries to increase and to diversify their exports of floricultural products" as well as "adapt their production and marketing activities to the requirements of the world market" (White 1997). China, Korea, and India are among the developing countries that have recently joined this world market with newly established export-oriented floricultural industries.[31] The Dutch flower industry has weathered fluctuating demand cycles better than its tropical region competitors for several reasons. First, it serves a large, relatively local but diverse series of markets; second, it enjoys a reputation for high quality and dependability; and third, it has enormous productivity and floral diversity. These advantages, as noted earlier, were established through decades of state support of horticulture and state investment in education, research, and infrastructure.

In contrast, Ecuadorian state support of its flower industry has been quite limited. The industry was established with partial help from subsidies provided under nontraditional export development programs and some state financial assistance.[32] However, most of these supports declined or disappeared by the early 1990s. The state regulates some aspects of flower farm employment and working conditions, including establishing a minimum wage and mandating lunch rooms, medical services, and protective clothing on larger farms (see below). Wage competition among growers is controlled, keeping wages low but also creating some stability for workers.

Growers everywhere grumble about state interventions. In Ecuador, however, growers may be justified in claiming that their flower industry thrives despite the government. Growers' complaints are numerous. They often mention a lack of state incentives for flower exports as well as the state's failure to stabilize bank lending rates that would facilitate expansion and innovation. The condition of the Quito airport, with its deficient structures, control systems, and security and its inefficiency, has been a continuing source of frustration for flower exporters. Growers claim that poor infrastructure and erratic government policies have discouraged cargo airline companies from adding Quito to their routes. Consequently, inbound and therefore outbound cargoes are limited and, in fact, by 2003 air traffic had declined to a third of its 1998 figure.[33] Therefore flower freight rates from Quito to Miami are far higher than from nearby Bogotá, allowing Colombian growers to sell their roses at lower prices in Miami (see the section on Miami in chapter 6).[34] Other state actions seem ill-considered with respect to this particular industry. In 1999, for example, all imported goods (most growing supplies, technology, chemicals, and many greenhouse coverings are imported) were subject to a 10 percent import duty. The Ecuadorian flower industry's relationship with government seems to duplicate the contentiousness that Fairbanks and Lindsay (1997) identified in their economic analysis of the struggling Colombian flower industry. In 1993 the Colombian state accused the private sector of mismanagement and private industry insisted the state had failed to create a supportive economic climate.

ECONOMIC AND POLITICAL STABILITY

Access to investment capital is a key factor in a grower's opportunities. The strong development of Dutch floriculture is partly attributable to the existence of early cooperative banking systems and to the flexibility of the current agricultural banks that emerged from that system. In Ecuador's short flower-growing history the availability of capital through formal channels has been uneven and interest rates sometimes high. In 2001, banks loaned money at rates between 15 and 20 percent—too high for expansion or innovation in a time of declining rose prices. Some Ecuadorian growers spoke enviously of what they presumed were low interest rates enjoyed by their global competitors in places like California and the Netherlands.

Yet according to several growers, Ecuadorian banking practice and regulation are so lax that at times loans without collateral were easy to obtain. As Marcelo Madrago, an Ecuadorian flower grower, explained, "The flower farm owner is friends with the person in the bank who makes decisions." The personal nature of some banks' investment policies provided opportunities to entrepreneurs to finance their entry into the industry in the second half of the 1990s. Rose ranges doubled between 1996 and 1998 from 800 to 1,700 hectares and to over 2,000 hectares by 2003.[35]

State and Structure

Many of these new growers were trying to take advantage of rising Russian demand for large-headed roses. Marcelo described how Russian intermediaries "with suitcases full of cash" arrived in Ecuador to arrange shipments of roses to Russia. In 1997 some growers exported as much as 22 percent of their production to Russia. With demand and prices high and production costs low, investors anticipated full return within three years. But that brief Russian rose bubble collapsed with the sudden decline of the Russian economy in 1998. Some Ecuadorian flower farms failed while others barely avoided collapse by negotiating new terms with their bankers.[36] In 1999 fiscal crises reached new levels. Sixteen banks that controlled 70 percent of total deposits failed and the government defaulted on its foreign debt. Widespread corruption among public officials further adds to political and economic uncertainty in Ecuador. Seven presidents rapidly succeeded each other in the decade 1995–2005, four of whom left office amid accusations of fiscal corruption.[37]

By 2005 some aspects of the Ecuadorian economy had improved. Inflation was a mere 3 percent, while interest rates, at 11 to 14 percent, were low enough to encourage at least a few growers to invest in diversification. Several switched from roses and began growing delphiniums, phlox, and other specialty flowers—not enough of them, however, to show up in export statistics. In 2005, Ecuadorian growers were far behind their diversifying Colombian colleagues who were growing specialty flowers such as hydrangea, mini calla lilies, and hypericum.[38]

MONETARY POLICY AND CURRENCY EXCHANGE

Ecuador's persistent high inflation and currency crises have often been resolved by devaluation. In early 1999 the sucre was devalued by 40 percent, bank deposits were frozen, and withdrawals restricted for more than a year.[39] Growers benefited from periodic devaluation through the pricing advantage it conferred in the international market, even though it increased the cost of essential imported goods.[40] Conversion to the U.S. dollar currency in April 2000 was an attempt to stave off hyperinflation. Prices rose by 25 percent in the succeeding two months and inflation for the year averaged over 90 percent, seriously affecting the country's flower growers along with the rest of the population.[41] Adopting the dollar currency amounted to a revaluation, dramatically increasing costs for growers at a time when close competitors like Colombia had lower inflation rates and lower freight rates and other costs.[42]

As more regions adopt stable currencies such as the euro or dollar, some volatility may subside. Ecuadorian flower growers who compete against Israeli roses in Europe or Colombian roses in the United States seemed to regret the loss of the marketing benefit conferred by regular devaluations of the sucre. However, the recent slide of the dollar gave Ecuadorian flower exporters a noticeable, if still uncontrollable, pricing advantage in their exports to Europe and the United States by 2004 (ECLAC 2004). Colombian growers, in contrast, were penalized by the rise of the peso against the declining dollar.[43]

A few global flower growers seek to cushion themselves against these shifts by investing in globally dispersed growing regions. Dutch bulb growers, for example, also produce bulbs in Chile. A handful of Latin American flower growers have farms dispersed in Colombia, Ecuador, Costa Rica, Peru, and other countries. They may also seek to enter new markets with a more favorable rate of exchange, higher prices, or other advantages but, as will be explained in chapter 5, once market choices are made, relationships established, and production tailored to those markets, adjustment can take many months or even years.

LABOR ARRANGEMENTS AND FARM WORKING CONDITIONS

In developing regions such as Latin America, parts of Africa, China, and other places, low labor costs are an important explanation for the initial development of labor-intensive cut flower industries. Growers in industrialized countries sometimes cite the advantage this gives their competitors in developing nations. Recent research has illuminated some aspects of flower farm employment in Ecuador and Colombia, including the benefits and risks for workers, and the contentious issue of worker health.

The Ecuadorian flower industry provided about 50,000 jobs in 2000, and Expoflores executives estimate that it supports about half a million people directly and indirectly.[44] Growers can justly claim they provide welcome employment and income especially for women, in rural areas historically characterized by underemployment. These jobs help to stem migration to urban areas and other countries and the related disruption of family life.[45] Ecuadorian farms average about twelve to fifteen employees per hectare, so the typical thirteen-hectare farm requires about one hundred and fifty to two hundred workers. On farms this large, the state mandates employee services such as medical facilities, and some farms go further by offering day care centers and subsidized meals and stores (Korovkin 2003).

Krupa (2001) describes the different forms of labor arrangements on these farms. In 2001 these included full-time contracts, temporary contracts, and *contratistas*, or labor hired through an intermediary contractor. This last group usually consists of unskilled labor hired for specific tasks such as the preparation of new planting beds. Those with full-time contracts are protected by law from casual dismissal. But Krupa points out that farm managers easily manufacture legitimate excuses for dismissal when they choose. Yet many of the growers I spoke with were quite concerned about retaining employees, particularly those trained in their preferred methods of cultivation, harvesting, packing, and so on. Friedemann Sanchez reported a similar concern among flower farm managers in Colombia. Employees themselves have reasons for preferring different contractual arrangements. *Contratistas*, for example, can avoid a rigid work schedule and take days off when needed to meet obligations in family or communal work projects. Not all farms use *contratistas;* some prefer to retain a larger permanent staff to handle occasional tasks.

FLOWER FARM WORKING CONDITIONS

Workers are generally selected after a three-month period of probation. Their hours are long as most work a basic forty-hour week spread over five and a half days and the majority work an additional four to six hours of overtime—stretching to ten hours in busy seasons—partly because workers want the extra income (Palan and Carlos 1999). In rose greenhouses workers are responsible for cultivating and harvesting a set number of rows of rose plants, but the number of rows assigned to each worker has increased substantially over the last decade or so (Korovkin 2003; Meier 1999). In both Colombia and Ecuador, employees describe this increased workload as a source of stress while employers characterize it as improved productivity. The more productive workers are rewarded with wage increases.

Steady work on flower farms attracts both local residents and Ecuadorians from the coastal areas to highland regions such as Cayambe because flower farms offer higher pay than alternatives such as construction work and domestic service (Krupa 2001; Korovkin 2003).

About 60 percent of farm workers are women. Women work in post-harvest care and flower packing, while men dominate irrigation, chemical fumigation, and maintenance. Men and women are equally employed in cultivating the ranges of flowers. From my observations, bouquetmaking—work that is understood to require creativity and a delicate touch—seems to be almost exclusively female work in Ecuador as it is in Miami and the Netherlands.

The majority of the women are young, often in the eighteen to twenty-five age range. Flower farm wages have changed the consumption patterns of young women and men and discount stores have appeared to satisfy their new consuming interests (Palan and Carlos 1999). Long work hours, income, and new ways of spending their time and money put young flower workers at odds with their families and rural community responsibilities (Meier 1999; Mena 1999; Korovkin 2003).[46]

Young women are also at an age of high fertility, but flower companies are reluctant to employ pregnant women for several reasons.[47] First, pregnant employees are more costly; Ecuadorian law specifies ninety days of maternity leave with the costs only partly paid by social services and the balance covered by the employer. Second, the farm loses the skills of a trained employee. Finally, well-publicized health concerns about exposure to certain types of agricultural chemicals have made both workers and employers sensitive to the possibilities of fetal injury.[48] Concerns about fetal health are probably part of the reason that some labor contractors in Colombia illegally test for pregnancy (Meier 1999). Reportedly, some Ecuadorian farms also discontinued farm-sponsored social activities that were thought to lead to unintended pregnancies and began offering family planning education (Meier 1999; Palan and Carlos 1999).

The possibility of occupational health problems is a source of anxiety for some flower workers. The media and nongovernmental organizations have paid considerable attention to illness and birth defects seemingly associated with exposure to agricultural chemicals. Some reports are carefully researched (Tenenbaum 2002; Smith et al. 2004) while some journalism seems poorly informed with minimal empirical research and weak knowledge of the floriculture industries.[49] Much of the debate about health effects depends on anecdotal evidence; no long-term detailed studies have been performed by the governments of Colombia or Ecuador or by the industries themselves.[50] Instead flower growers are encouraged by various bodies such as growers associations and international certification programs to institute safety practices of the sort already in use in flower growing in the United States, the Netherlands, and other industrialized nations (Meier 1999; Palan and Carlos 1999).[51] Occupational health and voluntary safety practices seem to be taken seriously by both management and employees on the larger, better-equipped farms, but on others they are probably ignored.

Women work at all levels in the flower industry, including in the middle ranks as social workers, doctors, secretaries, managers, and sales representatives, yet there is a noticeable racial hierarchy in Ecuadorian farms. Indigenous people are far less likely to achieve the education necessary for mid-level jobs; consequently, their opportunities are limited to cultivation, packing, and bouquetmaking. Mestizos are usually supervisors or office employees; most professionals, such as the agronomists, managers, and business owners, are white.

Despite the problems and drawbacks outlined above, regular flower-industry employment has produced benefits for women in both Ecuador and Colombia. Stable employment and increased income have brought autonomy and improved self-esteem and self-confidence (Friedemann-Sanchez 2002; Korovkin 2003). Friedemann-Sanchez's detailed study of women workers in the much longer established Colombian flower industry found that some women anticipated they would have long working lives in the industry and could plan accordingly. Flower industry employment offered them a greater degree of job security and greater benefits than the few alternative forms of employment, especially as permanent contracts and other improvements in hiring practices emerged as a result of pressure from national and international nongovernmental organizations. Furthermore, the Colombian floriculture industry aided workers by lending them money, mediating private conflicts and offering education; all services that are otherwise limited in the region.

Women, Friedemann-Sanchez explains, learn discipline and skills such as managing and planning their time. They themselves value these skills and put them to use in their domestic lives. Furthermore, Colombian women flower workers feel empowered by their exposure to a wider sphere and by the fact that their work at the farms is valued (in contrast to their work in the home). Some advance to supervisory roles, earning two or three times the minimum wage. In rural societies with marked domestic violence and inequality, permanent employment and a steady income afford women valuable bargaining power in the household, allowing them to establish greater equality and improve their domestic conditions (Mena 1999; Friedemann-Sanchez 2002). Some even choose to opt out of marriage and raise their children alone because their wage income permits this choice. All this has helped to reduce gender inequality, especially among the younger workers. Women remain in flower farm employment, Friedemann-Sanchez argues, because they "benefit both financially and in their quality of life" (Friedemann-Sanchez 2006, 176).

Furthermore, conditions improve for the children of female flower workers, since women usually spend their income on their children (Mena 1999; Friedemann-Sanchez 2006; Korovkin 2003).

RISING LABOR COSTS

In 2000, Ecuador's average wage for flower workers rose to about US$120 per month. At approximately US$1,400 per annum, it is far below the equivalent annual gross wage in the Netherlands of about US$17,000 for an agricultural worker.[52] Yet when these low minimum wages are combined with the costs of compulsory provision of various employee services, a few Ecuadorian growers worry that the comparative advantage of low labor costs is receding. Some see the need to invest in automated technology in order to reduce their employment costs and sustain their global competitiveness and profits.

The few Ecuadorian growers who are heavily invested in automated packing machines claim, like their Dutch colleagues, that automatic bunching, grading, and so on, is faster and less damaging to the flowers than the equivalent operations performed manually. Some consider new growing technology essential to survival and profit in the Ecuadorian flower industry. As Jorge Serrano commented during an interview, for a medium-sized grower "the market situation and competition are so difficult . . . if you are not competitive in costs and quality and if you don't control production carefully, it will be very difficult to survive." For others, weighing high interest rates and low flower prices, investment in labor-saving equipment or flower-growing technology was out of the question. For them, sustaining profits requires somehow obtaining higher prices for their flowers in their targeted international markets or improving productivity on their farms by investing in new higher-yielding or profitable flower varieties or by improving the efficiency of their workers (see chapter 5).

COMMANDING GLOBAL ADVANTAGE

Ecuador, Colombia, and some of the other flower-exporting nations are examples of Fernando Coronil's "nature exporting nations." These nations, he argues, are condemned to cycles of boom and bust as their economies respond to markets in the developed nations (1997). Fairbanks and Lindsay seem to agree. In their 1997 study of economic development strategies in Andean countries, they conclude that the Colombian cut flower industry's thirty-year, wealth-creation strategy of exporting "nature" and depending on the com-

93

parative advantages of natural resources like sunshine, soil, and altitude as well as low labor costs and proximity to the U.S. market could not be depended on in future. *Comparative advantage* proposes, in principal, that economic efficiency for each country is greatest when it makes the products at which it is most efficient, compared to other nations.[53] Theoretically flowers can be produced very efficiently in Colombia and Ecuador because they have ideal natural growing conditions and the advantage of lower costs for flower shelter, labor, heating, cooling, and lighting. Yet in Fairbanks and Lindsay's view, that strategy of depending on nature failed in Colombia in part because it was a mechanism through which much of Colombia's wealth was exported to other countries, mostly to the United States. The wealth was exported away because Colombia gave the United States the products of its earth, sunshine, and people's labor at subsidized rates through an undervalued exchange rate and artificially suppressed wages; and because, when the money was paid, it was paid to very few owners who declined to—or felt unable to—reinvest in Colombia and in the productivity of their fellow Colombians.[54] The Ecuadorian flower industry has generally followed a similar path, though some individual growers are exceptional in their efforts to reinvest in Ecuador.

In fact, the Netherlands, with its continuous improvements in technology and efficient division of labor into many specialized growers, produces flowers more efficiently than does Colombia or Ecuador—as measured by its returns in the global flower marketplace. The Netherlands' efficiency derives in part from its command of what the economist Michael Porter terms *high order competitive advantages* such as proprietary technology, product differentiation, "brand reputation based on cumulative marketing efforts," and continued access to customers (1990, 49–50). Colombian and Ecuadorian growers, in contrast, command the less desirable *low order advantages* including low labor costs and raw materials. The developmental Dutch state has aided the evolution of what Porter refers to as a "cluster" of world-class suppliers within the nation. Through "efficient, early, rapid and sometimes preferential access to the most cost-effective inputs" the flower-industry cluster aids "the process of innovation and upgrading" and contributes to its global competitive advantage especially through local cooperation that provides insights, information and new ideas (78). By commanding much of the innovation in new flower hybrids the Netherlands' flower industry also benefits from the upward, profitable phase of new flower product cycles (Vernon 1979) while growers in other countries are limited to the downward phase.

Grumbling growers in the Netherlands, California, and other places cite the low labor costs enjoyed by their competitors in Latin American and African nations. Yet they sometimes fail to appreciate their own proximity to clusters and the political and economic stability that affords them the security to borrow and invest in innovations that theoretically confer advantage in the global cut flower game.

Furthermore, the Netherlands dominates the stable and desirable segments of the global flower market.[55] In Europe—the major market for Dutch flowers—demand is steady and predictable. Unlike their counterparts in Ecuador and Colombia who focus principally on the U.S. flower market, Dutch growers (partly because of the auction system) have no need to depend on risky U.S. holidays like Valentine's Day when weather, transportation problems, and fluctuating demand contribute to risk and uncertainty for grower and trader.[56] In Ecuador and Colombia, some individual growing enterprises seem to divide the stable from the unstable market segments on a smaller scale, by dominating small but reliable market niches. This strategy is examined in more detail in later chapters.

Growers from many different regions with access to such stable and growing markets in the United States with whom I discussed the matter seemed convinced of the necessity for steady investment in cultivation-related technology in order to keep efficiently ahead of their competition. In every flower-growing nation and region there are growers who embrace cultivation and post-harvest technology and others who use little. Glass greenhouse growers invest more in growing technology than plastic-house growers or open-field growers. Larger growers invest more than small growers.[57] Since most flower-growing research is carried out in the Netherlands and aims to solve problems specific to the Netherlands' field-growing and glass greenhouse systems and flower types, resulting innovation is not always transferable to the more open plastic greenhouses prevalent in climatically-blessed areas of Latin America. Consequently investment in each new technology must be considered in relation to the cultivation requirements of the flowers being grown, the growers' marketing options and strategy, and the availability of capital and loans. Growers' technology decisions and their significance are explored in the next chapter.

There may be some risk that greater specialization and heavy investment in innovation and technology may eventually require impossibly high returns and constrain a producer's flexibility.[58] For the moment this does not seem to be a problem in the Netherlands, and current evidence from the Netherlands' flower industry lends support to the idea that firms that continually adapt and innovate in what they sell stay in the high growth and high profit zone. Yet in other regions capital investment is constrained and less rewarding. Grady Smith, a New York wholesaler and a long-term investor in Ecuadorian flower farms, offered the view that "as growing becomes more capital intensive, workers will need to be more educated on their jobs. If that happens, then the competitive labor advantage that Latin America had thirty years ago when the industry started [diminishes]." Later, Grady asked rhetorically, "Why would you invest in high technology growing there [when you] have to deal with the political and economic problems and pay [higher] transport costs?" He agreed that there are climatic advantages but felt that investing in Latin America might not be worthwhile.

Many factors—interest rates, corruption, instability, tariffs, and currency fluctuations—mold the complex national, supranational, and global structures in which export flower growers operate. The virtual inevitability of reverses in one or other major markets is another factor. Setbacks for one flower-producing nation may prove an advantage for another or seriously affect the fortunes of all. When the Russian market for roses collapsed in 1998, for example, Ecuadorian roses flooded the U.S. market. Prices for all flowers from all regions of the globe plummeted in the United States.[59]

Clearly a diversity of markets is desirable to reduce uncertainty and risk. But during the last decade as the share of exports sent to Europe by both Ecuador and Colombia declined, the share sent to North America increased— even after the dollar decline of 2002 impacted Colombian exports—to about 80 percent for Ecuador and 84 percent for Colombia. Exports from the Netherlands meanwhile were spread among a range of European nations, including Germany (36 percent), United Kingdom (14 percent), and France (14 percent). The United States, which accounts for 3 to 5 percent of its total cut flower exports, is a relatively minor market for the Netherlands.

Faced with volatile, uncontrollable conditions that structure their markets and opportunities, as well as uneven access to knowledge and technology, flower growers must devise strategies to ease constraints and improve their chances in the markets within their reach. The following chapter explores their experiences and strategies.

Five

Cultivating the Global Garden:
Local Growers in a Global System

In *The Botany of Desire* the horticultural writer Michael Pollan writes, "It was the flower that first ushered the idea of beauty into the world the moment, long ago, when floral attraction emerged as an evolutionary strategy." When seduced by the beauty of flowers, he suggests, desiring humans create new forms of the plant and spread them to new places, much as insects and birds do when they disperse pollen and seeds (2001, xviii).

Flowers conspire readily with these human desires when provided with precise conditions. Roses and carnations, for example, thrive in bright light, minimal diurnal or seasonal temperature variations, fertile soil, and even moisture. Many of these conditions are found in mountainous regions close to the equator, in countries such as Colombia, Ecuador, Costa Rica, and Kenya where climate permits year-round flowering and successive crops.[1] Other flower-growing regions, further from the equator like California and Holland, reproduce these conditions artificially to compensate for seasonal light and temperature variations. But they must accept greater crop seasonality and higher energy costs. Yet the satisfaction of desires for new flower forms and the search for cheaper and more perfect growing conditions has entailed new complications for commercial cut flower growers who are far from the consumers of their flowers. These complications revolve around spatial, temporal, and cultural barriers and the new competitors this global system has introduced. Greater times and distances to markets add costs and affect freshness and therefore the value of the flowers. Spatial and cultural barriers limit access to privileged scientific and cultural information, inhibiting quick responses to changes in taste, fashion, and competition that are vital in some flower market niches.

Solving these problems—overcoming these barriers—requires special knowledge streams. In this chapter I explore these barriers and the kinds of knowledge critical to flower growers. Scientific knowledge is essential—particularly knowledge about new flower types, new cultivation techniques, and new technology—and I examine how this is produced and shared. Success also hinges on market knowledge about competition and prevailing prices as well as certain cultural knowledge, especially about shifting consumer tastes.[2]

The means and costs of acquiring knowledge depend on a grower's market connections and relationships—both are a valuable and inexpensive source of information and market security. In pure economic terms, markets are abstract, anonymous, impersonal systems of exchange in which the social and cultural motivations of individual participants are irrelevant. Recently, however, social scientists have revealed the social component both of general economic behavior (Granovetter 1985; Block 1990; Heilbroner and Milberg 1995; Carrier 1997) and of market exchange (Dilley 1992; Carrier 1997; Slater 1997; Gudeman 2001). John Lie, for example, in his essay "The Sociology of Markets," disputes the economic ideal of "individual utility maximization with perfect information," citing markets such as Wall Street where networks, power, and socially acquired information distort that ideal (1997, 343–44). Anthropologists have attested to the social, cultural, and even moral elements of markets. Carrier suggests that it makes sense for market actors to "build and rely on stable, moral relationships rather than trying to meet each situation anew with fresh dispassionate calculations of the abilities and intentions of other firms" (1997, 12). Gudeman makes similar points about the cultural and social aspects of markets, arguing, "No trade or market system exists without the support of communal agreements such as shared languages, mutual ways of interacting and implicit understandings" (2001, 11). Recent anthropological research has illuminated some of the social and cultural aspects of contemporary global markets (Roseberry 1996; Tranberg Hansen 2000; Bestor 2001). The social nature of the cut flower trade is not really in question. Individual participants in the U.S. flower system, as noted in chapter 2, have historically depended on personal relationships established through consignment and other systems of exchange. What is interesting, however, is an apparent intensification of social networks of cooperation and trust and their global extension.

Gudeman complicates these notions of a social and cultural dimension to market exchange by identifying two processes that extend this dimension: innovation and reciprocity. In the process of innovation, Gudeman explains, the innovator creates "a relation to others" and as people mimic or "consume" the innovation their lives change and are indirectly affected by the innovator (2001, 146). He thus broadens the notion of innovation, offering a way to explore its social consequences. Innovation may consist in finding new markets or cheaper sources of supply or in creating new products, forms of organization, or methods of production (102–03). Reciprocity, on the other hand, is a direct tactical act. Extending reciprocity to others is "a way of groping with uncertainty at the limits of a community" (80). Gudeman limits reciprocity to nonmarket exchange that involves exchange "between persons of different communities. Falling in the sphere of communal transactions, it is never about objects alone but relationships forged through them" (81). However, the notion that transactions and objects forge relationships between individuals and between communities is also evident in market exchange. Reciprocity—conceived as a mutual exchange of favors that includes a sense of moral obligation—operates at many levels in the cut flower system. This behavior suggests both the existence of communities and individual acknowledgment of those communities. Indeed, many loosely networked communities are evident in the cut flower system; some are global, as I will explain in chapter 7. In this chapter and the following, however, I explore how processes of innovation and reciprocity both deepen the social and cultural dimensions of this market system and shape the distribution of information and competition—two elements animating the global cut flower system.

The flower growers who are the subject of this chapter engage with innovation and reciprocity in degrees varied by growing skills, informational transparency, competition, market strategies, and relationship strategies and modulated by geographic location and their individual objectives. In fact, the mix of these elements can be thought of as positioning growers along a strategic continuum. At one end of the continuum are growers who produce one or two varieties of a single flower species and invest little in seeking new knowledge, innovating, or fostering relationships and markets. At the other end are growers who assiduously seek new knowledge and markets and tend relationships as attentively as their most valuable blooms. They cultivate breeders, other growers, exporters, importers, and wholesalers. Through relationships they learn about innovation in technology and flower varieties, about new competitors and new consumer fancies. Between these poles are the majority of growers, who build certain relationships and acquire some new knowledge. All struggle with daily decisions about cultivation techniques, new plant selections, and the problems of selling a commodity whose value diminishes dramatically each day after harvest.[3] These differently strategizing growers may be found in each growing region mixing cooperation and competition according to the structural conditions and national state characteristics discussed in the previous chapter.

This chapter has two parts. Drawing on the experiences of many growers, I focus first on Dutch and then on Ecuadorian flower producers to describe their clustered geographic organization and to illustrate the interplay of the cultural, spatial, and knowledge barriers they face. I also examine their varied individual strategies and behaviors in relation to their personal production, markets, and competition. These elements shape growers' choices and contribute to the relative weakness of today's growers in the global cut flower commodity chain. Both sections explore these growers' distinct market options and show how their particular marketplaces condition their need for knowledge and relationships in a chain that is far from being the abstract market system referred to earlier. Instead, it resembles Braudel's second level of economic activity—the competitive sector of little workshops and small business enterprises. It is a rich competitive world of resourceful individuals and an arena of "inspiration, improvisation and innovation" (Braudel 1984, 631).[4]

I chose to concentrate on growers of roses because, as noted earlier, more roses are sold in the United States and in the global trade than any other single type of flower. Much of the information on cultivation, hybridization, and marketing in this chapter refers to roses. Yet I also encountered growers of many other types of flowers. I was especially interested in following the increasingly visible lives of lily, gerbera, and lisianthus. Today, lilies and gerberas have joined roses, carnations, and chrysanthemum to become major cut flowers, while lisianthus belongs with hundreds of other uncommon blooms in the specialty cut flowers category.[5]

The Netherlands

CULTIVATION

Burgemeester Kasteleinweg is a short straight road in western Netherlands that borders a landscape crisscrossed by canals dividing reclaimed land or polders. Running west from the Aalsmeer flower auction site, it passes through the village of Aalsmeer and leads to Schiphol International Airport five kilometers away. To the east, the road continues toward the villages of De Kwakel and Mijdrecht and bisects a geometric landscape of one-hectare rectangles studded with greenhouses. Paul van der Heiden grows gerberas in one of these greenhouses.

Gerberas, like other commercial cut flowers grown for the international trade, are undoubtedly the result of nature's processes (see figure 18). Yet, at the same time, they are a product of "civilizing processes" such as breeders' skills

18 Gerbera

and sophisticated cultivation technology that improve on nature. Paul van der Heiden, like most Netherlands flower growers, raises his flowers in a completely enclosed glass greenhouse where light, temperature, humidity, watering, and fertilizing are automatically controlled. Some of his neighbors, particularly those specializing in roses and lilies, have adopted more innovations, such as carbon dioxide enrichment and hydroponic cultivation.[6] His sophisticated cultivation and labor-saving technology enhance both the quality of Paul's blooms and his personal productivity.

In some Dutch greenhouses harvesting and packing are almost entirely automatic. Four hectares of rose ranges and packing rooms might be overseen by only two or three people. Several gerbera growers employ conveyor-belt growing systems that move plants past stations where workers cultivate and harvest the blooms. These save on labor costs since a single cultivator can tend 19,000 plants a day. A few years ago Paul enlarged and modernized his operations by buying his neighbor's property and building a new half-hectare greenhouse. Typically in 2000, new greenhouses with these basic growing technologies cost about two million dollars per hectare, a huge sum for a small agriculturalist. Paul, however, had little difficulty financing his expansion with a loan from a bank that formerly was an agricultural cooperative lending institution.[7]

No matter how automated a greenhouse, the plants themselves are always tended by someone like Paul or his wife, Chaya. Long work hours are typical for flower growers with small enterprises and Paul usually works six days a week, commuting in seconds from the family house adjacent to the greenhouse. Aided by part-time helpers—Chaya, his father, father-in-law, and a non-kin employee—Paul examines leaves and buds for insects and fungi, cuts and packs the blooms, and monitors automatic feeding and other systems. Carelessness about air temperature, disease monitoring, or, in the case of roses, their pruning dates can halve a crop's value or obliterate it entirely. Ceaseless attention to detail is crucial to success in all segments of the global cut flower commodity chain but the consequences of inattention are most onerous for growers. Consequently Paul and Chaya seldom take vacations or business trips abroad. A few years ago they visited a Dutch friend now growing flowers near Toronto, but in general they do not leave the Netherlands. In this they differ from some of their colleagues in Ecuador, Colombia, and other growing regions who may travel extensively in search of knowledge about new flowers and technology and to sustain their market relationships.

Paul has focused on gerberas for over twenty years while Hans Wijchman, a neighbor, has specialized in lilies for an even longer period—each growing about fifteen to twenty varieties within their chosen species. Other neighbors grow alstroemeria or freesia. Each of these flower types and the hundreds of others in commercial cultivation has its own set of complicated cultivation requirements, cycles, and treatments in order to reach the level of perfection in bloom and foliage demanded by the international trade. Consequently most Dutch growers specialize and invest years in acquiring knowledge and expertise in the cultivation of one flower species.

COOPERATIVE AUCTIONS

Such specialization is possible, in part, because of the cooperative auctions that are the marketplaces for almost all Netherlands' cut flowers.[8] Paul sends his gerberas to the Bloemenveiling Aalsmeer—one of the largest of the four remaining flower auctions—just a few kilometers from his greenhouse and the center of a vast flower-growing area. Here, about nineteen million flowers are assembled and sold daily. The auction complex itself occupies more than ninety hectares. Over ten thousand people work there—employed by the auction itself or by related businesses including exporters, wholesale flower buyers, transportation companies, banks, plant protection services, and many others. Through this spatial concentration of many elements in a floral horticultural complex, enormous volume, and rigorous quality control, the Netherlands auctions set standards for the global market in flowers.

Cooperative flower auctions share some similarities with the consignment systems described in chapter 2. The intermediary is a bureaucratic institution rather than an individual commission man, yet a grower still entrusts his flowers and waits to see what price is realized. The final price depends on the flower quality, grower's reputation, and demand and volume on a particular day. One major difference is that the final sale price is public information at the Netherlands auction, whereas in U.S. consignment systems that price is secret. The Dutch grower, however, cannot directly influence his return by negotiation because prices are determined by an impersonal bidding system. But by improving quality, monitoring auction prices, and carefully selecting among flowers known to generate high prices, he can indirectly influence his return.[9] Member growers like Paul and Hans benefit from the auction system in several ways. Quality standards, value, and adequate returns for growers are assured because auction inspectors use standard grades and set starting prices as well as the lowest acceptable price (below which flowers are destroyed), thereby assuring buyers of quality and avoiding destabilizing price fluctuations. The auction system also rewards growers with immediate payment.

Furthermore, auctions provide a largely local marketplace for local production since about 80 percent of the flowers traded through these auctions are grown in the Netherlands—the majority from immediately adjacent growers like Paul. This minimizes grower competition, both local and global. Gerbera growers are, in general, competing with a limited local pool of other gerbera growers on the basis of quality and variety. The transparent auction system theoretically allows every grower to inform himself about his competition since information about all growers' varieties, qualities, and resulting prices is readily available. This gives Paul the opportunity to differentiate himself from other growers. By incrementally tailoring his varieties and quantities with respect to those of other growers, he avoids the kind of direct competition that reduces prices and profits. By producing, sorting, and selling small volumes of specific flower cultivars, even a modest one-hectare enterprise like Paul's and Chaya's is viable and sustains the socially valued small-holding grower's way of life. Finally, the auction system relieves Dutch growers of the need to understand particular desires among distant consumers of their products or to design their output to satisfy them. As it aggregates a vast selection of blooms the auction ensures that the twelve hundred or so well-informed buyers can select grades, colors, species, and varieties to meet the demands of the varied global market sectors to which they are connected through their specific local or global networks. Flowers end up in the global market niches for which they are culturally appropriate and at prices their ultimate consumers are willing to pay. Additionally, the costs of reaching and using this market are reasonable. As Hans explained it: "My concern is getting a good price. . . . I get good prices on the auction [yet] it costs me only five percent to market my flowers through the auction, renting boxes, transportation and other things."[10]

Free of direct local competition and the business of marketing, Paul, Hans, and their fellow growers can focus on growing techniques and productivity, building relationships, gathering information, and improving their knowledge. Such freedom confers an extra edge for Dutch flower growers collectively in a highly competitive global market and contributes to the Netherlands' dominance of the global flower trade. This degree of specialization—division of labor—does not seem to increase risk for Dutch growers because the market for their flowers is huge and the auction system (and import tariffs) largely protects them from competition from other global growers.

CHOOSING NEW FLOWERS

Growers producing for the international market face multiple daily decisions. One of the most important, however, concerns upgrading their crops by adding new flower varieties. Many growers are concerned about improving the types, quality, and marketability of their blooms. Displays of new flowers and new cultivation technology always draw large crowds at the major international trade shows. Paul and Hans, like most growers, replace their plants and bulbs regularly. Replacement frequency depends on flower type. Chrysanthemums flower, die, and are replanted every few months while a rose shrub dependably produces flowers for ten years. The plant's nature is important but is only one factor. Growers also replace plants to adjust their variety mixes in response to the changes in market volume and consumer tastes that continuously alter flower prices. Paul's gerbera plants have three or four years of productive life but he replaces them after a year or two as colors or forms decline in popularity or as increased production by some of his competitors with larger greenhouses reduces prices below acceptable levels. Michael Starr, a California grower, once explained to me how growers who are "quick to pick up on new trends" can gain considerable financial advantage. Paul van der Heiden attends closely to trends and has adopted a process of almost continuous innovation—a process Piore and Sabel have labeled "flexible specialization" (1984).

Gerberas are readily reproduced through tissue-culturing, making it fairly easy for Paul to replace a proportion of his seventeen varieties every year to keep up with changing trends. Lily bulbs, however, propagate very slowly. For a grower like Hans, several years may elapse between choosing a newly hybridized lily and selling the resulting blooms at auction, by which time changing volume and other factors may have shifted prices substantially. "It is a gamble," he explained. "You don't know if you will get a good price for them."

Professional commercial growers agree that selecting a new flower variety is one of their most difficult decisions. "Gamble" is a frequent description since a poor choice launched onto an uncertain market can quickly eliminate previous profits. Decisions are further complicated by the fact that almost a hundred new gerberas (and over fifty new roses) may be launched in a year. How is a grower to judge which of these (or the hundreds and hundreds of existing varieties) are most likely to be profitable? The difficulty with such business decision, as Block points out in his analysis of the limitations of neoclassical economics, is that "individuals usually lack the information, the computational skills, and the time to act with perfect rationality" (1990, 25). Flower growers seldom (perhaps never) have the perfect information they need for a "rational" decision, or anything approaching it. Attempts to perfect their information depend on individual circumstances. Some Netherlands growers, possibly content with the financial return afforded by the efficient auction system, make little effort to gather formal information to guide their replanting decisions (Trip 2000). Instead, they may rely on intuition or a form of unconsciously reasoned decision-making. Intuitive decisions about such things as new flower variety choices, as the basis for economic action, are widespread in flower growing and trading. For growers, such decisions are shaped by mixtures of informal information—gossip and advice from fellow-growers and other social connections—and formal information, about price, productivity, and so on.

Paul and Hans, however, with their considerable investment in new varieties and technology, are concerned to ensure a higher return. Therefore they seek a range of formal information to guide their replanting calculations and to shape a distinctive position for themselves and improve profit. Ideally, Paul's gerbera gambles are guided by two sets of information, each requiring different sources and relationships to supply them.

The first area of knowledge is fairly concrete and encompasses the physical characteristics of new flowers. Like all commercial growers, Paul has basic productivity costs per square meter. These vary with each type of flower and are calibrated by the grower's skills, technology, labor and energy costs, loan repayments, capital investment, plant royalty fees, and so on. Consequently, accurate information about bloom yield per square meter and the potential market price per bloom is fairly critical. Details about bloom color, size, and susceptibility to disease in the grower's particular climate and growing conditions are also crucial. Auction statistics supply some pricing and demand information about existing and new cultivars, while physical characteristics, cultivation, and productivity information may come from breeders or from trade magazines. But according to Hans and others, "The biggest source of information for growers in Holland is talking to each other, going on tours [as well as] looking at each other's flowers." As explained in chapter 4, Netherlands growers readily exchange information through their species study groups. "Fifteen men come together every three weeks," explained Paul, describing the activities of his gerbera study group. "We tour each other's greenhouses [visiting] three of the group in an afternoon in a particular region."

Hans, the lily grower, also observes his fellow-growers. He, his brother, and his father (also lily growers) travel on Fridays "to 't-Zand in northern Holland where most of the lilies are grown. We walk around the greenhouses and look at the product" (see figure 19). These frequent, informative, social interactions between growers hint at both the degree of cooperation among these growers and the degree to which society and economy are integrated. These reciprocal exchanges of knowledge are also tinged with competition. As Hans noted, "They come here too . . . but by the time they see my successful lilies they are too late because they are two or three years behind. . . . Still, they like to see how the competition is doing. We say we like to shop." In short, through social observation of their fellow growers and by tracing color trends, prices, and demand through auction sales figures, Hans and Paul supply themselves with part of the information needed to help their selection of new flowers.

The second set of information Paul needs is more nebulous and concerns shifts in consumer and retailer tastes and desires. In theory, a sense of changing trends would allow him to focus on the most desired forms, colors, and other characteristics favored by consumers. Since about 80 percent of the flowers traded through the auctions are exported, chiefly to other European countries, both Hans and Paul cultivate relationships with middlemen exporters to gather information. Hans, who must invest for the long term because of slow lily bulb propagation, explained how he tries to reduce some of his risk by seeking and using information about lily trends:

19 Oriental lily

Mostly I depend on the exporters. They tell me what is selling well at a higher price. Every Monday and Friday I go to the auction and see the prices—you can see trends. For the last three or four years white has done better than pink. So for next year I have more white varieties than pink. . . . Exporters give me information about specific demands in different countries. For America they say, they want two, three, four big flowers on the stem and they like a big bloom. We don't sell stems with eight or nine blooms there because the topmost flower will then be too small. . . . The exchange rate is very important to me. If the dollar declines then they will buy fewer of our flowers. It is something you keep in the back of your mind. Right now I can buy bulbs that will produce three or four flowers [as opposed to seven or eight flowers] and if I think the dollar will continue strong next year with strong demand for flowers, then I will choose to buy the bulbs that will succeed in that market.

Paul, with much shorter cycles of innovation and with many more possible choices among gerbera varieties, found information gleaned from exporters of limited use. "If you go to ten [exporters] with ten new varieties," he explained, "each will choose something different because they have the Italian market, the German market, the U.S. market and all are different and specific. In the nineties the French wanted only pastel with a little orange and red. Russia wanted only bright red and orange and strong yellow. Italy wants big flowers. With Switzerland only quality counts . . . you can't grow for each market, so

Cultivating the Global Garden

you must gamble." In fact, Paul concluded that all his decision-making tools, while helpful, were really "never enough to predict future desires" with much accuracy.

Exporters, for their part, regularly visit innovative growers like Paul and Hans to observe their newest cultivars in the hopes of generating interest in these new (usually high-priced) selections among their own customers in advance of the actual harvest. Buyers also gather and exchange information—some of it unsubstantiated gossip and rumor—that will inform some of their purchasing decisions at the auction. This sort of social linkage across the boundaries of the usually separate communities of Dutch buyers and growers is probably uncommon. But a few innovative growers and exporters form these vertical relationships between their commodity chain segments, establishing competitive advantage and altering their market situations.

With taste changes difficult to anticipate, a more certain strategy for Paul to ensure his necessary return per square meter is to grow the newest varieties of gerberas. These are the most desirable "because people want what is new and different," Paul explained, and "then they are willing to pay [higher prices]." In pursuit of this strategy, Paul had patiently nurtured a relationship with an outstanding neighboring breeder. Every year he bought his new plants from that one breeder and frequently visited his test beds and discussed the trials. Finally the breeder reciprocated and recently chose Paul to grow and test-market some of his new gerbera hybrids. With approximately one hectare of greenhouse Paul hasn't the space to produce large volumes at low prices, so it was essential for him to "get something new and different and target a different market . . . to distinguish myself." By test-marketing the breeder's new varieties Paul has "an advantage of better prices. . . . Other growers, my colleagues, can learn from my experience and watch the prices the varieties are getting on the auction . . . the breeder gets testing of his new varieties in real growing and marketing conditions."

So a beneficial situation evolves for growers and breeders who establish relationships with each other and for the community of local growers who can observe the results of the collaboration, both during cultivation in a local greenhouse and later during sale at a local auction. But collaborating growers are a privileged few because breeders themselves are few. With only about five principal breeders of lilies and nine of gerberas in the world—most of them in the Netherlands—access is limited. Rose breeders are also scarce. There are about twenty major rose breeders in the world, with fifteen of them in the Netherlands, France, and Germany.

20 Alstroemeria

Not surprisingly, breeders offer new flowers to very few, usually local growers with the highest skills and standards so that the initial market prices are high because of quality as well as rarity.[11] "We start new flowers out in the Dutch market," explained Erik Piet, a salesman for an alstroemeria breeder, "and eventually they move to other countries" (see figure 20). This promotes interest in the new variety among potential traders, according to Erik, creating a market for (and incidentally among) increasing numbers of growers. With their huge production of gerberas, lilies, and roses, Dutch growers are breeders' major market, while growers in California, Israel, Colombia, Ecuador, and other countries are subsidiary markets. Because cycles of introduction, rising popularity, decline, and replacement have accelerated in the recent years, rose breeders now aim to persuade growers to buy and plant a new variety within a year or so of its launching. Beyond that short period "some varieties will already be too old for the market and other breeders will have launched similar types and colors to compete."[12] By the time growers in the "other countries" have acquired information about, and access to, a new rose, it may already be "too old" to be profitable in some market niches.[13] In a classic illustration of one aspect of the competitive advantages of clustering, proximity to the world-class research of breeders and their collaborating growers confers a distinct advantage on this fortunate few and on other local Dutch growers.

GROWER WEAKNESS

Dutch growers are, on the whole, securely positioned with respect to competition in the global flower trade. Yet recent changes in the Aalsmeer auction's activities and operations seem to be gently undermining that security. The authority of the institution itself has expanded and the interests of middlemen buyers seem to be favored over growers' interests. The Aalsmeer auction has historically handled the flowers of about four thousand neighboring grower members, but during the 1990s it also became the market place for a considerable portion of the production of Israel, Kenya, and Zimbabwe, among other places. In fact the auction has agreed to market the production of over three thousand nonmember foreign growers, who provide about 25 percent or more of the flowers passing through the auction. Imported flowers were originally intended to fill periods of low Dutch production such as the winter months—a benefit for buyers and others at the auction site. The Dutch auction buyer-member (who is in effect either a traditional wholesaler or an exporter) already benefited because he spent a minimum amount of time choosing from a vast daily selection of the highest-quality flowers in the world. He could concentrate on sales, service, and developing his customer base. Under the new arrangements, selection has been extended in volume, range, and season, and in 2004 the Aalsmeer auction turnover of cut flowers exceeded 1 billion euros.[14] Imports are concentrated in the winter months when Dutch production is lowest, but they also overlap the spring and summer months when Dutch domestic productivity is high. Such institutional innovation dilutes grower members' power while expanding the institution itself and its global authority.

Some rose growers complain, perhaps unfairly, that these auction innovations bring declining prices, thus favoring the buying middlemen over the growers. More pragmatically, rose grower Dick Vreeken argued that "we cannot stop their [foreign grower] production so we might as well try to channel it to our advantage" through the vast Netherlands flower-trading system.[15] Declining prices for some types of roses and other flowers are, as noted earlier, a general global phenomenon and partly a result of enormous worldwide production and stable consumption. Yet Dutch growers still have a pricing edge. The prices paid for Dutch blooms often exceed those for imports even of the same species and variety.[16] Differences in quality and freshness probably account for this, as well as the greater likelihood that the Dutch grow newer cultivars commanding higher prices. Yet as large volumes of these cheaper alternatives pass through the auction, they may eventually (and indeed, may already) affect demand and prices for Dutch blooms.

The relative anonymity and interchangeability of the foreign growers who

21 Viktor and Rolf sniffing out their new perfume. Photograph courtesy of Lisa Eisner.

trade through the Dutch auctions weakens their position in the flower chain and their competitiveness with their Dutch counterparts. At the auctions, flower lots are identified by the grower's name. Buyers are generally familiar with the quality standards of many growers and make purchasing decisions using that knowledge. But beyond that point in the journey, individual growers—Dutch and foreign—disappear as Dutch exporters or foreign importers repack the various bunches of flowers that constitute an order into their own branded boxes. These repacking processes often obliterate both the grower and the national origins of blooms. Unlike other globally sourced horticultural products such as grapes, peppers, and raspberries, labeling the country of origin is seldom required for flowers. Flowers from Israel, Australia, New Zealand, and Kenya may be imported into the Netherlands, purchased, repacked, and re-exported without national identification. They are simply anonymous blooms from the global garden.

Netherlands flowers, in contrast—while seldom identified with or branded by individual growers—are often clearly identified as Dutch or Holland flowers. The Flower Council of Holland, a division of the Netherlands Product Board for Horticulture with a multimillion dollar marketing budget, has been very effective in promoting Netherlands flowers in imaginative ways. It was surely not by accident that Dutch gerberas framed the Dutch fashion designers Viktor and Rolf in photos for a style article in the *New York Times* (see figure 21).[17] Indeed, U.S. retailers—who are sometimes hazy about the sources

Cultivating the Global Garden

of the flowers they sell—use the term "Holland" generically to signify specialty blooms or superior flowers, even if the flowers themselves are grown in Colombia. In contrast, "South American" in retail parlance often refers to commodity blooms such as roses, carnations, and chrysanthemums.

Ecuador

CULTIVATION

North from Quito along the Pan American highway, flower farms begin to dot the high Andean pasture land at about the seventy kilometers mark—around Tabacundo and Cayambe. Close to a hundred flower farms cluster here. The expanding industry flourishes in a valley with mild temperatures, fertile volcanic soils, and intermittent views of the Cayambe volcano. Plastic-sheeted flower houses shimmer throughout the valley. They are an Andean version of the Crystal City of glass houses that glittered in the Hudson River Valley one hundred years earlier. Jorge Vélez Serrano owns several flower farms, or "plantations," in this region. Like most of his neighbors, Jorge once specialized in roses. Now, however, he grows about eighteen different flower species including irises, lilies, freesias, gerberas, and asters.

Jorge, who has been in the business for close to twenty years, might have preferred to continue specializing in one flower for the advantages conferred in knowledge, quality, and range. However, several years ago, declining prices and increasing competition from expanding hectares of rose farms in Ecuador, Colombia, Kenya, Costa Rica, and other places prompted Jorge to expand and adopt new flowers and new growing and marketing techniques. He had learned that U.S. consumers paid more for new flower species, many of which were grown in California and the Netherlands. This knowledge also influenced his expansion decision. Not everyone shares Jorge's perspectives with respect to innovation. Some rose growers are thriving, but others are less prosperous or even insolvent. Yet these faltering farms continue to focus on roses because their owners are unwilling or unable to adopt new species or technology or because essential knowledge and capital are out of their reach.

While most of Jorge's flowers are raised in plastic-covered houses, a few "summer" flowers such as asters and delphinium are grown in open fields, taking advantage of the fertile soil and generous climate. Five hundred employees work on over forty hectares of covered houses, fields, and packing areas as well as in his management and sales offices. His three farms are well over the minimum size of about eight hectares necessary for an economically viable flower-growing business in Ecuador. A few Ecuadorian farms are considerably larger. However, like several others I spoke with, Jorge feels smaller farms allow him to maintain high quality in the flower species he grows.

Jorge's expansion was also influenced by difficulties in selling his flowers to wholesale florists, his traditional customers. Without a cooperative market like Aalsmeer, Ecuadorian growers must individually gain access to foreign customers and chains of distribution and establish their own quality standards. Some try to cooperate. Several years ago, Jorge and a few other growers formed a marketing group. However, differences in flower quality from different farms, as well as conflicts of personality and management style, eventually lead to its dissolution. A handful of group-marketing enterprises exist (some composed of kin groups, where issues of style and power are more easily resolved) but among Ecuadorian growers the spirit of competition is often far stronger than the spirit of cooperation. Flower farms are clustered together, but few of the recognized benefits of clustering have been realized. There is little trust and sharing and little dissemination of knowledge about new varieties and technology—certainly far less than in the Aalsmeer cluster. What flower knowledge exists, whether "tacit knowledge" about consumer tastes or "codified knowledge" about new varieties and growing technology, seems to be confined within each enterprise. It is not in the Ecuadorian grower's interests to risk his considerable investment in flower testing and marketing by sharing knowledge with other growers except perhaps at a later stage in a new bloom's product cycle. He needs to retain his hard-won competitive advantage.[18]

Broadly speaking, Ecuadorian flower growers have two marketing routes. They can send flowers on consignment to an intermediary importer in Miami who will eventually channel them to wholesalers, supermarkets, mass marketers, and bouquet-makers. Alternatively they can negotiate direct transactions with importers, wholesale florists, bouquet makers, or supermarket chains in the United States and Europe. A few U.S. bouquet makers have established bouquet-assembly plants in Ecuador in recent years; these may offer another option to some growers.[19] Flower quality, variety, and volume partly condition these marketing possibilities. Older flower varieties and those of poorer quality, for example, are generally sold on consignment while newer varieties and higher quality may follow either stream. Diego Salgado, one of Jorge's rose-growing neighbors, depends on the consignment system while Jorge tries to concentrate on direct sales. Both consignment and direct marketing are complicated, and direct marketing is also costly. As Humphrey and Schmitz, among others, have pointed out, these "sunk costs" create substantial barriers to new industry entrants (2000, 19).

CONSIGNMENT MARKETING

About 70 percent of the flowers passing through the Miami wholesale market are sold on consignment. Miami is a global market, like Aalsmeer, in the sense that flowers from many different growers and countries are gathered and offered for sale. But it is also a rather invisible, almost placeless market characterized by the secrecy of its transactions. About one hundred importer-wholesaler businesses cluster together in several city blocks adjacent to the Miami airport. Each firm handles and trades its individually negotiated shipments of flowers arriving from Quito, Bogotá, San José, and other cities. Buyers and sellers seldom meet to arrange their transactions; most trades are negotiated by telephone and e-mail. Competition is intense between importer-wholesalers trying to secure flower supplies at low prices (consistent with quality) and sell them profitably. Prices are private information, seldom shared. Consequently concrete knowledge about prevailing market prices and volume is scarce and transactions may depend on gossip and other factors that contribute to an intuitive or tacit feel for the current market.

The lack of transparency—the mystification of price and volume information—gives importers a considerable advantage in their dealings with growers. To overcome their relative disadvantages growers attempt to establish personal relationships in this market. Mark Granovetter offers several good reasons for this strategy. "Individuals with whom one has a continuing relation have an economic motivation to be trustworthy, so as not to discourage future transactions," he explains. Furthermore, "departing from pure economic motives, continuing economic relations often become overlaid with social content that carries strong expectations of trust and abstention from opportunism" (1985, 491).

An understanding with an importer helps the Ecuadorian rose grower Diego Salgado's marketing options in two practical ways. First such relationships sometimes involve "standing orders"—a verbal agreement to take regular shipments at a fixed price. Second, even under the basic consignment arrangements, long-term relationships—as Granovetter points out—build trust on both sides. Diego is trusted to provide dependable supplies of good roses, especially at holiday times. His importer-wholesaler, for his part, reciprocates by giving the consigned blooms sales priority, obtaining good prices (with a reasonable commission), and providing some stability for Diego in a highly competitive and volatile arena. All parties in these closely linked social networks enjoy a competitive advantage. Reputable importer-wholesalers and growers invest years in their relationships with each other, nourishing them with sometimes daily telephone conversations, e-mails, and regular meetings at trade shows. Occasionally, they even invest in each other's businesses. Such growers know, as Valerie Swift, a Miami importer-wholesaler explained, that "they get the best prices when that grower has a very close relationship with that wholesaler. It is not just a piece of paper."

Miguel Tejada, a middle-quality grower in Tabacundo, like many of his Ecuadorian colleagues, was convinced that "relationships [are] critical . . . this is a business of relationships. No question about it." Without such relationships, an importer may delay payment or cheat a grower on price or on the deductions for poor quality. He may also give sales preference to another grower's flowers or even to his own since many of the long-established and most powerful importing establishments in Miami are partially or wholly owned by other Ecuadorian or Colombian growers. Many Ecuadorian growers, Valerie explained, "want the fixed price, want the payment, want a guaranteed price on everything. But they can't get the commitment for it and they already have the flowers growing—so then what do you do?" Such growers would no doubt welcome the opportunity to grow their roses under a formal contract. Supply is so abundant, however, that there is little incentive for Miami importer-wholesalers or traditional wholesalers to offer such contracts. The grower without a verbal commitment, with poor relationships, may discover that his flowers have languished in an importer's cold room for several days, continuously losing value, before being sold cheaply for final retail in urban corner stores. Their condition may even deteriorate to the point where the grower receives nothing for them. Consequently, Diego seeks to entrust his flowers to an individual known to exchange them swiftly and handle them well.

Another part of the problem, noted earlier, is that standardized, industry-wide quality or freshness grades are still poorly developed in the U.S. cut flower trade. In effect, the ethics and reputation of networked individual growers, importers, and traditional wholesale florists act as a guarantee of quality and freshness. Relationships substitute for absent industry standards and help to preserve value for the grower. The economic importance of these relationships for the grower is evident from a brief examination of the charges and commissions levied under the consignment system in Miami.

Alberto Costa, who grows gypsophila and other flowers in Cayambe, explained the Miami consignment system. First, the grower pays the substantial air freight charges from Quito to Miami. This is a significant penalty for being several hours by jet, rather than two or three miles by road, from the principal marketplace. In Miami, importers levy handling (box) charges against the (selling) growers as well as the (buying) traditional wholesale florists or supermarkets. When a flower price declines from, say, $100 to $60 per box, the grower may effectively spend over 60 percent of that sales price on transportation and marketing costs (see table 8). As mentioned earlier, Paul van der Heiden spends 5 percent of his sales price on the same services.[20] Alberto argued that these charges offer incentives for importers to focus on high volume rather than the higher prices that benefit growers. Miami importers, he noted bitterly, "screw the growers left and right because they can." Roy Fish, a Miami importer with thirty years' experience, agreed with Alberto's assessment. He noted that "by dropping the price you can greatly multiply your sales. If an importer is short term greedy he will sell cheaper and try to sell more volume." With abundant supply from Colombia and Ecuador some flower importers are clearly tempted to focus on volume and low prices. Beneficiaries of this consignment system include other middlemen, that is, wholesalers, supermarkets, bouquet makers, corner stores, and New York Metropolitan Area consumers (see chapter 8). Theoretically, Ecuadorian flower growers have an alternative market. They might sell their flowers, especially roses, through the Netherlands auction system. But freight and other costs are high. In 2000, some Ecuadorian growers paid 52 percent of selling price in auction fees, transportation, and other costs for a return of about thirteen cents per rose stem after all deductions—a low return for a high-quality grower and probably insufficient to cover production costs.[21] Furthermore, since auctions demand high quality, a good grower might obtain a better return in the U.S. market for superior flowers in the winter season. Nevertheless, in late 1999–2000, Ecuadorian growers increased their shipments to the Dutch auctions by 70 percent. In that year they were the fifth largest importer to the auctions (after Israel, Kenya, Zimbabwe, and Spain), partly because roses were fetching lower prices in the United States. Increased production combined with only modest expansion in U.S. demand for flowers was partly to blame for the low prices. This problem increased after September 11, 2001, when parties and celebrations declined temporarily, slowing demand even more. Between 8 and 9 percent of Ecuador's flower exports went to the Netherlands in 2002 and 2004.

8 Sample importer-wholesaler fees and grower returns

	AVERAGE PRICE IN U.S. 40 bunches flowers at $2.50/bunch FOB Miami	LOW PRICE IN U.S. 40 bunches flowers at $1.50/bunch FOB Miami	% CHANGE In return between av. price and low price
Value of shipment	100	60	
Freight to Miami from Quito per box (paid by grower)	25	25	
Importer/broker charges			
15% commission (paid by grower)	15	9	
Handling charge to grower	3	3	
Handling (box) charge to wholesale florist	15	15	
Total return to grower	57	23	−60%
Total return to importer	33	27	−18%

Negotiating the second marketing route—direct transactions—as Jorge does, intensifies a grower's need for capital and often increases the pressure to innovate, gather information, and establish several kinds of relationships.

Formal contracts, as we have seen, are rare in the U.S. cut flower system; exchange is almost entirely based on verbal agreements.[22] Alonso Capel, a thoughtful Costa Rican grower, called them "gentlemen's agreements." They form the basis for a whole series of what Gudeman (2001) refers to as "implicit understandings"—expectations and obligations linking individuals along the commodity chain. Given the general reluctance to assume financial responsibility for a highly perishable commodity, this avoidance of binding or legal contracts seems rational enough. In some ways, "gentlemen's agreements" may offer a greater measure of security. When trusting relationships are the basis of exchange they deepen the social nature of the system. When moral obligation and reciprocal behavior condition exchange there is greater likelihood transactions will continue, whereas impersonal contracts expire or are broken. Fred Barents, a Miami importer-wholesaler, felt he had "a commitment to the farm. I am responsible for all the farms I do business with and the hundreds of people who work for those farms. Sometimes I have paid the farm more than I sold the product for. But," he added, smiling, "I am not Santa Claus."

Jorge's marketing innovation and diversification allow him to sell his flowers to a mixture of supermarkets, traditional wholesalers in the northeastern United States, and some Miami importer-wholesalers. Each market sector involves a range of relationships with different implied obligations, including sharing information and advice and offering assistance during setbacks. Andrés Pallares, who grows delphinium among his other summer flowers, explained his view that "personal connections carry a lot of weight . . . because it is all built on trust and good faith. We send him our flowers. If the guy is not scrupulous he can say—the flowers arrived bad, I am taking a fifty percent credit. But with a good relationship with a person, if he does say the flowers arrive bad, then the flowers probably did arrive bad—for whatever reason." Andrés added: "In times of pressure and competition like now, personal relationships are a tremendous help."

Carlos García, a high-quality rose grower, told a story of generosity among his wholesale clients to illustrate the way personal relationships cushion flower growers' risk. Following an unusually severe early frost, Carlos was forced to

Chapter Five

prune his roses at an unusual time. This set off an "up and down cycle that we had never had before" so that "all ten hectares came like crazy in February." With only a minor portion of the crop in red roses so popular around February 14 and the majority in other colors, there was little demand for most of these roses. "Fortunately," Carlos explained, "all our clients supported us and bought it. I didn't have to dump anything." That is why, he continued, you must "have a personal relationship. [Because we are] not like machines."

INNOVATION

Jorge's management of his harvests is complicated by his combination of traditional wholesale and supermarket customers. These distinct market sectors require different flower types, sizes, and pricing. These demands compel growers to tailor their crops to satisfy one sector even if they hope to spread risks by also partially serving others.

Growers consider direct transactions with traditional wholesale florists particularly desirable because wholesale florists pay well (if slowly) and assume freight charges—a significant benefit. Moreover, traditional wholesale florists often arrange standing orders to ensure quality and supply. Supplying wholesale florists, however, requires Jorge to attend to constantly changing tastes and trends and to innovate constantly and grow new flowers that will accommodate them. It is a challenging situation that the importer Roy Fish described during an interview as combining "all the constraints . . . of a perishable [business] with all the constraints of the fashion business." Tastes and demands vary for each nation, region, and season. Americans, for example, buy flowers for holidays such as Valentine's Day, Mother's Day, Thanksgiving, and Christmas, as well as for minor regional holidays. Outside these various holidays and the spring and fall wedding and celebration seasons, demand for particular flowers may be limited. To use an obvious example, red roses sell well on Valentine's Day and before Christmas but poorly for much of the rest of the year, while orange and yellow flowers are much in demand in the United States in October and November. As Carlos's story illustrated, roses must be precisely pruned and cultivated to meet these holiday dates, initiating a cycle that produces masses of red roses in February, and then again in May, August, and November—periods when there is little demand for red roses and prices for them are very low. Once flowers are being grown to satisfy target dates and channels, sale in other channels is limited. Carlos told another story to explain the difficulty in juggling these cycles between nations and regions.

"In Europe my standing orders are for the same colors in the same amounts year round. So they are not buying for seasons. My customers in Finland couldn't understand why Americans want orange roses in October. I explained the fall colors. They said they wanted the same colors year round. After October the next flush of orange roses is February, which is not a good month to sell oranges in America—I was trying to persuade the Finns to take oranges in February. But they wanted their usual selection. People are different."

Keeping pace with quite subtle shifts in trends and tastes is economically critical. "On any given day," explained the importer Roy Fish, selecting the current day's sales lists on his computer screen, different varieties of visually similar red roses of the same stem length "might sell at fifty cents, forty cents, thirty and twenty cents." One of the fifty-cent roses on Roy's list was the popular large-headed 'Charlotte.' Adding it to his range to satisfy his whole-sale customers would cost Jorge about $2.20 for each plant (about $150,000 per hectare) including royalty fees to the breeder—a large sum to risk at prevailing rates of interest (18 percent at the time). Furthermore, its popularity might be short-lived because, as María Gonzalez, one of his saleswomen, explained, "Two years [ago] we grew only one red rose. They developed well, were great in bouquets and then [suddenly] they were not in fashion any more, so they didn't sell well. So we pulled them out and planted 'Classy,' which was the red rose in fashion at that time. But the fashion lasted one year, now people aren't asking for it. They are asking for 'Charlotte' or big-headed roses. But we have a lot of 'Classy.' "

Such fashion trends (as opposed to holiday and seasonal cycles) are not significant at the level of chain supermarkets, where any twenty-cent red or yellow or white rose is as good as another. So 'Charlotte' might not sell profitably to Jorge's supermarket customers. Jorge established a direct rela-tionship with a supermarket chain, hoping to profit both from larger sales volume and from economies such as the use of his surplus May and August red roses in his supermarket bouquets. His supermarket relationships have brought advantages, but also fresh complexities. On the whole, Jorge likes his supermarket customers because they pay far more promptly than wholesalers. They also offer contracts which allow some forward planning and bring a measure of security. Jorge's arrangements with supermarkets, however, are unlike the contract farming common in horticultural chains, where, typically, the green bean, broccoli, or grape farmer contracts with an export company or some form of agro-industrial firm. Usually the contractor has some control over production, specifying such things as varieties, quality, quantities, delivery date, and so on. Contract farming in developing countries often involves peasant or small-holding farmers engaged in intensive production of a single horticultural crop. The contract binds them to agribusinesses sometimes with the lure of seed provision, credit, and modernization for the farmer (Cook 1994; Jaffee 1994; Little 1994; Freidberg 2004). Contract growers own their own land, yet Cook describes them as "effectively deskilled agricultural laborers working for a piecework wage for the contractor." Through these arrangements the contractor avoids—and the farmer bears—all the risks of farming such as disease, infestation, declining prices, and bad weather as well as labor disputes (Cook 1994).

Flower growers in Latin America also bear these risks but without even the small advantages described above. Very few have direct contracts with supermarkets and such contracts are often very short term. Flower growers also carry the additional burden of their crop's unusually delicate nature and vulnerability to blemish, fashion fads, and quick decay. In other respects, however, Ecuadorian flower growers have advantages over typical horticultural contract farmers. They are free to seek advice from different sources about new desirable varieties and growing methods and they may grow what they choose. Furthermore, they are never peasants. Instead, Ecuadorian growers are usually well-educated, prosperous, and influential enough to access the financial resources necessary to enter and remain in the capital-intensive business of growing cut flowers for export.[23]

Though rarely seen today, contract cut flower growing has been tried in the past. The Kenya government initiated a project in the mid-1970s primarily for political reasons. It survived for only two years and today Kenyan export flower growing is dominated by a handful of private, large-scale growing operations (Jaffee 1994; Hughes 2004). It is not completely clear from recent studies whether these large Kenyan flower growers have formal contracts with the United Kingdom supermarkets that are important customers. Perhaps, like the French bean growers of Zambia, they base their relationships with these supermarkets on trust (Freidberg 2004, 121). United Kingdom supermarket managers are said to influence the flower varieties produced at the farms to accord with their interpretations of changing flower fashions (Hughes 2000; Hughes 2004). However, only 16 percent of the country's flowers are exported to the United Kingdom while the remaining 84 percent are sold in the Netherlands and other countries, where demands may differ.

Growers, therefore, are likely to focus on the tastes of these larger markets unless they have contracts with United Kingdom supermarket buyers. In the United States, there are few incentives for supermarkets and other large retailers such as Wal-Mart and Sam's Club to deal directly with growers like Jorge. In fact, some retailers avoid taking ownership of flowers at any point in the commodity chain, preferring instead to pay suppliers only as flowers pass through the checkouts (see chapter 7).

However, supermarkets, together with mass retail stores, have captured substantial market share. They are forcing changes in flower retail and therefore change in the entire fresh cut flower commodity chain. These changes affect some growers by compelling them to abandon the ideal of specialization and struggle with diversification (see chapters 6 and 7). Thirty years ago, as explained in chapter 2, 90 percent of cut flower sales occurred through traditional retail florists. Today, less than 30 percent of cut flower stems pass through their hands (and therefore through traditional wholesale florists) while over 50 percent are sold through supermarkets and about 8 percent through lower-priced mass retail superstores such as Wal-Mart or Sam's Club. These important new retail segments—supermarkets and mass retail—have two characteristics that alter the fortunes of flower growers. First, some maintain their profits by requiring their suppliers to lower their margins and to assume all risk for the product. Often the suppliers are bouquet-makers or importers but sometimes they are flower growers themselves. Regardless of supplier, a lower return per stem is inevitable for the grower at the beginning of this chain. Second, these retail outlets concentrate on ready-made single-variety bunches (usually known as consumer bunches) or bouquets of mixed flowers.

There are still many bouquet-makers in the United States, but assembly of bouquets and bunches is steadily being pushed to the point on the commodity chain with lowest labor and ingredient costs—the Ecuadorian or Colombian farm. Jorge sells his own farm-made mixed bouquets to a midwestern supermarket chain. Consequently he has invested in growing a range of flower species to supply the component ingredients. He has also invested in more staff and technology such as bar-code labeling in order to meet the level of service demanded by supermarkets. In effect, the costs and complications of assembling a variety of flowers to offer to consumers, usually absorbed by retailers, wholesalers, and importers, are, in some instances, displaced to the grower at the beginning of the chain.[24]

Chapter Five

Each of the new flowers Jorge grows to satisfy his supermarket or wholesale customers has specific requirements for cultivation, different planting dates, and life spans. Each new flower "brings a new risk," he explained, and requires new knowledge that "costs money" to obtain. The costly process of testing new flowers often reveals a range of technical difficulties. Alberto Costa described a neighbor's problems in expanding his flower mix: "His farm is trying to diversify into tuberoses and anemones. [He] did not grow anemones in the correct location at first; they need to be higher [and therefore colder]. Also they bought the wrong anemones, Israeli hybrids instead of French hybrids."

Difficulty with new flower species is a common problem regardless of geographic location. Managers or agronomists at many farms I visited in different countries struggled with new, faltering flowers. A grower's tests and trials can take several years, by which time competing growers may have captured some of the potential market for that flower and demand may be disappointing. These factors help limit expertise in cultivating new flowers (other than large-headed roses). Moreover, few manage to match Dutch standards for these specialty flowers and gain access to high-paying markets in the United States and Europe. Jorge and his manager, Fidel Duran, worried about potential competition from local and global growers with respect to his newest flower, lisianthus (see figure 22). They began by mentally mapping the global growers linked by a shared interest in lisianthus. "No one else in Ecuador is growing [it] . . . California they are growing it—two farms," said Fidel. "But they don't have it year round," he continued, "and the stems are not as big as ours. The spray of our bunch is larger. I don't think anyone is growing it in Colombia. Certainly [they are] in Holland." The Netherlands is a constant reference point in Jorge's deliberations. From his trade-fair trips to Holland, he is aware that Dutch growers can produce many flowers year round but he also knows there are optimum natural production times for different flowers, seasons when quality is highest and production costs lowest. He now tries to focus his own lisianthus production to coincide with both U.S. holidays and the Netherlands and California counterseason.

In fact, his information was, inevitably, imperfect. Others in Ecuador, Colombia, and Brazil and over seventy growers in the United States were also producing lisianthus (Jerardo 2002). Furthermore, about 130 different varieties of lisianthus were offered at the Netherland auctions, some of them eventually reaching the New York Metropolitan Area. Indeed, its cultivation

123

22 Lisianthus

was featured in an Ecuadorian flower trade journal some eighteen months earlier. Yet, as Gudeman suggests, Jorge's latest innovation had placed him in a new relationship with other global growers. That relationship altered his behavior as he planned his planting times, land use, and harvests to minimize competition from their harvests. Lisianthus, in some ways, mediated the imagined relationship. Its beauty, the "evolutionary strategy" of plants, as Pollan (2001, xviii) puts it, had aroused the desire of flower consumers. Growers, learning of that desire, had in turn spread its cultivation to many parts of the globe.

RELATIONSHIPS

Adopting these innovations in flower production and market strategies requires Jorge to develop information about new flowers and their cultivation. The task of information gathering is harder for growers who are culturally and spatially distant from both the consumers of their flowers and from the Northern European center of flower industry innovation. Jorge, like other Ecuadorian growers, tackles these difficulties by using relationships with middlemen and other growers for information. Gathering this information is costly, yet essential for Jorge's survival as a flower grower. He and his sales staff travel frequently in the United States, Europe, and Latin America attending global trade shows to observe new hybrids and other growers' flower selections. Jorge also travels to shows and meetings to nurture his relationships with middlemen and to build new marketing links, relationships, and alliances.

The importer Roy Fish is fairly typical of the middlemen who are willing to share knowledge about changing tastes and the best gambles among new flower cultivars. "Growers are constantly asking for advice on what to grow next," explained Roy, who gathers his information through his own relationships with traditional wholesale florists and the retailers who guide and satisfy the whims and wishes of consumers.

Jorge finds that breeders are occasionally useful sources of knowledge about cultivation. But when it comes to guidance about new blooms, Jorge admitted that sometimes breeders "don't give you the truth. They always say you are the only one getting this flower." Dependable information from breeders appears to flow primarily to the handful of innovative, well-connected Ecuadorian growers who also invest in their own growing and marketing tests. Many others regard breeders and their information (offered in catalogues and conversations) with suspicion and resentment. My interviews yielded tales of breeders who entice growers to buy the seeds, cuttings, or plants of a variety that proves to have an unfashionable color, or heads too small or stems too short, or petals that shatter in shipping. Some Ecuadorian growers perceive that the breeder's interest lies in selling as many seeds, cuttings, or plants as possible with little concern for the grower customer who finds a saturated market and unrewarding price just as he harvests his new crop. Carlos García related what he regarded as a typical experience with breeders. "They offered one, 'Fancy Amazon,' I remember, a few years ago, as the best one, a good producer and it has three colors in one and the opening stage was beautiful and long stems. Everything a grower would want. Everyone in the United States and Europe wanted it [they said]." Carlos continued, "After you planted it you found out that the plant was no good, a bad producer. The market didn't like it because it opened too fast. So what do you do then? And they offered that to everybody in the world, not just in Ecuador but Colombia and Africa. Everywhere."

While breeders of new roses now often test them in Ecuador and Colombia, most other new flowers are bred and tested in distant Holland or other European countries with local growers and conditions in mind. An alstroemeria thriving in Aalsmeer may develop quite differently in Cayambe.[25] Breeders themselves claim tremendous difficulties in developing new flowers that will succeed in a wide range of climates and for growers with varying cultivation skills and different markets. Peter Kneppers, a salesman for a Dutch breeder, explained some of the problems: "We sell [flowers] in seventy-five countries—[we] can't test in all countries and there is tremendous variation both in climate and growing mediums. [We are] testing to eliminate the poor ones but it is a gamble with the rest. Is it also a gamble for the grower? We can't test if he can sell it—who knows—tomorrow red may not be a popular color. We can test only so many conditions . . . but we can't test for the market." These problems are real. I have seen samples of the same rose grown in the Netherlands and in Ecuador reaching different heights and bloom forms and emerging in substantially different shades. If flower breeders listed the global growers of their cultivars on their websites, allowing all growers to judge the extent of their personal competition, information might be more evenly distributed globally, as it is within the Netherlands. Yet breeders fear, understandably, that potential customers might be deterred from buying and planting a new flower by the knowledge that hundreds of growers around the world and down the road have already invested in that bloom. One Dutch rose breeder has begun offering information about a handful of growers producing its hybrids in the United States and Latin America, mostly for the benefit of wholesalers and retailers.

Like their Netherlands colleagues, Jorge, Carlos, and Diego also base their important new cultivar decisions on their observations of other growers. Without organized study groups, however, most Ecuadorian growers are limited to observing the cultivar choices of a handful of high-quality growers exhibiting at local trade shows. These choices are then imitated as the new varieties become more widely available. Emulative growers multiply the new blooms, eventually spreading them into supermarkets and convenience stores. As they do so, the fifty-cent rose may become a twenty-cent rose, no longer seen in the luxury market where new wants are identified and new cultivars with novel colors and characteristics are selected, propagated, and tested to satisfy them. This behavior helps shape markets for flowers at this level, lending some support to White's claim that markets are defined less by the behavior of buyers than by the observational behavior of producers who watch each other and determine their own actions from these observations "thereby reproducing the observations" (1981, 520–21).

Privilege and Improvisation

Forty years ago, a decade before offshore horticultural production of perishables began to be important, Raymond Vernon hypothesized that because "knowledge is not a free good," entrepreneurs in less-developed countries would be reluctant "to venture into situations which they know will demand a constant flow of reliable marketing information from remote sources" (1966, 202). Yet today many global flower growers are tethered to the end of an extended trading chain with spatial, temporal, and cultural barriers that constrain the technical, cultural, and market knowledge critical to entry and success in global flower exporting.

Many of these growers are affected by accelerating cycles involving competition, innovation and upgrading to reduce competition, relationships, new information, new costs, new competition through imitation and expansion, and new innovation/upgrading. The processes of innovation and reciprocity help shape these growers' local and global relationships, both real and imaginary, within the flower system. The more innovative and what I term "privileged" growers enjoy rich networks of relations with breeders, fellow-growers, importers, exporters, or wholesalers. These networks of sometimes reciprocal relationships support this market system by distributing information, cushioning competition, and offering security in volatile times. They help to smooth adoption of innovations, some of which are eventually copied by others I call "improvising" growers, who innovate at a slower rate. For some improvising growers, knowledge and relationships may barely extend beyond their local cluster of growers and suppliers and the institution or handful of people with whom they connect in the next downstream segment of the global commodity chain. They find themselves in a competitive relationship with other global growers whose innovations, strategies, and behavior often remain imaginary. In contrast, the innovative, networked privileged growers are more apt to see beyond the local, to consider the activities of other global growers on the basis of real rather than imaginary relationships, and to benefit from those relationships.

Market structures like the Aalsmeer auction, with its surrounding clusters of growers, breeders and buyers, seem amply equipped to allow specialization and facilitate "effective investment and *upgrading in small riskable steps*" (Humphrey and Schmitz 2000, 19; emphasis in original). They distribute information and manage global competition as well as competition within the cluster. Yet social networks are still a rich source of information and individual identity. Some Dutch growers have a strong informational and innovative advantage in their close relationships with and proximity to major breeders and new technology. They can follow the progress and performance of a new flower variety in the breeders' test area or in study groups or at the auction, tracking its characteristics and gaining knowledge before committing to grow it. This allows them to make decisions earlier in the breeding/growing/marketing cycle than, for example, a typical Ecuadorian grower who may encounter the new flower at a much later stage in its cycle when it is being produced by the breeder's propagating agent in Ecuador or by that grower's neighbors. People linked in these relationships are not simply exchanging flowers. Based on understandings of a moral obligation, they exchange information and favors. This behavior forms social ties and the identity of individuals as members of a small group linked by common norms, ethics, and interests. Thus the commodity itself, the cut flower, is not simply inert but rather, in the process of production, exchange, and consumption, it helps create social relationships and communities within the chain.

While perfect information is a fantasy, even partial information is undeniably difficult to use well because of the industry's volatility. In an almost organic process, innumerable independent daily decisions in all parts of the chain incrementally adjust and collectively modify the entire cut flower system. Gambles with new species and cultivars are one of the decisions that are often guided by gossip, speculation, and open or furtive observations, producing intuitive decisions that are multiplied thousands of times among the growers supplying the U.S. market. New flowers are cast onto the streams flowing to major consuming regions, like the New York Metropolitan Area. Some float into profitable sectors to be picked up with delight and appreciatively consumed; others soon disappear. Growers with better information and stronger relationships within the commodity chain are better able to reduce their risks by innovating and outpacing competition both from local growers and from other regions. They are powerful in terms of their social influence on other growers and within parts of the system. I cannot even guess if they are powerful economically since their finances and profits are secret.

The complexity of establishing concrete international relationships and acquiring and using knowledge defeats many global growers, leading to costly and puzzling market failures. Growers seek explanations for these disappointments in gossip and in speculation about the behavior of importers, breeders, and other growers and the unfathomable mysteries of "the market" that lies elusively and invisibly beyond the auction or the downstream importer or wholesaler in their commodity chain.

In this disorganized setting, the traders of these blooms in Aalsmeer and Miami enjoy advantage. While the one is an institution and the other a changing collection of small entrepreneurial businesses and individuals, both employ carefully crafted alliances and relationships to establish global networks linking many small, medium, and large enterprises. Both are now lodged at the center of global systems mediating access to downstream sectors of the fresh-cut flower global commodity chain. They influence production and orchestrate distribution in continuously changing configurations that connect with ever more growers in more countries, thus deepening their global nature. These networked structures allow skilled traders to orchestrate and select from a vast flexible assortment of fresh flowers ranging from fine and rare blooms to the commonplace and cheap, easily satisfying all kinds of market sectors. These trading middlemen, in the United States, are the topic of the next chapter.

129

Six

Specialty and Abundance:
Middlemen in a Changing System

> Now she is here, in the flower shop, where poppies drift white and apricot on long, hairy stems. . . . Clarissa chooses peonies and stargazer lilies, cream-colored roses, does not want the hydrangeas (guilt, guilt, it looks like you never outgrow it), and is considering irises (are irises somehow a little . . . outdated?) when a huge shattering sound comes from the street outside.—MICHAEL CUNNINGHAM, *The Hours*

In his novel *The Hours* Michael Cunningham recounts the thoughts and actions of Clarissa Vaughan, a Manhattan editor, as she buys flowers for a party in the late 1990s. Clarissa chooses among flowers that have been gathered from around the world and detached from their natural seasons. Shopping for out-of-season flowers, once a special privilege of the enormously wealthy, is not unusual at the end of the twentieth century, when quite ordinary New Yorkers may buy fresh flowers on any day at any hour. The United States is one of the world's largest cut flower markets. Each year it imports blooms valued at about $700 million. These and a smaller crop of domestically grown cut flowers are eventually sold at retail for around four billion dollars. The value of the flower trade in the New York Metropolitan Area (NYMA)—wholesale and retail together—is over a billion dollars.[1] Clarissa herself shares some of the spare statistical characteristics marking today's typical U.S. flower buyer: a college-educated woman between thirty-five and sixty-five with an income of between seventy-five and one hundred thousand dollars, usually living in a two-person household (Silvergleit 2001).[2] During the 1990s a greater number of Americans, potential flower buyers, occupied this age and income group, and between 1999 and 2003 the proportion of U.S. households buying fresh-cut flowers increased from 22 percent to 32 percent.[3]

Yet the typical NYMA flower buyer is probably not exactly like Clarissa because NYMA demographics differ from the U.S. pattern. New York City has many small households with almost 20 percent headed by women. Furthermore, Manhattan has more single-person households than anywhere else in the country.[4] During the prosperous 1990s many new immigrants nourished city and regional population growth and today immigrants and their offspring constitute over 55 percent of the city's population.[5]

In contrast to the waves of mostly European immigrants who populated New York at the beginning of the twentieth century, less than 20 percent of the city's end-of-the century immigrants came from Europe. Eighty percent are a complex mix of ethnicities and nationalities, with Mexicans and Bangladeshis among the fastest-growing groups by 2004. New immigrants favor Brooklyn and Queens where over 60 percent of recent immigrants are clustered. Ecuadorians and Bangladeshis prefer Jackson Heights, Chinese and Mexicans often choose Sunset Park, and many Salvadorians share life in Far Rockaway with Russians, Ukrainians, Haitians, Israelis, Nigerians, and Jamaicans. These groups vary in their income and home ownership levels and in household composition. About 80 percent of Bangladeshi households, for example, are married-couple families, compared with about 30 percent of the households of native-born New Yorkers. Many new immigrants make ends meet by gathering into multiperson households—even those with higher incomes and education levels. Home ownership rates also vary substantially between groups.[6]

These immigrants, with their different family compositions, household arrangements, and traditions, rapidly alter neighborhoods. They bring with them different flower customs so the work of the neighborhood retail florist differs from that typical in the rest of the United States.[7] NYMA flower buyers, moreover, depart from U.S. patterns in other ways. They enjoy wider choices of flower retail outlets, for example offering more varied types and variety of flowers. They also use these flowers in distinctive ways. New York Metropolitan Area flower consumers have wider flower choices because flower-trading channels have changed in the last twenty to thirty years. Two principal distribution chains evolved in concert with the developing global flower-growing regions discussed in earlier chapters. Governance of these dual chains resides primarily with a particular group of middlemen—the importer-wholesalers who coordinate and integrate the flow of enormous quantities of fresh flowers from all parts of the world. Other middlemen—traditional florists, floral designers, and traditional wholesalers—are also extremely influential for their communicative power and for their ability to shape tastes among consumers.[8] These dual distribution channels also differentiate flower consumers both socio-economically and in terms of an urban-suburban-rural divide. The chapter explores these recent developments in more detail.

Specialty and Abundance

Retailing Transformed

DISTINCTIVE BLOOMS

The poppies and peonies Clarissa considered are not offered to all U.S. flower buyers. In fact, the flower choices of New Yorkers are often quite distinctive. As explained in chapter 3, growers in the Netherlands, Colombia, Ecuador, and other places provide about 70 percent of U.S. cut flowers, with the balance supplied by domestic production, primarily in California and Florida. Each flower-growing region focuses to some degree on either specialty blooms or on the major cut flowers. Roses, carnations, and chrysanthemums, typical of the major cut flowers coming from Ecuador and Colombia, are imported through Miami and trucked up the East Coast to the NYMA in uncounted millions. Yet it is also worth noting which countries send flowers straight to New York's two international airports. Flowers arriving from Africa and Europe can travel on direct flights to many U.S. cities. The Netherlands, for example, ships flowers direct to over twenty cities in the United States including Philadelphia and Boston. It is reasonable to assume that most of the flowers arriving at the New York airports from Europe are sold in the NYMA.[9] Figure 23 shows the principal nations sending flowers directly to New York in 2004. It is apparent that a substantial portion of the imports of the Netherlands, Israel, Italy, and France—all important growers of specialty flowers—arrive through New York.[10] In effect, the NYMA, with 10 percent of the U.S. population in 2000, enjoys close to 30 percent of the uncommon imported cut flowers.[11]

NEW RETAILERS

Had Clarissa walked a block or two east from her apartment, she might have chosen to buy her peonies not from Barbara, the traditional retail florist she had known for years, but from a flower stand outside a convenience store. In the 1970s, the flower-selling convenience stores so familiar to New Yorkers today barely existed. Freelance floral designers and supermarket flower shops were also largely unknown. Yet by 2000, the majority of NYMA flowers were sold at these new outlets.[12] Together with traditional florists, they formed part of the two contiguous channels bringing fresh-cut flowers to the NYMA that I refer to as the specialty chain and the abundant chain. Traditional florists and freelance floral designers operate in the first stream—the specialty chain. Here exchange is structured around reciprocal relationships and is characterized by

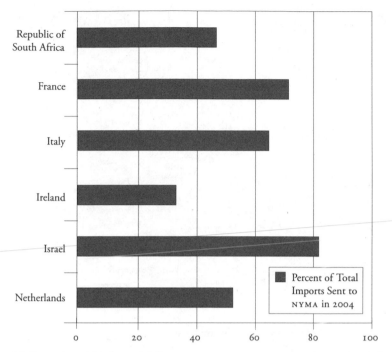

23 Countries with substantial direct exports to NYMA, 2004 – as a percentage of total imports. Source: USDA Economic Research Service. Trade Data Services.

close attention to flower innovation and the management and exchange of information. This specialty chain is being outpaced in terms of volume of flowers—although not necessarily in dollar value—by the second, which I call the abundant chain, where convenience stores, supermarkets, and mass retailers dominate. Personal relationships and knowledge exchange are much less important in the second stream. Instead, low prices and distribution innovations are defining features. Figure 24 illustrates the general structure of the middlemen linkages in these two streams joining the producers to the consumers of cut flowers. In the specialty chain at the left of the diagram, high quality and novelty are important, while at the right side, in the abundant chain, new and high quality flowers are less evident.

This chart greatly simplifies complex, fluid exchange relationships. Convenience stores, for example, buy many flowers from the mobile wholesalers described later in this chapter, but in the NYMA some convenience store flowers also come from upmarket traditional wholesalers. Supermarkets also

Specialty and Abundance

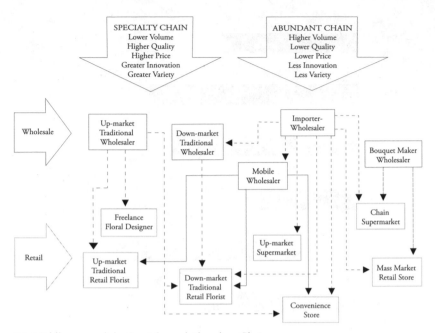

24 Middlemen and the Specialty and Abundant Chains

buy from traditional wholesalers although most of their flowers come from importer-wholesalers or bouquet-maker wholesalers.

Traditional florists enjoyed a monopoly in flower retailing for over a hundred years. At the end of the twentieth century, however, their dominance evaporated in the face of competition from convenience stores, supermarkets, freelance floral designers, and other new flower retailers.

TRADITIONAL RETAIL FLORISTS

Between 1977 and 1997 more and more Americans took up retail floristry and they appeared to prosper. Today, according to the 2002 U.S. Census Bureau Economic Census, there is an average of one traditional retail florist for every 13,000 Americans. Retail florist density relative to the U.S. average is a broad measure of local wealth; Manhattan, for example has one florist for every 6,800 people while the Bronx has one for every 42,000 residents (see table 9). The actual number of retail florists is higher since the Economic Census does not include small "mom and pop" retail florist operations without employees. Economic censuses and a recent industry survey indicated that

9 Traditional retail florist distribution in selected counties in New York metropolitan area in 2002

New York Metro Area Counties	# florists	Approx. population per florist	Sales per florist in thousands dollars
Bronx	32	41,645	211
Kings (Brooklyn)	107	23,040	264
New York (Manhattan)	227	6,772	540
Queens	112	19,905	216
Richmond (Staten Island)	33	13,446	418
Nassau	144	9,268	429
Rockland	20	14,388	310
Westchester	104	8,879	369
Bergen, New Jersey	90	9,824	355
Hudson, New Jersey	34	17,911	232
Union, New Jersey	42	12,441	400
Fairfield, Connecticut	79	11,172	385

Source: Department of Commerce Economic Census 2002

in the five years up to 2004 the national florists total had declined by 13 percent to 22,700. A similar decline was evident in the NYMA. Only about one third of these businesses are economically sustainable—those with sales over $120,000.[13] As an earlier Michigan study put it, many traditional florist establishments are essentially unprofitable "given the number of hours most owners work and the inherent business risk associated with the high level of competition." The costs of delivery, wire service work, labor, and rent often push retail florists into unprofitability (Collins et al. 1999).[14] Competition from new flower retailers is part of the problem for NYMA florists but so is a dwindling range of work.

CHANGING FLORAL WORK

By the beginning of the twenty-first century, much of the traditional florists' work described in chapter 1 had disappeared throughout the United States. Funeral work—the mainstay of the traditional retail florist for over a century—had declined substantially. Changing New York neighborhoods and customer characteristics were a major factor. Funeral work remained important in some neighborhoods but waned in others as new ethnic groups with simpler funeral traditions supplanted older Protestant, Italian, and Irish pop-

25 Funeral flowers for John J.
Gotti. AP Photo/Robert
Spencer.

ulations that emphasized funeral ritual.[15] Artie Christakos, an older Bronx
florist, lamented the decline in his funeral work. "Years ago the area was Irish
and Italian. When there was a death in the family, say the husband, not only
the wife but each child would send their own [funeral] piece, they didn't want
to be ashamed. Then it changed and now there might be just one piece from
the family." Artie explained, "Years ago they used to wake a person two or
three days, it was common. Now it is one day or overnight so a lot of people
think it is a waste." Furthermore, "The amount of flowers has changed. But
they are spending much more on quality flowers. Whereas in the fifties they
wanted mass, it was the amount of flowers." The deaths of notable Irish or
Italian New Yorkers still generate substantial funeral work for florists in
Brooklyn and Queens. "For florists who specialize in funeral arrangements,
few occasions are as momentous as the death of a mob boss," observed a *New
York Times* article describing the funeral of John J. Gotti in June 2002. Elaborate floral set pieces—gates of heaven, playing cards, a race horse, and even a
martini glass—attested to Mr. Gotti's high—albeit criminal—status in life and
recalled the elaborate New York funerals of fifty or one hundred years earlier
(see figure 25).

Chapter Six

Other flower rituals and traditional holidays have also adjusted to new populations. Some new immigrants adopt American holidays while also tending to preserve their traditional holidays and the floral customs associated with them. Hsiang-shui Chen's study of new Taiwanese immigrant behavior, for example, revealed that over 80 percent of the households in his sample celebrated Chinese New Year while about 50 percent celebrated Thanksgiving and 60 percent Christmas, although less elaborately than Chinese New Year. Most preferred to patronize Chinese-owned stores on the grounds of letting "my own people earn my money" (Chen 1992, 87), and Mai Wong, a Taiwanese florist I interviewed, claimed a very high proportion of Chinese customers. Other anecdotal evidence supports the idea of ethnic patronage within the New York City flower trade; many Korean-owned convenience stores, for example, buy their flowers from Korean mobile-wholesale businesses.[16]

As the work associated with funerals and religious and other holidays dwindled, wedding celebrations grew in importance. In the 1980s and 1990s weddings provided substantial work for florists with patience and a taste for detail. Yet at the same time, other forms of party and celebration work for wealthy individuals, institutions, and corporations were appropriated by the freelance floral designers discussed below. Today the most important work for the traditional florist in the NYMA and elsewhere is preparing and delivering gifts of flowers—as much as 60 percent in some cases. Customers rely heavily on the florist's skill, taste, and judgment to communicate cultural messages about the relationships and identities of both the giver and receiver that are embedded in gifts of flowers. Yet even this last bastion of traditional floral work is changing rapidly. Most of these gifts are ordered by telephone and to a small extent by Internet. This makes transaction easier but also reduces the personal nature of the exchange between customer and florist and the customer's commitment to a particular florist.

The gloomy assessment of the economic fate of many retail florists offered in Collins's Michigan study was supported by some of my interviews with traditional florists in the NYMA. The most vulnerable seemed to be those who had opened their shops during the prosperous decade of the 1990s. Some had entered the business with little experience, no business or floral design training, poor networks, and a romantic idea of retail florist work. Few, for example, understood the long hours and hard work involved.[17] Florists with several decades' experience who had adapted to local ethnic and economic changes appeared to be most stable. These were also the florists with a high proportion of funeral, wedding, and gift work. Funeral work is desirable because it occurs year round and profitably disposes of large quantities of the flowers that must be stocked for gifts and wire service work, as they age. Without funeral work these older flowers may never be sold. Weddings are also profitable because they often involve costly specialty blooms and elaborate presentations. The least prosperous-seeming of the florists I met lacked these steady mainstays, instead depending heavily on holidays, even though traditional floral holidays, such as Easter, Passover, Mother's Day, and so on today represent only about 16 percent of all fresh-cut flower transactions. Holidays and gifts began to dominate the work of traditional florists as long ago as 1977 when floral retail marketing groups began inventing many new holidays and "gift opportunities" to compensate for generally declining flower sales. This was some years before floods of global blooms introduced new forms of retail competition.[18]

For holidays, however, florists must invest in large inventories of flowers without any guarantee they will be sold. Even the most experienced can miscalculate. Poor weather and sudden economic downturns, among other things, can unpredictably alter sales. Peter Pomfret, a Jamaican immigrant florist in Brooklyn, was beset by problems linked, in part, to his increasing dependence on profits from flower holidays. "I don't know about Christmas and Easter—I don't know where the flower business went," Peter lamented. "I do it but no tip top business. . . . This store is basically a three time store—when those days come . . . Mother's Day, Valentine, Graduation . . . I know I have to put in a lot of flowers. Then I make it and save it for other times. I can put it all in my pot when Valentine comes." But, as he went on to explain, even "Valentine's and Mother's are going down, you do business but not like before." Peter attributed his problems to the neighborhood's ethnic composition, noting that "the neighborhood change . . . black people don't appreciate flowers that much." Competition from convenience store stands was another factor. "The flower business," he complained, "is messed up by the Koreans" because "in Brooklyn any hour of the night you can get flowers on Church Avenue and Flatbush. The Koreans have plants, food and flowers. I don't have nothing else besides flowers." His efforts to introduce a new line of products were frustrated. "I used to sell a few balloons" Peter explained, "I can't sell them anymore. A ninety-nine cent store opened right there, selling balloons. I can't sell them any more." The previous day during the quiet summer month when we met, he had discarded many unused flowers because "sometimes two, three months I don't get a funeral—so I don't get the chance to use [up] certain [older] flowers." Valentine's Day and Mother's Day are very important to many florists, generating over half their holiday revenues.[19] But that year, 2001, Peter Pomfret's Valentine's Day hadn't been particularly profitable and his summer was not going well. "Yesterday," he observed despondently, "when I finished work, for the whole day I make thirty-nine dollars. And I have three employees. What will I use to pay them?"

Dwindling profits and the declining relevance of flowers to some new consumers began to afflict traditional retail florists seriously in the NYMA during the 1980s as novel forms of retailing developed. Expanding supplies of cheap flowers from Latin America fueled this trend by encouraging the emergence of new types of middlemen who organized distribution to new competing retailers—freelance designers, convenience stores, and supermarkets. These new retailers, in turn, satisfied growing consumer interest in particular forms of flower consumption such as celebrations, gifts, and home decoration. These new retailers helped to expand the total numbers of flower buyers, but not those of traditional florists. Urban convenience stores were an immediate problem because they sold similar flowers and also deprived traditional florists of their walk-in cash business. "Florists relied on that cash business to pay employees and to avoid taxes," recalled Keith Corcoran, a former traditional florist, now a freelance floral designer. "Without cash all profits had to be declared" and marginal floral businesses became unsustainable.

As innovative freelance floral designers, urban convenience stores, and suburban supermarkets emerged strongly in the 1980s and 1990s, appropriating cash sales and predictable services such as planned celebrations, traditional florists were left with the riskier, uncertain, and unpredictable work including gifts for holidays, illness, and other occasions, often ordered and delivered on short notice. Only a few well-established florists retained profitable funeral work and weddings.

FREELANCE FLORAL DESIGNERS

Discouraged by the hazards and uncertainty of traditional retailing in New York City, former and new florists began to establish themselves as freelance floral designers in the early 1980s.[20] Freelance floral designers avoid the expenses that burden traditional florists. They shun permanent employees, operating a retail store (some work out of their homes), or stocking large quantities of flowers "just in case" a funeral, gift order, wire service order, or walk-in customer materializes. Freelancers eliminated some of the uncertainty of flower retailing by specializing in floral services for planned social events:

weddings, parties, charitable fund-raising events, and other celebrations for individuals and businesses. While some floral designers have permanent staff and working spaces, many are very flexible; they purchase their flowers and hire freelance staff a few days before the planned occasion. Most are very small businesses perhaps handling only twenty small weddings a year and sustaining themselves with steady corporate, hotel, and restaurant accounts.[21] A few orchestrate million-dollar celebrations where several hundred thousand dollars may be spent on flowers.

Freelance florists in New York City benefit directly from the way the economy of the city has become linked to what Sharon Zukin refers to as "symbolic production," especially the "growth of restaurants, museums and culture industries" such as the magazine and music industries (1995, ix). Their work is visible in the windows of expensive stores, at museums, and in up-market restaurants and hotels. Yet exposure to beautiful flower arrangements is not confined to the city's elite private spaces. For thirty years Macy's, a middle-range department store, has provided an extravagant spring flower show on its main floor. Hundreds of thousands of visitors—potential customers—visit the store to enjoy small gardens arranged with thousands of shrubs and flowers and view the confections of famous floral designers. The creations of the most famous floral designers also appear regularly on television shows, in the pages of magazines, and in the *New York Times*' periodic feature articles about cut flowers and floral design. According to a late-1990s *Times* article describing the work of the floral designer Robert Isabell, much of the demand for fresh-cut flowers in Manhattan today is linked to wealth—just as it was more than a century earlier—and to the existence of the many flower designers able to translate the desires of "New York society and people with enormous amounts of money."[22]

Freelance floral design work, however, is very vulnerable to recessions in both the "symbolic economy" and the general economy. Its practitioners prospered during the 1990s when the *Wall Street Journal* reported, "At private galas and corporate celebrations alike, guests couldn't see the other side of the table through the verdant gardens planted in the middle." But the early years of the new century, especially after September 11, 2001, was a period of economic contraction, and "rocks and apples" became favored table decorations at galas with declining budgets in some parts of the United States.[23] Such contractions, confirmed by my informants, seriously affected not only freelance florists but also the importer-wholesalers and the traditional wholesale florists who are their principal suppliers.

CONVENIENCE STORES AND STREET VENDORS

Buckets full of fresh flowers began to appear outside convenience stores in New York City in the late 1980s. Two factors encouraged the trend, both linked to innovative entrepreneurship. First was an increase in Korean immigrants who began to enter the small grocery or convenience store business in the early 1970s. Some even arrived with the intention and sufficient funds to start a small business, often a grocery store (Park 1997).[24] As Koreans opened grocery stores in many New York neighborhoods, Korean-Korean competition and high rents, especially in Manhattan, prompted some owners to offer new goods and services including labor-intensive salad bars and fresh flowers. A few penetrated produce—and flower—wholesale (Park 1997). By 1998, Koreans, with about 2,000 stores, controlled nearly 60 percent of all independent retail produce and convenience stores in New York City (Min 1998) (see figure 26).

The existence of a hundred-year-old stoop line law was a second factor. It permits licensing a space in front of a store, ten feet long and extending four feet into the sidewalk, to be used as part of the display premises. Perishable goods, such as fruits, vegetables, and flowers are one subcategory for which licenses are issued. With license fees in 2002 averaging only one dollar per square foot per year, stoop stands provide very inexpensive retailing space, far less than many traditional retail florists pay for store rent in the same neighborhoods. In some areas, in Chinatown and Washington Heights, for example, these stoop stands are devoted to fruits and vegetables. In other neighborhoods fresh-cut flowers are more important. Some, illegally, rent out the stoop line space to small flower-selling entrepreneurs, charging, I was told, as much as $3,000 a month in a good location like the Upper West Side. Flowers—as the unhappy florist Peter Pomfret observed—are available twenty-four hours a day in some neighborhoods and these long hours and prime locations on busy Manhattan streets ensure the sale of large quantities of blooms. I was told that a good stand may sell $17,000 worth of flowers a week, almost entirely cash transactions. However, since prices are low and profit margins minuscule, such flower selling probably provides a very modest living. In some parts of Manhattan these stands are so numerous and their flowers so varied that a virtual flower market is established. A motivated consumer may move from block to block searching for a lower price, or a new, unusual, or fragrant flower. They are now a familiar part of Manhattan existence. Sally, another character in *The Hours,* pauses to buy flowers at a convenience store stand:

Specialty and Abundance

26 Convenience store flower stand in New York City

[Sally] stops at the flower stand attached to the Korean market on the corner. It's the usual array, carnations and mums, a scattering of gaunt lilies, freesia, daisies, bunches of hothouse tulips in white, yellow, and red, their petals going leathery at the tips. Zombie flowers, she thinks; just product, forced into being like chickens whose feet never touch ground from egg to slaughter. Sally stands frowning before the flowers on their graduated wooden platforms, sees herself and the flowers reflected in the mirror tiles at the back of the cooler. . . . She is about to leave empty-handed when she notices a single bouquet of yellow roses in a brown rubber bucket in the corner. They are just beginning to open. Their petals, at the base, are suffused with a deeper yellow, almost orange, a mango-colored blush that spreads upward and diffuses itself in hairline veins. They so convincingly resemble real flowers, grown from earth in a garden, that they seem to have gotten into the cooler by mistake. Sally buys them quickly, almost furtively, as if she fears the Korean woman who runs the stand will realize there's been a mix-up and inform her, gravely, that these roses are not for sale. She walks along Tenth Street with the roses in her hand, feeling exultant. (Cunningham 2002, 183–84)

Chapter Six

Michael Cunningham's text encapsulates the pleasure of buying flowers as well as other experiential aspects of shopping in the NYMA at traditional florists, convenience stores, and greenmarkets.

Summer flower peddlers also claim sidewalk space to sell flowers discarded by traditional wholesalers or acquired cheaply from mobile wholesalers at the end of the day, much as child street peddlers did a century earlier (see chapter 2). They add to the sense of city streets and squares as spaces of pleasure and visual consumption, a form of "symbolic production" (Zukin 1995, ix) of the streets.

Greenmarkets scattered around the city also add to the city's visual display with their buckets of locally grown seasonal flowers. In the Union Square market, now more than a hundred years old, customers sometimes spend considerable time moving between flower sellers, examining and sniffing the blooms, before making a choice. These flowers—roses, peonies, lilacs, freesias, and others—grow nearby on Long Island or further north in New York state. They resemble Lizzie Hazeldean's roses in their freshness, fragrance, seasonality, and brief lives. Some might think of them as "real flowers."

The patrons of this market, while largely white middle class, also include the obviously poor and homeless and vary in age from toddlers with their mothers to schoolchildren, teenagers, and the elderly. Different age groups patronize the market at different hours of the day, with small children, their mothers, and the elderly evident in the quieter morning hours and office workers at lunchtime, while teenagers and others flock to the market in the late afternoon. Morning shoppers seem purposeful, but later strollers are ready to succumb to the pleasures of growing crowds, the stimulating smells of flowers, fruits, and vegetables, the unexpected and momentary pleasure of buying and eating a fresh small tart or muffin, or tasting cheeses, honey, and cider. Thrift is not a motive for shopping here. Larger bunches of roses and other blooms are available for less at nearby convenience stores. Instead these customers seemingly enjoy the pleasures of a live market; its "village" feel and the chance to choose from "authentic" flowers grown by local farmers or, in a few cases, wildflowers harvested from regional roadsides. Some flower buyers imagine the gardens and farms where these flowers are grown and reconnect to the real and imagined gardens of their youth and perhaps the promise of gardens in their future. Indeed, many fresh market shoppers mentioned reconnection to past memories as one of their reasons for buying flowers in general and certain flowers in particular. A middle-class white woman repeated the comments of many when she explained to me, "I grew up with flowers and they are a very important part of my life, almost as important as food." In a large, alienating city, shopping regularly at these local green-markets is also a way of establishing a "real" locality, a temporary sense of community based on a shared experience of everyday life. That kind of shopping, Miller explains (2001a), helps to mediate some of the contradictions of contemporary life. Shopping for flowers in an outdoor market is a way to circumvent the constant engagement with commodity goods and to connect with a "real" or "ideal" existence.

Market flowers are generally short-lived because they are often picked almost in full flower, displayed at the market on hot days, and carried home through warm city streets. But their colors, aliveness, and fragrance are at their peak in this market and their appeal is irresistible. Some customers buy flowers here as often as once or twice a week, including a woman in her early thirties who justified her frequent flower buying on the grounds that "they are very beautiful. They make me feel good and I love them." For such people, flowers have moved from luxury to necessity.

Some contemporary New Yorkers (probably the majority) are quite indifferent to these street displays of overflowing buckets of blooms, but I have observed many—usually women—pausing, admiring, and sniffing the blooms, taking pleasure even if they do not buy. Despite this frequently observed behavior, knowledge about flowers is quite rare. Clarissa and Sally show an uncommon level of consumer sophistication in their familiarity with flower names and understanding of the social meanings linked with particular flowers that is unusual among the flower buyers I've spoken with. Very few, for example, know anything about the origins of the flowers they buy from convenience stores. Cunningham's characters also capture some of the contemporary ambivalence toward consumption in general and the imagined origins of mass ("Zombie flowers") or artisanal production—"real flowers, grown from earth in a garden"—embodied in these various flowers and different retail outlets. In some cases flower-buying decisions are inflected with vague environmental concerns and ethical worries about the sources of the flowers—another contradiction of contemporary shopping. Megan Webster, a woman in her mid-twenties, for example, felt reassured by the abundant flowers at convenience stores. "I always buy from those grocery [convenience] stores," explained Megan. "I buy roses . . . I know roses grow very, very plentifully and they are not endangered like orchids. There must be millions and millions of roses. They are pretty and cheap. Also I love those lilies . . . the Stargazers, the oriental ones. I buy those because they smell amazing. I feel that is okay because they are very plentiful because they are on every street corner in New York . . . I definitely get tempted."

SUPERMARKETS

The introduction of supermarket flower shops also helped to undermine local traditional florists. Supermarkets first appeared in the United States in the 1930s and within a few years major chains like A&P replaced their traditional grocery stores with this new, profitable format (Wrigley and Lowe 2002). They changed the nature of everyday household provisioning as people were encouraged "to wait upon themselves" (Bowlby 1997, 93).[25] Ideas and emotions about cleanliness, modernity, class status, gender roles, and luxury gradually attached to packaged and branded goods. The meanings linked to a product rather than the product itself became the key to retailing (Burke 1996; Humphery 1998).[26] This turn was mirrored in "the transformation of what it means to be a consumer—the transformation from consumption as chiefly tied to material and social needs and goals to consumption as a process of personal pleasure and autonomous self-expression" (Humphery 1998, 33).

Bowlby and Daniel Miller among others, distinguish between "going shopping," an experience characterized by pleasure and possibly excess and transgression, and "doing the shopping," the boring, usually weekly, task of provisioning (Bowlby 1997, 102)—although in Miller's view even "doing the shopping" may be spiced with rewards, pleasure, and excess (1998, 6). After the late 1960s, supermarkets attempted to subvert the boring and transform weekly shopping into an experience of leisure and pleasure combined with efficient function (Bowlby 1997). First tested in California, pleasure-embodying floral departments in supermarkets spread through the United States in the 1970s (Haley 1972; Vogt 1972). Since supermarkets initially offered little service and their flowers were of poorer quality, few traditional florists felt threatened by this new form of retail even though it was expanding sales at twice the rate of florists.[27] The emergence of superstores and supercenters in the 1980s and 1990s, however, was more immediately troubling for traditional florists, because they forced supermarkets to innovate once more to make their stores more appealing. In the 1990s, conventional chain supermarkets in the United

States, faced with declining profits and rising competition from superstores, supercenters (see below), and each other, embarked on a fresh round of innovation. They spruced up stores, experimented with new retail formats, and targeted specific market segments or niches by offering (among other things) full-service bakeries and flower departments. At the end of the 1990s, customers visited supermarkets two or three times a week to purchase fresh produce, baked goods, and prepared foods (Humphery 1998, 156).

All these retail innovations had a tremendous effect on fresh flower retailing. In 1977 flowering potted plants and garden bedding plants were already widely sold at supermarkets, but cut flowers represented only 15 percent of floral sales at U.S. supermarkets, usually as self-service.[28] Over the next two decades increasing volumes of cheaper and cheaper flowers passed through supermarkets and by 1999 cut flowers constituted about 60 percent of their floral department sales. Furthermore, 60 percent of chain supermarkets floral departments offered full floral services; they were serious competition for some traditional retail florists (Floral Marketing 1999; Silvergleit 2001).

It is in these supermarket settings that the majority of fresh-cut flowers are purchased in the United States today.[29] By 2003 close to 50 percent of rose purchases occurred in supermarkets while sales of roses in florist shops declined from 37 percent in 1999 to only 22 percent in 2003. Some NYMA suburban supermarkets employ experienced florists and offer a range and quality of flowers that equals or exceeds those displayed in nearby traditional florist shops. Like the traditional florist, she or he observes and interprets customers' desires, offering new flower varieties and designs to pleasure-seeking up-scale customers. In one of our conversations, Betty Small, a full-time supermarket florist, marveled that just a few days earlier her flowers had been growing in Israel, the Netherlands, Ecuador, and other unidentified places. Indeed, she noted with pride how distribution innovations allow her to gather "all the flowers in the world" into her own tiny supermarket floral department.[30] It is even possible that her orders for lisianthus or gerbera link her with Jorge Vélez Serrano in Ecuador or Paul van der Heiden in the Netherlands.

SUPERSTORES AND MASS RETAIL

Superstores, often located in suburban areas or on the periphery of cities and large towns, offer at least 25,000 square feet of sales area and enjoy lower costs and higher profits than traditional supermarkets. Their higher profits derive, in part, from the inclusion of more "value-added" goods in departments such as pharmacies, photo shops, bakeries, and fresh flowers. By the early 1990s superstores accounted for almost twice the sales of conventional supermarkets because customers preferred the new outlets and also spent more money in these "one stop" shopping sites (Wrigley and Lowe 2002).[31] Superstores, in their resemblance to department stores, "put an end to the identification of food shopping as a definite task to be completed as quickly as possible. Now you can be doing the shopping and going shopping, getting the basics and enjoying yourself, all in one place and one time" (Bowlby 1997, 108).

Supercenters, a combination of the food superstore described above and general merchandise discount store, were originally conceived by the Meijer and Fred Meyer chains. The concept was adopted and developed by Wal-Mart in the late 1980s. By 2004 there were 1,500 Wal-Mart supercenters in the United States, each about 190,000 square feet and generating about $100 million to $120 million in sales each year (Dicker 2005). Again, the increased number of customer visits to buy food and the cross-over to purchases of other merchandise, including fresh flowers, helped to make these centers so profitable (Wrigley and Lowe 2002) (see chapter 7).[32]

Superstores, supercenters, and big box stores such as Home Depot now sell over half of all garden plants in the United States and garner about half of the $24 billion spent annually on lawns and garden plants in the United States.[33] In this process consumers become familiar with a wider range of plants and flowers. Orchids are a case in point. Once orchids were rare and an embodiment of class, taste, and expertise, but today they are easily propagated and are a popular potted plant and cut flower sold by the millions. At the same time, of course, the status formerly associated with the possession and display of now-common orchids is declining. New species and varieties of orchids in unusual forms and colors have been developed in response.[34]

These mass retailers' share of total cut flower sales is still quite small overall and an insignificant percentage of sales in the NYMA. Nevertheless, in the five years from 1999 to 2003 their percentage of total national sales of one particular flower—roses—increased from about 8 percent to about 15 percent. If present trends continue, these mass retailers may eventually become the "Big Buyers" of the cut flower trade and alter the structure of the U.S. cut flower commodity chain and individual flower choices.

Undeniably these new retail forms—supermarkets, convenience stores, and supercenters—have brought fresh-cut flowers into the lives of people who previously gave them little thought. Flowers have been liberated from the confinement of florist's shops that for economic, geographic, social, or emotional reasons were forbidding or inaccessible to many shoppers. In some ways they have extended the pleasures of the fresh market—often a limited urban or suburban phenomenon—to a broader group of consumers as they offer the sensual delights of fragrance and symmetry and the pleasure of choosing. In these self-service settings, shoppers select on the basis of price, appearance, and appeal without the discomfort (for some) of consultation with a florist. One consequence is that fresh-cut flowers are bought more often (see chapter 8).

INTERNET RETAIL

Internet and mail-order services fulfill only a tiny percentage of cut flower transactions.[35] The number of Internet flower-selling sites proliferated after 2000. Some of the best known in 2005 were 1-800-Flowers.com, ProFlowers .com, and FTD.com. Some orders are prepared and delivered by networks of florists or supermarkets in the locality of the gift recipient. In many cases, however, Internet sites simply gather orders that are then filled by independent bouquet-making companies in Miami, California, and other places in the United States. Dole Fresh Flowers and Wal-Mart briefly operated their own flower retail websites. By 2005, both had abandoned direct Internet retail, possibly because of poor returns and branding concerns—especially the difficulty in delivering flowers of adequate quality.[36] Wal-Mart still offers flowers at its websites, but these orders are simply passed on to FTD or another order-gathering firm, Post & Petal.[37] These order-gathering systems are made possible by new technology discussed in the next chapter.

My own tests of Internet-ordered flowers found them disappointing. Poor flower quality and high prices probably limit their appeal to time-pressed, wealthy consumers and to particular holidays such as Mother's Day. Indeed, holiday sales of cut flowers purchased on the Internet have increased slightly, probably because of their convenience for sending last-minute gifts to distant recipients. Internet sales may also be aided in part by periodic articles in New York magazines and newspapers—often close to Valentine's Day or Mother's Day—comparing flowers from different sources: mail order, Internet sites, and local traditional florists.[38]

CHANGING TASTES

Competition from freelance designers, convenience stores, and supermarkets has pushed the traditional retail florist "to give more; more design, quality and variety and service," observed Mike Stefalopatis, a Brooklyn florist with fifty years' experience. They also try to respond to change among their customers, aiming to "interpret their needs, feelings, and desires," as Mike put it. Many florists, especially those with wealthy, regular clients, pride themselves "on matching . . . arrangements to recipients' personalities."[39] Such attentive, interpretive behavior also changes the customers. As innovative traditional florists and floral designers give substance to their customers' desires with new flower types, they "are raising the taste level and awareness of the buying public. [They are] not willing to settle for mums and carnations any more," explained Keith Corcoran, a mid-level freelance floral designer, during our conversations. He noted that over time some consumers develop new knowledge and tastes and begin to "ask for specific things." This new consumer knowledge is one factor pushing retail florists and floral designers (to varying degrees) to seek out innovative flowers and presentations. Another is the desire for novelty in some consumer sectors. In upmarket retail, whether clothes, food, accessories, or flowers, novelty is a critical factor in managing competition. Floral designers seek the newest flowers both to keep their clients happy and to enhance their own creativity and reputation. "I like to use different flowers so people don't get bored," explained Marcus Bader, a high-level retail florist, because "sometimes people say, 'last year it looked so much better' . . . visually they have got bored with it. So I am always in search of new things to keep people's interest. It is important at my level of business. For my accounts, people want something different. They don't know what exactly, just different." Yet notions of the "new" or "different" in flowers vary among retailers, partly corresponding to urban-suburban as well as socioeconomic divisions. Some retail florists I interviewed considered oriental lilies and gerberas to be innovative, higher-quality flowers, while for others they were merely basic. Claudia Cimbon, a designer working for a Park Avenue retail florist, refused to use gerberas at all because she found their form "too rigid." Clarissa, in *The Hours,* is fleetingly concerned that irises are "somehow a little . . . outdated?" These different perspectives hint at the manner in which broadly increased consumption—the democratization of consumption— contributes to the evolution of tastes that discriminate between "the noble and the ignoble in consumable goods" (Veblen [1899] 1994, 74–75), and the ways in which retailers and consumers collude to shape those tastes.

A view of a more mundane, middle level of flower consumption is offered by examining recent changes in the styles and flower types offered by floral wire services in their style guides. Wire services and their member florists extend

Specialty and Abundance

throughout the United States. It is hard to judge how many designs selected from wire service style guides are bought by or delivered to recipients in the NYMA, but many florists use them. Customers choose a flower-arrangement design from among many photographed and displayed in these books and the order is passed to a distant member florist who prepares and delivers the gift arrangement. Florists also use them as style guides for their local customers. These pattern books are influential in the middle sectors of traditional floral retail, and changes are indicative of dispersing trends in colors, styles, and available flowers. I focused on changes in Teleflora stylebooks between 1992 and 2001.[40] Arrangements are designed with the expectation that included flowers will be available from traditional wholesale florists all over the country since many thousands of these styles are copied annually. Consequently the inclusion of a new flower type or variety suggests relatively large production and broad availability. Between 1992 and 2001 the number of specialty cut flowers used in Teleflora stylebooks increased by 50 percent, from thirty-nine to sixty-two species, with a range of varieties within some of those species. In that same period, the stylebooks omitted Easter entirely as a marked occasion for giving flowers and the pages devoted to funeral pieces declined slightly. Designs to be worn or carried by young women, on the other hand, expanded. High school proms became sufficiently important to merit their own pages of designs, alongside weddings. Through these stylebooks, even less discriminating flower buyers learned about new types of flowers and new ways to use them. Consumers are exposed to flower selections that vary significantly among outlets, between neighborhoods, and between city and suburb. Yet there is rather more mingling of the "Zombie" flowers rejected by Sally and the "real flowers" chosen with pleasure by Sally and Clarissa than might be imagined. Mother's Day is a holiday when sales are plentiful and the range of flowers offered is generally very wide. Figure 27 summarizes a survey I made of different flower retailers in the NYMA just before Mother's Day 2001.[41]

In middle-income areas many Mother's Day gifts of flowers come from traditional retail florists, so for this holiday they will stock larger quantities and possibly a greater range than usual. On the other hand, florist shops in upmarket locations, as well as supermarkets and convenience stores, are less likely to be the sources of Mother's Day gifts. Even so, a midtown Park Avenue florist (A) offers an enormous range of flower species and many different varieties within those species types—reflecting its typically large inventory rather than a pre-Mother's Day increase. But the next largest range was offered

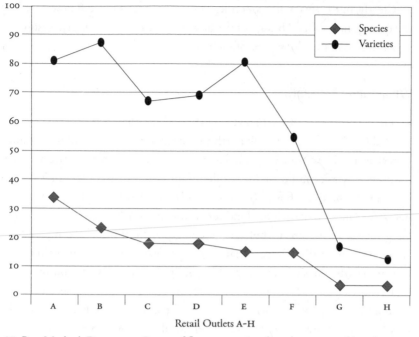

27 Pre–Mother's Day survey: Range of flower types in selected NYMA retail locations

by a convenience store on the Upper West Side (B). Two urban florists, one in a very poor neighborhood in the Bronx (C) and the other close to midtown Manhattan (D), offered the next largest selection. A midtown convenience store (E) and a suburban supermarket (F) showed a similar range of species but the convenience store had many more varieties. The poorest flower offerings were at a self-described "West Indian, American, Spanish, Mexican" grocery/convenience store in the Bronx (G) and a midtown urban supermarket (H).

Flowers are rarely refrigerated in corner stores or supermarkets but usually are refrigerated at traditional florists. For this and other reasons, quality varied between all these outlets. There were also great differences in the amount of space allocated to displaying flowers. The balance of specialty and commodity blooms also varied, reflecting both the neighborhood economy and the commodity chain connections of the retailer. The Park Avenue florist (A) had no carnations or chrysanthemums, for example, while the Bronx grocery convenience store (H) had *only* carnations and chrysanthemums and a few roses.

Specialty and Abundance

Clearly, in the NYMA all economic classes have access to fresh flowers.[42] Yet the quality, novelty, and beauty of the flowers—measured in variety, freshness, and aliveness of the blooms—is often linked to price.

Wholesaling Transformed

THE NEW YORK WHOLESALE FLOWER MARKET

Had Clarissa chosen to walk north for about a mile she would have found herself in the New York City wholesale flower market on 28th Street. Here traditional wholesale florist firms offer their retail customers a huge daily selection of the finest flowers from the global garden.[43] For those who shop here—freelance floral designers and retail florists—it is a creative resource. As Greg Rivers, a 28th Street wholesale florist, explained things, customers come "to get the inspiration. To see what is going to work at a particular time you have to see [the flowers]. The great thing about a market," Greg continued, is that "you can see alchemilla in my store for seventy-five cents and it looks good and you can walk down the street and see it for sixty-five cents and it may look just as good or even better. There is all this stuff. That is why you use the market." Yet the wholesale market too has changed substantially in the last twenty-five years. In its heyday in the 1920s almost eighty wholesale florists occupied several streets in the high 20s between Broadway and Seventh Avenue. In the 1950s it was still a large market with about fifty wholesale florists selling flowers grown within a hundred miles of the city as well as those from faraway states.[44] By 1985 the market comprised about twenty-four cut flower wholesale florists and by 2005 only about a dozen.[45] Mike Stafalopatis, the traditional Brooklyn florist, commented on the market's decline: "My father used to buy from Grady Smith's grandfather. I bought from [Grady's] father. There used to be a lot of wholesalers down there, now you can't even call it a market, just a handful of wholesalers now. It used to be from West 27th to West 29th from Broadway up to Seventh Avenue. All wholesalers. It used to be a pleasure to go down there. [I] used to go down there three or four times a week. Have breakfast, meet friends, it was crowded." Now, he continued a bit wistfully, "It's no longer like that. Changed tremendously . . . I don't go often any more; it doesn't pay." This nostalgia for the lost sociability of the early-morning urban marketplaces was fairly common among older florists and seems characteristic of changing fresh produce wholesale marketplaces in various settings.[46]

The "symbolic economy" is double edged. It contributed to vast increases in cut flower sales in the NYMA but also brought the local wholesale flower market into conflict with what Zukin refers to as the "cultural strategies of redevelopment" (1995, 2). After decades of patient efforts to rezone the flower market district from industrial to residential, developers succeeded in 1995, ensuring that the 28th Street neighborhood would no longer be hospitable to printers, furriers, flower dealers, and other small businesses. Notwithstanding local political commitment to confine residential development to the major avenues, leaving the small side streets untouched, the construction of several large apartment buildings adjacent to the flower market began to undermine its existence and future.[47]

Terminal wholesale flower markets, like produce markets, are active in the early morning. Twenty-eighth Street streams with dawn activity as florists bustle between Victorian storefronts, carrying bundles of colorful blooms and chatting with salesmen and other florists in an eager quest for the newest colors and freshest blooms for their day's creations (see figure 28). On the adjacent broad avenue, sterile sidewalks and monotonous frontages announce the new private apartments that are beginning to displace this busy morning market. New residents, vocal voters, complain about the early morning activity on the side streets and officials have become more assiduous in ticketing florists' vans parked on the street. Commercial rents are climbing rapidly, even doubling within a single year.[48] In the last five to ten years some middle-range wholesale florists have closed up or moved to other boroughs and nearby counties with lower rents. But the upmarket florists and floral designers who have grown with the symbolic economy have not followed them. An experienced floral designer, quoted in the *New York Times,* expressed his resistance to traveling outside Manhattan to select his flowers. " 'I'm not schlepping to Hunts Point,' he announced. 'I'm not in the fruit business. If you're not in Manhattan, you might as well be in Hong Kong.' "[49]

These zoning changes and the new forms of retail, especially supermarkets and convenience stores, have contributed to the shrinking of the 28th Street flower market because they took business away from mid-level traditional florists and consequently mid-level wholesalers.[50] These changes are among the factors that have encouraged a trend toward economic and geographic segmentation in cut flower distribution in the NYMA. The 28th Street flower market has come to be closely entwined with a specific local community of upscale retailers and upscale consumers.

Specialty and Abundance

28 View of stores at 28th Street flower market

Over the same period new competing forms of wholesale emerged to serve middle- and lower-priced retailing and consuming sectors. Bouquet-making wholesalers and importer-wholesalers—sometimes termed importer-brokers —are two new forms that proliferated as flower imports and consumption increased and distribution services improved in the 1980s and 1990s. Both new wholesale forms supply supermarkets and convenience stores. Importer-wholesalers also sell to regional wholesale florists and many types of retail (see figure 24). A third new competing flower wholesale form is the mobile wholesaler, operating primarily in urban areas. The recent trajectories of all four forms of flower wholesaling are described in the following section.

TRADITIONAL WHOLESALE FLORISTS

Peter Pearl, a chatty, articulate traditional wholesaler, runs the family business on 28th Street. For several generations it has provided retail florists with the important services described in chapter 2, namely, gathering and offering for sale flowers from a range of growers, providing credit, and selling in small quantities. Peter's firm prospered during the 1990s as the sales of the remaining traditional retailers in the NYMA increased by 25 percent and freelance floral designers and convenience store stands flourished. "Our sales volumes have increased dramatically," Peter explained. Yet his sales of the cheaper, major flowers had actually declined. "We used to sell three times as much [of those]," he said, while sales of the more expensive specialty flowers "like [large-headed] roses from Ecuador or the Dutch products and the stuff from Southern France" increased. In fact, he felt that these expanded sales of specialty blooms had "changed our whole way of doing business" (see figure 29).

During this transition, Peter has carefully distinguished himself by quality and type of blooms and has established particular relationships that will ensure territorial exclusivity. Each wholesale florist in the 28th Street market (and in the neighboring boroughs and states) deals with different Dutch or New Zealand exporters, different growers in California, France, Italy, Israel, Colombia, and Ecuador, and different importers in Miami.[51] Exporters, importers, privileged Latin American growers, and others are familiar with this local spatial organization. In the seven years of my research I noticed changes in these relationships, but for the most part wholesale florists seem to buy consistently from the growers, importer-wholesalers, exporter-wholesalers, and others with whom they have a long-term understanding. Even at Valentine's Day, when demand can shift prices substantially, local traditional wholesalers "don't necessarily shop around for the best price," Valerie Swift, a Miami importer-wholesaler, told me. Instead they give priority to preserving the association and "go with the person [they] have the best relationship with."

In the 1980s and 1990s, as the terminal market dwindled and changed and other wholesale florists became geographically dispersed in the NYMA, traditional florists made fewer and fewer visits to these scattered wholesalers to select their flowers in person. Consequently, telephone conversations with wholesalers became an important source of information about new trends and new flowers. Some retail florists (some of whom, as explained earlier, enter the trade without any previous training) also depend heavily on wholesalers' knowledge for basic information such as flower names and colors. In the words of several retail florists, traditional wholesalers became "their eyes." George Henning, a suburban florist, is very knowledgeable about flowers yet is typical in his reliance on his wholesaler relationships. "I will go and walk through the market once a month and see what is new," he said. Between visits, he relies heavily on his relationship with a wholesale florist at the 28th Street market who, in George's view, "is phenomenal. I thoroughly trust him.

Specialty and Abundance

29 New York wholesale flower store interior

I will say I've got to have things in bronze colors. [Or] if you've got anything different coming in send some up [to me]. If there is something specific [I need] he will get it for me," said George, concluding without hesitation, "I can trust Dick to pick things out."

Thus traditional florists, who often order by telephone, increasingly depend on a close interpretive relationship with a knowledgeable wholesale florist or salesperson. This friendly intermediary guides their telephone selections while considering the retail florist's local tastes, economic niche, and tolerance for innovation. If that salesperson moves to another firm, his florist customers will often choose to sustain the relationship and give their business to the new firm.

IMPORTER-WHOLESALERS

Importer-wholesalers emerged in Miami in the 1970s to organize the distribution of flowers from Colombia (see chapter 2). Colombian growers seeking secure markets for their flowers established several of the most important firms. In 2005 Miami had somewhere between seventy-five and one hundred flower importer-wholesalers.[52] Several of the pioneering importing enterprises

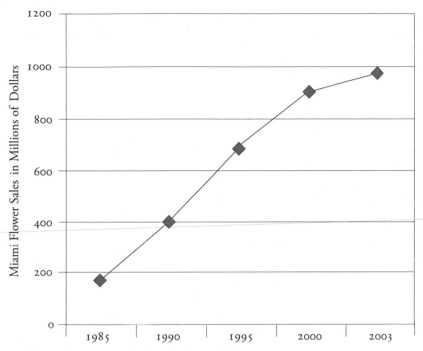

30 Value of importer-wholesaler sales through Miami, 1985–2003. Source: Association of
    Floral Importers of Florida.

are still important and some have added bouquet-making to their services.[53]
As figure 24 suggests, their collective customer range is wide. It includes
supermarkets, new mobile wholesalers, traditional wholesale florists, traditional retail florists, discount retailers, and bouquet-makers. Importer-
wholesalers often concentrate on specialized markets, for example, primarily
supplying traditional wholesale florists or supermarkets or convenience stores.
A few try to satisfy both traditional wholesalers and supermarket chains.
Collectively they serve a large geographic area including the middle and
eastern states. Traditional wholesale florists like those on 28th Street in Manhattan and in Queens, Brooklyn, and the Bronx, in turn, generally serve a
local customer base of retail florists and freelance designers. Because this
traditional trade is withering, some traditional wholesalers have also begun to
supply supermarkets—the expanding retail segment—especially those with
full-service florist shops. Traditional wholesalers can provide fresher bouquets
and unusual single-stem flowers to local supermarkets, often with just a day's

Specialty and Abundance

notice. With such a large customer and geographic base, importer-wholesalers govern a huge flow of flowers entering the United States. In 2004, imports into Miami were close to US$550 million while the sales value of flowers leaving that city was estimated at about US$967 million.[54] Figure 30 is suggestive of the growth in value (and volume) of flowers passing through Miami in recent years.[55] In 1985, sales of the much smaller group of importer-wholesalers of that time were about $180 million. In less than twenty years sales have more than quadrupled. This increased revenue developed from a huge expansion in volume of imported flowers rather than from increases in price per bloom, which were quite modest during that time.

BOUQUET-MAKING WHOLESALERS

Bouquet-making wholesalers emerged with the rise of supermarket and mass market flower retail and consumer acceptance of ready-made bouquets. Some are subsidiary enterprises of importer-wholesalers; others are independent bouquet-making enterprises. Most are located near important U.S. flower-growing regions or arrival points for imported flowers, such as Miami. However, as noted in chapter 5, bouquet assembly is steadily shifting to Colombia and Ecuador, where labor is cheaper and the majority of flowers for U.S. bouquets are grown. Currently, this developing trend takes two forms. Either bouquet-making enterprises establish assembly plants in Latin America or growers themselves manufacture their own bouquets from a range of flowers produced on their farms for direct sale to supermarkets.

Bouquet-makers manufacture three principal bouquet types: consumer bunches, (three, five, or ten stems of the same type flowers in a plastic sleeve); bouquets (one flower type such as roses with perhaps some ferns and gysophila); and mixed bouquets (an assortment of flowers arranged, tied, and sleeved together). Bouquet-makers save substantially on labor costs by designing a prototype of a mixed bouquet, or an arrangement in a container, for duplication by lower-cost employees. These employees do not experience the pleasure that is popularly and romantically associated with arranging fresh flowers. European and North American bouquet assembly lines are necessarily uncomfortably chilly and wet places, the better to preserve the freshness of the flowers. They are also rather solitary. Noisy conveyor belts transport flowers in water-filled buckets. Forklifts and other essential machinery also make enough noise to prevent conversation between the mostly female workers on the assembly lines. Conditions in the Latin American bouquet-making sheds

I visited were far more pleasant. They too were wet underfoot with water slopping out of buckets of flowers, but they were sometimes quiet, open airy sheds. With little noisy labor-saving machinery, conversation among these workers was at least possible. In both settings, I was told there is no shortage of applicants for the minimum-wage jobs on bouquet assembly lines.

Price and volume requirements in their market channels (primarily super-markets, convenience stores, mass retail stores, and consumer Internet orders) tend to limit both design and flower originality in ready-made bouquets. Upscale supermarkets, however, have higher-price thresholds and increasingly offer more expensive bouquets or arrangements with greater proportions of uncommon flowers that in many respects mirror the offerings at traditional retail florists.

Bouquet-making companies in the United States buy their ingredient flowers from many regions, including, in 2002, the Netherlands, California, and Israel as well as many Latin American countries. Faith Bickell, a Miami flower purchasing manager for a large bouquet-making company, described the global origins of one of her firm's bouquets: "In this bouquet we take a pom [chrysanthemum] from Medellín with a carnation from Bogotá with a green [foliage stem] and a bear grass from central Florida and a gyp [gyp-sophila] from Ecuador. The gerbera [in the arrangement] could come from many places." Faith also explained the mechanical process of creating the bouquets that will be given as gifts or perhaps centered on a family's table for a holiday meal. "We have product development people. They create a look depending on what the customer [supermarket] is looking for—or for a par-ticular holiday." After the look is approved, "They put it on a mix sheet or cost sheet—they lay out the plan [on paper] of what they want, then they make it and ensure it looks good, adjust it . . . and it becomes the product."

This brief description illuminates a moment when Sally's "real flowers, grown from earth" pause on their journey to the consumer and are trans-formed into the "Zombie flowers" that Sally resisted. No longer flowers, they are reclassified by Faith and her colleagues as "the product."

MOBILE WHOLESALERS

Many traditional wholesalers and importer wholesalers are small, private enterprises with significant capital investment, but with less than twenty permanent employees. Bouquet-making wholesalers tend to be slightly larger enterprises with more employees. Dole Fresh Flowers, a notable exception to this general pattern, is discussed in the next chapter. In addition to these permanent small flower-trading businesses, temporary traders—mobile whole-salers—provide an important layer of alternative service and supply in urban areas like the NYMA. Only a cellphone call away from their customers, they flourish and fade with the seasons, often exhibiting an ephemerality that mirrors the nature of the flowers they trade.

Mobile wholesaler appeared in the NYMA in the early 1980s. The form was probably pioneered by Dutch flower importers and they are still sometimes referred to as "Flying Dutchmen." After collecting flower shipments from the airport or an intermediary warehouse, these traders drive from retail store to retail store selling flowers from the back of a van. Dutch pioneers were even-tually followed by Korean, Israeli, Thai, Chinese, Ecuadorian, and Russian mobile wholesalers.[56] Some are individual entrepreneurs who operate only for specific holidays such as Valentine's Day. Others are orchestrated by large wholesalers in Brooklyn, Queens, and other locations. These specialized wholesalers gather great quantities of blooms and either sell them to indepen-dent small mobile wholesalers or operate their own fleets of van-driving employees who may compete with each other for profitable routes and work on commission.

Stoop stand flower selling benefited from this new form of wholesaling. By 2000, several of these larger orchestrating wholesalers were Korean, supplying —through mobile wholesalers—Korean-owned grocery and convenience stores as well as traditional retail florists and traditional wholesale florists. Ethnic connections are evident in trading. Mai Wong, the Taiwanese florist in Flushing, for example, regularly bought roses from a Chinese mobile whole-saler who appeared only for Valentine's Day and Chinese New Year.[57] Korean wholesalers buy flowers from many sources including Miami importer-whole-salers, exporters in Holland and Israel, or directly from growers in California, Colombia, Ecuador, and other places. With their huge volumes they can negotiate low prices. In fact, explained David Pang, a Korean wholesaler who had been operating his business for about six years when I spoke to him, "price, quality, and competition" are the factors that determine and adjust his activities and agreements. "We prefer to get the price that the flower requires at that particular time," David explained. Abundant supply is one factor that allows David Pang and his colleagues to focus on short-term profit and dis-pense with the reciprocal relationships that structure much flower exchange. Relationships form and dissolve rapidly in this segment, possibly contributing to New York's reputation among some Colombian and Ecuadorian growers as a market to avoid because prices are so low.

Mobile wholesalers are an elusive sector. In the years of my research a few of the largest orchestrating wholesale firms demonstrated their own mobility by dissolving and reforming into fresh companies or they simply disappeared. These hidden populations of the flower world with their own networks and relationships resist visibility and interviews. I managed to talk to a few only after many attempts and sometimes purely by chance. Most often they were alluded to rather than encountered. Ecuador is said to have a Korean grower and I was told about Korean exporters in both Ecuador and the Netherlands, but I was unable to meet them.

This mobile-wholesale sector, where transactions are entirely in cash, constitutes an informal flower economy in the NYMA often populated, as noted earlier, by new immigrants. Such informal trade includes immigrant street flower vendors—often Mexican. It flexibly and interdependently weaves its way into the formal regulated economy of licensed stoop stands, small supermarkets, and retail florists, allowing them to reduce their costs and sustain profit by buying cheaply and disposing of excess flowers. Informal urban economies with global links have been documented by other researchers and would repay future investigation in this case.[58]

Oscillating Chains

The twin chains of distribution, the specialty chain and the abundant chain, described in this chapter intersect at various stages in the life of the flower; most often at the moment of consumption, since Clarissa, Sally, and other flower buyers shop at all types of flower outlets. The chains continually influence each other, perhaps most obviously in the adoption of new flowers. Every year fresh flowers appear in the market, such as the unusual rose with "a mango-colored blush" that captured Sally's attention at the flower stand. When a new flower sells rapidly among high-level retail florists and freelance floral designers and is popular with their customers, they and their well-informed colleagues will reorder it. Their interest is communicated back along the specialty chain through a series of verbal reorders and elaborating conversations. Sufficient reorders for a new scarce rose will raise the price at a Netherlands auction or prompt a well-connected Ecuadorian grower to buy and plant more. Either response sends signals to observant competing and emulating neighboring growers. Some of these (as explained in chapter 5) will decide to risk planting new blushing roses and eventually offer them for sale through their own, probably lower-priced networks. Meantime, astute high-level wholesalers, anxious to fill orders for the blushing rose, will have spread the word about its popularity in many quarters of the globe, alerting other growers and traders to a developing desire for it in high-priced U.S. markets.

Thus demand for the new and the unusual, at the higher levels of the specialty chain, briefly draws or pulls a flower into the system. But growers who are connected to lower economic levels of the specialty chain, with scarcer knowledge of changing taste and fashion, must push it—sell it—through their networks in the trading system. The flower then reaches mid-level retail florists who may reorder, beginning another oscillation that eventually pushes the new flower into corner stores and supermarkets. This cycle, repeated for many flowers, together with the innumerable independent decisions that follow the circulation of this information and knowledge, including orders to propagators, further conversations, new relationships, verbal commitments, new standing orders, and so on, animates the entire system. At the same time, breeders may focus more attention on developing new roses with blushing qualities. These apparently mechanistic functions of demand and supply also rest on social and cultural bases. Complex personal relationships structure flower exchange as participants communicate knowledge about changing markets, competition, new flower types, and new consumer interests. Established middlemen, while arranging the exchange of flowers, give economic substance to abstract conceptions—new desires, changing tastes and practices. Others, the more mysterious and ephemeral immigrant entrepreneurs, smooth the flow of cheap blooms through an informal trading system that supports sectors of the formal flower economy in the NYMA. All these middlemen—like growers—expose themselves to financial risk and uncertainty that must be managed through social networks and innovative technologies. The following chapter analyzes their activities, networks, and strategies in this constantly adjusting system.

Chapter Six

Seven

Risk and Relationships:
Middlemen Strategies

The previous chapter explored the recent emergence of new forms of wholesaling and retailing within two parallel streams of global and local flower trading, the specialty chain and the abundant chain. In this chapter I examine the role and behavior of middlemen in these systems and I attempt to explain how and why economic and communicative power settled into these middle sectors of the Fresh-Cut Flower Global Commodity Chain (hereafter FCFGCC).

Several theorists have offered ideas about networks and knowledge that are useful in understanding the reconfiguration of the fresh flower commodity chain in the last twenty-five years. Manuel Castells has written of a new social structure he terms "informationalism" that appeared in the last twenty to thirty years—the period often termed postmodernity or late capitalism. The structure is *informational*, rather than simply information-based, because transformation of societies and institutions is part of the process. Knowledge and information technology are basic components of this structure that enable "information generation, processing, and transmission [to] become the fundamental sources of productivity and power" (1996, 21). The basic unit of "informationalism," according to Castells, is the network. Bennett Harrison (among others) has also shown an interest in networks and confirms an increase in networking among large and small firms. Harrison sees networking as a new way for firms to manage their global reach and to enhance the flexibility necessary for adjustment to market uncertainty, fragmentation, and intensifying production cycles. Timothy Sturgeon brings another dimension to the discussion of networks. He distinguishes between value chains that map "the vertical sequence of events leading to the delivery, consumption and maintenance of goods and services" and networks which, in contrast, highlight "the nature and extent of the inter-firm relationships that bind sets of firms into larger economic groups" (2001, 11). Networks, several authors agree, are also an important means of managing risk (Plattner 1989a; Castells 1996; Harrison 1997).

I argue that knowledge development, knowledge sharing, and the adoption of new technology by socially based global networks were important factors in the growing governance of the FCFGCC by middlemen in the last quarter of the twentieth century. Innovation and reciprocity—discussed in chapter 5 in relation to growers—also have a role in this middlemen segment of the FCFGCC. Innovation in both wholesale and retail distribution channels produced multiple permutations of flower distribution within the United States and in the NYMA in this period. In some sectors new information, logistical technology, and innovative product management permitted the circulation of greater and greater volumes of cheap fresh flowers to more consumers. At the same time, reciprocity is evident in chains of obligation, or what Plattner (1989a, 212–13) has termed "equilibrating" or balancing relationships. These relationships sustain social networks by helping to reduce uncertainty and risk in the precarious business of exchanging fresh flowers.[1]

In what follows I explore the presence and absence of social networks and reciprocating or equilibrating relationships as well as the links between knowledge sharing, innovation, and middlemen's economic and communicative power. Behavior in many of the flower-trading networks seemingly challenges Castells's contention that contemporary economic and social networks enjoy only "virtual" cultures that are insubstantial, "ephemeral," and lacking in "obligations" (1996,199). To the contrary, I suggest that in this particular system of provision, networks shape the identities of traders as they build relationships and small communities on the basis of their ethics and promises as well as kinship, class, ethnicity, and nationality. Gender is also an important factor in these relationships and alignments. The wholesale sector is clearly male dominated, and though the retail sector employs many women, fewer women than men occupy management roles.

In this chapter I am also trying to reveal precisely the ways in which the desires and preferences of flower consumers are communicated from retail outlets back along the chain to growers in an industry with little vertical integration. Miller (1995a, 5–7) has explained that integrated product coding systems allow retailers to capture information about consumer preferences and restock to satisfy their desires. Evidence from this study contradicts this assertion. In the cut flower system, networks of individuals, socially connected along the commodity chain—rather than electronically recorded data—communicate changing consumer choices to the growers. A numerically small but influential group of middlemen engages in this activity, acting as important cultural communicators. In the process they develop social and cultural power for themselves that converts readily into economic power. I analyze all these factors in terms of the two contiguous chains operating in U.S. fresh-cut flower distribution: the specialty chain and the abundant chain. In a final section I consider recent attempts at corporate restructuring in the middle sector and the ways in which these attempts appear to concentrate risk while, to their apparent detriment, disregarding existing knowledge and the benefits of networks in the exchange of fresh-cut flowers.

The Specialty Chain

Broadly speaking, the specialty chain brings flowers to a higher socioeconomic market sector where innovation and novelty are important (see chapter 8). High rates of flower innovation, the inherent fragility of the flowers themselves, and sales sensitivity to changing tastes and fluctuations in the larger economy add to the risks of trading along this chain. It demands careful management of uncertainty. Uncertainty in this context is a relative condition of not having sure knowledge—of having doubt.[2] Risk is understood here as the possibility of suffering loss or harm. Risk itself suggests a degree of uncertainty and implies knowledge of a causal relationship between certain conditions, possible decisions, and particular effects (Van Loon 2000, 166). Like many global traders, today's flower traders use cell phones and the Internet to connect with each other and with growers in local and global networks, forging a delicate balance between trust and risk as they arrange for fragile flowers to be placed in their care and travel partway around the globe.[3] The following sections explore the way knowledge, innovation, and vertical networks—in contrast to local, horizontal, or intracluster networks, which tend to be weak in the U.S. flower chain—help middlemen to balance risk and reduce uncertainty in the specialty chain and increase their economic and communicative power.

Knowledge, understood as a reasoned judgment based on sets of organized facts, to paraphrase Castells (1996, 17), has at least two benefits in the specialty chain. On the one hand, the exchange of knowledge serves to structure and sustain parts of the system and the relationships that knit it together. On the other hand, knowledge itself (about, for example, weather conditions in growing regions, new flower hybrids, newly emerging competitors, changing currency values, or a sudden passion for peonies in Manhattan) acts to alter and reshape the market for particular flowers. Middlemen's flower-related knowledge may be considered within three general categories: supply of flowers, demand for flowers, and outside factors affecting supply or demand.

KNOWLEDGE AND THE SUPPLY OF FLOWERS

The globalization of flower production resolved earlier problems of unstable supplies (see chapter 2) so that today, as Grady Smith, one of the NYMA larger traditional wholesalers, explained, "You can get any [flower] at any time—almost without exception." At the same time globalization of production has added enormous complexity to the governance of supplies intended to satisfy specific local demand. "In my father's time—when I started twenty years ago," Grady recalled, "we sold five or six rose varieties. Now it is sixty." This complexity adds to the risk of financial loss. Fred Berents, an importer-wholesaler based in Miami, connects to both middle- and upper-level markets in the specialty chain. Fred is typical of some importer-wholesalers as he constantly tracks and reorganizes a complex matrix of flower shipments from different quarters of the globe. He balances information and rumor about coming harvests with his knowledge about seasonal demands and weighs both against the risk that sudden oversupply will unfavorably alter prices for a certain pink lily or white peony. All the while he is conscious of temporal risk and the ever-urgent need to physically exchange flowers that are already dying. "You have to react fast," Fred explains. The quality and value of the crops he has committed to buy for his American customers decline continuously and precipitously after harvest so that "three days from now my product is worth nothing."

Most flower middlemen try to lessen both risk and uncertainty by making long-term arrangements through standing orders with growers, with other wholesalers, and with retailers they trust. Yet many decisions in the specialty chain are inevitably daily and short-term as trade in this chain responds to sudden needs and desires among consumers. Consequently, trading on the current or "spot" market offers, in Fred's words, "constraints and opportunities." In general, wholesalers can make last-minute purchases of many cut flowers with reasonable expectation of acquiring what is needed at a good price. Continually expanding global flower production and competition have kept the average prices of the common varieties of major cut flowers—such as roses, carnations, and gerbera—fairly stable for many years (Burket and Benedick 1980; Jerardo 2002, 2004). For the specialty flowers there is greater uncertainty because available quantities are generally smaller. Traders buy and sell both kinds of flowers rapidly, negotiating quantities and discounts and balancing trust, promises, and market speculation while at the same time manipulating tiny price margins in an effort to convert them into a profit.[4]

With good knowledge about the supply of flowers and the factors that may affect it and good global networks, wholesalers like Fred Berents, Grady Smith, and others coordinate and manage distribution. However, they and their networks cannot stabilize or orchestrate demand; they can only respond to demand. Furthermore, there is the additional risk, as Harrison suggests, that networks (whether of large or small firms) like these, by connecting global areas of production with markets, exacerbate the tendency toward global overproduction, eventually making it more difficult to coordinate supply with demand profitably (1997, 30–31). Very likely this was a factor in the overproduction and declining average prices of many rose varieties in the American and global markets between 2001 and 2004.

KNOWLEDGE AND THE DEMAND FOR FLOWERS

Wholesalers and retailers in the specialty chain are particularly attentive to local demands and the needs of their various customers. They are skilled at using direct personal contacts to gather information, develop knowledge, and rapidly assemble a range of blooms tailored to local desires in species, variety, and price. At the 28th Street market in Manhattan, for example, between 50 and 90 percent (depending on the wholesaler and his customer type) of customers—chiefly floral designers and traditional retail florists—select their flowers in person. As they do so, they chat with the wholesale owners, their salesmen and (the rare) saleswomen, and other florists and designers, exchanging personal gossip and news about novel flowers, styles, fashions, fads, and flower availability. Peter Pearl, the 28th Street market wholesaler (introduced in chapter 6), offered an example of the benefits of these direct social contacts when he described how the floral designer Robert Isabell's sudden interest in peonies in the late 1980s "made that the trendiest flower." Robert Isabell is among a small group of floral designers whose shifting flower preferences "have a big influence on what people buy—or what they buy from me for sure," and, according to Peter, his peony prices at the wholesale market soon quadrupled. Some years later when peonies from New Zealand began appearing in New York in November—peony is naturally a spring flower—at ten to twelve dollars a stem, Robert Isabell's clients "were clamoring for them" and as the *New York Times* reported, "the limited availability of the flowers . . . only heightens the craze."[5] Knowledgeable wholesalers like Peter are among those who benefit from crazes as they spread among other designers, retail florists, and their clients. By 2000, November peonies were commonly included in elite autumn weddings and other events and by then floral designers were beginning to focus on obtaining specific (distinguishing) varieties of November peonies.

Responding to such demands, Fred Berents and other wholesalers search the world for peonies. With the aid of a global map Fred energetically described to me how he orchestrates his peony supplies. "Peonies I bring from South Africa, also south of Santiago [Chile]. Mostly [in] November, December." He went on to explain, "I used to bring in more peonies from England and Holland [in early spring] but the United States peonies came up big time. [They start] in [the] Carolinas mid-May and then up to northern New York by the end of June [so] there is such a big production here now." The U.S. spring peony production Fred mentions expanded partly in response to the demand initiated by the new craze for peonies.[6] Similar shifts in fashions for flowers, often initiated by trend-setting floral designers and dispersed through magazines and word of mouth, influence the orchestration of supplies of many other flowers (see chapter 8). In recent years particular varieties of hydrangeas, cymbidium orchids, and calla lilies have become more important.

KNOWLEDGE AND OUTSIDE FACTORS

The globalization of flower growing for the U.S. market also increased the need for wholesalers to understand a range of outside forces and factors that constantly shift conditions and introduce uncertainty for growers, wholesalers, and retailers. Fred Berents had a ready example: "Look at Japan. They were buying from Australia, Holland, New Zealand, South Africa. Now they buy from Vietnam, Thailand, China where economies are not that strong and prices [are] lower. So now Australia, New Zealand, and South Africa are trying to come here [to sell their flowers in the United States]." Because the flowers of these newcomers shift the market, reducing prices and introducing fresh competition for the flowers Fred is importing from a range of other countries through his long-established networks, he finds this to be yet "another disturbing factor we have to deal with."

While these outside forces are quite beyond his control, an astute observer like Fred minimizes risk by paying close attention to changing structural factors and adjusting his decisions. He also explained how he shares his knowledge with other (not directly competitive) traders. "Freight rates are a big factor," he said, and "there are large-size [flower] companies selling strongly in the United States in mass markets—I keep warning them you have to look at worldwide production [not just your local competitors] because the moment the freight rate or exchange rate changes then the whole market changes." In 2002 and 2003 Fred expanded his relationships with Brazilian growers. He began importing large quantities of flowers from Brazil to Miami and at the same time reduced his imports from the Netherlands. One factor in this new development was a decline in the value of the dollar that made Dutch and other European flowers more expensive. Another was a new security surcharge of about 8 percent imposed at New York City airports after 2001 to cover the additional screening of flower boxes and the individuals who collected them. Shipments to Miami airport avoided that surcharge.

Yet another factor was the rising price of oil and increases in airfreight after 2001. By 2005, flower freight costs per kilo from Amsterdam to New York had more than doubled over rates prevailing in the late 1990s. Popular Dutch hydrangeas are large-headed, subtly colored, and very heavy; they now cost wholesalers $11–12 per stem delivered to the United States. So tastes for off season hydrangea blossoms are now sometimes satisfied by smaller, lighter, less colorful hydrangeas from Brazil and Peru. These reach Miami importer-wholesalers for about one third the price of the Netherlands hydrangeas. Such responses and the behavior of Fred and other importer-wholesalers have the effect of opening new markets to flower growers in new supplying regions such as Brazil, or even to growers in the United States and Canada who rush to meet the demand for colorful hydrangeas. The new growers, in turn, following Fred's suggestions, gradually improve the quality and range of their flowers and, at least in theory, improve their own competitiveness while also adding to the sum of global competition as they seek to satisfy Fred and other wholesalers of his caliber.

As an importer-wholesaler, Fred sells quite a few flowers to a large traditional wholesale enterprise in the NYMA where Bill Blake is a manager. But Fred is only one component of Bill's own large network of suppliers. Importer-wholesalers in Miami, exporter-wholesalers in Aalsmeer, as well as growers in California and several Latin American countries, are all linked by their relationship to Bill Blake and his firm. This large network helps to manage uncertainty or risk for his firm. Bill described his own complicated arrangements to ensure ade-

Risk and Relationships

quate supplies of just one single flower, the calla lily (see figure 36). Many come "from Colombia and Ecuador. We get local calla lilies from Pennsylvania [and we also] get them from Holland. [They are] very big but they don't ship real well, so we depend on local sources for the big ones . . . right now we are getting them from Australia and New Zealand." A month earlier Canadian and California crops had supplied his calla lilies but rainy weather in California [where calla lilies are field-grown] speckled the white calla blooms with dirt, so he was forced to scour other global regions for replacements. Calla lilies, of course, are only one of the hundreds of flowers to be tracked, acquired, and passed along the chain on a daily basis.[7]

Like many in the FCFGCC, Fred Barents claims to make decisions based on intuition. "You have to follow the market constantly and what is going on in the world—you filter the information and absorb what is important," Fred explained. "It is important for me to keep the finger on the pulse—that is why I am still also selling. You make so many decisions based on your experience. That is why I travel a lot and am on the phone a lot, [I] follow the market developments. Then act on that, making decisions on feelings." In fact, his decisions are based on tacit knowledge. Fred develops knowledge through his (possibly unconscious) reasoned judgments about particular sets of facts, then buys and sells on the basis of that knowledge and subtly and incrementally alters the market for various flowers.

The knowledge that Fred and his colleagues and competitors develop becomes a social and economic asset in this market system and has two important uses beyond informing Fred's personal decisions. First, he can share it with Bill Blake, Grady Smith, or Peter Pearl, all of whom are linked together by their personal networks. By sharing his knowledge on a reciprocating basis Fred uses it to sustain relationships, build trust, and indirectly limit his risk. Bill, Grady, and Peter in turn may pass Fred's ideas about new flowers, price shifts, and new seasons of availability to retailers in their networks and later reciprocate by giving Fred news about fading fads and fashions. While these social networks of relations are a mechanism for gathering and sharing knowledge, the degree of sharing is calibrated to some extent by consumption level. At the uppermost socioeconomic level, the wholesale-retail information exchange is more intense.

Second, Fred's knowledge and experience may be sold or exchanged as part of a service, possibly to a supermarket or another retailer in the abundant chain where knowledge about flowers and trends is limited. In fact, Fred is already starting to market his knowledge and expertise in this way.

Networks of relationships have three principal characteristics that make them especially appropriate systems for exchanging flowers. First, they distribute risk by encouraging cooperation and trust; second they are flexible and responsive; and finally, they diffuse information critical to improving competitiveness. Long-term relationships abound in the specialty chain networks, often between globally dispersed individuals. Tales of help through bad times were fairly common along the specialty chain middle sector, probably because networks must be well-maintained to diffuse risk efficiently. People move around within the industry but sustain their connections and the portable economic value conferred by their knowledge of flowers and by their ethics and relationships. New forms of communication seem not so much to displace these relationships as to strengthen already existing ones. Fred Berents, the Miami importer-wholesaler, was one of many in this chain who discussed his currently strong position in terms of relationships. "I think relationships are important in this way," Fred observed. "The people I do business with in my company are old relationships and strong—we have pretty much had these strong relationships since the beginning [mid-1980s] with a high level of trust. You take care of each other. I believe in it strongly."

Relationships are sustained through socialization. At trade shows, postshow social drinking and dinners are common ways to exchange ideas. Some traders and growers with close relationships attend sports events together, while others have planned brief family vacations together. A command of English and a familiarity with American culture confer advantage. Not surprisingly, growers and traders who have worked in the United States or been educated there seem far more successful at developing strong relationships along the chain. Equally, language and social advantages for some may conspire to exclude others. Newcomers to the industry, with poor English and little experience of the United States, may find it difficult to penetrate long-established networks. This type of exclusion from strong networks may partly account for the failures of some apparently experienced wholesalers. For example, Sarabeth Coombs, also a Miami importer-wholesaler, explained how, following the collapse of USA Floral Products Inc. (see below), "a lot of [displaced former employees] are trying to open their own businesses as a result of all that [disruption]." However, many were unsuccessful despite their experience in the industry because, as Sarabeth assured me, "It is a difficult thing to do if you are unsupported by others [in the industry]."

171

Risk and Relationships

In the FCFGCC, as explained in chapter 5, the value of blooms is frequently uncertain and subject to renegotiation along the chain. Because of this uncertainty and the necessity for rapid transit along the chain, agreements in the specialty chain are entirely verbal and money is not exchanged (except at the consumer stage) until well after the flowers and their value are a mere memory. Cooperation and trust are consequently important, and network forms—in contrast to the unrestrained self-interest of hypothetical "free markets" and the central management of vertically integrated corporations—encourage reciprocity and cooperation as governing principals (Plattner 1989b; Harrison 1997, 132).

Networks shape trust among individuals and reduce market complexity, while also establishing mutually acceptable standards of behavior and conduct (Granovetter 1985; Plattner 1989b; Boden 2000). The importance of mutual trust and related standards of conduct seems to be widely understood in the specialty chain. Piet Wessel, a salesman with an Aalsmeer exporter-wholesaler, described the "chain of obligations" within which he functions, explaining that verbal agreements supersede other market considerations. For example, even if the auction price of a flower is unfavorably high relative to a previous agreement, "you must pay it to keep your relationship with your customer," insisted Piet, because "you need to fulfill your commitment and price obligations irrespective of what it costs you." Because Dutch exporters are responsible for absorbing deductions for poor shipments (charges that are absorbed in Latin America by the growers), they are especially careful about choosing customers they can trust to be honest about the condition of received blooms.

The anthropologist Stuart Plattner uses the term "equilibrating relationships" to describe such long-term relationships and the balancing processes that reduce risk in multiple back and forth transactions. In some cases, Plattner explains, these long-term relationships are like partnerships and although the actor's objective is self-interested, sustaining the relationship is given greater weight than a short-term profit. Imbalances in an agreed price, as Piet Wessel is certainly aware, can be addressed in later transactions to achieve satisfaction for both. In a market system like the FCFGCC where uncertainty, frequency of transaction, and capital investment are all high, equilibrating relationships make a lot of sense.

Networks are also responsive and flexible exchange systems. Flexibility, in this sector of the commodity chain, means the ability to acquire quickly many different types of flowers from varied sources. Flexibility is an important quality for a high-priced traditional wholesaler like Peter Pearl, whose relationships with his retail customers hinge on access to a great variety of high-quality, unusual blooms and his ability to deliver them on short notice. Peter consequently telephones as many as twenty growers each day because "I like to talk . . . I like to talk to get a feel." To enhance his flexibility, he also invests time, energy, and money in building and sustaining his large networks of relationships among growers with small specialty farms. "I have always gone out and traveled [to make connections]," explained Peter. "Like Albert Bellini [a grower of Swiss origin with farms in Ecuador and Colombia]. It took me two years to get him to send me those roses. Two years it took me." Peter recalled how "I have been stood up at hotel lobbies by him. I sat there for three hours one day when I was in Bermuda at one of these [wholesalers'] conventions. But finally I was able to corner him and he loves me now." Peter emphasized the personal nature of his industry ties, "like my French tulip supplier and my Italian . . . I always went [to see them] and everything is hands on. So I always have personal relationships. . . . It is very important, because they know what I like, they are my eyes."

Finally, networks efficiently diffuse information that sometimes becomes "stuck" within vertically integrated and free market systems (Harrison 1997, 132). Wholesale florists, retail florists, and floral designers networked in the specialty chain travel together to the major global trade shows looking for the new and interesting, pooling their expertise, and socializing with each other, with growers, and other traders. Peter Pearl is among those who take their knowledge gathering and sharing seriously.

> Every year I go to Aalsmeer [trade fair]. It is very important because you see all the new varieties you are going to see two years down the road. You meet everybody. All the people I deal with are there. It is the number one event. I was there with Albert Bellini about two years ago and we are talking about what do you think of this rose variety and what do you think of that variety—because he buys thirty or forty thousand plants at a time. He asks me, "Do you think this will be a hot seller?" I told him oranges are big, so he put in a lot of different oranges. That will pay off for him. It is a hot color—orange right now. Because everyone is asking for it—the designers.

Risk and Relationships

Fred Berents is also serious about his knowledge-sharing obligation to mid-level traditional wholesale florists who lack direct connections with growers yet need to gather information about new flowers or changes in the supply. "Companies like ours, small to medium, are the backbone of this industry," claimed Fred. "The average [traditional] wholesale house is not big enough, [has] not enough time, experience and knowledge. They depend on us for knowledge."

Well-networked wholesalers thus fulfill a significant role as the "eyes and ears" or knowledge conduits for the small local wholesaler and linked retail florists. Where retail florists and their local wholesalers are poorly networked, flower knowledge and innovation may disseminate very slowly. Suburban florists, for example (discussed in chapter 6), make most decisions about the flowers they will offer to their customers on the basis of what they hear from their primary traditional wholesalers rather than on the basis of what they see. Some, operating on very small margins and with poor business training, are slow to innovate, frequently choosing to reduce risk and uncertainty by sticking with inexpensive familiar flowers. Such behavior contributes to urban-suburban-rural as well as socioeconomic differentiation in flower choices and tastes. Knowledge (and its absence) thus has a social and cultural, as well as an economic, value.

TECHNOLOGICAL INNOVATION

As wholesalers of all kinds embraced continuous innovation in species and varieties, seeking new, unusual, and high-quality flowers in different parts of the globe, they also increased their need for innovative technology and accelerated its rate of adoption. Even mid-level wholesalers felt pressed to adopt new technology, especially those who began supplying supermarkets and convenience stores with bouquets and bunches. Firms found new ways to use computers to communicate, to monitor and manage distribution and information, and to coordinate wide-ranging activities such as custom-packing boxes of flowers for individual retailers at the farm. These innovations reduce the need to handle the flowers during transportation and improve flexibility and service. In fact, orchestrating flower exports, imports, and trade has become a matter of complex logistics.

Cellular and satellite telephones allow individuals in the FCFGCC to maintain constant communication outside traditional business hours. Importer-wholesalers, traditional wholesale florists, and growers telephone each other constantly. Retail florists call their traditional wholesale florists morning, afternoon, and (in emergencies) evening. In fact, all along the chain every hour of the day is now an hour in which to do business. E-mail has speeded and improved communication, facilitating placing and withdrawing orders on very short notice, generating questions, invoices, and so on. Yet the adoption of new communication technology is far from universal. Extensive technology in some firms coexists with the persistence of pencil and paper order taking, estimating, and calculation in other, usually smaller wholesale and retail businesses. However, during the seven years I have been following this industry, several of the small "pencil and paper" firms have gone out of business, perhaps because their owners' unwillingness to adopt new technology undermined their usefulness to technologically adjusting networks.

The development of computerized flower inventory systems generally lagged behind the explosion in varieties. Peter Pearl, like Grady Smith, handles hundreds of flower varieties and noted, "When I first started you ordered gerbera daisies by varieties because there was only about fifteen or twenty. Now you can't keep track. . . . You used to order red roses or yellow roses—now they [designers and traditional florists] specify 'I want "Aalsmeer Gold," I want "Oceana," I want "Red Velvet." ' The retailer has become more educated and you have to be able to keep on top of things." With new computer systems Peter can really keep on top of things. "Computers changed us," he acknowledged. "We can track what is selling well." Today he monitors the hundreds of flower types in his inventory and his daily sales and plans some future orders with computer-generated reports.

As new computerized inventory and flower-tracking systems have increased efficiency they have speeded order processing and flower "picking and packing," favoring a sort of just-in-time supply of fresh flowers. As a result, even small regional wholesalers and retailers can depend on geographically distant suppliers without endangering their business, provided they are linked in trusting relationships. Beth Dalton, an experienced importer-wholesaler in Miami, explained that as "a wholesaler in Rhode Island orders the product [from Beth] . . . it appears in his computer inventory. He works way ahead—he is confident I can get that product to him." Furthermore, Beth explained, the wholesaler "is selling [it] before it is even cut. So I have to make sure I don't promise what I can't deliver and that I deliver what I promise. So I have to have a tremendous relationship with the farm. Retailers have been destroyed because they weren't buying from a trusted [importer-wholesaler]

Risk and Relationships

source." Dependability is critical for distant traditional wholesalers, explained Beth, because if "they receive poor product, they can lose all the money they need to make during holidays."

Yet as new tracking and inventory systems reduce risk for smaller wholesalers, they encourage larger exporters, importer-wholesalers, and traditional wholesalers to take bigger risks. Some speculate by buying overproduction at low prices and holding larger and larger short-term inventories. In some cases, as much as 70 percent of total inventory is purchased on speculation while only 30 percent of purchases fulfill existing orders. This behavior permits a higher level of service and increases sales volume by reducing restocking time for their clients. Improved inventory tracking allows better risk management, and Internet communication speeds "special sale" offers along the FCFGCC. Yet an enterprise holding larger and larger flower inventories is assuming greater and greater risk. Moreover, since network systems respond to rather than orchestrate demand, these trends toward holding larger and larger inventory may aggravate a tendency toward global overproduction and contribute to an increasing imbalance between supply and demand (Harrison 1997, 30–31).

The Abundant Chain

A recent celebratory article about perishable retailing innovation in *Produce News* claimed, "Forward-thinking companies are developing higher-value products that cater to specific consumer wants." It explained that supermarkets and other retailers of perishable goods are looking for "that one product that can take them out of the doldrums of commodity pricing to the loftier location occupied by the value-added niche products."[8] Fresh-cut flowers are just such a "niche product" and have been embraced by the two retailing segments that, in the NYMA, constitute the abundant chain—that is, convenience stores and supermarkets. Both retail forms bring similar flower types, qualities, pricing, and presentations to generally lower-priced markets. Here, however, flower innovation and novelty diffuse more slowly than in the specialty chain.

The *Produce News* article implies that matching supply to specific consumer demands is a fairly new concern of the perishables industries. Fresh flowers industry experts, however, confidently predicted in 1972 that growers and suppliers to supermarkets would soon have access to marketing data that would closely track consumers' flower preferences and identify their wants.

Furthermore, consumers themselves were expected to demand more information about the flowers they were buying.[9] Little of this predicted innovation in supermarkets occurred in the succeeding thirty years. In fact, according to Humphery, supermarket retailers have been "less powerful in design and effect" and less rational and scientific than many suspect and rather naïve in their understanding of consumers (1998, 208). Even if they wish to—and notwithstanding the existence of appropriate technology—retailers in the supermarket section of the abundant chain only accidentally manage to match supply to demand with respect to fresh-cut flowers. Furthermore, they seem incapable of catering "to specific consumer wants."[10]

These deficiencies result in part from widespread inflexibility, poor flower knowledge, and resistance to certain types of innovation. These characteristics are, in turn, linked to particular characteristics of supermarket industry structure in the United States, especially intense internal and external competition, hierarchical corporate organization, conservatism, and aversion to risk. These structural traits limit the development of networks of equilibrating relationships and the diffusion of knowledge about flowers and local flower consumers. In contrast to the specialty chain, networks of relationships in the abundant chain, although sometimes long-term, are usually based on purely economic transactions rather than personal, cooperative ties. In fact, in supermarket corporate structures, personal ties between buyers and suppliers are sometimes considered unethical or improper.

INNOVATION

Supermarket flower retail expanded as foreign production generated huge supplies of cheap blooms and distribution improved. Two notable marketing innovations also substantially increased the quantities of flowers being sold through supermarkets. First, in contrast to the traditional retail form of selling single flower stems or custom-designed arrangements, supermarket flowers are generally sold prepackaged. They come in variously sized bunches of the same flower (consumer or grower bunches) or increasingly as mixed bunches or bouquets.[11] This innovative packaging, begun as early as 1968 in California supermarkets, allows shoppers to make quick selections from a simple supermarket display.[12] A later innovation of the 1980s, still widely used today, was the introduction of "three bouquets for $10"—that is, a customer may buy one bunch of flowers, conveniently sleeved in plastic, for $3.99 or three for $10. This marketing novelty soon raised the average supermarket flower sale from less than $5 to $10.[13] It also encouraged the development of bouquet-making wholesalers to satisfy rising demand for ready-made bunches and bouquets. In turn, other new firms emerged to supply sleeves, colored papers, and distinctive wrappings for bouquets—much as violet-colored and scented papers were used more than a hundred years earlier for distinctive presentation (see chapter 1).[14]

Several technological innovations also helped supermarkets' sales of cut flowers. Scanable barcoding is potentially one of the most important. It is widely used to track boxes of flowers from grower to wholesaler to supermarket hub and even to individual stores.[15] Universal Product Codes (UPC) may also be assigned to each flower stem, bouquet, or bunch to register its sale. Data from this immensely useful system may, as Miller points out, be employed to analyze the choices of consumers and to restock the supermarket to satisfy their apparent preferences. The system has great potential for tracking local consumer flower preferences. For example, a taste among Bronxville, New York, supermarket shoppers for yellow roses and violet lisianthus could be tracked. Then the Bronxville supermarket floral or produce manager could reorder flowers to satisfy these local desires.

However, this opportunity to observe and "cater to specific consumer wants" has been largely ignored. By 2000, only about half of U.S. supermarkets used the UPC "category management" tool to track grocery sales at all (Floral Marketing Association 1999). Furthermore, in the case of flower sales, most grocery stores with the UPC system simply note that *flowers* rather than *yellow roses* have passed through the checkout.[16] Greater detail about the types of flowers sold is very rarely registered.[17] In practice it seems that UPC scanning systems merely track different flower suppliers ("vendors") and their assorted bouquets and bunches rather than the detailed preferences of local consumers.[18] Speaking of his supermarket customers, Sam Hopewell, a Miami bouquet-making wholesaler, explained, "What they tell me is 'I want to buy your four-pack arrangement' and they give me one SKU and one UPC. But it is my job to make sure that every time it goes into that store it is different but still with the same SKU and UPC number to make things easier for the category manager." Sam continued, "They are relying on [my] expertise for color [and] style. It is my job to make sure it sells. If it doesn't sell the client tells me."

KNOWLEDGE

Supermarkets typically invest little in specialized personnel training and flower knowledge is scarce among supermarket employees. Poor knowledge constrains innovation in flower types. While big chains employ knowledge-able flower buyers, in smaller chains and independent stores the flower buyer is often a store's produce manager, who will "order a rose, a sunflower and alstroemeria because they know them," explained Alyssa Framingham, a bouquet-making wholesaler. Such buyers will rarely risk ordering an unfamiliar flower. The produce manager may be a good judge of Peruvian mangos but he or she seldom knows anything about Peruvian hydrangeas or lilies. Furthermore, box stores such as Sam's Club, one supplying wholesaler explained, generally order the same flowers for an entire region with no local differentiation.

Many supermarkets compensate for their untrained store employees by subcontracting flower supply. In some cases wholesale or retail firms take complete responsibility for stocking, staffing, and maintaining supermarket and box store retail (such as Sam's Club) flower departments, whether full service, limited service, or self-service.[19] In effect, supermarkets hire (or "in source" to use Friedman's 2005 terminology) the design expertise, flower knowledge, and logistical expertise of importers, bouquet-makers and other kinds of wholesalers. Bill Blake, a previously mentioned manager at a large traditional wholesale firm, summarized his experiences supplying flowers to supermarkets by observing that "they don't know the secret to making it work." Wholesalers, in fact, are sometimes far more observant about the shifting flower tastes of supermarket shoppers than are supermarket flower buyers (or produce managers). Alyssa explained, "If I look at my sales [to a particular supermarket store] and see they are stagnant, I know I have to change something in my bouquet recipes. Sometimes they [the supermarket flower buyers] don't want to change a bouquet even though I see that the sales are dropping—people are getting bored. . . . Marketing becomes a lot easier if you have something that is not on every street corner." But, she elaborated, supermarket floral managers are resistant even to such small changes because "it is a hassle for them to . . . change the [UPC] code," consequently "they don't want to change the bouquet."

Some wholesalers offer supermarkets a form of just-in-time inventory management. They sell supermarkets their wide knowledge of varieties, their skills in orchestrating supply—including consolidating shipments and import documentation from multiple offshore farms—and their command of computerized inventory management, among other techniques. This service allows supermarket managers to make very-last-minute decisions to buy or not to buy. Steve Kulkins, a NYMA bouquet-maker wholesaler, offered an example:

Risk and Relationships

"I have a very large [supermarket] customer. They will call up and say I want a hundred boxes of something in two hours." This additional layer of activities and services provided by highly competent middlemen compensates for the supermarket produce or floral manager's inability to manage fresh-cut flower variety and inventory. It helps the store to respond—somewhat imprecisely—to "consumer wants."[20]

RISK, TRUST, AND RELATIONSHIPS

While selling knowledge and service to supermarkets may be regarded as an opportunity for the wholesale sector, the risk is intensified because of the greater quantities of flowers involved and the uncertainty of fluctuating store sales. Large supermarkets (sometimes functioning in small store-level units) displace, rather than share, the risk and uncertainty of retailing fresh flowers by transferring it to upstream segments of the FCFGCC. Usually risk is transferred to wholesalers and sometimes further along the chain to growers (see chapter 5). Alyssa explained what happens to the grower at the beginning of the chain when her supermarket customers are inattentive to their shifting sales. "If the farm is used to selling fifty boxes of roses a week and the next week it goes down to ten [because the supermarket hasn't notified Alyssa in advance that the roses aren't needed] then you are stuck with that product. The farm hasn't sold it or put it on the open market because we are expecting that grocery store chain to take it." As a result, Alyssa said, "We sell it at a loss [on the spot market]. But the supermarkets get to call the shots. So we write that off." When supermarkets suddenly stop large orders, those extra flowers offered cheaply cause price swings that temporarily destabilize the specialty chain as well as the abundant chain.

Many wholesalers are prepared to accommodate supermarkets because of their high volumes and prompt payments. These relationships between supermarkets and their suppliers require that supermarkets invest a certain level of trust in those suppliers. John Brooks, a supermarket analyst, considers that "relationships play an important role in [supermarket] buying decisions because of the need for trust in your business partners" and the need to ensure "quality, availability, and the ability to deliver on time." Consequently, according to Brooks, "Buyers have a relationship with those who have performed well for them" and "over a long period of time [this] leads to personal relationships, rather than strictly impersonal business relationships." Yet from the flower wholesaler's perspective, relationships with supermarket contacts are often impersonal, strained, and tainted with "ill-will and lingering uncertainty."[21] "There is a lack of cooperation and not working as partners," explained Alyssa, who supplies bouquets to mid- and upper-level supermarkets in Florida. "There is an attitude 'you are trying to screw me' or 'you'll do what I say.' " She contrasted this absence of trust and cooperation with her relationships with growers and breeders who "will call me and ask me what I think about a particular color and what do I see happening at the stores . . . we share information." From Alyssa's perspective, "There needs to be more information, cooperation, and stronger relationships [with supermarkets]." Steve Kulkins, the NYMA bouquet-maker, described his supermarket customers as "a bit of a tough bunch." He found them to be deeply "concerned about competition and . . . time pressure . . . they are off the phone in a few seconds." My own experiences with supermarket flower buyers were similar; they have little time to chat and, perhaps understandably, are reluctant to discuss improved methods or novel procedures that could be relayed to their competitors.

Thus U.S. supermarkets, with their hierarchical structure and resistance to risk, change, and investment in employee training, are poor conduits of knowledge about new flowers or new consumer tastes. Relationships in the abundant chain, while not strictly impersonal, are seldom characterized by reciprocity or the sharing of risk and knowledge evident in the specialty chain. Instead supermarkets tend to use external networks of knowledgeable suppliers with whom they forge economic alliances rather than equilibrating relationships, in order to exchange products and displace risk.

Knowledge about consumers' tastes consequently remains untapped in supermarket systems. In some respects, then, this situation in U.S. supermarket retail does not accord with Daniel Miller's contention (1995a) that consumers engaged in weekly provisioning (supermarket shopping) shape the nature of demand—at least for this consumer good in this particular system of provision. Miller argues that consumers ultimately collude with producers to mold a "demand-led capitalism" that in turn leads to "a shift in power from production to consumption." Miller's mechanism for collusion is the consumer's choice registered at the checkout, or point of sale, through technology such as the scanable UPC that allow vertically integrated retailers to employ this information to "match exactly supply to demand" (1995, 7).

There are several reasons why this "collusion" is not evident in the trade of fresh-cut flowers in U.S. supermarket retail. Miller bases his argument on the four or five supermarket chains that dominate United Kingdom supermarket retailing. Of these, two supermarket chains (Tesco and Sainsbury) command 60–70 percent of supermarket retailing in prosperous southern England. Such limited competition may permit more latitude in floral selection and pricing and better tracking of consumer tastes. In the United States, however, the supermarket industry tends to be regional and far less consolidated and integrated than in the United Kingdom.[22] In 2000 there were about 30,000 supermarkets of which approximately one third were independent and the balance distributed among more than seventy-five chains.[23] By early 2005, despite a handful of publicized acquisitions, there were still over seventy supermarket chains. These individual and chain supermarkets often compete with each other on price and, as noted above, invest little in gathering knowledge, sourcing flowers, and training employees.

Another major difference contributing to different outcomes for producer-consumer collusion is that United Kingdom chains sometimes directly source their cut flowers. According to Alex Hughes, United Kingdom supermarket retailers must comply with the 1990 Food Safety Act and its requirement for traceability in the supply chain. This is an important reason why supermarket chains deal directly with flower farms in Kenya (and perhaps other places), a rare practice among U.S. supermarket chains.[24] Such supermarkets work primarily with two or three very large growers who can provide great quantities of flowers and be easily monitored and audited. These direct links afford British retailers such as Tesco better communication with growers and greater control over production and perhaps also over quality, pricing, and variety. Such retailers are thus in a far better position than their American counterparts to control what is produced for their stores. They are also apparently confident that they understand the "needs and requirements" of their customers (Hughes 2000, 185). Armed with such critical information and possibly, as Miller suggests, with "instant knowledge of the pattern of purchases" provided by "point of sale electronics" (1995, 4) these supermarkets seem well positioned to keep their customers happy.[25]

While this is seldom the case in the current U.S. system of cut flower provision, things may change. They could do so quite rapidly if Wal-Mart becomes more involved in flower retailing. Wal-Mart's enthusiasm for collecting and analyzing UPC data and restocking its shelves in response to local preferences (Dicker 2005) could do precisely what Miller suggests if applied to its cut flower sales. Theoretically, such data collection, combined with Wal-Mart's requirement that some suppliers use radio frequency identification

(RFID), could track and monitor flower shipments and their temperatures. Then its customers' flower choices and their quality could improve substantially and set new standards for other cut flower retailers. However, the current cost of implementing RFID—estimated at more than half a million dollars for a medium to large fresh produce supplier—probably puts the technology out of reach for the flower growers and middlemen supplying Wal-Mart stores.[26]

One effect of the failure to establish a close linkage between supply and consumer demand is evident in flower wastage (or "shrink," in the industry jargon). Each segment of the FCFGCC aims to keep its wastage well below 5 percent, but in supermarkets it averages 12 to 15 percent.[27] Fifteen percent waste would be unacceptable even in traditional cut flower retailing with its high markups. Ignorance of consumer wants is partly responsible. So is poor knowledge at the store level. Flowers are wasted when employees don't know when or which flowers to order or how to treat and care for them when they arrive. Flowers from Colombia, Ecuador, and other places (see chapter 4) are available at such low prices that it makes better economic sense to expend them—in the process of meeting the broader objective of attracting affluent, niche customers to the supermarket—than to invest in expensive employee training. Besides, some of the cost of wastage is eventually passed down the chain to growers in the form of the lower prices negotiated in later transactions. Yet high wastage and correspondingly poor flower department profits may be a factor in a reported trend toward reductions in employee and space allocation for supermarket floral departments.[28] As noted earlier, some mass-market retailers such as Costco solve this waste problem by refusing to take ownership of the flowers. Instead, bouquet-making wholesalers take full responsibility for the care and replacement of fading bouquets inside the store. Wholesalers are paid only for the bouquets that are sold. This seems to be a developing trend with more wholesalers now offering these costly, riskier services to supermarkets also.[29]

STRUCTURAL REORGANIZATION
AND VERTICAL INTEGRATION

As flower growing for the U.S. market became a global industry, competition between growers, traders, and retailers increased along with market differentiation and cycles of flower innovation. Historically, as noted in chapter 2, the U.S. flower industry was based on local networks of relationships. As production became global and risks multiplied, social flower networks also extended globally.[30] Throughout these developments there have been few examples of vertical integration in the industry either nationally or internationally. This contrasts with other horticultural commodities, such as fruits and vegetables, where a degree of vertical integration is common. Granovetter has pointed out that vertical integration is generally less likely to appear in industries where flexibility is required. Instead, networks are favored for mediating transactions, spreading risk, and generating standards of behavior between firms (1985, 503). Occasionally, large, vertically integrated corporations have attempted to participate in cut flower production and distribution but have seldom persisted, perhaps because they were insufficiently flexible.[31] Yet in the last years of the 1990s, three large corporations, USA Floral Products Inc., Dole Fresh Flowers, and Gerald Stevens Inc., attempted structural reorganization in the U.S. flower chain. These efforts to restructure the industry had various motivations but the suddenness of the trend and the scale of the attempts may support Harrison's contention that "in the context of a global system populated by big companies perpetually on the prowl for new profitable opportunities . . . the very success of a district can itself bring about changes that give rise to its opposite" (1997, 23). The success of Colombian flower growers and the Miami flower-trading district may have prompted some of these attempts at consolidation.

The following section focuses on two of the three restructuring efforts: USA Floral Products Inc. and Dole Fresh Flowers.[32] USA Floral Product's brief history is suggestive of the importance of relationships and knowledge of the system of provision. The formation of Dole Fresh Flowers, on the other hand, raises questions about the advantages of vertical integration versus network forms of organization in an industry where supply is plentiful, prices low, and flexible responses to unpredictable consumer shifts are desirable.

USA FLORAL PRODUCTS INC.

USA Floral Products Inc. was the creation of a businessman who had successfully formed US Office Products through consolidation. It emerged in 1997 in the heady days of abundant venture capital. USA Floral's objective was to acquire, control, and consolidate the Miami importer-wholesalers, bouquet-making companies, and regional wholesalers that supply supermarkets and traditional wholesalers. No doubt aware of abundant flower supplies, the company chose not to acquire any farms. Initially it honored the standing-order commitments of its newly acquired subsidiary importer-wholesalers, but gradually it would accept flowers from growers only on a consignment basis. Higher-quality growers refused to ship on consignment and sought other trading channels. Other flower growers responded to USA Floral's insistence on consignment flowers by tailoring their costs of production to the expected lower prices in a market increasingly dominated by a single buyer. Plants were closely spaced to produce more flower stems per square meter per year and given less fertilizer, thus yielding weak-stemmed blooms with smaller heads. Having undermined relationships with the better growers who found alternative chains for their flowers, USA Floral soon had access only to these low-quality consignment flowers. Distribution also slowed in this less-flexible corporate setting and flower quality declined. Traditional wholesale and supermarket customers ignored these poor-quality aging flowers and USA Floral's sales dropped. Returns on the venture capital invested in the enterprise were considered inadequate in a period when alternative investments could produce high returns. As performance declined, investment support was withdrawn.[33]

When USA Floral finally collapsed in 2001, Ecuadorian, Colombian, and other growers were owed millions of dollars and were left without a marketing system for their crops. Many sold their flowers on short notice at very poor prices. The numbers of importer-wholesalers increased substantially as displaced employees and growers without channels established their own importing-wholesaling firms, sometimes by buying subsidiaries of the former USA Floral enterprise. For some time, Latin American growers with poor networks suffered from this disruption in established systems of exchange. A few months after the collapse of USA Floral Inc., Peter Pearl, the 28th Street market traditional wholesaler, described some of the immediate consequences: "All of a sudden these growers have nowhere to ship their flowers, so they are really dumping. There is no market on carnations or poms [chrysanthemums]. Even on the holidays. When I worked here back in high school [about twenty years earlier] you would see South American pompons four dollars a bunch on Mother's Day. You can't get two dollars today. That is because people don't want them as much and the quantities coming in are incredible."

USA Floral Products crumbled partly because it failed to integrate its subsidiaries. It also ignored valuable entrepreneurial skills and carelessly disregarded the networks of relationships that smooth the flow of flowers in the specialty chain. Even before its collapse, predictions of its demise were plentiful. Bob Cone, a mid-sized NYMA wholesaler, was one of several who shared his views on USA Floral during its rise and fall. Bob declared it would never succeed because "the flower industry is too personal, it is too entrepreneurial, and there are too many factors and too many farms. There are thousands of farms and thousands of varieties of flowers." What many outsiders don't understand, he continued, is that "it is not like growing peas or potatoes."

Resentment of USA Floral Products derived in some instances from its executives' disdain of the carefully acquired knowledge and experience and the system of relationships that had sustained the chain prior to their arrival. " 'I don't know anything about flowers,' these businessmen said to me," recalled Alyssa, the bouquet-making wholesaler, whose previous firm was merged into USA Floral Inc., "as if it was an irrelevant female thing and they had this superior business knowledge." Sandra Webb, another Miami importer-wholesaler, predicted that corporate consolidations like the USA Floral project would fail because "it is a [business of] tremendously personal relationships—you can't just depend on numbers—it is the personal network of relationships in the floral industry." Consolidators fail, Sandra continued, because they "try to turn it into a cookie cutter."

Many seemed to view USA Floral's collapse not just as an affirmation of the importance of their knowledge but as testimony to the value of their individual ethics, commitments, and relationships. "A lot of relationships [are] built into this industry," agreed Daniel Burnett, whose family operates a long-established flower-trucking service. "With USA Floral and Gerald Stevens it became [only] the dollar."

DOLE FRESH FLOWERS

The risks associated with global competition, accelerating new flower cycles, and poor information are often most burdensome for growers (see chapter 5). This raises questions about trading firms that choose to become producers of flowers rather than acquire them through some form of contract or a "spot," or current flower market that is widely acknowledged to have abundant supplies and stable prices. By becoming growers, traders increase the possibility of profit through more efficient exchange of knowledge and reduced transaction costs, yet they also concentrate the risks of exchanging fresh flowers in one firm rather than spreading them among many.

In 1998 the Dole Corporation bought four large flower farms in Colombia, together with one of the largest importer-wholesale establishments in Miami, and formed a new subsidiary, Dole Fresh Flowers.[34] It is responsible for about 20 percent of flower imports into Miami, but every year the Fresh Flowers division, while still a public company, posted "disappointing" earnings and sustained losses. Like USA Floral Inc. and Gerald Stevens Inc., Dole Fresh Flowers eventually replaced the original management of its purchased flower businesses with new managers from Dole Food Company Inc.'s California headquarters. The new managers, of course, had little experience with flower growing or trading, and since its formation Dole Fresh Flowers has had a succession of chief executive officers.

Dole Fresh Flowers supplies supermarkets and traditional wholesale florists and, in 2002, opened a $30 million headquarters, warehouse, and processing center in Miami. For many companies, such an investment might create pressure to increase volume or product range to help amortize the investment. However, the parent company, Dole Food Company Inc., has vast resources and its chairman, David Murdock, was confident in March 2002 that "we will become the dominant seller, marketer and growers of flowers in the United States."[35] Early in 2003, Murdock paid $2.5 billion to purchase all of Dole Food Company Inc.'s stock, making him its sole owner and freeing him of "the short-term pressures and constraints of the public equities markets" and incidentally the need to operate profitably in the short term.[36] It is possible that a vertically integrated flower growing and trading company like Dole Fresh Flowers, with enormous resources, huge investment in flower transportation logistics, and apparent commitment, may be able to capture a large market share and dominate the industry. In that case it may also be able to correct one of the industry's long-term problems by increasing fresh-cut flower consumption through sustained advertising (see chapter 8). Yet it would also need to be nimble and responsive to shifts in consumer tastes and practices.

As noted in chapter 6, Dole Fresh Flowers initially attempted to extend its vertical strategies through the chain by reaching consumers through its consumer website, Flowernet.com. The site offered boxes of Dole flowers to be arranged by recipients but was suspended after a few years, possibly because the majority of Internet flower purchases are intended as gifts and buyers overwhelmingly prefer flowers arranged in vases and other containers.[37] Dole Fresh Flowers may also have encountered some of the difficulties associated with branding implied by the sale of its own flowers at its dedicated website. Branding is a much-discussed issue in flower growing. Some think of it as a way of increasing the visibility and market power of quality growers who hope that retailers (or even consumers) will ask for their flowers by farm or grower name or, at least, by country. Others say that branding is irrelevant for flowers because they are so perishable and people judge and buy purely on the freshness or openness of the flower at first sight. In fact, only a few growers specifically brand their flowers, because they must be certain that quality will not suffer on the trip to the consumer. Indeed, I have found expiring bunches of zombie-like flowers at convenience stores sadly bearing the brand labels of growers I know to be excellent. Rio Roses, an importer-wholesaler, is a recent example of a firm planning to advertise its brand to increase awareness among consumers. Yet the inability to distinguish any difference—except degree of freshness—between roses of the same species and variety, whether branded or not, is widespread and a substantial hurdle to branding. As one retailer put it in a recent industry magazine interview, "I can't tell the difference between a Rio Rose and a rose."[38]

The persistence of a large-scale producer like Dole Fresh Flowers and large buyers like Wal-Mart and Sam's Club may eventually determine pricing and consequently the types and qualities of flowers that are produced by a shrinking number of growers.[39] This in turn could reestablish a tendency toward uniformity and limited choice for many American cut flower consumers. Nevertheless, flower prices are likely to remain far lower and choice far greater for the majority than they were twenty years earlier.

There is some precedent for a degree of vertical integration in the fresh flower chain. Several larger Colombian and Ecuadorian growers have established their own importing-wholesaling firms in Miami. Such small-scale forward linkages in the chain have continued to evolve and have usually been based on close personal, ethnic, and kin relationships that reduce the risks and uncertainties of distribution and marketing.[40] Individual wholesalers have also attempted backward linkages. Some became investors or partners in flower farms either to ensure consistent supply or because, as the importer-wholesaler Fred Berents explained, "I could not find enough growers who went along with my ideas about what to grow for the future."[41]

These smaller vertical linkages appear successful. However, in some respects the objectives of growers and wholesalers conflict since growers want to sell at high prices and wholesalers want to buy at the low prices—sometimes leading to internal differences between the grower partner and the wholesaler partner. It appears that wholesaler involvement in growing to orchestrate larger counterseasonal production of specialty flowers or to ensure access to newest varieties (generally high-value flowers) is helpful because in that case a supply of special blooms rather than the lowest price is the wholesaler's objective. But when innovative linkages are formed simply to ensure supply at low prices, the benefits, in light of the vast global production, have been doubtful. As Grady Smith, an experienced NYMA traditional wholesaler who had invested in Ecuadorian farms, explained it, "The reason we became growers was to ensure a consistent supply chain with quality and volumes from the nursery. In retrospect it was a serious error. Because the economics of growing are such that often it is cheaper to buy the stuff from other growers." After a moment, Grady added, "If I had a chance to make that decision again, I would not have done what I did. There are no real advantages in this business to being a grower as a wholesaler."

Commodities and Identities

In the FCFGCC—as with other contemporary global commodity trading systems (Boden 2000; Bestor 2001; Freidberg 2004)—social relationships, technological innovation, and specialized knowledge help shape new global social and cultural interactions. Innovations, networks, and above all the knowledge that diffuses through the specialty chain or is sold as expertise in the abundant chain have all been instrumental in the expanding importance of middlemen in the FCFGCC. But much of this knowledge is developed and shared through social networks of middlemen rather than through electronic data collection and analysis. Even in the abundant chain, serving a broad market of flower consumers, electronically gathered information about consumer preferences is, at the time of writing, either very limited or trapped within chain segments. Such behavior lends little support to Miller's (1995) contention about the mechanisms for collusion between consumers and producers—at least for this particular commodity.

Current behavior in the networked specialty chain of the FCFGCC also seems to contradict Castells's contention that because networks—which he sees as the basic component of the informational society, displacing individuals as well as collectivities such as corporations—are altered by "each strategic decision, creating a patchwork of experiences and interests" (1996, 199), they have an insubstantial, ephemeral cultural component.[42] In the system examined here, individuals have not been displaced. They are the basic unit of a networked system. They skillfully develop and deploy their knowledge to mediate between the distinctively different interests and knowledge of con-

Risk and Relationships

sumers and growers. Many of them speak of obligation and reciprocity, tailoring behavior and decisions according to a broadly understood reciprocal code of conduct. Even in the abundant chain, where personal trading relationships are weaker, there are economic and practical incentives for maintaining common standards of ethical behavior.

The power to communicate cultural change, shape taste, and push innovation in design and favored flowers in new directions, and its accompanying economic benefits, rests with elite traditional and freelance floral designers and some traditional wholesale florists. These cultural communicators are numerically tiny in terms of the entire U.S. flower system but are a significant force in the NYMA. Their networks of relationships are pivotal in the exchange of knowledge and the command of a varied supply of favored flowers from the global garden. To a degree, the cultural component in this network is linked to the identity of the "things" being traded and of the individuals responsible for their exchange. The journey from grower to consumer reshapes both the identity of the flower and the identities of those to whom it is entrusted. Kopytoff observes that a commodity may be seen as such by one person, and at the same time, "as something else by another." Such shifts in the commodity's ascription reveal "a moral economy that stands behind the objective economy of visible transactions" (1986, 64). The biography of the global flower is, as Kopytoff has suggested for other commodities, a story "of classifications and reclassifications in an uncertain world of categories whose importance shifts with every minor change of context" (90).

With branding uncommon, most flowers are progressively deterritorialized on their journey to the consumer. At each stage of exchange flowers may be reinscribed with the identity of the individual who currently bears their intrinsic risk until they are finally and fully inscribed as part of the identity of the consumer (see chapter 8). In conversation, flowers proceeding along the specialty chain metamorphose from grower—"Jorge Vélez Serrano's lilies"—to importer-wholesaler—"Fred Berents's lilies." A florist referring to her traditional wholesale florist supplier might say, "I always get my roses from Peter Pearl or from John at ABC Flowers." Once in possession of the flowers, a retail florist, while arranging them, will often refer to them as "my flowers." Finally, a consumer may concur with this ascription by referring to them as the florist's flowers, as in "I usually get my flowers from Betty at Parkway Florist." This process of reinscription is probably peculiar to flower exchange. Even in the abundant chain, a supermarket produce manager may show a preference for "Alyssa's bouquets" although more often the bouquet is simply "the product" described by the bouquet-maker Faith Bickell in chapter 6. The personal nature of the risk assumed and degree of care invested in each exchange are probably factors in this phenomenon. But one effect is the total mystification—or fetishization—not only of the relations of production but also of much of the exchange process. Consumers rarely regard the flowers they buy as commodities. Instead, as discussed in the following chapter, they impart yet another new identity to the flowers, often imagining their origins in local nurseries and tangling the history of the blooms they buy with childhood experiences of people, gardens, nature, and rural life.

In the specialty chain (and to some extent in the abundant chain) the terms of exchange often involve a moral equilibrating component that opens up possibilities of negotiation about ethics and relationships as well as price. Middlemen construct aspects of their identities in these personal relations through their negotiations and gifts of knowledge and their promises and ability to fulfill them. Thus in constructing trading relationships that reduce risk, a trader's identity assumes great significance. His identity is defined by his ethics, behavior, morals, and social category—class, nationality, social networks, or kinship.[43] "The drama here," as Kopytoff (1986, 90) puts it, "lies in the uncertainties of valuation and identity," both of the commodity and the traders themselves.

At the end of the flower's journey consumers employ it in their own processes of constructing and sustaining relationships and shaping group and individual identity. These final stages in the life of the flower and the concluding relationship between flowers and their final consumers are examined in the next chapter.

191

Eight

Self and Signs: Flower Consumers

Fragrant 'General Jacqueminot' and 'Maréchal Niel' roses disappeared from New York florists shops years ago. Their heady scent, an indicator of short floral life, ensured their departure from the flower trade. The new cut flower chain wanted long-lived sturdy blossoms that survive journeys from California, Colombia, and Ecuador. Scentless but exquisitely colored hybrid roses supplanted them. Lizzie Hazeldean's silvery-pink rose metamorphosed into a dozen tones of violet, fifty hues of salmon, four dozen tints of delicate pink, and a hundred shades of red. Luxuriant rose bouquets of deep maroon or pale ivory tinged with mineral pink entice today's strollers on city sidewalks. Brilliantly colored blooms also appeal to busy supermarket shoppers or peek demurely through the windows of traditional florist shops. These new roses brighten dim tables in luxury restaurants or form bouquets that duplicate or complement the hue of any bridesmaid's dress. These roses did not exist thirty years ago. Then, people chose their roses from a few varieties and a handful of colors and used them for obligatory cultural purposes—funerals, birthdays, and weddings. But few desired flowers for themselves.

Practices: Shaping the Self

In earlier chapters we saw how new flowers evolved with competitive global flower growing and trading. Consumers' changing tastes and practices rippled through the Fresh Cut Flower Global Commodity Chain, prompting shifts in growers' activities. In this chapter I begin by examining these consumer tastes and practices and seek to understand why and how they are changing. Then I briefly explore the way the magazine industry influences some consumers as they formulate the meaning and significance of fresh flowers in their lives. Ultimately, what and how we consume, the way we employ consumption for our own purposes, resisting standardization, ignoring commercial messages, and deriving satisfaction and pleasure from the work of consuming, is an individual matter.[1] This, I argue, is as true for choosing, buying, and using flowers as it is for other forms of consuming.[2]

CONSUMPTION AND IDENTITY

Consumption is simultaneously a social and cultural activity and an economic activity. In contemporary societies, goods, like clothes, cars, and fresh flowers, help to make visible the intangible understandings of culture and help organize societies by classifying people into recognizable groups.[3] In these processes special meanings become attached to consumer goods. Theorists debate whether consumers themselves are active in establishing the cultural meaning and value of the goods and commodities that populate their materials worlds. For some authors, consumers are simply the inactive terminus of the commodity chain. They are represented as passive, manipulated recipients of ideas offered by advertisers, marketers, and producers of goods (Harvey 1989; Rutz and Orlove 1989; Appadurai 1990; Firat 1991). Others consider consumers to be active agents in both market systems and the construction of commodities, suggesting that their shifting values and related choices influence what is produced and marketed (Schneider 1994; du Gay 1997; Campbell 2005). Miller points specifically to the cultural changes of the 1970s. These, he writes, prompted consumers to reject the homogenized commodities typical in previous decades of modernism.[4] As consumers sought more diversity and difference in commodities and services, producers developed new technologies and products to satisfy and profit from these demands (Miller 1997, 60).

I share the view of Miller, du Gay, Campbell, and others that consumers help to establish the social and cultural value of particular goods in their daily practices. (Mintz 1985; Miller 1995; du Gay 1997; Miller 1998; Campbell 2005). The meanings invested in commodities are particularly important to consumers living in complex contemporary societies that offer many messages but insufficient guidance for what is normal. People seek to build consensus and distill the normal from their own consumer practices, the media industries, and the behavior of others (Miller 2001). They also collude with producers, distributors, and marketers to mold the meanings of goods directly through the ways they use them in their everyday lives.

Consumers of fresh flowers help to confirm the meanings and cultural value of flowers by discarding certain flower customs and adopting or extend-

193

ing others. For example, one increasing practice is the presentation of a bouquet of flowers as a publicly agreed sign of respect, acknowledging exceptional achievement in athletic, artistic, or academic endeavors. This bouquet-giving ritual occurs in many settings, including at Olympic Games and at graduations (see figure 31). Today it has been revived and extended to encompass all kinds of performances and levels of achievement including children's ballet recitals and middle school musical concerts.[5] Another example is the way people ignore, accept, or reject the flower holidays promoted by floral retailers. Many are proposed but consumers adopt and celebrate only those few that are significant to them as individuals or as part of a community. Valentine's Day wins approval, but what about Secretaries Day or Mother-in-Law's Day?[6] Through such practices and customs, fresh flowers join a whole range of goods infused with meanings in early-twenty-first-century life. They come to have value as commonly understood signs. They become part of stories we tell ourselves and others about who we are, where we belong, and the lives we would like to live. They help to create and sustain identities.

The notion of identity, as we think of it today, emerged in the early twentieth century as identity was seen as a fluid, rather than a fixed, aspect of the self. For middle-class women, consumption and its promise of "sensory excitement, sexual expressiveness, and emotional release" challenged the fixity of a Victorian ideal of identity (or true womanhood) achieved through work and self-denial (Traube 1996, 140–41). What "being a person means" changed as consuming goods became a commonplace activity (Mintz 1985, 214). Female identity gradually came to be a "matter of merchandising and performance . . . built around commodities, style and personal magnetism" (Peiss 1996, 312). This identity evolution gained strength after World War II in concert with the freedom "gained when the standard social hierarchies, ideologies and the deeply conventionalized politics and morality that characterized a previous cultural era . . . dissolved under the steady processes of consumer and social democratization" (Lee 1993, 164). By the end of the twentieth century, individuals were fully engaged in self-creation (Giddens 1991).

Identity today is an aspect of lifestyle.[7] Contemporary individuals often participate in multiple lifestyles and in the corresponding behavior and identities that are appropriate for home, work, clubbing, and so on. To add to the ongoing narrative or story they construct about themselves—a story that may be revised sometimes in quite small ways, to maintain coherence—individuals braid together strands taken from lots of materials, sources, and discourses.

Chapter Eight

31 Olympic medalists. Photo: Charlie Booker.

Roles, fantasies, traditions, collective memory, and ideas derived from media and advertising and from consuming itself—all are part of this active process of constructing and maintaining the self and the self's story (Bourdieu 1984; McCracken 1988; Lee 1993; Bowlby 1996; Mintz 1996; Castells 1997; Slater 1997; Miller 2001; Campbell 2005).

While indisputably creative, self-creation is not a smooth or simple process. A number of theorists point out the difficulties and demands of the struggle to create a coherent experience of the self in the face of tendencies to standardize experience and consumption (Giddens 1991). As individuals engage in a search for fundamental reassurance about who they are and how they fit in, they experience a loss of "fully centred subjectivity" (Lee 1993, 165). The possibility of plural identities and lifestyles is itself "a source of stress and contradiction in both self-representation and social action" (Castells 1997, 6) because it requires each of us "to compose individually the continuity which society can no longer assure or even promise" (Bauman 2001, 24). Popular media reprocesses this condition of uncertainty, indefinition, and anxiety as marketers, producers, advertisers, and editors offer consuming as a solution. For example, some magazines now present traditional gender roles as an ideal while others celebrate the flexibility, autonomy, and bricolage of modern urban existence (Gauntlett 2002). Magazine readers may seek discursive guidance for either lifestyle perspective by gleaning ideas from *Martha Stewart Living, Real Simple,* or *Paper.*

Creation of identity is an activity fundamental to several of today's widespread fresh flower practices. But as we will see in the following sections, concern about pleasure, status, and belonging are also woven into the contemporary culture of flowers.

THE UNAMBIGUOUS SIGN

Contemporary Americans draw on three main sources of inspiration when they use fresh flowers for identity creation and other cultural purpose: media metaphors, personal background, and floral tradition. Advertisers, marketers, magazine editors, and filmmakers draw on traditional meanings when they employ floral imagery as metaphors for luxury, femininity, sexuality, status, romance, community, life-cycles, and kinship. These meanings, commonly shared and constantly recirculated, have been extended into new cultural practices, but they have undergone little fundamental revision over the last century. Flowers are thus visible, unambiguous symbols of meanings that are widely understood but rarely altered by the industries employing them and seldom changed by consumers themselves.[8] This symbolic stability is one of the attractions of fresh flowers for cultural purposes, especially when compared to the contested and manipulated meaning and symbolism of many other commodities.

Widely shared, traditional floral practices are also a factor in contemporary flower usage. People learn through collective and individual experiences that flowers are appropriate at weddings or funerals, or as a gift to signal love or to comfort the sick. People draw on their awareness of these collective floral traditions—sometimes without much previous direct personal experience of them—to shape their own flower-consuming behavior.[9]

Personal background is a third critical factor in involvement with fresh flowers, as it is with other goods. This encompasses all those individual elements of upbringing, education, and background that contribute to identity, a sense of social place, and the tastes for particular things.[10] These components of identity help condition the value and cultural relevance of fresh flowers in an individual's life. A taste for flowers as domestic decorations, for example, depends "on your class" according to Louis Varmus, a floral designer. In Louis's early life "we had flowers [growing] in back but no appreciation to bring them into the house in that way. Other things affecting us were a little bit more important," Louis recalled, noting, "You must have the leisure to see and think about that. If you are thinking about putting bread on the table you are not giving much thought to flowers." Indeed, a 1991 investigation of flower consumers in Pennsylvania confirmed the class aspects of involvement with flowers. The study suggested that knowledge of flower types—itself a distinctive form of what Bourdieu (1984) calls "cultural capital"—is heavily weighted to the educated, upper-middle, and upper classes (Behe and Wolnick 1991).

Drawing on these sources—media metaphors, personal background, and floral traditions—for inspiration, Americans today use flowers in various activities that are symbolically intensified with abundant flowers. Among the most popular of these activities are decorating their homes with flowers, giving gifts of flowers, and using them in rituals such as weddings and, to a lesser extent, funerals. These practices bring sensuality, pleasure, and luxury into people's lives and help to shape aspects of their own and others' identities and social worlds. They are explored in the following sections.

FRAGRANCE, MEMORY, AND SENSUALITY

People want floral fragrance. When we approach flowers, a common response is to sniff the blooms and smile. People seem to seek—and receive—a shot of pleasure from the scent of a flower. A recent study suggests that floral fragrance (evident in many manufactured perfumes) induces pleasure especially when combined with the symmetry evident in most flowers. Indeed, humans are thought to be "biologically primed to associate flowers with happiness." Furthermore, the "sensory elements of flowers . . . such as visual symmetry, color, odor, and pheromones . . . affect moods" (Haviland-Jones et al. 2005).[11] Women put fragrant flowers in their living rooms and at their bedsides, claiming they make a difference in mood and to the way they feel in general. Megan Webster, a journalist in her mid-twenties living in lower Manhattan, recalled the pleasure induced by the fragrant flowers in her wedding bouquet as it lay by the bedside on her wedding night. "We slept with the smell of these gorgeous flowers—the lilac and the gardenia." Megan remembered, "As the gardenia dies the smell becomes more pronounced."

Sometimes the mood inspired by floral scent is linked to particular memories. Megan is especially fond of gardenias and lavender because they were grown by her mother and grandmother. Their fragrances, she explained, "are a connection to home and make me happy." Other women also spoke of memories of childhood or happy relationships revived by lilacs, peonies, and other scented flowers.[12]

Both men and women react to the presence of fresh flowers with smiles and pleasure despite the widespread understanding that women are more responsive than men to flowers and emotion (Haviland-Jones et al. 2005). Statistically, however, men buy few flowers for their own homes or their own enjoyment, probably because of the strong associations of flowers and the home with femininity. Limited availability in some parts of the United States may also be a factor. In the NYMA inexpensive flowers tempt men at convenience stores, in seasonal fresh markets, and in supermarkets. In my interviews, some men easily admitted to buying flowers for themselves for sheer pleasure. As one middle-aged market stroller put it, "I just think flowers are beautiful." Other men, however, made a point of disassociating themselves from the flowers I observed them buying, carefully explaining they weren't flower people themselves but were buying for wives or girlfriends.

People also use flowers to induce feelings of happiness in other ways. Giving themselves a little reward or a "treat"—to use Miller's (1998) term—by buying flowers on the way out of the supermarket or on the way home from work acts as a self-reward, especially among women, possibly because they are more receptive to shaping self-identity through pleasure and consumption.[13] Cheap visible and accessible flowers make treats easier and probably more frequent. Sidney Krauss, a retiree who divides his time between New York and Florida, explained how cut flowers had now become a part of his life. He and his wife buy flowers at their supermarket "on impulse if we see something we like. It is just so easy because they are there. I can pick up a quart of milk and there are the flowers." Once Sidney purchased flowers only occasionally from florists for gifts, but today, he explained, he buys them often because "they are lovely to have and to look at. I am partial to it. Be nice to have flowers all the time." Sidney is not all that unusual. Once I brought up the subject, several older men acknowledged that with retirement and increased leisure they had begun buying flowers regularly as a means of enhancing their homes and bringing pleasure to their daily lives. In all cases, convenience and the low cost of the flowers (from supermarkets, big box stores, and corner convenience stores) were important factors in their frequent purchases. Sidney's wife, Patricia, offered her view that buying flowers is "an impulse thing, especially for women. At the end of their big shop they will say, I am going to have this for me." For at least some of these consumers, buying flowers for themselves seems to be a way of caring for the self and of making a home for the self both materially and symbolically.[14]

Yet for other shoppers I spoke to, fresh flowers remain something desired and pleasing but rarely purchased for themselves or others.[15] People under twenty-five, for example, are statistically less likely to buy flowers, perhaps because of limited discretionary income. People over fifty, on the other hand, are more likely than younger people to regard fresh flowers as a seasonal, limited luxury. In some cases these ideas seem conditioned by youthful notions of flowers as an expensive luxury. They may also be part of a continuing concern among older shoppers about the ephemeral, nonutilitarian, wasteful nature of flowers that Goody (1993) attributes to a persistence of "puritanical ideas, especially in America."[16] Geographic location and limited access to cheaper flowers may also be factors. In my interviews, these ideas about seasonality and luxury seemed slightly more prevalent in suburban areas where retail sites are fewer and flowers are more expensive. The cheaper flowers offered in urban convenience stores appeared to encourage flower buying among those who formerly had considered them a luxury. Furthermore, some people may prefer to continue to regard fresh flowers as a rarity or luxury. In that way, flowers retain their value as a special reward for the self, or a special gift that also implies sacrifice on the giver's part.

DOMESTIC DECORATION

American women buy flowers for themselves more often than in the past. Today, most buy at supermarkets or convenience stores. Sales of flowers for home decoration in U.S. supermarkets increased by about 40 percent between 1993 and 2000 (see figure 32).[17] It is reasonable to assume similar growth in sales at convenience stores.[18] Megan Webster explained, "I like choosing my own flowers [and] . . . those stalls are pretty hard to go past and not buy something." Lily Fable, an advertising executive in her late twenties, began to buy flowers only after moving to New York. "They are cheaper here. For five dollars you can get a really nice little bouquet. It is nice to be able to buy flowers." Both Megan and Lily chose flowers for their apartments at convenience stores, often "when people are coming to visit" because, as Lily explained, "it looks as if you are excited about them coming." This added social dimension—using flowers to communicate an emotion to others rather than buying them strictly for oneself—may make it easier to justify the expenditure.

Megan, Lily, and Sidney, along with many others I spoke to, enjoyed choosing flowers for their home; they believe fresh flowers transform domestic space. Flowers have become a component of Sidney's conception of his home and his pleasure in it. "It makes a difference to me to have flowers in the

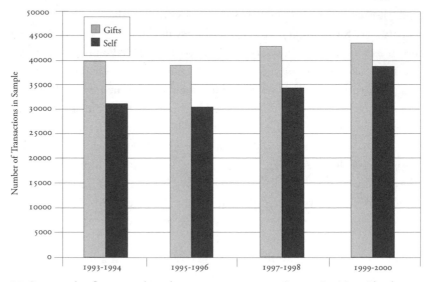

32 Supermarket flower purchases by purpose, 1993–2000. Source: American Floral
Endowment's Florastats Consumer Tracking Study 2001.

apartment, it enhances it," he explained. Megan too valued the beauty fresh
flowers brought to her home but also commented on the perceived health
benefits of flowers and plants as "better for the air. I think plants in the house
make the air cleaner . . . [they bring] humidity into the air. I just think it is
better for you." Others spoke of the importance of bringing nature, represented by fresh flowers, into their homes and lives.

Younger people were more conscious than older buyers of selecting flowers
for themselves to express an aspect of identity. Megan noted how flowers, and
the act of buying them herself, changed both her emotions and her conception of herself. "[If] I'm feeling miserable I go and buy some flowers . . . and it
cheers me up. It makes me feel a bit more like a homemaker. It makes me feel a
little bit more grown up and as if I am looking after myself and creating a little
nest." Sam Springer, a postgraduate student in his early thirties who had also
recently moved to Manhattan, was quite explicit about their value for self-
construction, noting that "flowers have a sense of celebration to me because of
the colors and everything." He went on, "I think you really are marking your
space that way. By putting something into it that you have chosen that you
feel perhaps is a piece of you."

Sam's ideas and behavior represent a refashioned idea of appropriate male interests and practices with respect to fresh flowers. This may be an urban phenomenon, guided by changing conceptions of maleness in new men's magazines (Gauntlett 2002) and television programs celebrating flexibility in the gendered nature of the self. Sometimes the identity constructed with fresh flowers deliberately contrasts with an earlier self. For Sam, flowers are a luxury from which he derives pleasure but they are also "a way of distinguishing yourself from your background." His childhood home was a place where fresh flowers were never purchased because "flowers would die in three or four days so to them [my family] it was a waste of money." Instead, he explained, "We had plastic." Older people like Sidney Krauss were less explicit about shaping the self, perhaps because at his age—mid-sixties—identity is more fixed than in younger people. His focus was on the pleasure derived from his flower purchases, especially color. "Color appeals to me. They have some beautiful colors and I look for things that will go with our color scheme."

Much flower-consuming behavior seemed learned from older women. Mothers, aunts, and most of all, grandmothers commonly inspired a delight in having flowers in the domestic space and a desire for certain flowers in particular. Class also shaped floral experience. A solidly middle-class background drew more often on pleasant childhood floral memories. Perhaps not surprisingly, considering the long history of associating flowers with women and the domestic sphere, these recollections were highly gendered; invariably women recalled and related their childhood experiences with older female relatives.

GIFTS OF FLOWERS

Lily likes to give flowers for birthdays, sickness, and other customary occasions. During one period when I spoke to her, she had recently given flowers to a sick grandmother in the hospital, to her boss who was leaving the firm, and to her boyfriend after a quarrel. Megan too gives gifts of flowers for birthdays, and "when people have babies and things like that. I get so much pleasure out of choosing beautiful flowers for them." Megan expressed a view common among givers of flower gifts: "It is not just . . . nice for me, I think it makes people happy . . . women love receiving a bunch of flowers—it makes them feel as if they are loved, I think."[19] Although Lily and Megan may not have thought about it in this way, their gifts perform social functions. Bringing flowers to the sick and giving flowers in thanks for a dinner invitation are ways of acknowledging social obligation. Gifts also construct social solidarity by appropriately recognizing ritually important occasions such as births. Such gifts also shape the boundaries of social groups through inclusion and exclusion.

Gifts also offer the recipient a particular conception of his or her identity through implied characteristics. Frequently, floral gifts confirm a gendered role such as mother, wife, secretary, or hostess and signal a "feminine" aspect of identity such as sensitivity, creativity, or desirability. When these gifts are visibly consumed—as most gifts of flowers are when they are prominently displayed—they communicate information about the giver and the receiver including social location and roles, group membership, taste, and identity (Scammon et al. 1982; Lamont and Molnár 2001).[20] Fresh flowers—simple, ephemeral, and with no practical use—embody many of the characteristics of the ideal gift (Carrier 1995). They communicate sentiment rather than utility or monetary value. (Although signaling extravagant expenditure may be part of the message embedded in some floral gifts; see below.) Because flowers fade quickly their ephemerality implies no obligation. These qualities are perhaps one of the reasons why gifts of flowers are increasing in the United States. As other floral practices have declined—especially religious observations such as Easter and extended funeral rites—gift giving has expanded.

Florists welcome this growth in gift giving. "Today about sixty to seventy percent of our business is everyday [gifts] . . . birthdays, anniversaries, somebody wanting to send flowers," said George Henning, a suburban Westchester florist, as he explained the transformations of the last twenty years. For the Brooklyn florist Wayne Collman, the three major gift-giving holidays are "Mother's Day, Valentine's, and Christmas." In Wayne's changing neighborhood, "Thanksgiving has become almost a nonholiday and Easter less and less important every year." Funerals and weddings constitute about 50 percent of Wayne's work and "the rest is gifts."[21] In New York City today the popularly observed flower festivals are often secular and they celebrate the individual. This contrasts with the predominantly collective and religious observations of a century earlier when Easter ruled the floral calendar. Valentine's Day is now the busiest flower day of the year, followed by Mother's Day and Secretaries' Day.[22] All require gifts. Valentine's Day is immensely popular even in poorer and immigrant neighborhoods. "[This neighborhood is] now ninety percent Latinos" observed Richard Hopper, a Queens florist, as he explained his shifting customer base and their practices. "Valentine's has grown all of a sudden, just like that, in the last ten years. A lot of lovers out there, especially the Spanish people."

Observing St. Valentine's Day has a long tradition but became more important after 1900.[23] The *New York Times* noted the local popularity of giving cards, flowers, and candies as early as February 9, 1908. By 1911 the *Weekly Florists' Review* was encouraging its readership to promote and advertise this holiday to the flower-buying public. Growing consumerism and a popular emphasis on romantic love in the twentieth century were also important factors in this holiday's growth.[24] Bunches of fragrant purple violets were common St. Valentine's Day gifts to young women until well into the 1930s.[25] Roses too were desired, but their cultivation required more costly heat and light. Production lagged behind demand in the early twentieth century. As farmers in California and Colorado began to produce abundant quantities of a few flower species, red roses and red carnations emerged as the favored flowers for Valentine's Day. In 1969 the Catholic Church removed St. Valentine's Day from its official liturgical calendar, but this did not diminish commercial and popular enthusiasm for the holiday now secularly known as Valentine's Day.[26] However, as Richard Hopper noted, substantial growth in this flower holiday came in the 1980s and 1990s with increased flower imports, declining prices, and the greater visibility of flowers on New York streets.

New York City is fertile ground for romantic love. Manhattan has an unusually large population of single people for whom romance has special significance. NYMA florists and restaurants promote Valentine's Day heavily, while magazines and newspapers suggest ways to celebrate and ideas for gifts. The *New York Times* offers at least one love-related article each February, as it has done every year since the 1920s. Even the sober *Wall Street Journal* has given a nod to the holiday of love.[27] A February 15 survey of a class of seventeen undergraduate students in New York City in 2005 revealed that fifteen had exchanged gifts or acknowledged Valentine's Day in some fashion. Twelve had exchanged cards and eight had exchanged gifts of flowers including a tiny fraction of the 120 million red roses sold in the United States for Valentine's Day (out of an approximate total of 350 million roses and other flowers). At an average national price of $73 for a dozen roses arranged in a vase (up from $63 in 1998), expressions of love were not cheap.[28] In New York, however, they could be purchased for far less at city convenience stores and suburban supermarkets, where a dozen red roses (without vase) were offered for $20 and sometimes less. Men bought most of these flowers and the great majority gave them to a partner or desired partner. By 2004, however, women's flower purchases for Valentine's Day had grown to about 35 percent of the total. They gave to their mothers, daughters, and other female kin as well as to friends. Sometimes they simply enjoyed the flowers themselves.[29] Fewer than 20 percent of their floral gifts were intended for husbands or male partners.[30] They were changing the nature of the holiday with gifts that nurture largely nonromantic relationships.[31]

These gifts of flowers also announce community and *belonging* since they are usually exchanged within a relatively small kin, social, or professional group. This claim to belong to a particular social or kin group is an important aspect of the exchange. Participating in the Valentine holiday itself and the community solidarity participation expresses may also be a factor, especially in large urban settings where relationships are sometimes impersonal.

Finally, choosing and giving a gift of flowers for this widely shared holiday is uncomplicated and raises little anxiety about misunderstood signs. For almost everyone red roses (or other red blooms) will unambiguously signal romantic love. All other flowers generally indicate other forms of love and relationship.

Whatever type of the love is being acknowledged with such gifts, its expression has, according to Miller, become more complex and demanding. Miller argues that "love today is a practice or technology of care and intimacy in which extreme sensitivity to the particular individual object of our love is at a premium" and the quality of the love is equated to some degree with detailed effort in its expression (2001b, 184).

Conversations with flower buyers pointed both to the importance of gifts of flowers in nurturing relationships and, in some cases, to the care put into selection. The growing abundance of floral choice appears to have increased the complexity of expression. A careful choice of flowers is a way of illuminating the giver's sensitivity to enigmatic signals about the nature of the relationship and the identities of giver and receiver communicated by the gift. Lily Fable, for example, described how she "bought flowers for [my boyfriend] twice when we had a fight. Because I felt bad I was being kind of unreasonable. I bought him tulips because roses seemed a little bit like—you wouldn't give roses for a fight really unless it was a really bad fight I guess—and the other stuff seemed too friendly. I thought tulips seemed a little bit in-between, a little romantic, but not like red roses, you know—so Valentine's Day or something."

Lily's care in selection and concern about the messages sent by her gift choice is not uncommon among flower buyers with a certain level of flower knowledge and a degree of self-awareness. My interviews suggest that shoppers are attracted to new flowers or to familiar flowers in new colors and they will buy a novel flower for themselves. However, they seem less likely to choose unknown flowers for gifts. They look with suspicion on unfamiliar flowers or those that seem to introduce ambiguity into the symbolism of their gift. Recently developed "black roses" are an example. Introduced in the late 1990s, black roses are very dark red rather than truly black and generally are rarer and more costly than other roses. By 2000 they were gaining in popularity as gifts for men because, as some florists observed, the color imparted "a masculine edge" and for Valentine's Day implied sentiments that were not "too mushy." Some giftgivers, however, were reluctant to embrace the new bloom. "You've got to be careful who you give black roses to," noted one potential flower buyer in a *New York Times* report. "I think black roses send a real message," he continued, "and I'm not sure what that message is exactly."[32]

On the other hand, my interviews suggested that certain groups of people are more apt to embrace new flowers for gifts as well as for themselves. These include people who can afford to play with signs and are concerned with trend setting, communicating their economic status, or distinguishing their own from the common tastes. However, since very few flower buyers are familiar with more than a handful of flower types, florists and floral designers are important intermediaries in this self-conscious signaling of self.

Mary Coggins, an employee at Perfect Posies in Manhattan, explained the gift-giving practices of her celebrity clients. They "give bigger and better than most people. [For Mother's Day it is] three baskets, one to the grandmother, one to the mother, one to the mother-in-law and they are five hundred dollars apiece." Messages about the donor's status are an important aspect of these gifts and the flowers they contain. "They feel the need to do a little bit more because often they have new found money, new celebrity status, and they want to be able to show it off. A lot of being a celebrity is showing off how big you have become, how famous you are. They do that by spending more money and giving high-priced gifts that say 'look I've made it.'"

In modern consumer societies such as the United States, status is maintained through competition and the use of positional goods to communicate tastes, appearances, and lifestyle preferences. Particular tastes in clothing, food, cars, or rare flowers differentiate among classes and sectors and serve as "markers of class" and of group identity (Bourdieu 1984; Schneider 1994; Slater 1997; Warde 2000).[33] In New York City, a single, expensive florist is sometimes the choice of many members of a particular ethnic or social sector. In such cases, gift givers make no claim to cultural capital through implied

Self and Signs

knowledge of particular flowers in a gift arrangement. Rather, their choice of floral designer implies social location, taste, and other aspects of the giver's identity. "People want to impress," explained Kenneth Dixon, a midtown florist. "We are in an echelon and people know it is expensive, so if it has our [Park Avenue Florals] tag on it . . . it's like 'we paid a lot of money.'" He also noted the way his clients use these positional flowers selectively. "They say 'if I have to send a thank you to Mrs. So and So it has to come from you.' It has to have a [Park Avenue] Floral's tag." In some ways the choice of florist is a claim to *belonging* or admission to a social group.

These florists and designers are themselves deeply invested in promoting novelty blooms and in signature styling that differentiates them from other floral designers. They must also struggle to impart characteristics that distinguish the donor in sometimes highly competitive spheres of gift giving. For example, bouquets of flowers are popular gifts for movie stars since, as one Los Angeles florist explained, "You can't give chocolate and food because they're all on a serious diet." Around Oscar time nominated stars are "engulfed with flowers," receiving dozens of bouquets a day sent to congratulate, compliment, court, and console. A skillful arrangement of rare blooms and uncommon colors—sometimes composed of several hundred flowers—can cost thousands of dollars. Each donor requires that his or her gift be exceptional enough to impress the fortunate star, who has probably already received dozens of bouquets. By 2005, this competitive giving had become "a lot more intense" than previously, said a stressed Los Angeles florist trying to meet the challenge of ensuring that "different senders get different looks."[34]

Unusual flowers have joined other consumption goods as being positional and announcing status and they have become a part of a complex of new status signifiers. Thus at high social and economic levels, there is a call for new flower-arranging styles and distinctive flower colors and types, which in turn trigger ripples in the flower chain. Disdain for the commonplace—such as carnations and chrysanthemums—echoes attitudes in New York a century earlier (see chapter 1). The trajectory of *Phalaenopsis* orchids is an example. A century ago these orchids were stripped from tropical trees for the enjoyment of wealthy collectors. Their cost and complex propagation and cultivation requirements sustained their value as signs of cultural capital, status, and wealth (see chapter 1). Improved propagation methods dramatically increased production over the last decade or two. Declining prices encouraged their use as decorative flowering plants and as cut flowers.[35] Americans have purchased hundreds of thousands and perhaps millions of *Phalaenopsis* orchids from supermarkets and supercenters such as Wal-Mart (see chapter 6). As *Phalaen-opsis* became a common interior design accessory, visible in local supermarkets as well as in the pages of house and garden magazines, desire for them faded among the cognoscenti who sought new forms of orchids. As one prosperous, middle-aged woman confessed during our conversation, "I think I am getting a little tired of orchids." But her feeling was vague and she was unable to explain exactly why orchids no longer appealed.[36]

WEDDING FLOWERS AND IDENTITY

About two and a half million weddings take place each year in the United States, and they generate forty to fifty billion dollars for the wedding indus-try.[37] By 2004 the average U.S. wedding cost about $22,000 (an increase of about 20 percent since 1999) and about $38,000 in the NYMA. Flowers account for between 5 and 10 percent of the total expenditure.[38]

As the scope and scale of weddings have grown more luxurious, so have sales of wedding flowers. Retail florists and freelance floral designers, them-selves an important part of the wedding industry, agree that wedding flowers have become more elaborate and costly in the NYMA over the last ten to twenty years. Several described weddings in which millions of dollars were spent including substantial sums on lavish displays of fresh flowers.

"There was a late eighties period when it was 'show as many flowers as you can to show we spent a fortune,'" recalled Robert Rickman, a Manhattan floral designer with many years of experience at the high end of floral con-sumption. "It was status display and social climbing. I would say in the last fifteen to twenty years at least [expenditures have greatly increased]." He reflected, "People are more sophisticated and wiser now" even if they are "still spending plenty of money [on weddings]." Yet Mike Stefalopatis, the Brook-lyn florist mentioned earlier, did not see any evidence of wiser expenditure on weddings. Instead he deplored some recent wedding excesses: "We have a lot of status [to deal with]. It is all show. X had his daughter's wedding at the Waldorf—he rented the grand ballroom for a week. He had the carpeting changed. The room draped with different fabric. . . . He spent over a million dollars on decorations." Mike asked me, "Why rent the Waldorf Ballroom if you are going to change it? Why not rent a barn? We draped *Dendrobium* orchids everywhere. Gives you an idea of the type of work they expect of us."

Such spectacular and excessive displays of fresh flowers communicate high social status today just as they did at the Gilded Age wedding of Cornelia Martin described in chapter 1. Less spectacular wedding consumption also

207

Self and Signs

sends signals about a high level of disposable income as well as "displaying and communicating" the status of bride and groom "as sophisticated, discriminating wedding consumers" (Boden 2003, 156).[39]

Otnes and Pleck argue that extravagant weddings have become pervasive (in promotion and performance) in part because they "legitimate lavish consumption through the 'ethic of perfection'—or the standard that includes the desire for both flawless beauty and perfect performance" (2003, 8). Boden's research among marrying couples in Britain—many of whom did not have especially lavish weddings—showed that they were highly conscious of the manipulation by the wedding industry (including wedding magazines, florists, and other service providers) in their choices and decisions. Yet "rather than turning away from the new commercial world of weddings . . . [they] repeatedly commit themselves to it." This purposeful involvement implicates them in their own manipulation by the wedding industry. But as Boden points out, by "further fuelling the imagination, [this manipulation] itself produces pleasure" (2003, 156).

Most brides, knowing little about flowers, kindle their imaginations by seeking guidance from cultural mediators such as magazines and floral designers. In this interactive, synergistic process, magazines play a large part. Fashion, identity, and symbolism intertwine. New bouquet and other wedding flower styles often designed and prepared by New York City floral designers are regularly featured in bridal and other magazines. Florists attest that brides increasingly compose an imaginary bridal self from images in these magazines. Some brides may draw inspiration from the bouquets carried by celebrities in lifestyle and wedding magazines featuring the ceremonies and celebrations of "the famous and the semifamous."[40] Images from these magazines help to shape a vision of their wedding-day appearance and experience.[41] Such images have been important since early in the twentieth century when movie fan magazines and newspaper photographs of celebrity weddings offered largely unattainable models of bridal presentations (Otnes and Pleck 2003). Yet the allure of celebrity appears to have intensified in recent times, as the advertising and magazine industries have increasingly focused on the power of images—especially celebrity images—to compel consumers.[42] The success of celebrity images also may be partly a consequence of rising incomes and declining prices for luxuries such as flowers that puts them within reach of more brides.

Brides and other flower buyers interviewed often acknowledged that celebrity, lifestyle, and other magazines fueled their imaginations, yet none wished to copy the icons depicted in their pages. On the contrary, all were intensely concerned with ensuring that their bouquets and wedding flowers reflected aspects of their own identity and expressed personal meanings. Most felt that wedding flowers should communicate their personal conception of their celebration and themselves.

The choice of flowers for the bouquet is important. The bouquet symbolizes the bride's important role in a life-cycle ritual. Florists confirm the importance to brides of "having a meaningful type of flower, like, 'my mother had this flower in her bridal bouquet,'" as Manhattan florist Randall Grange put it. Most importantly for recent brides like Megan and Lily, the bouquet embodied important aspects of their identities.[43] This often took the form of a connection with traditions or association with living or dead relatives. Megan wanted lavender in her bouquet because "at my grandmother's house there were long, long hedges of lavender . . . and the smell always calms me down." Another bride's ceremony flowers included "tons of hydrangeas. We had them because they were Granny's favorite flower and as a tribute to Granny."

Lily's bouquet had no such tradition behind it, but it actively expressed aspects of her identity. She explained that she had looked "through magazines and I did a lot of research, but I also felt that my bouquet was probably the most reflective, in some ways, of me. . . . Flowers are the statement of the wedding in some ways." Her florist first suggested roses, but she declined. "I didn't want roses, I felt like roses were so overdone . . . [and] they didn't reflect any aspect of my personality."

This desire for a bouquet expressive of the bride's identity or personality is evident across ethnic and economic strata. Brides who are the children of new immigrants sometimes want bouquets expressive of their connection with mainstream culture rather than with their ethnic traditions. They too seek guidance from magazines and intermediaries. Mai Wong, the Taiwanese florist in Queens with a largely Chinese clientele mentioned earlier, said, "Now many brides look in magazines before they come to me. The [other] Chinese flower shops around here don't do [individual] designs. I do something different. I create it for them individually." These desires sometimes lead to difficulties, Mai explained. "Young people don't care so much for the tradition of using red flowers for celebration and weddings. Sometimes the bride will come in and say she wants all white flowers then the mother-in-law comes in and says 'red.' The old people don't like white because white is for funerals."

Self and Signs

Yet while the bouquet should be personalized by colors or types of flowers, the actual bouquet *style* seldom departs from a prescribed form. "Few people want to go off the path, they want to be the same as everyone else," said Karl Pepper, a Manhattan florist. "They don't want to take a chance and do something different. . . . They all follow the same pattern when it comes to [bridal] flowers." Almost all the brides I spoke to followed the current bouquet form, possibly because it simplified one of the hundreds of decisions to be made in the course of preparing a contemporary wedding. Yet each carefully selected the colors and flower varieties incorporated in that prevailing bouquet style.

Lily was different. "I didn't really like the pictures" of bouquets and arrangements that florists offered as models. "The people whose weddings they had done, their taste was so different from mine." Instead, Lily decided: "I didn't want an arrangement, I just wanted one type of flower, tied together. I wanted it to feel very natural, like I had just picked up the flowers and carried them around . . . it was like a bushel of flowers. I felt they were very free looking, unusual."

Megan, too, put a great deal of thought into the meaning of her bouquet. For her the most important aspect was "all about my childhood really, and what I like about my family." The bouquet, following the current style, was a compact, round arrangement stuffed with blossoms. "I was very sure about having gardenias," she recalled. "I remember my grandmother having that plant and my mother as well. So I knew I wanted gardenias." Megan recalled her romantic vision of the bouquet and the wedding day. "I knew that once they were cut they would only last twenty-four hours and they have very short stems as well so they have to be wired and then they can't drink any water. But I thought that for the one day we got married [it didn't matter] if they died after twenty-four hours. It was quite a romantic idea that they didn't last very long. They were beautiful, but then they died." More knowledgeable about flowers than many brides, Megan ensured that all her favorite, meaningful flowers were included. "In the end we had, tulips, lilac, ranunculus, some beautiful white roses . . . [but] it was mainly all about the gardenias, they were the main things."[44]

Lily was unusual in demanding a different form of bouquet. Changes in bouquet styles are seldom initiated by brides. Occasionally cultural icons will prompt new styles. For example, cascading bouquets became popular following the wedding of Princess Diana. More recently, bouquets have been small and tightly packed with blooms. Randall Grange assured me that this is now such a strongly preferred style that "if you see a large bouquet, people look at you like you are crazy. [Brides] want a small, lush, French style. Wispy looking. Not something that is going to cover their whole stomach."

Yet Randall admitted that the current desire for a smaller lush bouquet is partly the product of the explosion in new flower types and colors described in previous chapters, especially "tea roses, *Dendrobium* [orchids, and] freesia" and a desire on the florists' part to form bridal bouquets from the newer specialty flowers. "Even florists get bored with flowers," explained Randall. "If you see something new and beautiful there is no way you are going . . . to go with what [you] had last year." It seems then that new needs in bouquet styling have evolved and taken shape partly because new flowers are available and they appeal to florists, perhaps more than to brides who must depend on these experts for guidance.

Furthermore, the wedding magazine industry's constant need for new images and ideas also influences bouquet styling and the imaginations of brides and florists. In early 2002, Sally Plimpton, a leading designer at Perfect Posies, detailed to me the year's distinctive trends, noting, "People are very much into white, into clean, structural, environmental, organic arrangements." Organic arrangements demanded green flowers "such as viburnum, which is a citrus lime green, and celery-colored flowers like bells of Ireland." These uncommon blooms subsequently appeared in a series of green and white bridal bouquets that Perfect Posies designed for *In Style* magazine's spring 2002 wedding issue. Florists and magazine editors thus favor the new.

BELONGING AND IDENTITY

In her study of contemporary brides and grooms in Britain, Boden offered the view that one role for commercial wedding consumption is to allow today's marrying couples "to have the event they want, an event appropriate and relevant to them, and expressive of their current personal or social situation should they so desire (or alternatively to escape somewhat from mundane reality into a Cinderella-like romantic fantasy). In short, wedding consumption provides an avenue for couples to *think through and enact what the whole occasion means to them*" (2003, 157; emphasis added).

I would add two cultural functions for the lavish wedding. First, weddings, like other rituals, are symbolic as well as social actions that establish "visible public definitions" (Douglas and Isherwood [1976] 1996, 43). Costly ritual trappings such as the long white dress and bouquet help to fix the meanings attached to the ritual. They momentarily confirm "traditional" female and male roles, identity, and other aspects of the self that have become contested and contradictory in recent years. Wedding consumption is "women's work" and "an extension of their domestic role" that Boden avows is "willingly and happily undertaken by most brides" (2003, 157).[45] This work of emphasizing the wedding and its ritual adjuncts may serve, as Douglas and Isherwood put it, to "contain the drift of meanings" and minimize at least for a day some of the contradictions of modern existence.[46]

Second, weddings ritually acknowledge social relationships and establish a sense of belonging because the wedding gathering symbolically constitutes a social group and affirms its values. This kind of consumption is a part of the concrete processes of "cultural reproduction of social relations" (Slater 1997, 148). Today's larger, more costly weddings bring together the geographically dispersed friends and families of an older, better-educated bride and groom. By the beginning of the twenty-first century, those friends and family members—especially in the educated middle and upper classes more apt to spend on lavish weddings—were likely to be widely scattered across the United States and even around the world. A wedding celebration ritually calls on them to confirm their kin connections and social communities.[47]

Such relationships and family life itself have a fundamental social purpose: to make clear who we are. "We not only live with families," Gillis points out, "but depend on them to do the symbolic work that was once assigned to religious and communal institutions: representing ourselves to ourselves as we would like to think we are" (quoted in Miller 2001b, 55). The growing significance of wedding celebrations and the rituals surrounding them is, I argue, a part of this symbolic work. At these gatherings of kin and kin-like friends, celebrants perform the cultural and social work of confirming community membership, making clear who we are and how we fit into a social group— where exactly the bride and groom, and others, belong.

Lily Fable expressed these ideas herself—and echoed the sentiments of most of the brides I talked to—when she explained, "The best part was having everyone come to the wedding . . . just about everybody you have ever cared about in one spot . . . high school friends, college friends, family . . . it is overwhelming to have everybody there . . . I don't think you would ever feel that much love again in your whole life."

Elaborate wedding rituals thus become a form of social action that compensates for the dwindling nature of some social institutions by increasing others in importance and reinvigorating them as signifiers of stable collectivities and identity. From this perspective, flowers formed into arches, garlands, and table decorations create a welcoming and celebratory atmosphere for the guests as the bridal couple publicly confirms new identities and responsibilities within their kin-like group.

At the same time bridal crowns and bouquets signify a momentary embrace of a traditional, romantic, emotional female identity that on the one hand is contested by new social and economic changes but on the other is celebrated and fantasized in representations of the feminine in popular television programs and especially magazines. The following section examines the way magazines influence the three dominating floral practices discussed in the first half of the chapter.

Persuasion: Shaping Taste and Meaning

THE WEAKNESS OF FLORAL ADVERTISING

Historically, advertising and retailing have been critical in revolutionizing middle- and working-class consumption. Advertisers and marketers gradually differentiated consumers into narrow market sectors and targeted them for messages about desirable goods and services (Fine and Leopold 1993). Fresh-cut flowers must compete with many other discretionary goods for attention in this environment, yet direct advertising, for reasons outlined below, has had very little impact on flower consumers.

The cut flower industry, as explained in chapter 6, is still a fragmented network of small, medium, and large businesses. Different segments of the cut flower system pursue individual forms of flower marketing. For example, many traditional florists advertise locally while supermarkets include information about weekly flower promotions in flyers and local newspaper advertising. Most of this local advertising *assumes* rather than *creates* consumer interest in the social and cultural uses of flowers.

Furthermore, this industry fragmentation has limited large-scale or industry-led floral advertising, and the few broad campaigns of recent decades have been brief and ineffective (Ward 1997). In 2000 a few Colombian and American flower growers created the Flower Promotion Organization to persuade the public that flowers are an important part of daily life and to encourage regular flower buying. The organization's annual budget is about four million dollars. The two major floral wire/Internet services, Teleflora and FTD, together spend about $100 million annually on national advertising, largely to the floral retailers who are their principal market, and to a lesser extent, to flower consumers.[48] These budgets are very small compared with those for marketing other discretionary consumer goods. In the sportswear industry, for example, five million dollars secures the endorsement services of only a single celebrity, and one company alone, Nike, spends close to 1.4 billion dollars annually to persuade consumers of the desirability of its products.[49]

Leaders in the fresh-cut flower industry are clearly concerned about the lack of advertising to shape meaning for consumers and stimulate individual flower consumption. "We spend more money advertising to ourselves than to the consumer," John Brooks, an industry analyst, lamented during our conversation. "Without industry promotion," complained Bill Gouldin, a leading U.S. florist, "our ship is without a rudder and it's finding its natural course: very seasonal, very price intensive . . . we're drifting toward becoming a commodity."[50]

ICONS, IMAGES, INTERMEDIARIES

The weakness of direct floral advertising is partly offset by the indirect effects of two other common means of shaping consumer tastes—consumer magazines and images of celebrities in television, movies, and print media. Both constantly remind potential flower buyers of the customary meanings and the ritual and symbolic functions of fresh flowers.

Images of flowers as metaphors for luxury, sensuality, purity, emotion, status, romance, femininity, nature, tranquility, and domesticity saturate movie, television, and print media (see for example, figure 33). These images embody many of the traditional meanings of flowers, employing what Poole has described as "relationships of referral and exchange among images themselves" (1997, 7). Roses, for instance, are a common—and traditional—symbol for luxury and romance, while in the contemporary print media images of anthuriums are a frequent visual metaphor for sexuality. Figures 33 and 34 are examples of "the pleasures of looking" (Poole 1997, 17) and of the ways in which the recirculating symbolic imagery of flowers gathers value and force from widely shared traditional meanings. In some images new meanings have been attached to unfamiliar flowers. The arresting advertisement for a Kohler faucet, for example, seems to transfer notions of exoticism (of both the African woman and the anthurium flowers) and purity (of water, nature, and the line of the carefully placed blooms) to the contemporary faucet (see figure 34).

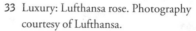

More space.
Our new First and Business Class.

Lufthansa

33 Luxury: Lufthansa rose. Photography
courtesy of Lufthansa.

Such powerful images imprint the consuming imagination, contributing to a complex process of shaping the "specific ways in which we see (and represent) the world, determine how we act upon that world and, in so doing, create what that world is" (Poole 1997, 7).

At least since the 1920s and 1930s, as noted previously, advertisers depended on images of the urban wealthy and of "fashionable society" to sell products. These images emphasized class distinction, focusing on portrayals of the upper middle class and above (Marchand 1985, 198). Formerly, such icons were members of the wealthy or aristocratic social elite, but today they are more likely to be popular entertainment and sports stars. The launch of *People* magazine in 1974 with an initial readership of about one million marked an intensification of popular interest in celebrities and the celebrity lifestyle. Today, the magazine's average circulation is over 3.5 million, two-thirds of them women.[51]

In the last few decades print media and popular television shows intensified their detailed reporting of the lives enjoyed by an economic elite. An expanding group of well described sports, entertainment, political, literary, and other icons offers models of lifestyle and forms of consumption which, Schor argues, guides the consumption decisions of the middle three-fifths of the population (Schor 1999).[52] Whether as sources of emulation or as guides

34 Exoticism: Woman, *Anthurium*, and Kohler faucet. Photograph courtesy of Kohler Co.

to behavior, images of celebrated people abound in lifestyle and other types of consumer magazines. "Celebrities are the last people we all have in common," Martha Nelson, the founding editor of *In Style* magazine, reportedly observed.[53] Movies, television, the Internet, newspapers, and magazines intertwine in their focus on celebrities.[54] Here, I focus on consumer magazines, because many of them directly and indirectly offer abundant ideas and images of the flower-saturated lifestyle and because readers of particular consumer magazines and frequent flower buyers share statistical similarities. I argue that growing popular consumption of certain categories of magazines coincides with and influences the burgeoning flower practices—domestic decoration, gift giving, and extravagant weddings—described in previous sections.

CONSUMER MAGAZINES

About 25,000 magazines circulate in the United States, with a thousand new consumer magazines introduced annually.[55] Consumer magazines—in contrast to other categories such as trade, hobby, and professional magazines —aim to advise readers on the complex business of consuming and how certain goods and services fit their lives and identities. Guidance in consum-

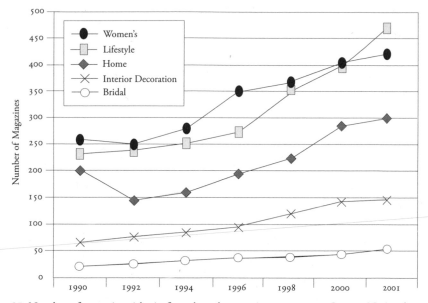

35 Number of magazine titles in five selected categories, 1989–2000. Source: National Directory of Magazines 2001.

ing fresh flowers is offered primarily in the home (including cooking), interior decoration, lifestyle, women's, and bridal categories.[56] Home and interior decoration and design magazines are often referred to collectively as "shelter" magazines. All five categories expanded substantially during the 1990s (see figure 35).

Each year about fifty new titles emerge in the home category while the number of lifestyle magazine titles more than doubled in a decade, effectively expanding and fractioning the consumer magazine market into narrower sectors with more specialized wants and needs. Consumers seem to welcome them, possibly because one of the functions of any "smart new magazine," according to one editor, is to meet "a need that people did not know they had."[57] New magazines in these categories seamlessly blend advertising and editorial content in which "well-informed shopper-editors" select and present commodities to the reader together with buying information.[58] A desire for fresh flowers is cultivated in editorial content that assumes flowers are a component of the creative, nurturing, feminine identity and in images of ideal worlds where gardens and interiors are always flower-filled and bouquets identify brides and their attendants as they participate in flower-laden celebra-

Self and Signs

tions. Flowers are important signifiers of the imaginary lives purveyed in the pages of these immensely popular magazines.

To explore the association between representations of flowers in these magazines and flower consumption, I examined distribution of the top-selling magazines in all five categories and focused on a total of thirty-five magazines.[59] The twenty best-selling magazines in these categories in the United States and in the NYMA in 2000 are shown in table 10.

An index of circulation illustrates the degree to which circulation matches population in a particular area. An index of 100 is an exact population match while an index of 130 indicates the readership is 30 percent higher than the norm.

It is clear from table 10 that magazine reading is popular. The favored magazines in these categories in the New York/Northern New Jersey Metropolitan Statistical Area differ substantially from the U.S. norm. The top seven magazines in the United States list compose the group known as the "Seven Sisters"—home and family magazines that have traditionally targeted married, stay-at-home mothers. This is a dwindling demographic group since about 73 percent of women with children under eighteen are in the labor force, either part-time or full-time. Only one of these magazines appears in the NY/NJMSA list, perhaps because the target audience is underrepresented. Instead, upscale lifestyle and home magazines are preferred and more widely consumed, as indicated by the higher numbers.

The target demographic group for the majority of the magazines popular in the NY/NJMSA is fairly affluent women, who are predominantly college-educated, between twenty-five and fifty years old, and with household incomes over $60,000.[60] These demographics correspond closely with those of the typical fresh flower buyer. More detailed local differences in the interests of women readers in the NY/NJMSA may be inferred by indexing magazine choices in several smaller statistical regions.[61]

Table 11 illustrates the immense popularity of lifestyle magazines such as *Vogue* and *In Style* and home magazines such as *Town and Country* and *Elle Decor* in certain areas. Some indexes are in the 200 levels, that is, more than double the norm. Differences between areas relate to demographics such as wealth and education and the higher proportion of single women and African American and Latina women in the NYMSA and nearby New Jersey.[62] They also suggest something about regional values or lifestyle. The bridal magazines listed here have broad popularity throughout the NY/NJMSA, suggesting keen

10 Twenty top-selling magazines in selected categories in United States and New York / New Jersey Metropolitan Consolidated Statistical Area. Indexed by circulation.**

	U.S. TOP-SELLING MAGAZINES IN SELECTED CATEGORIES		N.Y./N.J. MSA TOP-SELLING MAGAZINES IN SELECTED CATEGORIES	
Rank	Title	Index U.S.	Title	Index NYMSA
1	Better Homes and Gardens	274	Latina*	204
2	Family Circle	180	Gourmet*	189
3	Good Housekeeping	162	Working Woman*	184
4	McCall's / Rosie	151	Vanity Fair	183
5	Ladies' Home Journal	150	Harper's Bazaar	182
6	Woman's Day	150	Vogue	178
7	Redbook	84	Town and Country*	169
8	Martha Stewart Living	83	Bon Appétit	162
9	Country Living	59	Architectural Digest	160
10	In Style	57	Elle Decor*	158
11	Cooking Light	52	Essence	156
12	Bon Appétit	44	Metropolitan Home	137
13	Vogue	40	Brides Magazine	137
14	Vanity Fair	38	Woman's Day	137
15	Country Home	38	In Style	135
16	Essence	36	House Beautiful	134
17	Home*	36	Home*	129
18	Victoria	35	House and Garden*	129
19	Gourmet*	32	Colonial Homes	125
20	House Beautiful	31	Modern Bride	123

Source: Magazine Publishers of America Fact Sheet and ABC Magazine Market Coverage Report 2000

* 1999 statistics
** The Office of Management and Budget divides the United States into 350 metropolitan statistical areas for demographic, census, and other statistical purposes. These MSAs are used by Standard Rate and Data Service as the unit basis for their Magazine Market Coverage Reports by publication and market area on which some of my analysis is based. The units used here, are taken from the New York/Northern New Jersey metropolitan consolidated statistical area. A smaller unit, the New York metropolitan statistical area (NYMSA), also used here, includes the five New York City counties, as well as Westchester, Rockland, and Putnam counties (Consumer Magazine and Agri-Media Rates and Data, December 1991).

11 Top-selling magazines in selected categories in four smaller regions of the NYMSA. Indexed by circulation.**

Rank	NYMSA	Index	Nassau/Suffolk, N.Y.	Index	Jersey City, N.J.	Index	New Haven/Stamford, Conn.	Index
1	Latina*	340	Working Woman*	522	Latina*	500	Gourmet*	273
2	Elle Decor	306	Gourmet*	258	Elle Decor	290	Town and Country*	237
3	Home*	286	Vanity Fair	235	Vogue	250	Bon Appétit	233
4	Essence	265	Vogue	206	Vanity Fair	185	Architectural Digest	231
5	Vanity Fair	256	Town and Country*	197	Essence	175	Vanity Fair	193
6	Vogue	243	Bon Appétit	185	In Style	175	House and Garden*	193
7	Harper's Bazaar	243	Harper's Bazaar	180	Harper's Bazaar	170	Colonial Homes	190
8	Metropolitan Home	208	Architectural Digest	173	Brides Magazine	150	House Beautiful	180
9	Architectural Digest	185	Ladies' Home Journal	165	Bridal Guide	135	Martha Stewart Living	172
10	Town and Country*	184	Brides Magazine	165	Modern Bride	130	Metropolitan Home	168
11	Gourmet*	166	Elle Decor	152	Working Woman*	125	Cooking Light	166
12	In Style	134	Modern Bride	151	Metropolitan Home	125	Traditional Home	165
13	Working Woman*	125	Bridal Guide	147	Woman's Day	115	Vogue	162
14	Brides Magazine	125	House Beautiful	146	Gourmet*	95	Harper's Bazaar	155
15	House and Garden*	125	Metropolitan Home	143	Architectural Digest	95	In Style	153
16	House Beautiful	114	In Style	142	Town and Country*	90	Modern Bride	152
17	Bon Appétit	100	House and Garden*	135	Martha Stewart Living	90	Elle Decor	142
18	Modern Bride	93	Traditional Home	131	Bon Appétit	85	Working Woman*	142
19	Martha Stewart Living	83	Better Homes and Gardens	129	House Beautiful	85	Country Home	133
20	Bridal Guide	76	Today's Homeowner	127	House and Garden*	85	Family Circle	130

Sources: Magazine Publishers of America Fact Sheet and ABC Magazine Market Coverage Report 2000

* 1999 statistics

** Index of circulation is percentage of circulation divided by percentage of population indicating the degree to which circulation matches population in that area. Such a population index illuminates the popularity and resonance of particular magazines in certain areas. Some of this is to be expected, such as *New Jersey Monthly* being popular in New Jersey and *Essence* popular in regions with high African American populations and *Latina* and *People in Español* more widely read in regions with higher Latin American and/or Spanish-speaking populations. Other patterns may map onto age and income demographics and suggest something about values or "lifestyle."

interest in the wedding ritual, and sell particularly well in suburban Nassau and Suffolk counties on Long Island and in Jersey City.[63] *Martha Stewart Living,* a magazine that perhaps more than any other in the list focuses on the domestic uses of fresh-cut flowers, is most popular in the New Haven–Stamford area that includes the wealthy suburb of Fairfield County in Connecticut, where supermarkets are amply stocked with fresh-cut flowers.[64] In all areas, popular lifestyle and home magazines are generally upscale choices reflecting greater affluence in some cases but also the interests, aspirations, desires, and fantasies of Metropolitan readers.

Supermarkets are important purchasing sites for these magazines as well as for fresh flowers. Over 60 percent of single-copy magazine sales occurred through supermarkets in 2000.[65]

MAKING MEANINGS AND SIGNS

Magazines profit by delivering their readers to advertisers. To do so, they must first entice, capture, and retain their readers' interest.[66] A principal means of retention, as Inge Stole explained in an essay about the failures of early television programming and advertising, "is to make consumers aware of their shortfalls and to offer them products with which to redeem the problems" (2003, 77)—in other words, to create new needs and then satisfy them. In creating new needs, consumer magazines (and their advertisers) continually emphasize new and changing social circumstances, behaviors, and styles.

At times the magazine industry notices evolving needs in its audience and responds with an entirely new magazine. The recent expansion of consumer magazines aimed at women attests to magazine producers' skills in identifying what Martyn Lee describes as the "highly segmented tastes, needs and sensibilities" of modern consumers and has led to an increasingly segmented magazine market that permits advertisers to target consumers more precisely (1993, 115). The magazine industry's facility for identifying narrow sectors of consumers is exemplified by the emergence of *Real Simple,* a lifestyle magazine launched in 2000 (for which reason it does not appear in the tables in this chapter). Its circulation reached 1.9 million by 2005, even as circulation of the previously popular *Martha Stewart Living* declined. The magazine's development has depended on close attention to the needs of its readers, who are targeted as busy women "who are seeking to bring some order to their increasingly chaotic lives." Researchers identify these needs not only through typical focus groups but by actually visiting readers and observing them as they shop, cook, and get their children ready for school.[67] Readers are counseled on purchasing solutions to daily dilemmas. As one advertising executive explained a few years ago, magazines like *Real Simple* are never about "consuming less"; they are only "about consuming more selectively."[68] They offer the illusion that the increasingly complicated lives of women in the United States can be managed by fine-tuning behavior and self-presentation through more rational consumption. It is an approach that resonates with millions of women.

This emphasis on the importance of the continuously new, or as Appadurai puts it, the "valorization of empherality," is, he argues, a foundation of modern consuming (1996, 83).[69] In Appadurai's view "the aesthetic of ephemerality becomes the civilizing counterpart of flexible accumulation and the work of the imagination is to link the ephemerality of goods with the pleasures of the senses" (85). In this respect, fresh-cut flowers—pleasurable, evanescent, and always in need of replacement—are the perfect commodity.

Yet desires for "new" things must also develop within a framework of relevance to the consumer's own purposes and of cultural meaning that is shaped not only by outside forces such as magazines and other media but also by individual location, experience, imagination, and judgment (Lee 1993; Slater 1997; Miller 1998). David Gauntlett explored the relevance and effects on women's identity of some of the messages contained in popular women's magazines. Readers, it seemed, did not take all magazine messages seriously (although readers in their thirties were more discriminating than teenagers). He concluded that women's and men's magazines "suggest ways of thinking about the self, and propose certain kinds of lifestyle, which are then actively processed by the readers as they establish their personal biography, sense of identity and technologies of the self." Furthermore, "those who fear for the reader-victims of these publications are overemphasizing the power of the texts and underestimating the ability of readers to be selective and critical" (2002, 206).

Reader/consumers, then, appear to be engaged in a sort of filtering process, seeking general patterns that help them make sense of and construct their lives and identities. The increasing segmentation of the magazine industry and the intensification of the process of targeted advertising aid this process. Readers can observe patterns and select ideas from among a range of magazines more precisely tailored for them. Magazine content includes useful decision-making tools and ideals (or fantasies), which may include flower-decked living rooms or romance, with which to organize an ideal world of relationships and belonging and their own individuality.

MEDIATING MEANINGS AND SIGNS

Ideas about flowers and their uses generated in magazines begin with top-tier floral designers. Many such designers are found in Manhattan, a locus of cultural agency and innovation and the headquarters of most bridal, house and garden, and lifestyle magazine. The floral designer Robert Rickman described the dual importance for notable floral designers of establishing relationships with magazine editors and the "creative energy in New York." He also described the mechanism for "a trickle down of ideas from the big designers to everyone else. Ideas are disseminated through shelter magazines . . . *Fine Gardening, Town and Country, House Beautiful.* They will pick out a designer for spring and, say, do ten wedding bouquets and [they] will feature wedding bouquets as an article. So in those wedding bouquets they will have a new flower or a new color or a new way of doing it—that is the way the word spreads."

The styles and flower types circulating among tastemakers then diffuse to a popular level. George Henning, a suburban florist, was one of several who confirmed the importance of home magazines in diffusing ideas about new flowers and new ways to use flowers in domestic settings. "Shelter magazines are extremely important, because all of these [clients] read shelter magazines," George explained. "Sometimes they thumb through them and sometimes they seriously read [them] . . . and many times they'll just look at the covers. And most good covers on shelter magazines have floral somewhere on the cover. So that makes a very big difference." George himself depends on these magazines for education. He noted, "I study the trends and I know what the trends are [from] what I read in magazines."

Paul Yellen, a traditional florist in Harlem—a revitalizing but still poor district in northern Manhattan—acknowledged similar diffusing effects from both television and consumer magazines. "People may have seen an arrangement of calla lilies on the [television] show and [they] come in and describe the flowers to me that they saw on the show," he said. Later Paul commented on the changes he had noticed in his customers over the last twenty years "The consumer is much more educated now—you don't have to travel around the world to see things now. There are magazines—*House and Garden*—all these magazines that depict a fine way of living." Paul acknowledged the taste-

36 Calla lilies

transforming aspects of media, noting that "now you just can't give people a bunch of gladiolas." They have learned there is something better (see figure 36).

Magazine production and magazine consumption, therefore, can be seen as a process of collusion between consumers and magazine creators and content providers. Mid-twentieth century conceptions of mass media depicted it as a means of social control and suppression of identity in which choice is illusory and consumers are passive (Horkheimer and Adorno [1944] 1997). Yet, recent research suggests audiences are actively employed in selecting among media offerings for subjective purposes (Traube 1996; Verdaasdonk 2002). It is a dialogue or a trade in which magazine buyers consent to their own commodification. Editors and advertisers offer carefully selected content; consumers accept or reject it—voting at the newsstand and generating a tiny economic and cultural frisson through the vast system of capital and markets. This type of commodification may be, as Ohmann argues, "a close ally of hegemony" (1996, 362). However, I suggest that consumers, especially urban consumers, are active participants in these hegemonic processes. They are willing to engage in a dialogue as long as they have the freedom to choose and as long as (to rephrase Ohmann) the yoke is light and the inducements are sweet (350).

How much influence do media images have on the way Lily, Megan, Sidney, and Sam think about and consume flowers? My conversations with them and other flower consumers suggest that they are influenced to some degree by print, movies, and television and to some extent by class background. In most cases, a middle-class upbringing in America provides basic ideas about using flowers as domestic decorations and gifts. Several people from working-class backgrounds, however, became aware of these flower practices from watching movies and television shows. Their notions about giving flowers as gifts or using them to decorate a home developed from media representations of romantic behavior and respectable middle- and upper-class life.

CONSERVING AN UNAMBIGUOUS SIGN

Consuming fresh flowers in New York is still assumed to be the work of women, but its practice has changed in several important ways since Lizzie Hazeldean bought roses on Broadway in 1870. For one thing, women rather than men are the principal buyers of flowers today. They use them to express and construct aspects of identity, for pleasure, and to confirm relationships and community. Flowers are still employed to signal status through quantity, or distinctive variety and presentation, just as they were a century ago. Today, however, a shared profession or a common range of interests are as likely as ethnicity or religious affiliation to define the status group that spends on luxurious floral displays and gifts.[70] Fresh flowers are still a luxury for the majority, but in large urban areas they are a luxury that has been democratized. And the particular luxury of enjoying out-of-season flowers is now shared by all.

Forms and degrees of participation in the contemporary culture of flowers are still conditioned by age, class, income, and gender, but these restraints weaken when flowers are cheap and within easy reach as they are in contemporary metropolitan areas. Men start to buy flowers not only as gifts for women but also for themselves. Older people begin to reconsider their fixed views of flowers as a seasonal luxury. Women buy freely for their own sensual pleasure, when the sum involved is small. Poorer people occasionally escape the bounds of necessity and enjoy a luxury themselves or the luxury of giving a gift, when a bunch of carnations costs three dollars.

Finally, intrinsic qualities of fresh flowers make them especially well suited to their role as agents in a variety of cultural and social activities. Flowers are not transformed as they are traded, like cotton into clothing or sugar into chocolates, consequently, commercial cut flowers are seemingly identical with their untraded cousins—the flowers that grow and flourish in gardens, parks, and meadows. Very few buyers of today's flowers know their origins. Sidney Krauss's comments were typical: "I never think about where the flowers come from," he responded, surprised by my question. "I assume they are grown locally. There are a lot of nurseries. Where do they get flowers?"

This pervasive vagueness about the blooms' beginnings allows people to imprint fresh-cut flowers with their own notions of nature, pleasure, or luxury and with memories of people, places, and other times. In effect, the ideals and meanings of uncommodified flowers are conferred on commodified blooms, transforming them into objects of special value because they seem to exist (as if by magic) outside capitalism and commerce. Fresh flowers fulfill their cultural roles because they are pure and their messages unambiguous. This half-conscious process of masking fresh-cut flowers' commercial nature ensures that a thing with culturally marked value for gift exchange and rituals is preserved as an uncontaminated sign for nature, femininity, love, romance, luxury, and so on. Culture itself "ensures that some things remain unambiguously singular, it resists the commoditization of others; and it sometimes resingularizes what has been commoditized" (Kopytoff 1986, 73).

Conclusion

During the twentieth century, the culture of flowers, once the privilege of a small wealthy group, diffused to a larger population in the United States. In this study, I traced this process and followed fresh flowers over time and space as they metamorphosed from a local to a global phenomenon. This idiosyncratic commodity—highly perishable and subject to all sorts of risks and limitations—changed in the process. It transformed from a delicate fragrant perishable luxury into a sturdy, scentless "affordable luxury" that brought pleasure to many in the middle classes.

I found three frameworks to be helpful. Commodity chain analysis was primary, with its focus on the economic and social organization of exchange systems. Fine and Leopold's systems of provision framework was also useful. It similarly explores economic and social organization but acknowledges the influence of cultural systems on consumption (2002, 7). Finally, Goody's notion of a culture of flowers crystallized this essential cultural component through his exploration of the meanings assigned to flowers, the spreading knowledge and enjoyment of flowers and their rich contribution to cultures.

At the same time governance of the fresh-cut flower commodity chain altered. First consumers, then growers, and eventually middlemen influenced the types of flowers produced. I have focused on this middle sector of this chain—exporters, importers, wholesalers, and retailers and their relationships with each other and with the growers and consumers of flowers—to explain how and why this change occurred and the consequences for today's flower growers and consumers. The chain eventually split into two channels—the specialty chain and the abundant chain. These channels evolved partly through changes in growing and marketing, but alterations among the consuming classes and in the larger economic and social systems also influenced their development.

Following the rose, lily, and lisianthus over time and space—along their personal global commodity chains—revealed some of the subtler elements of commodity chain function and relationships. It is clear that social relationships structure the exchange of flowers. External forces such as trade agreements and tariffs, trading institutions, and currency exchange also foster or constrain these exchanges and their accompanying relationships.

Innovation and the flow of knowledge proved to be critical to the health of the system. Essential knowledge might be codified or formal knowledge, such as information about new flower cultivars or new growing technology. Knowledge could also be tacit or informal, such as a "feel" for the market or changing consumer wants. In fact, knowledge of changing consumer meanings, practices, and tastes is the sap of the system, flowing up and down, generating change and profit and power for a few. Innovation and knowledge sustain the chain and nourish the spread of the culture of flowers.

Fine and Leopold suggest that as forms of distribution alter and the cultural construction of the meaning of the good being consumed is changed, so production adjusts and vice versa. Each sector of each chain changes the others (Fine and Leopold 1993, 15). This study shows how that happens in this commodity system. On the one hand, a developing mass consumer taste for red roses on February 14 prompted many growers to concentrate on raising roses to bloom for that particular date. Wholesalers and retailers also focused much effort on meeting the demands of Valentine's Day. On the other hand, the changing tastes of a small group of wealthy, trend-conscious consumers—a desire for distinctive types of roses, for example—also set in motion a quite different series of activities among particular growers and traders. Middlemen communicate these changing consumer interests and preferences in ways that allow consumers to influence—through intermediaries—what is produced. These interactions eventually improve the choices of most flower consumers.

The Fresh-Cut Flower Global Commodity Chain

As the fresh flower chain expanded into a global industry after 1970, increased competition among growers and traders helped to generate differentiated markets. Related changes included a dramatic increase in the quantities of flowers grown and consumed, the commercial development of many new types of cut flowers, and, in some markets, swift obsolescence of colors and flower varieties. At the same time, in the NYMA, new kinds of distribution and retailing gave greater visibility to fresh-cut flowers, dramatically reduced prices, and removed barriers to purchase that deterred consumers under older systems of provision. All these changes together presented consumers in metropolitan areas with a great bounty of new, varied, and inexpensive flowers that helped to extend and democratize the culture of flowers. Most people are still unfamiliar with many varieties of flowers. Ignorance, however, does not appear to limit pleasure, and besides, there is a great range of inexpensive, well-known flowers such as roses, carnations, chrysanthemums, lilies, and gerberas.

Participation in the culture of flowers is also a factor of geography and the distribution of floral retail. Buying opportunities favor urban dwellers. In rural areas spottily distributed traditional florist shops and other retail outlets sell flowers at higher prices than in cities. Even in urban areas, poorer districts offer few flower choices and poorer quality.

Flowers forge relationships along the chain in the process of market exchange and among consumers through gift exchange. Furthermore, when chain participants assume responsibility for this fragile commodity, they sometimes experience subtle identification with the flowers themselves. Thus the commodity itself, the cut flower, is not simply inert but rather, in the process of production, exchange, and consumption, it shapes culture and people's conceptions of themselves and creates social relationships and communities within and beyond its system of provision.

Flower Growing

Today's flower growers produce a huge range of qualities and varieties. More common flowers—roses, carnations, chrysanthemums, and lilies—recognizable by the average consumer, are associated, within the trade, with Latin American growers. Uncommon and high-quality blooms such as lisianthus, stocks, and delphinium are associated with European and U.S. flower growers. Yet exquisite, unusual flowers also come from Latin American countries. So this perceived dualism of production is partly an inaccurate perception—a consequence of distribution limitations in the Latin American commodity chain—rather than a uniform condition. Latin American growers who innovate and focus on specialized blooms and establish reliable trading relationships and distribution systems are changing this perception.

Flower growers willing to change prospered in the period covered in this study. In mid-twentieth century those who moved to cheaper growing areas and produced large quantities of cheap flowers did well. As global competition increased in the last decades of the century, American growers survived if they had knowledge about new flowers and the skills to grow different species.

Conclusion

Foreign export growers found their greater times and distances to markets added costs and affected freshness and ultimately the value of their flowers. For some, spatial and cultural barriers limited their access to essential scientific and cultural information essential for innovation. These same barriers inhibited quick responses to changes in taste, fashion, and competition that are vital in high-priced markets.

In some countries such as Ecuador and Colombia where flower growing is clustered but not cooperative, larger growers seem to be favored because they can compensate for local structural and institutional inadequacies. They establish relationships for marketing and monitoring new consumer developments; they gather formal, scientific information and they have the resources to innovate and apply new knowledge and methods. Most are flexible enough to accommodate short and diverse product life-cycles. These larger growers are likely to be the most successful in the long term.

Very large growers may also impact their local cluster. Perez-Aleman (2003) has shown how the arrival of an Italian multinational corporation influenced upgrading in a cluster of Nicaraguan dairy producers and promoted local partnerships. The arrival of Dole Fresh Flowers, noted earlier, must have changed its Colombian cluster. Flower growers in Colombia and Ecuador have been successful in global markets, but they are limited by their competitive, rather than cooperative, local structure. This inhibits the spread of knowledge and slows upgrading in flower varieties and growing methods. No doubt growers are adjusting to the presence of a dominant producer like Dole. It would be useful to discover, through further research, how this multinational corporation has changed its flower growing cluster and whether the changes include improved cooperation and transfer of knowledge and what types of knowledge. Such research would aid understanding of the varied ways knowledge is diffused within clusters—especially clusters producing the same commodity in different global regions. In turn, this could help refine conceptions of the role of knowledge in the global competitive advantage of horticultural clusters.

Middlemen

Like growers, traders must cultivate relationships. Their networks of social relationships have an economic foundation but they are also a basis for social communities and cultural understandings. Relationships are also an element of their individual identities because trading communities have common ethics, understandings, and norms of behavior. Reciprocity and obligation help to balance and sustain relationships and reduce uncertainty and risk. Middlemen play a crucial role in the health of the system by circulating knowledge—about crops in particular growing regions, new flower hybrids, newly emerging competitors, changing currency values, or a developing desire for mini calla lilies in Manhattan. Members of these communities affect each other as they share knowledge and through their daily decisions and choices. They must constantly adjust to the consequences of their own innovations, decisions, and actions and those of others connected through the chain.

Small, well-placed groups of traditional florists, freelance floral designers, and traditional wholesale florists shape taste, push innovation, and communicate changing consumer culture. These cultural communicators are a significant force in the NYMA. They initiate cycles in favored flowers and at the same time attempt to command a supply of the favored flowers. Their power is social, cultural, and economic. Furthermore, to some degree, this group of middlemen communicates social and cultural change and also fashions it. They encourage growers to produce a new flower, for example, but then they offer it to some consumers but not others.

The traditional middle sector of wholesalers and retailers is shrinking, however, as new forms of flower distribution and retail are growing. How will potential big buyers like Sam's Club and Wal-Mart alter this system of provision? If they continue to expand their fresh-cut flower marketing activities they could change the chain substantially. Superstores and box stores could become such a powerful market sector that they set standards for price, variety, and quality for many producers. They could, for example, increase demand for small hybrid flowers with long post-harvest lives that slip easily into bouquets. The number of supplying growers might shrink, leaving only those able to innovate and produce in cost-effective large quantities. Superstore demands might also lead to greater uniformity and limited selection for the majority of flower consumers. Novelty may come with different wrappings and presentations rather than different flowers. Consumers in prosperous New York would be little affected since superstores and big box stores have limited urban presence. Wholesalers and retailers will still supply consumers in this and other large urban centers from their diverse sources around the world, but suburban and rural flower buyers may find their selection reduced. If large Latin American growers become more tightly connected to price-

Conclusion

conscious big buyers, fewer new and unusual flowers may circulate between the dual chains. Would consumers, then, tire of uniform flowers and refuse to buy them as they did in the 1960s and 1970s? Would the urban-suburban-rural divide in flower choice, quality, and practices intensify—perhaps symbolically expressing other differences in values and interests?

Consumers

In this study, I have also explored the motivations of today's flower consumers to discover what makes flowers useful to these middle classes. Why are more of them buying flowers than in the recent past? Are they simply responding to marketers' urgings to buy or do they buy flowers to satisfy their own purposes and needs?

Fresh flowers satisfy consumers' desire for beautiful things. Ideas generated by movies, magazines, and television feed consumer imagination and promote the pleasures of newness. Consumer desire for novelty is an important factor in the operation of the fresh flower chain. At all market levels it is evident that new flowers and new colors are a source of delight and desire. Markets and profits grow when consumer desires are met. They are met by improving distribution, thus ensuring that flowers are fresh. They are met when new retail outlets put flowers in front of more consumers. They are met with appealing new varieties or colors and with fragrance.

As noted several times in this study, the whims of a few elite consumers are analyzed, communicated, and acted upon by social networks of growers and traders. These whims and responsive activity in the commodity chain influence which flowers are grown and ultimately which flowers reach various sectors of consumers in the United States. Elite groups have a long history of demonstrating practices associated with particular commodities and establishing an accompanying range of meanings. Other sectors of society have then adopted, emulated, or reformulated these practices and meanings within the boundaries of their particular social and economic constraints (Bourdieu 1984; Mintz 1985; Goody 1993; Veblen [1899] 1994). The possession and enjoyment of fresh flowers has always been a way of "distinguishing the richer from the poorer" in any society (Goody 1993, 428). All this is still true to an extent. One important difference, however, is that out-of-season flowers are no longer the luxury and privilege of a tiny elite. Today these flowers grow for the pleasure and cultural needs of a large middle class. Furthermore, growers and traders respond to their widely shared desires by, for example, providing roses for Valentine's Day or orange blooms for Thanksgiving. However, the more obscure, daily desires of most middle-class flower consumers—unlike those of the rich—are poorly understood and receive little attention. Nevertheless, today's consumers have many uses for fresh flowers.

Women and men have grasped this unambiguous symbol of love, domesticity, nature, luxury, and femininity. They have used it in ways that suggest an embrace of fresh flowers' primary cultural function: to clarify and communicate social and cultural meanings. They have abandoned many of the floral practices associated with the traditional elite sector, reformulated others and adopted new ones (some from the turbulent sphere of celebrities) that reflect contemporary concern with gender, relationships, group memberships, and identity.

As noted earlier, wider consumer enthusiasm for fresh flowers developed along with new forms of production and retail. It also evolved in concert with an intensifying focus on identity and lifestyle. Magazines and other media cultivated this focus, neatly linking it with consumption.[1] Clearly, consumption is one of many sources of identity, but it is an important one, especially in metropolitan areas. Consumers accept that aspects of identity are purchasable and flower buying and use make particular aspects explicit while also sending additional signals. Weddings, for example, are a performance—as well as a ritual—in which the bride presents, with her dress and flowers, a certain identity and sees that identity confirmed in the gaze of others. Yet these flower saturated celebrations also involve a powerful impulse to belong and to confirm a place within a social group.

Some new flower practices may reflect a distaste for—or at least ambivalence toward—the forces that insistently commercialize so many aspects of contemporary urban life. Many American consumers are vague about the origins of their fresh-cut flowers. Subconsciously they detach them from their commercial foundations and connect them to fantasies of natural beauty, gardens, and idealized existences—conceptions that make fresh flowers ideal for some cultural purposes. Gifts of flowers acknowledge the cultural value of important life stages, relationships, and a variety of traditional gender roles. Buying and placing flowers in the home creates an ordered environment filled with personal meanings and statements about the self. This haven and its flowers fortify a connection with a—possibly imaginary—stable past or ideal future and may temper the often conflicting and confusing signals offered by

Conclusion

commercial and popular culture. The popularity of shelter magazines and buying flowers for the home suggest that the ideal of the home as a haven for the self resonates with a lot of people, especially women. Finally, most flower uses also confirm the waning of older protestant values such as thrift. Flower buying for oneself and for gifts seems to be part of an evolving cultural embrace of luxury, pleasure, and reward—something that all purveyors of luxury goods would, no doubt, like to see more widely accepted.

Whatever the motivation for individual flower consuming impulses, it is undoubtedly true that more women and men than ever before are able to use flowers in a "culturally appropriate way" which means they participate and "experience the culture directly—becoming part of the medium of signs that constitutes that culture" (Csikszentmihalyi and Rochberg-Halton 1981, 51). They can give material expression to their cultural conceptions of themselves and others by buying and sharing a six-dollar bunch of roses from a convenience store.

All these ever-changing cultural factors—meanings, distinctive desires, physical pleasure, identity, and relationships—interlace with the economics of flower production and trade. The chain alters when Sidney Krauss gathers up three bunches of small ochre-hued gerberas to bring nature and exquisite colors into his apartment, or when Lily Fable confirms her bridal conception of herself by rejecting roses and carrying a "bushel" of gloriosa lilies, or when the grower Jorge Vélez Serrano takes a chance that a new shade of lisianthus will be popular. Their actions—these tiny gestures of the self—shiver through the chain, shifting it once again.

Notes

Introduction

1   The names and events in this description are fictitious, although based on real people and places.

2   In this kind of analysis the boundaries of culture and economy blur and interweave, an argument Paul du Gay makes very clearly (2004a).

3   This thirty-year period corresponds with the late-twentieth-century period sometimes referred to as "postmodernity" "late capitalism," or "post-Fordism." Around this time, forms of production changed from an earlier rigid "Fordist" phase of mass production to more flexible structures tailored to respond quickly to changing market demands. Innovations in technology, organization, and marketing were an important aspect of these changes. Labor organization became more flexible; new labor relations and new social formations developed. Capital was invested for shorter periods and in various industries and ventures around the globe. Production of many consumption goods shifted to developing countries. These alterations all contributed to what Harvey (1989) refers to as a new regime of "flexible accumulation" (see Lash and Urry 1987, Harvey 1989, and Blim 2000). At the same time, individualism and concern with self-identity became more pronounced conditions of existence—at least in urban centers of developed economies (Giddens 1991). Characteristics of popular culture also changed in postmodernity or late modernity and were typified by diversity, pastiche, fragmentation, depthlessness, and transience (Jameson 1991).

4   Producer-driven chains are usually capital- and technology-intensive mass industries supplying such commodities as cars, computers, and aircraft. These chains are vertically integrated and control is exercised from the headquarters of transnational corporations that own the factories. In this model, production patterns often shape consumer choices. In buyer-driven chains, brand-name merchandisers and large retailers play an important role by managing production and utilizing subcontracting networks.

5   This omission is in part attributable to the authors' concern for particular aspects of global commodity chain structure, operation, or effects. For example, the role of state policies or production innovation (Korzeniewicz et al. 1995) or the role of multinational corporations and international institutions (Talbot 1995), or peasant resistance to innovation in marketing channels (Stanford 2000a). For authors

acknowledging the importance of middlemen, big and small, and suggesting they shape the market context for producers and the choices of consumers, especially in agricultural systems, see Cook (1994), Goldfrank (1994), and Gereffi and Korzeniewicz (1994a). Talbot's study of coffee (1995), Collins's exploration of relations among Brazilian grape growers and traders (2000), and Stanford's analysis of long-term change in the California and Mexican avocado industries (2000b) also reveal something of the institutions and activities of trading middlemen and their effects on producers.

But governance, even of these agricultural chains, is still assigned principally to big buyers including supermarket chains, food industries, food service industries, and large institutions such as prison systems. The fresh-cut flower global commodity chain constitutes an alternative form, a chain with multiple branches and drivers. Parallel branches, some governed by large buyers and others by small middlemen, supply diverse forms of retail that, in turn, serve sometimes distinct and sometimes overlapping consumer markets. Such patterns have been observed in the trading of fresh fruits and vegetables, cocaine, specialty coffees, spices, and Asian small manufactured goods such as toys, apparel, hats, and fashion accessories. See Jaffee (1994), Raynolds (1994), Wilson and Zambrano (1994), Talbot (1995), Min (1996), and Freidberg (2004).

6   They also helpfully outlined the conditions that determine which of these four types will emerge within a chain.

7   See Lee (1993, xii-xiii) for a discussion of the social implications of commodity production, distribution, and exchange. Lee draws attention to "a certain logic of capital which *requires* that human needs change over time" and "the transformational nature of capital and its effects on everyday life" as well as the idea that capital and consumption articulate, forming a relationship "which is ultimately condensed into the form of the commodity" (emphasis in original).

8   This is a much-discussed question. See, for example, Marchand (1985), McCracken (1988), Fine and Leopold (1993), du Gay et al. (1997), Miller (1997), Baudrillard (1998), Klein (1999), and Douglas and Isherwood ([1976] 1996).

9   See Miller (2001a), among others.

10 Within New York City most purchases are made at traditional florists and corner convenience stores. Fewer purchases—although far more in dollar amounts—are made through freelance floral designers. In the suburbs most flowers are bought at supermarkets and traditional florists.

One ❧ Tastes, Traditions, and Trade

1   At department stores, as Miller points out in describing the Bon Marché in Paris (1981), all the trappings of bourgeois existence were visible and tangible—the linen could be felt, the silks sampled. Department stores provided a pattern of middle-class life for all those with the means and desire to emulate it. In disseminating this model the department store contributed to the homogenization

of the class. Through catalogues, just as through the magazines of a slightly later period, forms of dress and home decoration appropriate to the successful middle-class person were identified and made available at the lower prices afforded by mass production and swift turnover. Both upper and lower bourgeoisie patronized department stores. They came for the prices, the events, or because they imagined the store as a link with their lifestyle or a style of life they dreamed of.

2   See Goody (1993) for a thorough and engaging analysis of the way symbolic meanings attached to individual flowers and how they were formalized through lists, dictionaries, and advice books into a "language." Traditional meanings of flowers were first systematized in France, then spread throughout Europe and the United States. This "language" was primarily a means of communication between the sexes.

3   The heyday of this style and the somewhat similar, but later, Picturesque School was roughly from 1755 to 1840 (Fleming and Gore 1979). Today several of these large landscape gardens remain, largely preserved by the professional hands of the National Trust.

4   All three were of humble origin and self-taught. Loudon, for example, was a farmer's son who taught himself Italian and French and drawing. He founded two important gardening magazines, the *Gardener's Magazine* and, in 1838, *The Suburban Gardener and Villa Companion,* intended for the owners of the smaller suburban gardens of the middle classes. Hyams (1966) describes Loudon's garden design as embodying the best qualities of "an eighteenth-century man of taste as well as . . . a nineteenth-century man of science and business." Jane Loudon continued garden writing after her husband's death and is credited with encouraging gardening as "the essential past-time for women that it has remained ever since" (Fleming and Gore 1979).

5   By the end of the eighteenth century a general process of farm enlargement through land acquisition had created more and more landless villagers. They survived by hiring out their labor and growing vegetables around their cottages. Cottage gardens were a necessity for the rural poor who grew food on the bit of land surrounding their cottages or in nearby "allotments." More prosperous cottagers might also include a few flowers among the densely planted vegetables.

6   Many small local horticultural societies emerged and became another important medium for spreading knowledge about flowers and plants.

7   Notably in Downing's *A Treatise on the Theory and Practice of Landscape Gardening* (1841); also *Cottage Residences* (1842) and the gardening magazine *The Horticulturalist.* See also McGuire (1989) and Plumptre (1993).

8   Especially in his book *The Wild Garden* (1870). Robinson also began some influential gardening journals including, beginning in 1879, *Gardening Illustrated,* intended for small or cottage gardeners.

9   At the time, it was considered inappropriate for Jekyll, a gentlewoman, to pursue a profession. She designed hundreds of gardens and wrote a number of garden design books—many of them still in print today—while remaining always an

amateur. Active during the last quarter of the nineteenth century and first quarter of the twentieth century, Jekyll was the forerunner of a number of professional women garden and landscape designers. In America these included Rose Standish Nichols, Ellen Biddle Shipman, and Beatrix Jones Farrand. Largely self-taught, these important women designers interpreted and transformed English and European garden design to suit wealthy Americans (Fleming and Gore 1979; Brown 1982).

10   These included the economical Siemens regenerative furnace (1863); the Beivez cooling oven, which allowed cooling in thirty minutes (1870); and the Siemens tank furnace (1873), which made glass melting a continuous process. See History and Highlights of Pilkington at http://www.glasslinks.com/newsinfo/pilk_his tory.htm and A Historical Look at Glass, PPG Industries, Inc. at http://www .glasslinks.com/newsinfo/histppg.htm (both accessed December 15, 2005).

11   Most plant hunters were Dutch, English, or German but little is recorded about their lives or "how they found their way around the world when finding your way around the world was not an easy thing to do, or how they taught themselves to identify plants that were nearly unknown. Obviously they were all adventure-some and able-bodied. Apparently they had a good sense of direction, mastery of a few foreign languages, and a tolerance for being alone" (Orlean 2000). They were so numerous that remote places in Malaysia, South America, India, and China were sometimes crowded with orchid hunters, and their depredations—chopping down trees to strip them of orchids—reportedly resulted in devastation of the forests.

12   The terrarium principle was discovered by Nathaniel Bagshaw Ward, a physician, amateur botanist, and Fellow of the Royal Society. He designed a glass-topped wooden case that could be stored on deck. It protected plants and watered them purely with the moisture that condensed on the glass during the warm daylight hours and dripped down at night (Brockway 1979).

13   The Royal Horticultural Society became "royal" in 1861. Kew, originally a royal garden, became a state institution in 1842. From 1804 the Royal Horticultural Society's display gardens were at Chiswick, moving at the beginning of the twentieth century to their present location at Wisley, Surrey. Both institutions are still immensely influential in English botanical, plant, and garden circles.

14   Today several of the world's most important rose breeders are French. See chapter 5.

15   In 1902 Gertrude Jekyll listed thirty-eight species of garden roses originating from China, Siberia, America, Persia, Japan, and the Himalayas among other places (Jekyll and Mawley [1902] 1983).

16   The orchid had been known and cultivated in China, where orchid guides were published in the thirteenth century, for thousands of years (Reinikka [1972] 1995).

17   "Orchidelirium" brings to mind the "Tulipomania" of the seventeenth century, although much of that earlier delirium related to speculation in bulb prices rather than desire for the blooms themselves. See Schama (1987) and Goody (1993).

18 "Money Spent for Flowers: Enormous Sums Expended in a Season," *New York Times,* March 5, 1899.

19 Philip Burne-Jones, *Dollars and Democracy* (New York: D. Appleton, 1904), quoted in Dunlop (2000).

20 In support of conspicuous consumption the wealthy commanded flowers to be gathered at great distances. Dunlop (2000, 29), for example, quotes the *New York Times* description of a party given by Mrs. Bradley Martin in 1897: " 'a great army of poor folks in Alabama have been engaged in gathering clematis vines for the affair' and florist J. H. Small told the Herald that the other greens 'consisted chiefly of smilax, galax and 'royal' asparagus vines. The smilax came from the swamps of Florida. Our agent down there at once engaged fifteen men, their wives and children, who plunged into the swamps and got this. It took four days and the continuous use of six wagons.' " Yet the consumption of distant fresh flowers by the wealthy was not a nineteenth-century innovation. Goody refers to Suetonius's story about a friend of the Emperor Nero who gave a party that required four million sesterces worth of roses. Local production of forced flowers was supplemented with roses imported from Egypt and Campania for this event (Goody 1993). Fragrant rose petals rather than fresh-cut rose blooms may have been the objective.

21 "Money Spent for Flowers: Enormous Sums Expended in a Season," *New York Times,* March 5, 1899.

22 In 1880 a mild winter forced roses into bloom before they were needed. At the same time, increased prosperity encouraged more weddings and other receptions. There was such a shortage of flowers that florists feared growers would not be able to produce enough of the white flowers needed for the coming Easter demand.

23 "The Flowers of New-Year's Day," *New York Times,* January 1, 1878.

24 Mabel Osgood Wright, *The Garden of a Commuter's Wife* (New York: Grosset and Dunlap, 1901), quoted in Seaton (1988).

25 "Science Evolves New Types of Flowers: Floral Marvels in Color and Form Encourage Mass Production in the Garden," *New York Times,* June 28, 1925.

26 Donzel (1997) writes that "Charles Worth, who pioneered the idea of haute couture on both sides of the Atlantic, produced the sublime and voluminous ball gowns of the 1860s that were trimmed with large bunches of fresh flowers from bust to train."

27 "Camellias and Carnations: The Trade in Cut Flowers," *New York Times,* April 10, 1870.

28 The roses of this period were substantially more fragrant than most modern roses. Fragrance is associated with senescence, that is, decay; hence fragrant flowers generally have short lives. Late-twentieth-century rose breeding for the commercial cut flower trade favored characteristics such as longer post-harvest life, and in making that choice, eliminated fragrance.

29 Violet growing was not confined to the Rhinebeck region. A Mrs. R. E. Darbee was reported to be growing violets commercially at about this same time, 1886, in

Colma, California (*Weekly Florists' Review,* 100th Year Collectors' Edition, 1997). Commercial cut flower growing had developed around most major United States cities by this time.

30 Americans buy about three hundred and fifty million flowers (not all roses) today on February 14. But in the late nineteenth century, the production of so many blooms to coincide with a single spring festival was a considerable achievement.

31 "Union Square in Bloom," *New York Times,* March 29, 1893.

32 "Valentine Vogue Is Inaugural Blue," *New York Times,* February 13, 1933.

33 Goody (1993) suggests that America's Puritan foundations slowed the adoption of many European flower-related customs and traditions until after the Civil War.

34 Other uses of flowers for weddings included garlanded arches and wedding bells formed of flowers and fresh flowers on the bridal cake as well as various kinds of vase arrangements. An American bridal guide book of the late nineteenth century advised the bride to "budget $100 for decoration of a small church and $500 to $1,000 for a large one" (*Manual of Good Form in All Matters Connected with the Marriage Ceremony,* quoted in Money-Collins 1997).

Two ⊛ Favored Flowers

1 According to Treadway (1997), the floral trades in New York City were well established by the 1860s and floristry undoubtedly expanded rapidly after 1870. Lower Broadway was the main commercial district until about 1890, when fashionable shops began to move north of 23rd Street (Homberger 1994).

2 "A Scarcity of Flowers: Fine Roses Selling for Fifty Cents Each," *New York Times,* February 11, 1880.

3 Many of these earliest flower growers were immigrants trained in England, Scotland, and Germany, often as estate gardeners. Peter Henderson, who published a book on commercial flower growing in 1868, had more than four acres (about one and a half hectares) of glass greenhouses in Jersey City around this time. Possibly Peter Henderson is the same grower who sold 100,000 roses, but that is not certain (Treadway 1997).

4 Roses were gaining in popularity; one florist of the period estimated that twenty-four million cut roses were sold in the United States in 1885 (Treadway 1997). General Jacqueminot and Maréchal Niel were among the most popular roses for commercial cut flowers and for garden growing. "A Scarcity of Flowers: Fine Roses Selling for Fifty Cents Each," *New York Times,* February 11, 1880. See also Jekyll and Mawley ([1902] 1983).

5 Flower growing for prosperous urbanites has a long history. A Roman writer observed that "it is profitable near a city to have gardens on a large scale; for instance, of violets and roses and many other products for which there is a demand in the city." Violets in this reference are thought to be stocks (*Matthiola incana*) rather than the fragrant violets (*Viola odorata*) we think of today (Goody 1993).

6 "Camellias and Carnations: The Trade in Cut Flowers," *New York Times,* April 10, 1870.

7 Ibid.

8 "Union Square in Bloom," *New York Times,* March 19, 1893.

9 Often street vendors were children or young girls. Child flower vendors, employed by flower farms, were paid seventy-five cents a day or a 25 percent commission. Other young flower sellers bought the end of the day stock from flower stallholders and in the early evening sold it to men going home from work. Flower girls, if they were neat and pretty, developed regular customers among men leaving their offices and could earn as much as two dollars a day selling little nosegays for five to ten cents. "Street Flower Girls," *New York Times,* October 21, 1871.

10 Goody describes similar types of flower selling in ancient Rome (Goody, 1993).

11 A few wholesale florists existed in New York in the 1870s, and an 1898 issue of the *Weekly Florists' Review* included photos of a floral wholesale establishment in Chicago (Treadway 1997).

12 In *Land of Desire* (1993), his book about the growth of United States department stores and the rise of consumer capitalism between 1880 and 1930, William Leach notes an expansion of the brokering class around 1895 as the economy grew. Intermediaries like wholesale florists fall into this group that is "interested in expanding markets and volume turnover, in the movement of commodities from producer to consumer, in money, not people." Leach sees amoral and undesirable aspects to the emergence of brokering intermediaries since their role requires "repressing one's own convictions and withholding judgment in the interest of forging profitable relationships." Furthermore, in his view, their presence negatively shaped twentieth-century American culture and life by fostering an increasing obsession with pleasure and desires and an "amoralism essentially indifferent to virtue." While clearly seeking profit, flower wholesalers and other middlemen also provide a service by smoothing the circulation of larger and larger volumes of flowers. In doing so they may foster "pleasure and desire" but it is difficult to judge whether this is obsessive and amoral. My thanks to Sharon Zukin for bringing Leach's observations to my attention.

13 "Great Show of Cut Flowers: Beautiful Specimens at the Newly Opened Market: Many Greeks in the Business," *New York Times,* September 4, 1895.

14 Violets, camellias, and a range of other delicate, fragrant blooms were still raised in local greenhouses, while large quantities of gladiolus, freesia, and ranunculus continued in seasonal field production for local markets in California, the mid-Atlantic states, and Massachusetts (Carbonneau et al. 1997).

15 Florida's subtropical climate with high summer temperatures and humidity limits production of most commercial cut flowers to the winter months, roughly October to the end of May.

16 Prices paid to growers often depended on distance from market. New York wholesale florists paid freight costs when buying (direct) from a grower or shipper

in California, while local growers, who sold on consignment, paid the (smaller) freight costs. If the New York wholesaler paid a local grower twelve cents for a rose and freight and commission costs for a rose from California amounted to three cents, then the California rose grower might receive only nine cents for his roses sent to New York. For the California grower, then, the New York market may have been less attractive than closer customers.

17 Cooling systems were not necessarily as energy-intensive as modern air-conditioning; Colorado greenhouses were cooled by using fans to draw air over wet straw.

18 As production grew, support systems also developed. Cuttings suppliers emerged, offering a dependable source of baby plants for chrysanthemum and carnation growers. Larger growing enterprises required more seeds, chemical fertilizers, insecticides and herbicides, sprayers, and a host of other new items. Horticultural brokers, such as Fred C. Gloeckner and Co. Inc., generally supplied these. Trucking systems also improved, and by the 1970s, long-haul express services with refrigerated trucks dominated delivery, especially in the eastern region.

19 *Florist* magazine 1979, quoted in Scammon et al. (1982).

20 Another possible factor in this apparent shift involves the limitations of the 1959 and 1970 floricultural censuses, the basis of these early statistics. These censuses did not include farms with less than $2,000 in sales ($1,000 was the bottom limit for the 1950 census). Small farms and greenhouses may have produced more specialty and garden flowers but were not reflected in production statistics.

21 Presently commissions are about 15 percent.

22 In a government report, Burket writes, "Grower-shippers initially were flower producers exclusively, but subsequently . . . expanded their operations to include shipping flowers produced by other growers. In many cases, grower-shippers also have expanded product lines to cover a full line of fresh cut flowers to satisfy the needs of mass merchandisers and retail florists." Another variation of this new intermediary was the wholesaler-shipper who established a purchasing center in a major growing area in order to obtain and supply the complete variety of flowers needed by supermarkets and retail florists (Burket and Benedick 1980). Mellano and Company of southern California is a contemporary example of the grower-shipper. Established in 1925, Mellano currently grows twenty-seven different flowers but also consolidates and ships to wholesalers the flowers of other growers both domestic and imported.

23 There is not always a precise division between these systems. A grower who generally negotiates prices and quantities in advance of shipping might also send remaining unsold flowers to a wholesaler on a consignment basis.

24 It has not entirely disappeared. Even today local growers send flowers to New York City's 28th Street market on a consignment basis.

25 Coaxing (or *forcing*) flowers to produce blooms outside their natural seasonal boundaries was not a novelty. This method was the basis of winter production for the Gilded Age wealthy in New York City. But mass producing spring and

summer flowers all year round was considered impractical, in part because flowering in many plants is triggered by day length as well as temperature.

26 Since these early years are not well documented, I depend here on several informants, some of whom were members of the pioneering flower-growing families or were in some way concerned with initiating the Colombia–United States flower trade.

27 Several long-established Colombian growers assured me that Edgar Wells was the industry's pioneer. Another explanation suggests that an American university agronomist, David Cheevers, started the industry. In this account Cheevers's graduate research indicated that the Andes offered an excellent climate for year-round flower growing. In 1962 he traveled to Colombia and spoke about flower growing to a group of U.S.-educated wealthy Colombians. While this version is not consistent with the explanations of my informants, undoubtedly David Cheevers and two other Americans, Harmon Brown and Thomas Keeler, were involved in the early development of the Colombian cut flower industry (Carbonneau et al. 1997). Cheevers subsequently started his own flower farm in Colombia and apparently still grows flowers there, as does Edgar Wells.

28 These were transported to the northeastern United States by a well-established flower trucking company and traded through a large East Coast wholesale florist, the S. S. Pennock Co. of Philadelphia. At about the same time, in 1965, Michael Thomas, an American from a Florida flower-growing family started a farm in Costa Rica that today is one of Costa Rica's largest flower exporters.

29 Wages are about $120 to $130 per month today in Ecuador and Colombia.

30 By 1970 eight landowning Colombian families had diversified into flowers with total production of about twenty hectares. A 1971 Colombian government report offered compelling economic reasons for others to join them. It suggested that Colombian flower growers could earn profits of 57 percent of revenues by exporting cut flowers to the United States (Fairbanks and Lindsay 1997). Colombian growers quickly out-produced emerging Latin American rivals such as Costa Rica and Mexico and by 1977 thirty-five growers were exporting to the United States, filling three daily cargo flights with fifty to eighty tons of flowers (First Research 1978). Colombia prospered by adding chrysanthemums to its carnations and by 1980 was the second largest flower-exporting country in the world after the Netherlands. See Kirsten Bosnak, "Pride of the Andes" *Supermarket Floral,* April 1993.

According to a report prepared by the Colombian Flower Council, about 450 Colombian growing enterprises existed by about 1990, but fewer than fifty firms produced most of the flowers (Bruce Rubin Associates 1993). Many of those early growers are still important today. Several expanded their influence by investing in large importing and trading offices in Miami.

31 Some of these early investors were of European or American origin, as well as Colombian and Ecuadorian.

32 "Flower Growers Ban Cheap Blooms," *New York Times,* September 25, 1925; "40

Notes to Chapter Two

Firms Attacked as Flower Trust; Federal Action Begun Charging Plot to Compel City to Buy Hothouse Blooms Only," *New York Times,* December 16, 1925.

33 Leonard Neft, "Crisis in the Flower Industry," *San Jose Mercury,* August 3, 1973; Mary Hughes, "ITC Begins Hearings on Cut Flower Imports," *Florists' Review,* May 5, 1977; First Research (1978).

34 Neft, "Crisis in the Flower Industry."

35 Government agencies dutifully responded. In 1974 the Department of Treasury held a countervailing duty proceeding to determine whether Colombian government payments to Colombian flower growers were an unfair subsidy. No violation of the Tariff Act of 1930 was identified because the Colombian government immediately stopped paying growers directly and instead subsidized an "agency that assists producers" (Burket and Benedick 1980). In 1977 the United States International Trade Commission considered a request filed by the Society of American Florists for some form of import relief for growers. Testimony from those hearings offers glimpses of the divisions between the interests of United States growers, Miami importers, wholesalers, and retailers. See Burket and Workman (1977) and Mary Hughes, "ITC Begins Hearings on Cut Flower Imports," *Florists' Review,* May 5, 1977. In 1979, Roses Inc., a forty-year-old rose growers' organization, filed another petition claiming imports of fresh cut roses were injuring domestic growers. The commission found no evidence of injury to domestic growers, citing stability in domestic production. Furthermore, according to the commission, the value of domestic production had increased almost 30 percent in a period of several years. Higher prices for both domestic and imported roses were attributed to higher quality and increasing demand (Burket and Benedick 1980; First Research 1978).

36 Mary Hughes, "ITC Begins Hearings on Cut Flower Imports," *Florists' Review,* May 5, 1977; Floral Trade Council newsletter, January 1992; Roses Inc. Bulletin, September 1997.

37 Several northeastern growers, established in the early twentieth century, persisted through these disturbances by introducing new flowers and/or targeting niche markets. These include the Pinchbeck Nursery in Guilford, Connecticut, specializing in roses, and F. W. Battenfeld and Son in Red Hook, New York, formerly a violet grower but now specializing in anemones. The Montgomery Rose Company in Hadley, Massachussetts, has grown roses since 1909, as well as delicate and uncommon gardenias and stephanotis.

38 The total number of flower growers of all types (including flowering potted plants) is difficult to estimate before 1985. Growing establishments were reported by crop and one farm might grow several different flowers. However, it is likely in 1970 there were more than 8,000 and by 1987 the number had fallen to about 4,500, rising again by 2003 to more than 4,700 (Johnson 1990; Jerardo 2002). Current statistics include growers with more than $100,000 in revenues in 36 surveyed states. Of these, 548 were cut flower growers only, down from 829 in 1997. However, these statistics do not include the thousands of farmers earning

less than $10,000 from flower growing. Cut flowers may be one of several crops or sources of income for these farmers.

39 This problem recurred, less severely, between 2002 and 2005.

40 The next detailed survey of floriculture crops will appear after the 2007 Census of Agriculture (Jerardo 2004).

41 Gladioli were not among the imports because freight rates are high for such a heavy bloom. They also have more onerous cultural requirements that limit their appeal to some growers. For example, the bulbs need chilled storage before planting and production requires large land areas. Demand for gladioli slowed following a steady decline in demand for funeral flowers with which they were popularly associated.

42 The wholesale flower market on 28th Street between Sixth and Seventh avenues moved to its current location in the 1920s. At that time, it included some of the firms still important in the region's flower trade today such as Paul Meconi and S.S. Pennock (Carbonneau et al. 1997).

43 Major terminal markets at the end of the 1960s included Boston, New York, and Philadelphia in the Northeast; Chicago, Cleveland, Detroit, and St. Louis in the Midwest; Los Angeles and San Francisco in the West; and Atlanta, Baltimore, Dallas-Fort Worth, and Washington, D.C. in the South (Goodrich 1972). The Miami terminal (import) market emerged later and became important by the 1980s.

44 These wholesale florist statistics should be approached with caution since some floral wholesalers sell only "hard" supplies, such as ribbons, wrappings, floral foam, vases, etc. to retail florists. The statistics do not distinguish between wholesalers of hard goods and perishable goods because many wholesale florists sell both.

45 Another survey conducted in the late 1960s suggests that wholesalers outside major metropolitan areas combined wholesaling with retailing or flower wholesaling with flower growing. These wholesalers were more prosperous (Carpenter 1972).

46 For example, in 1961 a California carnation was 5 cents and a Long Island carnation was 6.4 cents. A standard chrysanthemum from California cost 12 cents and a Long Island chrysanthemum cost 20 cents. Roses went for 6.9 cents in California and 9.1 cents on Long Island. Of course, prices for different varieties and qualities varied, as did freight and possibly grower-shipper charges (Fossum 1973, table 100).

47 This was much higher than the national average of consigned flowers. In 1972 the New York Metropolitan Statistical Area (MSA) had 288 wholesalers comprising 25 percent of the United States total. Their $92 million in sales constituted 20 percent of United States sales (First Research 1978).

48 Wholesalers at the 28th Street market in Manhattan have precisely the same complaints today as their predecessors of the 1970s.

49 Retail florists established several professional organizations including the Society

of American Florists, founded in 1884. They enjoyed a lively professional press including the *Weekly Florists' Review,* a still flourishing Chicago publication that began in 1897. Finally, many wire and telephone services linked florists and facilitated distant delivery of fresh flowers. Florists' Transworld Delivery (FTD), founded in 1910, was the first and Teleflora followed in 1934. These pioneering services were joined by Telegraph Delivery Service (TDS) and Florafax International in 1960, American Floral Services (AFS) in 1970, and Redbook Floral Services in 1976. Wire services apparently functioned well. Between 1950 and 1970, 50 percent of retail florists were members of FTD (Fossum 1973).

50 Averaging roughly one retail florist for every 10,000–12,000 people between 1948 and 1997. Urban areas had greater concentrations of retail florists.

51 In 1950 the value of flower crops was $200 million with consumers spending $650 million on all types of floricultural crops including potted plants. So wholesalers and retailers together accounted for $450 million in sales. By 1970 the value of flower crops had increased to $500 million while consumer expenditures were two billion dollars. Thus total wholesale and retail sales roughly tripled in that period, with retail florists apparently benefiting more than wholesale florists (Fossum 1973).

52 Summer blooms still appeared in street markets but street vendors dwindled in the postwar period, possibly because of better education and work opportunities. Prewar protests against street vending by the robust association of professional retail florists may also have had some effect. "Flower Sales Debated," *New York Times,* March 30, 1935.

53 This florist regretted the disappearance of inexpensive bleeding hearts, for example. Formerly he "sold clusters of them to young men who took this means to express their love." He commented furthermore on the number of expensive new varieties being offered in hothouse flowers, including roses. For a man to spend "thirty or forty dollars on flowers" was "only an incident of daily business," he reported. "Modern Fashions and Flowers," *New York Times,* May 17, 1925.

54 A postwar surge in marriages and a trend toward earlier marriage were partly responsible for this increase.

55 In concert with the trend in almost all agricultural and horticultural products, the prices of many cut flowers fell, relatively, during the twentieth century. In New York in March 1899 a dozen 'American Beauty' roses cost between $6 and $10 ("Money Spent for Flowers: Enormous Sums Expended in a Season—American Beauty Roses and Violets Always in Favor," *New York Times,* March 5, 1899). This is precisely the price asked for a dozen roses today by many Manhattan corner stores.

Three ☙ Fresh Flows

1 Many farms legally classified as corporations are family-owned and run businesses. Many use wage laborers, others depend largely on family labor. Mann classifies farms with more wage workers than family workers as capitalist enter-

prises. Under such a strict definition all farms in Colombia and Ecuador and many in the United States are capitalist enterprises. Many in the Netherlands are not. Yet for this industry, the definition does not seem entirely appropriate since it includes many growers who would be surprised to find themselves described as capitalist enterprises. In the United States, for example, there are thousands of small, sometimes part-time flower growers serving local markets and farm stands and satisfying unstable, unpredictable demand (a dualism described in Berger and Piore 1980). These activities bring the average small American flower grower about $3,000 per annum. As table 3 indicates, these thousands of fresh-cut flower growers accounted for only 1 percent of the total value of United States cut flower farm sales in 1997. (Recent estimates, from 2002, put the contribution of small growers as high as 6 percent.) When not automated, flower production is labor intensive, and contemporary small families can seldom supply all the needed labor. Furthermore, in many flower-growing families, the younger generation is well-educated and has a range of career choices so they are less apt to contribute their labor. Consequently, these small flower growers are often family-run, unsophisticated enterprises that depend on wage labor for their harvests of "uncivilized" flowers that are still largely determined by natural annual cycles and unpredictable conditions.

2   See also Ross Wehner, "Valentine's Day, and All Is Not Rosy: Ecuadoran Flower Workers' Health Failing from Regular Use of Pesticides on Roses for U.S.," *San Francisco Chronicle,* February 13, 2003; Ginger Thompson, "Behind Roses' Beauty, Poor and Ill Workers," *New York Times,* February 13, 2003.

3   According to the classifications in the Human Development Index for 2005 that uses data from 2003.

4   The precise order varies from year to year but the Netherlands and Colombia have been first and second for many years. In 1998 this group comprised nine countries. The top three have since increased their exports and Israel, Zimbabwe and Thailand's exports have declined. In Zimbabwe, political uncertainty was a major contributor to this decline. Marta Pizano, "Zimbabwe: Still Blooming," *Floriculture International,* December 2004.

5   That is, 70 percent of flower *stems* are imported. In dollar values imported cut flowers represent about 60 percent of U.S. consumption because domestically produced flowers are generally the less common and higher-priced blooms.

6   This trend continues. One of California's largest rose growers converted to orchid growing in 2005. Mary Westbrook, "Why Orchids," *Floral Management,* November 2005.

7   I interviewed this grower in March 1999. He immigrated to California in the late 1970s after selling his farm in Holland.

8   These observations are based on an examination of California Cut Flower Commission's *The Cut Flower Guide,* 1997, the Colombia Flower Council Catalogue, 2000, and data available from the California Cut Flower Commission website http://www.cfc.org (accessed April 2005).

9   Based in Ohio, the Association of Specialty Cut Flower Growers helps all United States growers of commercial cut flowers. Its membership includes a number of California growers. See http://www.ascfg.org (accessed December 15, 2005).

10 See http://www.rosesinc.org (accessed December 15, 2005).

11 Joan Silverman, "The Well Traveled Bouquet," *Horticulture,* March 1982. Alstroemerias are commonly known as Peruvian lilies and, like Brodiaea, are a type of lily. Ixiea are closer to iris and gladiolus.

12 Mary Westbrook, "Colombia Today," *Floral Management,* December 2005.

13 Jerardo (2002).

14 There are fewer large United States cut flower growers than there were a decade ago. California currently produces about 70 percent of the cut flowers grown in the United States. In 1998 California had 460 important flower growers but by 2003 there were less than 300 (Prince and Prince 1998; Jerardo 2004).

15 All regions have improved their productivity per hectare in recent years, with Ecuador doubling productivity by 2003, but the relative differences remain. *Floriculture International,* January 2005.

16 United States flower growers brought suit in the late 1990s against Colombian growers for dumping flowers on the American market at lower than cost prices. The dispute was temporarily settled when Colombian flower growers agreed to contribute $3 million to an advertising fund aimed at increasing the market for cut flowers in the United States.

17 Dumping involves selling export goods into another market for less than fair value. Fair value is usually based on the selling price in the producer's home market. Countervailing duties are imposed when the grower's home government transfers funds to the grower; often in the form of export subsidies or special financial aid to growers. In the case of Costa Rica in the 1980s, flower growing developed as a nontraditional export industry and the tax credit program Certificado de Abono Tributario (CAT) was structured by the United States Agency for International Development (USAID). The ITC then penalized Costa Rican growers with countervailing duties because of their participation in the subsidy program. Negotiation led to a gradual phasing out of government support after 1987, ending entirely in September 1999. These incentives contributed to rapid growth in Costa Rican flower exports to the United States between 1985 and 1995. *Florida Ornamental Growers Association Newsletter,* July/August 1987; "Asocolflores, AFIF, Express Concerns re: Commerce Dept. Findings on Methods, Rates," *Flower News,* January 27, 1990; *Association of Floral Importers of Florida Newsletter,* February/March 1992.

18 Debbie Hamrick, "Colombia Wooing the Unusual," *FloraCulture International,* January 2002, 12.

19 Flower exports from Colombia, Ecuador, and Peru increased considerably in the 1990s but there is little evidence that coca exporting declined.

20 An extension of the act was passed in 2001. Subsequently it was amended to become the Andean Trade Promotion and Drug Eradication Act (ATPDEA),

which expired in December 2006. The objective of the act is to "promote broad based economic development, diversify exports, consolidate democracy and defeat the scourge of drug trafficking by providing sustainable economic alternatives to drug crop production." Second Report to Congress on the Operation of the Andean Trade Preference Act as Amended, April 30, 2005. Available at http://www.ustr.gov/Trade_Development/Preference_Programs/ATPA/Reports/Section_Index.html (accessed December 15, 2006). See also *El Nuevo Herald,* January 4, 1990, section 4B; *New York Times,* January 24, 2002, section W1; *South Florida Sun-Sentinel,* February 10, 2002.

21 Canada has had a free trade agreement with the United States since 1989. Its flower exports to the United States have grown steadily since 1994.

22 The Agricultural Plant Health Inspection Service (APHIS) examines flower shipments at every United States port of entry. Infested shipments may be fumigated or returned to the sender but often they are simply destroyed since both fumigation and returning flowers are expensive options that may also damage flowers. About 5,000 infestations are reported annually in Miami. This does not seem excessive considering more than 30,000 boxes of flowers pass through the Miami airport each day, increasing to 60,000–70,000 boxes a day before Valentine's Day. Sherri C. Ranta, "Airport Area Business Blooms with Flower Power," *Miami Today,* February 8, 2001.

23 Hartmut Fischer, "European Union: Stringent New Phytosanitary Requirements for Cut Flower and Plant Imports," *FloraCulture International,* August 2002, 8.

24 As early as 1935 air transportation was being used to export violets from New York to Dallas, New Orleans, and Kansas City ("Violets Travel by Air," *New York Times,* April 17, 1935). By the 1940s, gladioli were being flown from Florida to the Northeast (Joan Silverman, "The Well Traveled Bouquet," *Horticulture,* March 1982), and by 1950, cut flowers grown in California and destined for northeastern and midwestern markets were United Air Lines' leading cargo ("Flowers Lead in Air Cargoes," *New York Times,* August 25, 1950). Following World War II, the formation of several cargo airlines by former war pilots vastly increased the quantities of cut flowers that could be shipped from California to eastern markets in the 1950s.

25 Air service changes after September 11, 2001, are an example. Passenger flights are often a preferred means of transporting cut flowers because their scheduled departures are more reliable than some cargo departures. A decline in passenger traffic in the six months following September 11 prompted many airlines to eliminate flights and destinations, so time-distance for some cut flower shipments was increased. These flight reductions limited cargo space so much that not enough flowers could be shipped to New York to meet Mother's Day demand for flowers in 2002.

26 This was a recent problem for Australian growers who ship 90 percent of their exported cut flowers to Japan, United States, and the Netherlands ("Trade hit by US Attack," *FlowerTECH* 4, no. 7 [2001]).

Notes to Chapter Three

27　Those early gladioli plantings helped established a truck transportation system from Florida to Philadelphia, New Jersey, and New York that still dominates today. "Flower Growers, Point to Big Losses, Protest Union Drive to Enlist Truckmen," *New York Times*, February 13, 1950; Joan Silverman, "The Well Traveled Bouquet," *Horticulture*, March 1982.

28　One important method adopted widely among Latin American growers air-freighting flowers to the United States is known as *dry shipping*. It involves cutting the flowers in tight bud and standing them in a solution of nutrients (predominantly sugar) for several hours before packing them in carton boxes without water. They are rehydrated in special solutions on arrival at their final destination. This contrasts with the *wet shipping* method (flowers standing in buckets of water) widely used in Europe, where most cut flowers are transported in trucks rather than planes.

29　Individual growers, importers, and wholesalers establish and follow such standards, but they are exceptional.

30　By 2003, Internet flower purchasing between retailers and importer-wholesalers seemed to be growing (Jim Leberris, personal communication).

31　Much as the Japanese shape tuna fisheries around the world (Bestor 2001).

32　Peter T. Kilborn and Lynette Clemetson, "Gains of the 90s Did Not Lift All, Census Shows," *New York Times*, June 5, 2002.

Four ❧ State and Structure

1　Castells (1996) and Blim (1992), among others, draw attention to the importance of state policies in positioning national industries in global systems of production and trade.

2　Quoted in Arrighi (1994).

3　Differences in social organization in different areas also influenced variable agricultural development. In coastal districts farmers either owned or rented land on favorable terms and profited from land improvement and intensification of agriculture. In contrast, in the eastern part of the country the social structure was persistently tied to feudalism and common lands. Poor soil, a shortage of fertilizer, and poor transportation also limited agricultural development in that region (Huizinga 1986).

4　Continuing the trade initiated at the beginning of the seventeenth century, the Netherlands is still the world's largest exporter of butter and cheese as well as of flowers. Capital is another major export: At the end of the twentieth century Holland was the third largest investor in the United States and Canada (Hooker 1999).

5　Almost ninety percent of the population is ethnically homogeneous. Of the other 10 percent, most are immigrants from the former Dutch colonies of Surinam and Indonesia. More recent arrivals include "guest workers" from Turkey and Morocco as well as former Yugoslavians who migrated in the 1990s. The Dutch welfare state guarantees a minimum income for all, sometimes supplemented by disability and other allowances. By the 1980s, payments for social insurance and social services consumed about one third of the GNP. Reforms reduced the numbers of recipients and the amounts received. Today's economy is considered to be recovering strongly from the decline of the 1970s and 1980s. About 6.7 million are employed. Some of these work the standard thirty-eight-hour week but many, especially women, have part-time jobs. Country briefings, Netherlands fact sheet, Economist.com, January 2002 and April 2005; "Modelmakers: A Survey of the Netherlands," *Economist,* May 4, 2002; Hooker (1999).

6   United Nations Statistics Division, Commodity Trade Statistics Database 2003.

7   Flower Council of Holland, http://www.flowercouncil.org (accessed December 15, 2005). An additional 25,000 hectares of open fields are devoted to growing flower bulbs for sale around the world.

8   By one account there were 26,000 growers of vegetables and flowers in 1968 (Jaap N. Kras, personal communication).

9   Its annual budget in 2000 was about one hundred million dollars and is about equally divided between technical research, market research, and promotion of Dutch flowers at home and abroad.

10 Jaap Kras, "Dynamite?," *FloraCulture International,* January 2005.

11 The European Economic Community (EEC) was created in 1957 with the Netherlands one of the six founding nations. Ten years later the European Community was established with additional countries joining over succeeding years. In 1992 the European Union was created. Agriculture was important in the economies of the six founding nations but only the Netherlands had a net foreign trade balance in agricultural products at the time (Hasha 1999; Zobbe 2001).

12 The Common Agricultural Policy (CAP) came into effect in 1958 with the Treaty of Rome and the founding of the European Economic Community (EEC). It was gradually implemented through the 1960s (Hasha 1998; Zobbe 2001). An important policy (with amendments) for forty years, its original objectives were to improve agricultural productivity and ensure food supplies at reasonable prices and a fair living standard for farmers. Free trade within the community, common financing, and preferences for community goods were important principles of the policy that supported the production of major food products through various kinds of interventions including subsidies. In recent years the policy has been criticized for high costs and its contribution to environmental damage, overproduction, and inequality in global trading opportunities ("Cleansing the Augean Stables," *Economist,* July 11, 2002; "Europe's Meagre Harvest," *Economist,* January 23, 2003). Some supporters claim that its original objectives are still valid and important today. Bertie Ahern, "We Must Stand by the Common Agricultural Policy," *Financial Times,* September 26, 2005.

13 The Dutch government recently reduced its financial participation in flower-related research in favor of environmental research, maintaining that the Dutch flower industry is economically strong enough to finance its own research. A. Priel, "Mission to Reshape Israeli policy," *FlowerTECH,* 5, no. 1 (2002).

14 Growers grumble occasionally about the activities of the Product Board for Horticulture, perhaps resenting their mandatory contributions and involuntary membership.

15 See Fairbanks and Lindsay (1997).

16 Jacob M. Schlesinge and Craig Karmin, "No Safe Haven: Dollar's Slide Reflects Wariness about U.S.," *Wall Street Journal,* June 3, 2002.

17 Purchasing power parity puts this at about $4,000, still not a princely sum. Country Briefing, Economist.com, April 2005.

18 Country Briefing, Economist.com, May 2001; "Optimism after the Chaos," *Miami Herald,* November 7, 2000.

19 In contrast, the average European cow receives about $2.50 per day in subsidies. Edmund L. Andrews, "Rich Nations Criticized for Barriers to Trade," *New York Times,* September 30, 2002.

20 Several people I spoke to estimated that about 70 percent of current capital investment in flower farms is from Ecuadorian funds. A large part of the remainder seems to be supplied by Colombian growers who have extended their business interests into Ecuador partly in response to growing civil unrest and insecurity in Colombia. Some growers simply moved to Ecuador.

21 These export figures are taken for 1985 and 1990 from Salamea and Waters (1995). 2004 figures come from Expoflores at http://www.expoflores.com (accessed December 15, 2005).

22 Their conversation recalls Dutch growers' similar enthusiasm for the superiority of rose-growing technology that improves on nature. Artificial soil mixes, hydroponic cultivation, and carbon dioxide supplements are some of the explanations for the superiority of Dutch blooms.

23 In Colombia, a larger percentage of flower growing hectares are owned by non-family private corporations including Dole Fresh Flowers, now a privately owned (but not necessarily family-owned) multinational corporation (see chapter 7).

24 CEPAL, *Annuario estadistico de America Latina y el Caribe,* 2004.

25 Some cut production but not enough to raise prices. Bankruptcies increased ("La Floricultura uno de los negocios más rentables del siglo XXI?" *Marketing Flowers* 19 [2001]). Russian demand for Ecuadorian roses increased again by 2003.

26 Global statistics don't distinguish between types of roses so this statistical decline could be the result of the current mix of roses worldwide. For example, a high proportion of lower-priced "sweetheart" roses would lower the average return per stem. If the mix shifts in favor of the much higher-priced large-headed roses, then the average return per stem would rise.

27 Nancy Laws, "World Commerce in Cut Flowers and Roses," *FloraCulture International,* April 2002, 23–25.

28 Jaap Kras, "Ode to the Rose, Consumer Favorite," *FloraCulture International,* April 2002, 40.

29 Fairbanks and Lindsay analyzed the Colombian flower industry. They used it as an example of the developing world pattern in which initial success occurs in

some enterprise that depends on cheap labor, local resources, and government assistance but is subsequently halted by an inability to convert initial success to competitive advantage that confers rising standards of living on citizens. Developing countries, they suggest, will need to make a transition from comparative advantage of natural resources and cheap labor (easily duplicated in many nations) to competitive advantage by making strategic choices and drawing on their resources of innovation, knowledge, and human capital.

30 The association attempts to educate growers about new species and cultivation techniques, as do various trade magazines. Expoflores also lobbies government departments over such important issues as high freight rates, the continuation of favorable trade agreements, and the intellectual property rights that affect growers' royalty payments to breeders.

31 Sometimes these are established with the aid of Dutch experts trained in the Netherlands.

32 In some countries such as Colombia and Costa Rica tax credits supplied through export certificates or Certificados de Abono Tributario (CAT) were the means of subsidy. See Fairbanks and Lindsay (1997) for Colombia and Edelman (1999) for Costa Rica. I do not know whether credits were specifically used in Ecuador.

33 CEPAL, *Annuario estadistico*.

34 "La Floricultura uno de los negocios más rentables del siglo XXI?" *Marketing Flowers* 19 (2001).

35 Expoflores 2000 and *Production and Marketing of Roses* 2 (2003).

36 Instability and volatility affect many flower-growing regions. Israel and Zimbabwe are examples of nations with formerly thriving, expanding cut flower industries that have declined during recent political turmoil. California growers in 2000 and 2001 were in dire straits because of energy shortages and rising energy prices that greatly increased their production costs. Curiously, Colombia's thirty years of turmoil has had little long-term effect on flower production and export. The dollar value of Colombian flower exports has generally risen during the last twenty-five years. Between 1992 and 2000 alone, exports increased around 50 percent in value.

37 "Politics in Ecuador: Taken for a Ride," *Economist,* August 3, 2002, 31; "A Coup by Congress and the Street," *Economist,* April 23, 2005.

38 Colombian floriculture is relatively dispersed with about five hundred growers providing 75 percent of exports—especially compared to some regions such as Kenya, where flower production is dominated by only three growers (Hughes 2004). However, it is not clear from statistics how many of these five hundred growers are diversifying into specialty flowers and away from the traditional rose, carnation, and chrysanthemum crops. It is quite possible that a single large grower, Dole Fresh Flowers, currently producing about 25 percent of Colombian flower exports, is responsible for much of the shift to specialty blooms evident in export and import statistics.

39 Fairbanks and Lindsay comment that when nations undervalue their currencies

to aid competitiveness they are "exporting the wealth of their countries to richer countries. That is, purchasers in the United States, for example, would get to buy Andean flowers at very low prices, thus capturing the wealth of those countries cheaply" (1997, 105).

40   "La Floricultura uno de los negocios más rentables del siglo XXI?" *Marketing Flowers* 19 (2001).

41   "Dollar Politics," *Economist,* March 16, 2000, and "Divided about the Dollar," *Economist,* January 4, 2001.

42   "Optimism after the Chaos." Furthermore, at least during the 1970s and 1980s, Colombian growers may have enjoyed the benefits of an undervalued peso as well as access to investment capital generated by the drug trade, portions of which were returned to Colombia and channeled into the formal economy partly through local banks' investment in nondrug businesses (Naylor 1987). "Squandering an Unlikely Recovery," *Economist,* September 15, 2001; "Ecuador Bounced Back with the Dollar: Argentina Could Too," *Wall Street Journal,* November 2, 2001.

43   Mary Westbrook, "Colombia Today," *Floral Management,* December 2005.

44   These estimates are based on data from Expoflores and Korovkin (2003).

45   For analysis of the gender question in Latin American flower farm employment, see Flores and Quintana (1995) for Mexico, and Salamea and Waters (1995) for Ecuador. For the effects of flower farm employment on Ecuadorian people and communities, see Mena (1999), Krupa (2001), and Korovkin (2003).

46   Korovkin (2003) describes the "psychological and social problems that are likely to haunt young flower plantation workers: the anxiety generated by increasing productivity targets and high labor turnover rates, identity crises caused by the clash between communal norms and individual achievement orientations and frustration associated with greatly increased but thwarted individual aspirations." Furthermore, mothers working on the farms share stresses experienced by working mothers almost everywhere. They feel anxiety, guilt, and stress when they cannot give the same attention as previously to their children, to caring for livestock and domestic crops, and to the community organizations that are the foundation of rural civil society

47   This form of gender discrimination also occurs on Colombian and Kenyan flower farms (Smith et al. 2004).

48   Corporación Cactus in Colombia has been very active in drawing attention to these health issues, among other things.

49   See, for example, Ginger Thompson, "Behind Roses' Beauty, Poor and Ill Workers," *New York Times,* February 13, 2003, and Ross Wehner, "Valentine's Day, and All Is Not Rosy: Ecuadoran Flower Workers' Health Failing from Regular Use of Pesticides on Roses for U.S.," *San Francisco Chronicle,* February 13, 2003.

50   A four-year study by CEAS (Centro de Estudios y Asesoria en Salud) in Quito, funded by Canada's International Development Research Center and under the guidance of Dr. Jaime Breilh, is nearing conclusion. One of its objectives is to

promote an awareness of floriculture's health risks and to suggest laws and other means to encourage sustainable floriculture. A preliminary report describes the prevalence of subtle health problems among flower workers. These include stress and disorders affecting the neurological, blood marrow and liver systems and genetic stability that are linked to continuous levels of exposure to agricultural chemicals. They are most evident among workers in cultivation and post-harvest. Exposure is of low intensity on farms that comply with international protection standards but it can be high on plantations where the codes of conduct for pesticide use and worker protection are not met (Breilh 2004).

51 An important recommendation is the provision and use of clothing such as masks, gloves, hats, and body-suits to protect workers against chemicals on the plants. On many farms I visited, employees were well supplied with protective clothing. On others, employees wore little protection, even when actually spraying chemicals on plants. Protective equipment is required by law, Krupa explains (2001), but workers he interviewed complained that it is not always provided, especially when damaged equipment needs replacing. Mena's study (1999) indicated that more than a quarter of workers received no protective equipment at all and very few were given information about health risks associated with chemical exposure. Managers, on the other hand, insist that some workers refuse to wear or use the protective equipment provided.

52 Sources: Expoflores and Statistics Netherlands, Voorburg/Heerlen, 2002, http://www.cbs.nl/en/figures/keyfigures (accessed April 2005).

53 A nation can theoretically benefit by importing goods that can be produced more efficiently at home than abroad so long as it concentrates on products at which it is even more efficient (Baumol and Blinder 1994).

54 Furthermore, the continuous instability caused by civil war and the drug trade have an unmeasured impact on the flower industry by encouraging Colombian flower professionals to move themselves and their money to other nations and by discouraging experts and investment funds from traveling to Colombia.

55 Berger and Piore (1980) described the importance of market division into stable and unstable segments. The basis of this duality, as they see it, is productivity that is dependent on the division of labor, which, in turn, is a function of market size and stable demand. A single firm (or national industry), they suggest, may emerge to separate and govern the stable and predictable market while many small firms (or nations) would satisfy the fluctuating portion of demand. Firms in the stable segment are capital intensive because stability encourages investment. They use extensive division of labor and specialized resources while the unstable component uses less specialized capital and labor that can move in and out of other activities in response to variation in demand and increased uncertainty. When very few firms occupy the stable segment, Berger and Piore argue, additional concentration is minimized by tacit understandings and fear of severe competition between firms.

56 This geographic differentiation in markets is common. In Kenya, for example,

dominant growers send 90 percent of their flowers to just three countries, with most going to the Netherlands and much smaller quantities to the United Kingdom and Germany (Hughes 2000, 2004; Smith et al. 2004). A tiny fraction of Kenyan flowers reach the United States.

57 A survey of California greenhouse growers suggested that, of large growers (with more than ten acres or four hectares), over half used computerized environmental controls and hydroponics, while a third had carbon dioxide injection, water recycling, and soil heating and cooling (Prince and Prince 1998).

58 I am thinking here of Daniel Luria's analysis of 3,000 small manufacturing plants in the United States. He assessed firms according to three scales of innovative behavior and then divided them into a tripartite hierarchy. Luria observed that the middle group takes market share from the upper (most innovative and highest prices) and lower (least innovative and lowest prices). Those with high investment in equipment, training, and innovation are less able to generate the returns needed. The winners in this competition are the worst of the low-level group and the best of the middle group. So "good" producers are not rewarded by the market. Furthermore, decline in "good" producers means the industry as a whole suffers from declining quality, variety of products, and lower productivity and technical change. See Luria, "Why Markets Tolerate Mediocre Manufacturing," *Challenge,* July–August 1966, 11–16. In the Netherlands the implicit difficulties for "good" producers may, at times, be alleviated by partial state funding of new cutting-edge automated systems. See "Moving Flowers," *FloraCulture International,* March 2001, 28–31.

59 According to some Ecuadorian growers, average prices for roses, between Russia and the United States, were about thirty-five cents per stem in 1996–97, with average costs of production about sixteen to eighteen cents per stem. By 2001 average prices were twenty-two cents while average costs had crept closer to twenty cents.

Five ⊛ Cultivating the Global Garden

1 High altitude equatorial sunlight is both powerful and directly overhead. This helps develop particularly strong plants and stems as well as larger rose blooms.

2 I follow Castell's distinction between knowledge and information. He defines knowledge as "a set of organized statements of facts or ideas, presenting a reasoned judgment or an experimental result, which is transmitted to others through some communication medium in some systematic form," while information is "data that have been organized and communicated" (1996).

3 Many flower growers produce for purely local markets. They do not face the same concerns about technology, relationships, and capital financing as growers for international markets and they are not generally included in this study. Some of the local United States growers in California, in the mid-Atlantic states, and in other regions are a bit different. They may grow to the high standards necessary

to compete with imported flowers while also selling some of their lesser quality flowers through local farmers' markets and other outlets.

4 It seems to me that the great majority of those engaged in growing and trading cut flowers in the global system that delivers flowers to U.S. consumers correspond to this second level of Braudel's three-tiered model of economic activity, that is, the competitive sector of small business enterprises sandwiched between monopoly capitalism at the topmost level and a lower, informal economic sector functioning outside the authority of state and market where fraud, barter, and moonlighting operate. However, all three levels coexist in the fresh-cut flower value chain.

5 The major cut flower category discussed in chapter 2 expanded during the 1980s. Today major flowers in United States trade, by volume, are rose, chrysanthemum, gerbera, lily, carnation, and alstroemeria. California growers add iris, delphinium, snapdragon, and gladiolus to the above list to make a ten-bloom major cut flower category. California growers also include about 100 additional types of flowers in their specialty cut flowers category (Prince and Prince 1998).

6 Carbon dioxide enrichment increases yield by stimulating photosynthesis. In some greenhouses carbon dioxide may be double the normal or natural levels. In the Netherlands it is often generated in association with heating systems or in cogenerators that supply heat, electricity, and carbon dioxide. In hydroponic systems, plants mature in pots filled with a loose compound of shredded coconut husks, rockwool or some other nonsoil or "substrate" substance. These lightly textured mixes encourage strong roots, while nutrient-enhanced water periodically feeds the roots through a flexible piping system attached to each pot. Roses, gerberas, carnations, and other flowers flourish because the technique eliminates the risk of fungal diseases (and related insect infestations) to which they are very susceptible if water lingers on foliage or buds. Yields may improve by 20–25 percent. However, installation adds 10–40 percent to the costs of traditional beds in soil. Marta Pizano, "Zimbabwe: Still Blooming," *FloraCulture International*, December 2004.

7 Rabobank was formed in 1972 from the merger of two cooperative farmers' banks—the Cooperative Central Raiffeissen Bank and the Cooperative Central Farmer's Credit Bank ("Boerenleenbank")—both originally established in the late nineteenth century. Rabobank remains a cooperative membership institution, much as it was 100 years ago. It is owned by the central Rabobank, its subsidiaries, and local cooperative banks in the Netherlands and profits are reinvested in the growth of local businesses. Now among the world's largest banks, it offers financial services in thirty-seven countries. See http://www.rabobankamerica.com (accessed December 15, 2005).

8 Flowering plants in pots, also important crops in the Netherlands, are more likely to be traded outside the auction system.

9 G. Trip's excellent study of decisionmaking among Netherlands chrysanthemum growers (2000) showed how prices vary between different cultivated varieties of

the same flower since different shapes, sizes, and colors differ in popularity. Constantly choosing to grow the most popular color rather than the least popular color in each monthly period was calculated to increase the grower's annual return by 13 percent. Trip's study showed that some Dutch growers were reluctant to track prices in this way and base their new planting decisions on resulting information.

10 The auction makes money on renting out the carts, buckets, boxes, etc., and on a percentage of the turnover of both growers and wholesale buyers. Therefore, some argue, there is little incentive for the auction to encourage higher flower prices. Increased flower prices would help growers (but not the wholesale buyers) substantially more than, say, reducing the costs of cooperative auction membership has done. Jaap Kras, "Flower and Plant Cooperatives," *FloraCulture International,* October 2005.

11 Delbard Roses, for example, placed their new 'Red Intuition' rose with only three growers in the world. *FloraCulture International,* January 2002, 8. These growers were given exclusive growing rights for five years, later extended for a further two years. In such cases growers may calculate breeder royalties on the basis of blooms produced rather than per plant, which is typical.

12 Edward Bent, "The Price of a Good Rose," *FloraCulture International,* June 2001.

13 There are exceptions. 'First Red,' hybridized by the French breeder Nirp International, had already been in production for eleven years in 2001 when it was said to be the most widely planted rose in the world. Edward Bent, "The Price of a Good Rose," *FloraCulture International,* June 2001.

14 Total turnover of cut flowers and plants for all the Netherlands auctions in 2004 was about 3.6 billion euros. Jaap Kras, "Frans Kuiper Leaves the VBA," *FloraCulture International,* July 2005.

15 Quoted in Jennifer Neujarh, "The Health of the Dutch Auction System," *FloraCulture International,* December 2005.

16 Jeremy Pertwee, "Right Decision Can Save a Small Fortune," *FlowerTECH* 5, no. 5 (2002).

17 Román Alonso and Lisa Eisner, "Double Dutch: The Fantasy Life of that Famous Fashion Duo Viktor and Rolf," *New York Times,* December 8, 2002.

18 See Pinch et al. (2003) and Tewari (1999) for more on the competitive advantages of geographical clusters and the way knowledge may or may not be disseminated between firms within clusters and chains.

19 Some growers do not attempt direct trade in the international market, consigning instead to a local grower-shipper in Ecuador. The local grower-shipper is spatially and sometimes culturally closer and, over the long term, apparently economically preferable. Poor floricultural knowledge (many newer Latin American growers have little experience in floriculture although most hire an agronomist for technical knowledge), poor flower quality, and bad experiences in earlier trading relationships are some of the reasons growers gave me for this choice. This additional node in the commodity chain reduces returns, but growers balance that loss

against the insuperable complexities of gathering reliable market knowledge and establishing trustworthy international relationships across vast spatial and cultural barriers. In this respect they have much in common with other small agricultural producers, for example, Brazilian grape growers. See Collins (2000). The risk of abuse may be less than in dealing with unknown importers in Miami who may assess unreasonable credits or simply never pay.

20 Other Netherlands growers estimated that total costs with delivery and various other fees are somewhat higher. In 1995 a developing country producer selling through the Dutch auctions could expect to spend much more. Total fees and charges amounted to about 20 percent of sales price plus the cost of air freight to the Netherlands (White 1997).

21 Exporting flowers to the Netherlands auctions can be costly for many foreign growers. See Franklin Tulcanaza de la Torre, "Mercadeo de rosas," *La Flor de Ecuador,* May 2001; Aaron Priel, "Currency and Competition Depress Israel's Growers," *FlowerTECH* 4, no. 2 (2001).

22 Netherlands growers and buyers have formal contracts with the auctions.

23 Growers of potted flowering plants are more likely to produce under contract. Because potted plants are too heavy for airfreight, virtually all are grown in the United States or Canada.

24 This inconvenience may be balanced by increased profits and possibly by reductions in flower wastage, for the grower. Since 2001, this strategy of growing a mixed variety of flowers has spread among other Latin American growers with whom I have maintained contact. The demand from supermarkets and the decline of traditional wholesale and retail was the reason for this change (Michael Thomas, personal communication).

25 The newest rose, gerbera, or alstroemeria is seldom totally new but rather a refinement of an existing cultivar. It is created (as are most cut flower cultivars) using traditional methods of cross-pollination. Hundreds of thousands of crosses and five to seven years of trials are needed to produce a handful of marketable new flowers. In some cases these varieties are marketable in only a few growing regions. A tall alstroemeria, for example, would probably not be bought by Netherlands growers since the extra height would require more expensive and scarce labor in tying and training, a factor that would not discourage an Ecuadorian grower who may welcome a variety not being grown by the competition in the Netherlands. A successful rose may support a rose-breeding enterprise for many years and sustain investment in the thousands of crosses and trials that disappoint.

Many people assume that new cut flowers are the result of gene manipulation. But the huge cost of licensing and using gene technology cannot be recovered in the sales of rose plants for commercial cut flower growing or even through a licensing fee on individual stems. A flower produced with gene technology will have particular, selected characteristics that may have limited global appeal. Different markets seek roses with different characteristics, and individual growers themselves look for yet another range of characteristics. Often a particular rose variety will be selected by a limited number of growers in a particular growing region because it does well in their conditions and sells in the markets they connect to. Other growers will prefer other roses. The 'Blue Moon' carnation is the only genetically modified flower in commercial cut flower production today. It seems unlikely that others will be introduced in the near future. A long-standing effort to produce a blue rose using genetic modification has so far been unsuccessful. *Society of American Florists Floral Trend Tracker,* Summer 2005.

Some research is being conducted on using biotechnology to restore lost scent to various flowers such as snapdragons (*Antirrhinum*), but it will be many years before such research has commercial applications. There appears to be rather more biotechnological research into genetic manipulation of various flower characteristics for flowering potted plants and bedding plants—a far larger and more uniform market.

Six ◈ Specialty and Abundance

1 I conservatively estimate the total value of the wholesale trade in flowers in the NYMA in 2005 at over $500 million. Local retailers then sell these same flowers and other wholesale floral items to consumers for more than a billion dollars. These estimates are based on the United States Census Bureau (a division of the Department of Commerce) Economic Census 2002 data on wholesale and retail florists, other statistics, my observations and anecdotal evidence.

2 Only about one-third of cut flowers sold in the United States today are bought by men, traditionally the purchasers of most flowers (see chapter 1). The majority of male purchases today are made at Valentine's Day. In the NYMA, however, the proportion of male flower buyers seems higher and their reasons for buying may differ from those of the typical American male (see chapter 8).

3 Nicholas Kulish, "Snapshot of America 2000: Small Census Survey Finds Richer, More Educated, Multilingual Nation," *Wall Street Journal,* August 6, 2001; Eric Schmitt, "Census Data Show a Sharp Increase in Living Standard," *New York Times,* August 6, 2001; American Floral Endowment data, Society of American Florists, quoted in *Floral Management,* June 2004, 10.

4 Janny Scott, "The Census—New York; Households Grow and Fewer People Live Alone, Data Show," *New York Times,* May 22, 2001.

5 More than 43 percent of the foreign-born arrived after 1990, and 80 percent after 1980. The foreign-born also account for about 20 percent of the population in surrounding Metropolitan Area counties. Nina Bernstein, "Record Immigration Is Changing the Face of New York's Neighborhoods," *New York Times,* January 24, 2005.

6 Ibid.

7 In 1980 the New York City white population was 52 percent. By 1990 this had shrunk to 43 percent. Sections and neighborhoods changed at different rates. In

the Elmhurst-Corona district of Queens—the location of several of my retail florist encounters—alteration was more dramatic, with the white population shifting from 98 percent in 1960 to 18 percent in 1990. Irish, Italians, Jews, and others of European extraction now live alongside Chinese, Colombians, Haitians, Indians, Koreans, and many others. While such changes are more evident in U.S. coastal cities than in the middle of the country, nevertheless, as Sanjek points out (2001), the United States citizenry is undergoing a great transformation.

8   I follow the broad definition, given in the U.S. Census Bureau Census 1997, of wholesalers as those organized to sell or arrange the purchase or sale of goods for resale, that is, goods sold to other wholesalers or retailers.

9   Whereas with fewer direct flights to East Coast cities with USDA animal and plant hygiene (phytosanitary) inspection facilities (see chapter 3), flowers arriving by air from Central and South America must enter (at the time of writing) through Miami, Savannah, Washington, or New York.

10 Values are quite small in some cases. For example, Zimbabwe and South Africa each sent about US $300,000 worth of blooms in 2000. By 2004 Zimbabwe's exports to United States had declined to about $58,000.

11 California also sends large quantities of specialty cut flowers to the NYMA.

12 As discussed later in this chapter, mass retailers like Wal-Mart and Sam's Club were also unknown in 1970s. Superstore or box-store retailers like Home Depot are gaining ground in flower retailing in some parts of the United States, especially in their sales of flowering potted plants. However, in the NYMA their cut flower sales lag far behind the other retail forms.

13 *Floral Management,* January 2005. Also reported in *Floral Cuttings,* February 2005, and the Economic Census, 2002.

14 In 2000 (and in 2002) total United States retail florists sales amounted to about $6.5 billion (Silvergleit 2001). But the actual quantity and value of fresh-cut flowers is a small portion of these totals because these figures include sales of other types of gifts (potted plants, teddy bears, balloons, ornaments, etc.) as well as charges for delivery, vases, wrappings, labor, and so on.

15 According to the IPSOS/AFE Consumer Tracking Study 2004, funerals (or "sympathy") averaged 23 percent of florists' sales in 2003. But in many regions it is considerably less. *Floral Management,* February 2005.

16 Other immigrant groups have contributed to New York City flower retail in other ways. Greek wholesale and retail florists were important for most of the twentieth century and remain so. Today, Latin American immigrants often supply the cheap unskilled labor needed to unpack and prepare flowers and clean up flower-selling spaces. The mobile-wholesalers described later in this chapter also are often immigrants.

17 Most I interviewed worked six days a week and sometimes seven with fifteen-hour work days common in advance of important flower holidays

18 Mary Hughes, "ITC Begins Hearings on Cut Flower Imports," *Florists' Review,* May 5, 1977. The holidays observed by the retail floral industry today include

"Random Acts of Kindness Week," "National Good Neighbor Day," "Reconciliation Day," and "Employee Appreciation Day" (presumably for non-secretaries). *Floral Retailing,* March 2001.

19 See http://www.aboutflowers.com (accessed December 15, 2005).

20 Patti Schuldenfrei, "A.M. New York: In the Heart of the City and Out in the Suburbs, New York's Floral Distribution System Is Entering a New Day," *Florists' Review,* September 6, 1984.

21 Throughout this book I follow the classification of the Organization for Economic Cooperation and Development (OECD) for business size described by Bennett Harrison (1997). Very small firms have fewer than twenty employees. Small companies have twenty to a hundred employees. Large firms have more than a hundred employees.

22 Elisabeth Bumiller, "A Star Floral Designer's Flights of Fancy," *New York Times,* December 22, 1998.

23 Robert J. Hughes, "Galas for Less: The New Rules," *Wall Street Journal,* June 7, 2002.

24 By the late 1990s over 50 percent of New York City's Korean immigrants were self-employed, with a further 30 percent working in Korean-owned businesses. Language difficulties are often a factor in this unusual employment pattern (Min 1998).

25 du Gay (2004b) has pointed out that some shop assistants welcomed the impersonality of the self-service system as a liberation and a release from "servitude."

26 Retailing had begun selling nonmaterial fantasies and shaping class identity as early as the mid-nineteenth century (Miller 1981; Ohmann 1996).

27 Edmund Estes et al., "Retailing Florist Crops through Mass-Merchandising Outlets in Four Western Metropolitan Areas," *Florists' Review,* June 30, 1977.

28 Monica Humbard, "Competition, the Competitive Nature of the Business," *Super Floral Millennium Issue,* 1999, 24.

29 Interviews and statistics derived from the American Floral Endowment Consumer Tracking Study support this contention.

30 Not surprisingly, the large chain supermarkets (self-distributing) are more likely than small independent supermarkets (not self-distributing) to operate full-service departments. However, full-service floral departments have proved to be expensive to operate and future departments may be more likely to be self-service (*Floral Marketing,* 1999).

31 Similar developments have affected cut flower retail in the United Kingdom. Five grocery chains—Tesco, Sainsbury, Safeway, Morrison, and Asda (purchased by Wal-Mart in 1999)—are heavily involved in superstores and dominated 90 percent of the United Kingdom market by late 1990s. Particular firms also enjoyed regional dominance. In southern England, for example, Tesco and Sainsbury governed 60–70 percent of grocery retail (Wrigley and Lowe 2002).

32 As Wrigley and Lowe point out, there is no certainty that this supercenter model will prevail in the United Kingdom and United States during the twenty-first century, since small-format retailing is gaining ground in some regions.

33 Bart Ziegler, "From the Runway to the Side of the Driveway," *Wall Street Journal,* April 15, 2005.

34 Mary Westbrook, "Orchids Worth Ogling," *Floral Management,* February 2005.

35 About 2 percent in 2004. *Floral Cuttings,* December 2005.

36 Dole Fresh Flower Inc.'s direct-to-consumer website, http://www.flowernet.com, was still functioning in 2001 but subsequently disappeared and was not replaced. See also chapter 7.

37 These were the fulfillment firms listed in July 2005 at http://www.walmart.com.

38 See, for example, John Leland, "The $100 Posy Race. Critics Decide Which Bouquets Speak the Language of Love," *New York Times,* February 6, 2003; Nina Siegal, "Tulip Mania for Mom," *Wall Street Journal,* April 29, 2005; and Charles Passy, "Roses of a Different Color," *Wall Street Journal,* February 3, 2005.

39 Olivia Barker, "A War of the Roses Erupts at Oscar Time," USA Today, February 24, 2005.

40 These style books have been issued for decades but I was unable to track down copies prior to 1992.

41 There were eight locations in all. Three retail florists, one suburban and two urban, three urban convenience stores in different boroughs, and two supermarkets, one urban and one suburban.

42 In rural areas there are far fewer retail sites for buying flowers. Often they are limited to widely dispersed traditional florists (and to Internet sites)—a form of exclusion from an area of shopping and consumer culture and one of the socio-spatial inequalities of retailing. For more on this concept, see Williams et al. (2001).

43 About 330 large wholesale firms (10 percent of the total), each with annual sales over $5 million, are responsible for close to 60 percent of United States wholesale flower sales.

44 "Flower Growers, Point to Big Losses, Protest Union Drive to Enlist Truckmen," *New York Times,* February 13, 1950; Patti Schuldenfrei, "A.M. New York: In the Heart of the City and Out in the Suburbs, New York's Floral Distribution System Is Entering a New Day," *Florists' Review,* September 6, 1984.

45 A further twenty or so wholesalers sell silk flowers as well as the vases, ribbons, and other "hard goods" needed to arrange flowers.

46 See, for example, Freidberg (2004).

47 David W. Dunlap, "In the Flower District, a Crop of High-Rises," *New York Times,* October 10, 1999.

48 Cara S. Trager, "Flower Market on Shaky Ground," *Crain's New York Business,* July 10, 2000. Patrick O'Gilfoil Healy, "Flower District Working on a Move," *New York Times,* October 12, 2005.

49 Terry Pristin, "Flower District Considers a Repotting: Wholesale Market Feels Pressure as Neighborhood Is Transformed," *New York Times,* November 1, 2000.

50 The United States Census Bureau Census statistics indicate the number of traditional retail florists businesses declined about 13 percent between 1992 and 2002 both in the United States and in the NYMA.

51 Some traditional wholesalers refuse to buy from Miami importer-wholesalers, arranging instead to buy directly from Latin American farms. The flowers are shipped to them in New York either on direct flights or through Miami, where an agent handles inspections and ensures that they are swiftly trucked to New York.

52 The Association of Floral Importers of Florida gives these numbers. This association's members include the major Miami importers, who, in 2000, accounted for about 85 percent of import volume. The number of importers has declined from 130 or more, in 2002, when USA Floral Products, Inc. collapsed and former employees established small importing businesses in Miami. See chapter 7. A few importer-wholesalers are also found in other cities but I have little information about them.

53 Bouquet-makers are probably included in these total numbers.

54 Exporting and importing statistical sources use different bases for their statistics. As noted in chapter 5, many flowers, especially from Latin America, arrive on consignment, so the value of the shipment is estimated and true value is not always known until after it is sold. USDA import statistics are based on extrapolations from inspections and accompanying shipping documents. In contrast, export statistics supplied by flower export associations in various countries are based on members' estimates of sales and the values may be higher than the estimates given on import documents. While confusing and sometimes contradictory, these varied sources are nevertheless useful to describe trends.

55 Over 70 percent of flowers imported into the United States pass through Miami.

56 The original Dutch mobile wholesalers of the 1980s depended on personal connections in the Netherlands for their flower supplies, and this special connection with a supplying country still fuels some of these enterprises. For example, I met a Thai mobile wholesaler who receives regular shipments of Thailand orchids at JFK airport and drives them around to wholesalers, florist shops, and corner stores until all are sold (Amwat Nan Raviwangse, personal communication).

57 These traders buy at very low prices and their markup is often only 15–20 percent compared to the traditional wholesaler's 30–50 percent on higher-priced flowers.

58 See, for example, Alárcon's description (2000) of the chain connecting Asia, Los Angeles, and Mexico City that supplies clothing. Alárcon explains the interplay between adjacent levels of distribution—formal, semiformal, and informal (*tráfico de hormiga*)—that assemble huge quantities of goods and distribute them globally.

Seven ֎ Risk and Relationships

1 This form of social, relational exchange depends a lot on reciprocity, obligation, and trust. It shares characteristics with the *guanxi* market model of Hong Kong and Taiwan that Alan Smart (1997) has described as integrating small, medium, and even large firms through networks of alliances. It also corresponds with Castells's description of Asian market models (1996). See also Blim (2000) for other types of capitalism and exchange.

2   This is a simpler formulation than the (Keynesian) economic understanding of uncertainty in the "sense of unquantifiable risk" and the related issue of whether uncertainty "represents an absence of knowledge in some absolute sense, or whether it is a relative concept referring to the degree. . . . of rational doubt" (Dow 1994).

3   My thoughts about risk, trust, and uncertainty in this chapter draw heavily on Boden (2000).

4   Wholesalers and retailers often work with markups, while supermarkets and a few wholesalers plan around gross margins. Gross profit margin is a percentage factor of sale price. If a one-dollar flower is sold for $1.50 the *margin* is 33 percent. Markup, on the other hand, is a percentage of the cost price. So a one-dollar flower *marked up* 33 percent would sell for $1.33.

5   Kimberley Stevens, "Fairest Bloom of the Season," *New York Times,* November 2, 1997.

6   Few mid-level retail florists buy the costly November peonies; their high prices generally confine them to the elite levels of consumption.

7   As these examples suggest, different types and qualities of bloom become associated with different producing regions: carnations with Colombia, short tulips with Holland, tall tulips with France, delphinium with California and France, fine lilies with the Netherlands, large roses with Ecuador, *Dendrobium* orchids with Thailand, and so on, much as simpler market systems associated different products with different villages. Grower organizations try to capitalize on these associations to establish a distinctive global position for their flowers (at least within the trade and more rarely among some consumers), as with "Ecuadorian" roses and "Holland" flowers.

8   Tim Linden, "Opportunities for 'High-Value' Produce Explored at Marketing Conference," *Produce News,* March 3, 2003.

9   George Vogt of Bachman's European Flower Markets made this prediction in 1972 when Bachman's, a Minnesota retail florist chain, operated leased flower departments inside supermarkets. At the time, Bachman's was owned by the Pillsbury Company. In 1989 Bachman's, no longer owned by Pillsbury (which is itself now owned by General Mills), closed its supermarket operations. Recently Bachman's opened floral stores inside Byerly supermarkets, a small upscale chain in Minnesota. Vogt, along with others, accurately predicted great increases in the number of flowers sold through supermarkets. See http://www.bachmans.com (accessed December 15, 2005).

10 Convenience stores in the NYMA are more responsive to local preferences because of their loose network structure. In other cities and suburban and rural areas, convenience store supply may be somewhat less responsive to consumer choices.

11 Upscale supermarkets with full-time floral department employees also sell flowers as single stems and as custom-made arrangements.

12 Monica Hubbard, "Competition: The Competitive Nature of Business," *Super Floral Millennium Issue,* 1999.

Notes to Chapter Seven

13 Dawn J. Grubb, "Marketing to the Masses," *Super Floral Millennium Issue,* 1999.

14 These wrappings, often designed in the Netherlands or the United States, are sometimes manufactured near bouquet-makers in Colombia, for example, but more often are themselves imported from Italy and Korea, among other places.

15 This was slowly adopted by supermarkets after its introduction in the 1960s and is still not in place in some smaller stores. The United States flower industry began wider use of bar coding only in the last ten years.

16 In my casual testing of supermarkets in the NYMA, even stores with very detailed and sophisticated UPC coding for almost every other item will use only a "general produce" or "miscellaneous" category for a flower purchase.

17 A few supermarket chains track flower sales by species but they are exceptional. And whether they use this data to guide future flower orders is uncertain.

18 The lack of industry standards for names, sizes, and qualities of blooms noted in chapter 2 contributes to poor tracking in the supermarket sector. Codes for flowers were introduced in 1992 but seem to have limited use (Kirsten Bosnak, "Pride of the Andes," *Supermarket Floral,* April 1993). The Produce Marketing Association's recently formed Floral Data Standardization Task Force, with a membership of United States growers, distributors, and supermarket retailers, may eventually remedy this. Cindy Long, "Category Management: Good, Educated Decisions Based on Data and Common Sense," *Produce News—Floral Marketing,* April 7, 2003.

19 Cindy Long, "Petals Distributing Offers Valuable Service to Supermarket Floral Departments," *Produce News—Floral Marketing,* May 5, 2003.

20 The degree of dependence on such service varies with the supermarket. Sometimes it is a small part of a supermarket's total purchases.

21 Cindy Long, "2003 WF&FSA Convention Brings Insight," *Produce News—Floral Marketing,* May 5, 2003.

22 Although there are some big players; the Dutch firm Royal Ahold, for example, is a multinational corporation that owns several supermarket chains in the northeastern United States and in many other countries. See http://www.ahold.com (accessed December 15, 2005).

23 Also about 55,000 convenience stores, according http://www.supermarketnews.com (accessed December 15, 2005).

24 Furthermore, it is my understanding that Tesco also obtains a great many flowers from bouquet-making intermediaries based in Europe.

25 Moreover, other less powerful innovations that Miller contends contribute to consumer differentiation and indirectly to consumer agency are clearly evident in the United States cut flower provisioning system. These include the development of socioeconomic market niches and subcontracting to supplier networks.

26 Tim Linden, "Shippers Shouldn't Delay move to RFID, Says Wal-Mart's Bruce Peterson," *Produce News,* August 1, 2005.

27 "How to Manage Your Cut-Flower Shrinkage," *Superfloral Retailing,* June 2002.

28 Freddy Perkins, "Floral Notions," *Produce News—Floral Marketing,* January 13, 2003.

29 Cindy Long, "Petals Distributing Offers Valuable Service to Supermarket Floral Departments," *Produce News—Floral Marketing,* May 5, 2003.

30 This general globalizing process is described by Piore and Sabel (1984), Castells (1996), and Harrison (1997), among others.

31 Earlier unsuccessful efforts to participate in a United States industry that appears to offer profitable opportunities included the Pillsbury Company and United Fruit in the late 1960s and 1970s (Boydston 1972; Haley 1972; Vogt 1972). In Kenya the Brooke Bond Company and later Unilever entered and eventually abandoned cut flower growing (Jaffee 1994).

32 The third, Gerald Stevens Inc., was formed to consolidate traditional flower retailers. Operating between 1998 and 2001, it failed in part because of a business plan based on poor knowledge of the industry and because the individual entrepreneurial owners of the large traditional florist firms consolidated together were unable to function in a corporate structure.

33 I am indebted to Manuel Aragón of Teqflor Inc. for much of this account and to his article on USA Floral Products in *Flower News,* August 2001.

34 In 2000, Dole owned about 800 hectares of flower farms in Colombia, Ecuador, and Mexico (Dole Annual Report, December 30, 2000).

35 "Dole Fresh Flowers President Unveils New Facility," *Floral Management,* March 2002.

36 Society of American Florists, *Dateline,* April 11, 2003.

37 See Doreen Zavad, *Buying Floral Products on the Internet.* American Floral Endowment Report prepared by Ipsos-NPD, April 2002. Walmart.com also offers flowers and seemed to become aware of this preference in mid-2005. Many of its orders are filled by bouquet-making wholesalers, but by mid-2005 the site had partnerships with two order-gathering firms, FTD and Post & Petals. FTD supplies the flower arrangements in containers offered at the Walmart.com site and delivers them through its network of traditional florists. Given Wal-Mart's focus on low prices and the higher costs of working with traditional florists, it is hard to see how Walmart.com profits from this arrangement.

38 Mary Westbrook, "Rio's Grand Plan," *Floral Management,* June 2005.

39 Sam's Club is owned by Wal-Mart.

40 The other large importer-wholesale firms in Miami—Falcon Farms and Queens Flowers—also own hundreds of hectares of flower farms. Falcon Farms began as an importer-wholesaler but now owns over 200 hectares of farms in Colombia and Ecuador and also provides in-store flower services—stocking flower departments and supplying personnel—to about 300 supermarkets and other stores. Cindy Long, "Falcon Farms Takes Flight: Innovative Thinking Drives Company's Success from Farms to Supermarket Floral Departments," *Produce News—Floral Marketing,* April 7, 2003; Cindy Long, "Petals Distributing Offers Valuable Service to Supermarket Floral Departments," *Produce News—Floral Marketing,* May 5, 2003.

41 Recent innovations at the relatively new company Plantador Cía Ltda. suggest

yet another form of backward and forward linkage. Plantador, with nurseries in Ecuador and Colombia, is a propagating and sales agent for some of the most important European and United States rose breeders. It offers financing to potential growers and recently opened a Miami wholesale office to market the flowers of those same growers.

42 Castells's focus is on the economic and social changes following recent economic globalization and instantaneous communication. He seems to view *culture* as a minor aspect of the social but does not appear to define it. His view of the insubstantial cultural components of networks is linked to his vision of a contemporary breakdown in social communication that causes "social groups and individuals [to] become alienated from each other, and see the other as a stranger, eventually as a threat. In this process, social fragmentation spreads, as identities become more specific and increasingly difficult to share" (1996, 3).

43 Possibly this is a reason for the widespread preference in the FCFGCC for forming networks that include the same kin, ethnic, or national group.

Eight ⊛ Self and Signs

1 The role of consumer has come to rival in importance—and perhaps supplant— the traditionally important role of producer or worker. Discussion about "consumer confidence" and "consumer responsibility" in sustaining economies shows this shift. As Rachel Bowlby puts it, "We are all addressed as 'consumers' now, and the term is assumed to imply individual rights and respect that are lacking for those who are merely regarded as parents, patients, voters, omelet eaters and so on. The consumer is fast becoming the model of citizenship itself" (1996, 363).

2 For more on this perspective, see Giddens (1991), Miller (2001), and Boden (2003).

3 For consumption, see, among others, Bourdieu (1984); Baudrillard (1998); McCracken (1988); Dilley (1992); Campbell (1995); Miller (1995a); Carrier (1997); Clammer (1997); du Gay et al. (1997); Canclini (2001); Veblen ([1899] 1994); Douglas and Isherwood ([1976] 1996).

4 These changes followed the new social movements—students,' women's, civil rights, and ecological—of the 1960s and 1970s.

5 Giving bouquets to children for musical performances seems to have been customary in the late nineteenth century (Donzel 1997).

6 Some flower holidays are regionally popular. Memorial Day is one flower holiday virtually abandoned in the New York area, but in Utah it rivals Valentine's Day in importance for florists. Sweetest Day, established in 1920s to recognize orphans, soon included friends and co-workers. It did not catch on in New York but is immensely popular in Ohio. Other proposed flower holidays—Sweetheart Day, Good Neighbor's Day, and Mother-in-Law's Day—did not take hold anywhere (Noland 1997).

7 According to Castells (1997), among others, identities assemble through indi-

viduation and internalization and are "stronger sources of meaning than roles" because they are self-constructed. Social roles, in contrast, are shaped and confirmed by structure or "outside forces" (Mintz 1996).

8 The greeting card industry is another that depends heavily on floral metaphors and images.

9 These traditional meanings are what Burke (1996)—describing the growing importance of another cultural commodity, soap—calls "prior meanings." He has shown how immensely important they can be in enhancing a commodity's social and cultural power and therefore its commercial value.

10 Bourdieu (1984) calls this "habitus" and has shown it to be a powerful organizer of taste and society.

11 The authors also hypothesize that some plant and flower odors may mimic sex hormones, increasing the possibility that they prime positive moods.

12 Fragrance is one of the qualities of flowers that allow them to act as bridges to happy memories and what McCracken refers to as "displaced meaning." McCracken describes displacement of meaning as a cultural strategy for dealing with the inconsistency between the real and the ideal. People preserve their ideals by shifting them to any number of locations including a past "golden age" or a glorious future. Industrial urban societies, for example, praise rural and pastoral ones. Individuals may displace meaning to a happy childhood summer in a frictionless family or to a future with a more fulfilling occupation or more time to devote to gardening. Miserable situations can be tolerated by "the judicious displacement of certain hopes and ideals" (1988, 109). When meaning is relocated in space or time, in this fashion, it is protected from empirical test. Flowers' impermanence is useful in this respect. They act as very brief bridges, offering only short-lived contrast with present reality and the ideals it denies.

13 A study of flower-buying habits conducted some twenty years ago concluded that women who bought flowers for themselves did so impulsively at new convenient outlets such as supermarkets. Usually they were younger professional women in the 20–44 year age group (Scammon et al. 1982). A 1990 study of self-gifts (not flowers specifically) revealed a ritual aspect to the practice. There were rules of conduct and sacrifice as well as temporal spacing to ensure that the treat did not lose its value (Mick and DeMoss 1990; Miller 1998).

14 For more on this conception, see Slater and Binkley (2002).

15 A 2005 survey of floral gift giving conducted by the Society of American Florists found that 35 percent of respondents considered flowers "too much of a luxury" possibly because of flowers' perishability. Mary Westbrook, "10 Things Your Customers Aren't Telling You," *Floral Management,* May 2005.

16 As an example of this persistence Goody mentions requests in Europe and America for contributions to a charity as an alternative to funeral flowers (1993, 281).

17 Ipsos-AFE Consumer Tracking Study, 2001.

18 There are no statistics on flowers sales through convenience stores.

19 Other interviewees made similar remarks. Furthermore, a recent study of flower

gift giving conducted between 2002 and 2004 demonstrated that people give flowers primarily to make the recipient "feel special." Communicating feelings between the donor and recipient was the second most important reason followed closely by a third factor—the pleasure the donor received in choosing and giving flowers. Ipsos-AFE Consumer Tracking Study 2005.

20 A recent study (Haviland-Jones et al. 2005) suggests that flowers are still most likely to be placed in the communal spaces of a home, probably on the family dining or living room table.

21 The Society of American Florists, underscoring the importance of gift work for florists, recently commissioned another study of floral gift giving. *Floral Management,* May 2005.

22 Mother's Day appeared about 1907. A congressional resolution in 1914 officially established observance for the second Sunday of May. Initially, respect for mothers was marked by increased church attendance and the male practice of wearing a white carnation in a buttonhole. But Mother's Day observances eventually took the form of presenting gifts to mothers, usually flowers and often corsages. In May 1917 the Chicago Florist's Club placed an advertisement promoting the new holiday in an issue of the *Literary Review.* The magazine's 700,000 subscribers were considered by the florists to be "a desirable class of people" (Noland 1997). It was the first cooperative promotion among American florists and Noland credits this advertisement with establishing the floral holiday although it seems unlikely that a single advertisement, rather than a sustained promotion campaign, would have such an effect.

Secretaries' Day was introduced by floral retailers in the 1950s and was initially suggested by officials of the National Secretaries Association and the Dictaphone Corporation. Their intent was "to recognize good performance and increase the integrity of secretaries" (Noland 1997, 252). The holiday, extended and renamed Professional Secretaries Week, became popular and profitable for florists in Manhattan and other urban centers in succeeding decades, despite public confusion after attempts to change the name to Administrative Professionals Week. *Floral Management,* February 2005.

23 Religious holidays became increasingly commercialized in the late nineteenth century. "The Easter Parade, once a religious promenade, had become a fashion show" by late century, Gary Cross explains. The "commercialization of the festive calendar was in fact a smooth transition from the Victorian's romantic and aesthetic understanding of religious, moral, and even patriotic holidays" (2000, 52).

24 Romantic love was not in itself new. The notion that love alone should determine the choice of partner has carried weight at least since the eighteenth century. It expanded with the developing fashion system, with the spread of novel reading as a leisure activity, and with a general identification of women with sensitivity, gentleness, and emotionalism. Campbell argues that romanticism fueled consumerism and the taste for newness since it "legitimates the search for pleasure as a good in itself" (1987, 201).

25 "Valentine Vogue Is Inaugural Blue," *New York Times,* February 13, 1933.

26 Deirdre Carmody, "St. Valentine's Day Survives His Fall," *New York Times,* February 14, 1970.

27 See, for example, "Risky Proposals and Sweetheart Deals," *Wall Street Journal,* February 14, 2005, or Andrew Jacobs, "In City of Excess, Saying 'Marry Me' Can Be a Spectacle," *New York Times,* February 14, 2005.

28 Compared with prices in the early part of the twentieth century for Valentine's Day flowers these may not be so extravagant. In the late 1920s, according to the *New York Times,* "some lovers thought nothing of spending $50 to $100 for bouquets for their sweethearts." During the depression, however, $10 for a corsage of two or three orchids or roses at $1.50 to $12.50 a dozen became "adequate expressions of affection." See "Valentine Vogue Is Inaugural Blue," *New York Times,* February 13, 1933.

29 Ipsos-INPD for American Floral Endowment Consumer Tracking Study, 2004, and *Floral Cuttings,* January 2005.

30 Sending St. Valentine's Day greetings to someone other than a sweetheart was not that unusual in mid-twentieth century, when about half the greeting cards, usually of the joking sort, were sent to business and personal friends (Peggy LeBoutillier, "Hearts and Dollars," *New York Times,* February 13, 1949). But I believe giving flowers was, until fairly recently, confined to amorous gestures.

31 Cheal (1988) shows that women from all social classes are involved in a "discourse of relationships" and in relational cultures in which gift giving is important. Women are far more likely than men to give gifts, many to other women. Several theorists have shown the primary objective of gift giving is the construction or maintenance of a *relationship.* This is more important than the nature or value of the gift itself. See Gregory (1982), Cheal (1988), Mauss (1990), and Carrier (1995).

32 Kimberley Stevens, "Neighborhood Report: New York Valentines; For the Truly Avant-Garde, Black Is the Color of a True Love's Rose," *New York Times,* February 13, 2000.

33 Bourdieu demonstrated that status markers involve access to certain decoding skills that give admission to secondary and tertiary levels of meaning that lie beyond those immediately graspable by direct experience. Those who share these decoding skills occupy different social niches from those who do not share them. In this way, tastes both unite and separate and act to shape groups and their boundaries and to reproduce an individual's social status. In short, as Bourdieu famously observed: "Taste classifies, and it classifies the classifier." In the flower world, these decoding skills are shared by few people, so distinction often depends on the obvious extravagance of the presentation and the status attached to using particular florists.

34 Olivia Barker, "A War of the Roses Erupts at Oscar Time," USA Today, February 24, 2005.

35 New orchids are propagated through a tissue-culturing method discovered in 1963 (Reinikka [1972] 1995). This laboratory process produces thousands of iden-

tical orchids from a parent plant. Today many orchids destined for final consumption in Europe and the United States are cultured and partially raised in China, Costa Rica, and other places around the world.

36 See also William L. Hamilton, "The Half-Life of Must-Haves," *New York Times,* September 26, 2002.

37 See Laura M. Holson, "For $38,000, Get the Cake, and Mickey, Too," *New York Times,* May 24, 2003, and Ellyn Spragins, "Putting Your Wedding on a Pedestal," *New York Times,* June 1, 2003.

38 See Jennifer Saranow, "To Have and to Hit Up," *Wall Street Journal,* May 6, 2005; Lauren Lipton, "The Copycat Wedding," *Wall Street Journal,* May 21, 2004; and "Wedding Costs across the Nation," *Floral Management,* March 1999.

39 An *Economist* article about an increase in costly, fantasy weddings—evident in both the United Kingdom and United States—pointed out that middle-class women who once postponed childbearing to accommodate a career now also seem to delay marriage for the same reason. With an increase in later marriage, the marrying pair has higher average income than earlier couples and they are choosing to spend it on celebration ("Wedding Costs: For Poorer," *Economist,* June 14, 2003). Extravagant weddings occur in all classes, each with distinguishing features. See Otnes and Pleck (2003).

40 Alex Kuczynski, "The Curse Of the In Style Wedding," *New York Times,* June 2, 2002. The volatility of celebrity marriage and the lead-time required for publication are such, however, that bride and groom sometimes file for divorce before the issue celebrating their marriage appears at newsstands.

41 See, for example, *People* magazine's coverage of the "top secret," "surprise" wedding of Britney Spears and Kevin Federline in the October 4, 2004, issue. Thirteen pages of photographs showed details of dresses, accessories, and the thousands of red and hot pink roses employed to decorate the wedding space. The wedding of Donald Trump and Melania Knauss, celebrated "amidst family, friends and some 10,000 flowers," qualified for only eight pages in the February 7, 2005, issue. Dresses, food, and decoration, all reputedly donated to the fortunate couple, were photographed and described in detail.

42 The appeal of celebrities and other cultural icons and of associated goods such as fresh flowers is not new. Joseph Epstein explains that celebrity was an established phenomenon in late-nineteenth-century Paris, where "the Abbé Arthur Mugnier . . . wrote in his journal: 'What I like in society is the setting, the names, the beautiful homes, the reunion of fine minds, the contact with celebrities'" (2002, 195).

43 The brides I interviewed were overwhelmingly white, well-educated, and middle class, ranging in age from twenty-five to sixty.

44 Like many brides, Megan preserved flowers from her bouquet. The sentimental significance of the bouquet is evident from this common practice. Dried petals from the bouquet are sometimes incorporated in the wedding photograph album or some other form of remembrance.

45 The bridal role is one of many now commodified and purveyed by consumer magazines and this obviously has some effect on the current enthusiasm for it.

46 García Canclini (2001) makes a similar point about the way excessive consumption expenditures on rituals help to order and secure society.

47 Otnes and Pleck (2003) make similar observations.

48 Society of American Florists, *Dateline,* December 18, 2002.

49 See Erin White and Maureen Tkacik, "Spend It Like Beckham," *Wall Street Journal,* June 19, 2003, and Joe Pereira, "New Balance Sneaker Ads Jab at Pro Athletes' Pretensions," *Wall Street Journal,* March 10, 2005.

50 Bill Gouldin Jr. quoted in Debbie Hamrick, "Eye Level: 49 Percent of American Households Don't Buy Flowers, Plants," *Green Profit,* September/October 1999. Gouldin uses "commodity" in the sense of something uniform, substitutable, and lacking in special meaning.

51 See http://www.people.com (accessed December 15, 2005). The site also offers details of recent celebrity weddings.

52 Miller, Gauntlett, and others persuasively argue that the constant demand for celebrity news and opinions (as well as for sitcoms, soap operas, and magazine guidance on social behavior) is part of a need to understand how we should behave with others and how they should be behaving with us. In Miller's study, a dominant concern of shoppers is anxiety over reconciling discourses with other individuals and also in developing some self-confidence in determining for themselves what such persons are supposed to be like in the first place (Miller 2001b; Gauntlett 2002).

53 David Carr, "The News Media: In Style's World of Fashion," *New York Times,* February 25, 2002.

54 Martha Stewart, for example, is both a celebrated representative and a cultural disseminator of the tastes and lifestyles of the upper classes. The dispersal of her brand-name products in stores like K-Mart has also helped to democratize the furnishings and accessories of the upper social sectors. Martha Stewart gave coherence to a flower-filled lifestyle in her lifestyle magazines, television programs, and Internet flower shopping sites. The economic and cultural synergies between such celebrity opinion leaders and lifestyle magazines are also evident from the launch of Oprah Winfrey's Magazine *O* and the renaming of *McCall's* magazine *Rosie* after Rosie O'Donnell, a popular talk-show host.

55 David Carr and Lorne Manly, "At Star-Crazy Magazines, Brand's the Thing," *New York Times,* March 10, 2002.

56 Just five of the more than two hundred categories recognized by the National Directory of Magazines in 2001.

57 David Carr, "Technology and Media: Nimble Magazines Adjust to Fast Pace," *New York Times,* December 16, 2002.

58 David Carr, "The News Media: In Style's World of Fashion," *New York Times,* February 25, 2002.

59 I concentrated on glossy monthly magazines, omitting popular weeklies like *First*

for Women, as well as purely fashion and beauty magazines. The latter are popular in NYMA but rarely feature fresh flowers in editorial content or advertising. Some magazines like *Vogue,* although primarily concerned with fashion, also feature celebrities, popular culture, and aspects of "lifestyle" including fresh flowers, and were therefore included.

60 See Alex Kuczynski, "Media: Glimpse of the AOL-Time Warner Future," *New York Times,* March 13, 2000, and William L. Hamilton, "They've Got Your Numbers," *New York Times,* August 15, 2002.

61 Based on the magazines contributing reports to Audit Bureau of Circulations (ABC) that certifies circulation information (rate base) and readership demographics (age, home ownership, income, industry, job title, children, and so on) guaranteed to potential advertisers.

62 NYMSA is the New York Metropolitan Statistical Area defined by the Office of Management and Budget and includes the five New York City boroughs, Westchester, Rockland, and Putnam counties.

63 Regional wedding magazines issued annually and filled with local advertising also sell well, for example, *Connecticut Weddings, Atlanta Weddings,* and so on.

64 Also true in Monmouth and Ocean Counties in New Jersey, which were not included in this sample.

65 Magazine Publishers of America Fact Sheet 2001, Audit Bureau of Circulations (ABC) Data. Consumer magazine statements for December 2000. Certain categories such as bridal magazines that are of interest during a relatively brief life-cycle stage are almost entirely sold as single copies while the majority of home, lifestyle, and women's magazines are sold by subscription

66 This is not new. Readers' anxieties, aspirations, desires, daily needs, and attention were being sold as "use values to unseen third parties," that is, to marketers and advertisers, before the end of the nineteenth century (Ohmann 1996, 8). In the process, brand names, slogans, and packaging became familiar to a readership that identified them as signs that helped them to imagine and construct themselves as a particular segment of the middle class with particular economic and educational levels and certain patterns of consumption. Demographics about age, income, and so on enhanced this commodification of readers. The recent development of "psychographic data" correlating readers' attitudes, beliefs, lifestyles, and values with specific zip codes has refined that process while also improving magazine distribution and sales to advertisers (Magazine Publishers of America, glossary of circulation terminology, http://www.magazine.org/retail/2154.cfm, accessed December 15, 2006). This may also be a later refinement of "clustering demographics." See Schneider (1994).

67 James Bandler, "Real Competition: Real Simple is Now a Real Rival to Martha Stewart Living," *Wall Street Journal,* December 28, 2004.

68 Stuart Elliot, "The Media Business: Advertising: Time Inc. Decides a Magazine about Simplifying Life Might Strike a Chord among Harried Readers," *New York Times,* February 18, 2000.

69 Various writers similarly point out that constant change is an essential means of reshaping human needs in the service of capital expansion. See, for example, Harvey (1989), Lee (1993), and Cross (2000).

70 Quite possibly membership of such status groups is only a few hundred, just as it was in the Gilded Age.

Conclusion

1 As Ohmann (1996) points out, this is a process that has been underway since the end of the nineteenth century, but it has intensified in recent debates.

Note to Conclusion

Bibliography

Alarcón González, Sandra. 2000. "El tianguis global." In *Globalización: Una cuestión antropologica,* edited by Carmen Bueno Castellanos. México D.F.: Centro de Investigaciones y Estudios Superiores en Antropología Social.

Appadurai, Arjun. 1990. "Disjuncture and Difference in the Global Cultural Economy." *Public Culture* 2, no. 2: 1–24.

———. 1996. *Modernity at Large: Cultural Dimensions of Globalization.* Minneapolis: University of Minnesota Press.

Arrighi, Giovanni. 1994. *The Long Twentieth Century.* London: Verso.

Auslander, Leora. 1996. "The Gendering of Consumer Practices in Nineteenth-Century France." In *The Sex of Things: Gender and Consumption in Historical Perspective,* edited by Victoria de Grazia and Ellen Furlough. Berkeley: University of California Press.

Baudrillard, Jean. 1988. "Consumer Society" in Jean Baudrillard, *Selected Writings,* edited by Mark Poster. Cambridge: Polity Press.

———. 1998. *The Consumer Society: Myths and Structures.* London: Sage.

Bauman, Zygmunt. 2001. "Consuming Life." *Journal of Consumer Culture* 1: 9–29.

Baumol, William J., and Alan S. Blinder. 1994. *Economics: Principles and Policy.* New York: Harcourt, Brace.

Behe, Bridget K., and Dennis J. Wolnick. 1991. "Market Segmentation of Pennsylvania Floral Consumers by Purchase Volume and Primary Retail Outlet." *HortScience* 26, no. 10: 1328–31.

Berger, Suzanne, and Michael J. Piore. 1980. *Dualism and Discontinuity in Industrial Societies.* Cambridge: Cambridge University Press.

Bestor, Theodore C. 2001. "Supply-Side Sushi: Commodity, Market, and the Global City." *American Anthropologist* 103, no. 1: 76–95.

———. 2004. *Tsukiji.* Berkeley: University of California Press.

Blim, Michael L. 1992. "Introduction: The Emerging Global Factory and Anthropology." In *Anthropology and the Global Factory,* edited by Frances Abrahamer Rothstein and Michael L. Blim. New York: Bergin and Garvey.

———. 2000. "Capitalisms in Late Modernity." *Annual Review of Anthropology* 29: 25–38.

Block, Fred. 1990. *Post Industrial Possibilities.* Berkeley: University of California Press.

Boden, Deirdre. 2000. "Worlds in Action: Information, Instantaneity, and Global Futures Trading." In *The Risk Society and Beyond: Critical Issues of Social Theory,* edited by Barbara Adam, Ulrich Beck, and Joost Van Loon. London: Sage Publications.

Boden, Sharon. 2003. *Consumerism, Romance, and the Wedding Experience.* New York: Palgrave Macmillan.

Bonarriva, Joanna. 2003. USITC Industry and Trade Summary, Cut Flowers. Washington: United States International Trade Commission.

Bourdieu, Pierre. 1984. *Distinction: A Social Critique of the Judgment of Taste.* Cambridge, Mass.: Harvard University Press.

Bowlby, Rachel. 1996. "Soft Sell: Marketing Rhetoric in Feminist Criticism." In *The Sex of Things: Gender and Consumption in Historical Perspective,* edited by Victoria de Grazia and Ellen Furlough. Berkeley: University of California Press.

———. 1997. "Supermarket Futures." In *The Shopping Experience,* edited by Pasi Falk and Colin Campbell. London: Sage Publications.

Boydston, Charles B. 1972. "Problems and Opportunities in Developing Foreign Production of Ornamental Foliage Plants for United States Markets." Minneapolis: National Colloqium on Marketing Horticultural Crops.

Braudel, Fernand. 1984. *The Perspective of the World: Civilization and Capitalism, 15th–18th Century.* Vol. 3. New York: Harper and Row.

Breilh, Jaime. 2004. Ruptura del ecosistema floricola e impact en la Salud Humana en la Cuenca del Granobles: Abordaje participativo hacia un ecosistema saludable. Primera Fase del Proyecto. Technical Report. Quito: Centro de Estudios y Asesoria en Salud.

Brockway, Lucille H. 1979. *Science and Colonial Expansion: The Role of the British Royal Botanic Gardens.* New York: Academic Press.

Brown, Jane. 1982. *Gardens of a Golden Afternoon.* New York: Van Nostrand Reinhold.

Bruce Rubin Associates Inc. 1993. *Colombia Flower Council Industry Report.* Coral Gables, Fla.

Burke, Timothy. 1996. *Lifebuoy Men, Lux Women: Commodification, Consumption, and Cleanliness in Modern Zimbabwe.* Durham, N.C.: Duke University Press.

Burket, Stephen D., and Clark M. Workman. 1977. *Fresh Cut Flowers: Report to the President on Investigation No. TA-201–22 under Section 201 of the Trade Act of 1974.* Washington: United States International Trade Commission.

Burket, Stephen D., and Gerry Benedick. 1980. *Fresh Cut Roses: Report to the President on Investigation No. TA-201-42 under Section 201 of the Trade Act of 1974.* Washington: United States International Trade Commission.

Campbell, Colin. 1987. *The Romantic Ethic and the Spirit of Modern Consumerism.* Oxford: Basil Blackwell.

———. 1995. "The Sociology of Consumption." In *Acknowledging Consumption,* edited by Daniel Miller. London: Routledge.

———. 2005. "The Craft Consumer: Culture, Craft, and Consumption in a Postmodern Society." *Journal of Consumer Culture* 5, no. 1: 23–42.

Canclini, Néstor García. 2001. *Consumers and Citizens: Globalization and Multicultural Conflicts.* Minneapolis: University of Minnesota Press.

278

Carbonneau, Marvin, Carolynn Van Namen, et al. 1997. "Growing, Wholesaling, and Importing." In *A Centennial History of the American Florist,* edited by Frances Porterfield Dudley. Topeka, Kan.: Florists' Review Enterprises.

Cardol, Goossen. 1988. "Ruimte voor Agribusiness-Complexen: Structuur, positie en dynamiek van het Noordlimburgse tuinbouwcomplex vanuit functioneel, geografisch en regionaal perspectief." *Geography and History.* Nijmegen: Catholic University.

Carpenter, William J. 1972. "Cost of Doing Business: A Survey of Wholesale Florists." Research Report for Wholesale Florists and Florist Supplies of America.

Carrier, James G. 1995. *Gifts and Commodities: Exchange and Western Capitalism since 1700.* London: Routledge.

——, ed. 1997. *Meanings of the Market.* Oxford: Berg.

Castells, Manuel. 1996. *The Rise of the Network Society.* Oxford: Blackwell.

——. 1997. *The Power of Identity.* Oxford: Blackwell.

Cheal, David. 1988. *The Gift Economy.* London: Routledge.

Chen, Hsiang-shui. 1992. *Chinatown No More: Taiwan Immigrants in Contemporary New York.* Ithaca, N.Y.: Cornell University Press.

Clammer, John. 1997. *Contemporary Urban Japan: A Sociology of Consumption.* Oxford: Blackwell.

Collins, Carolyn A., Barbara Fails, and Oliver Schabenberger. 1999. "Analysis of Michigan Full-Service Retail Florist Businesses by Annual Gross Sales." *HortScience* 34, no. 1: 144–48.

Collins, Jane L. 2000. "Tracing Social Relations in Commodity Chains: The Case of Grapes in Brazil." *Commodities and Globalization: Anthropological Perspectives,* edited by Angelique Haugerud, Priscilla M. Stone, and Peter D. Little. Lanham, Md.: Rowman and Littlefield.

Cook, Ian. 1994. "New Fruits and Vanity: Symbolic Production in the Global Food Economy." In *From Columbus to ConAgra: The Globalization of Agriculture and Food,* edited by Alessandro Bonanno, Lawrence Busch, William H. Friedland, Lourdes Gouveia, and Enzo Mingione. Lawrence: University Press of Kansas.

Coronil, Fernando. 1997. *The Magical State.* Chicago: University of Chicago Press.

Cowan, Ruth Schwartz. 1983. *More Work for Mother: The Ironies of Household Technology from the Open Hearth to the Microwave.* New York: Basic Books.

Cross, Gary. 2000. *An All-Consuming Century: Why Commercialism Won in Modern America.* New York: Columbia University Press.

Csikszentmihalyi, Mihaly, and Eugene Rochberg-Halton. 1981. *The Meaning of Things: Domestic Symbols and the Self.* Cambridge: Cambridge University Press.

Cunningham, Michael. 2002. *The Hours.* New York: Picador USA.

Dicker, John. 2005. *The United States of Wal-Mart.* New York: Tarcher/Penguin.

Dilley, R., ed. 1992. *Contesting Markets: Analyses of Ideology, Discourse, and Practice.* Edinburgh: Edinburgh University Press.

Donzel, Catherine. 1997. *The Book of Flowers.* Paris: Flammarion.

Douglas, Mary, and Baron Isherwood. [1976]. 1996. *The World of Goods.* London: Routledge.

279

Dow, Sheila C. 1994. "Uncertainty." In *The Elgar Companion to Radical Political Economy,* edited by Philip Arestis and Malcolm Sawyer. Aldershot, U.K.: Edward Elgar Publishing.

Dudden, Faye E. 1983. *Serving Women: Household Service in Nineteenth-Century America.* Middletown, Conn.: Wesleyan University Press.

du Gay, Paul. 2004a. "Devices and Disposition: Promoting Consumption." *Consumption, Markets and Culture* 7, no. 2: 99–105.

———. 2004b. "Self-Service: Retail, Shopping, and Personhood." *Consumption, Markets and Culture* 7, no. 2: 149–63.

du Gay, Paul, Stuart Hall, Linda Janes, Hugh Mackay, and Keith Negus. 1997. *Doing Cultural Studies: The Story of the Sony Walkman.* London: Sage.

Dunlop, M. H. 2000. *Gilded City: Scandal and Sensation in Turn-of-the-Century New York.* New York: HarperCollins.

ECLAC. [United Nations Economic Commission for Latin America and the Caribbean]. 2004. *Social Panorama of Latin America.* New York: United Nations.

Edelman, Marc. 1999. *Peasants against Globalization: Rural Social Movements in Costa Rica.* Stanford, Calif.: Stanford University Press.

Epstein, Joseph. 2002. *Snobbery: The American Version.* New York: Houghton Mifflin.

Eskilon, Melissa Dodd. 1997. "Plants and Flowers." In *A Centennial History of the American Florist,* edited by Frances Porterfield Dudley. Topeka, Kan. Florists' Review Enterprises, Inc.

Evans, Peter. 1995. *Embedded Autonomy: States and Industrial Transformation.* Princeton, N.J.: Princeton University Press.

Fairbanks, Michael, and Stace Lindsay. 1997. *Plowing the Sea: Nurturing the Hidden Sources of Growth in the Developing World.* Boston: Harvard Business School Press.

Fine, Ben. 2002. *The World of Consumption: The Material and Cultural Revisited.* London: Routledge.

Fine, Ben, and Ellen Leopold. 1993. *The World of Consumption.* London: Routledge.

Firat, Fuat A. 1991. "The Consumer in Postmodernity." *Advances in Consumer Research* 18: 70–76.

First Research. 1978. *Marketing and Economic Analysis of the Floriculture Industry in the United States.* Miami, Fla.

Fleming, Laurence, and Alan Gore. 1979. *The English Garden.* London: Michael Joseph.

Floral Marketing Association. 1999. *Report on Mass-Market Floral Operations.* Washington: Food Marketing Institute and Floral Marketing Association.

Flores, Sara Maria Lara, and Ofelia Becerril Quintana. 1995. "Reestructuración productiva y mercado de trabajo rural: El caso de la floricultura de exportación en el Estado de México." In *Globalización, deterioro ambiental y reorganización social en el campo,* edited by Hubert C. De Grammont. México D.F.: Juan Pablos Editores.

Foner, Nancy. 2000. *From Ellis Island to JFK: New York's Two Great Waves of Immigration.* New Haven, Conn.: Yale University Press.

Fossum, M. Truman. 1973. *Marketing Facts for Floriculture.* Washington: Society of American Florists.

Freidberg, Susanne. 2004. *French Beans and Food Scares: Culture and Commerce in an Anxious Age.* Oxford: Oxford University Press.

Friedemann-Sanchez, Greta. 2002. "Challenging Patriarchy in the Transnational Floriculture Industry: Household Economics, Identity, and Gender in Colombia." Ph.D. diss., University of Minnesota.

———. 2004. "Assets, Wage Income and Social Capital in Intrahousehold Bargaining among Women Workers in Colombia's Cut-Flower Industry." Paper presented at the Workshop on Women and the Distribution of Wealth, November 2004, Yale Center for International and Area Studies.

———. 2006. *Assembling Flowers and Cultivating Homes.* Lanham, Md.: Lexington Books.

Friedland, William H. 1994. "The New Globalization: The Case of Fresh Produce." In *From Columbus to ConAgra: The Globalization of Agriculture and Food,* edited by Alessandro Bonanno, Lawrence Busch, William H. Friedland, Lourdes Gouveia, and Enzo Mingione. Lawrence: University Press of Kansas.

———. 2001. "Reprise on Commodity Systems Methodology." *International Journal of Sociology of Agriculture and Food* 9, no. 1: 82–103.

Friedman, Thomas L. 2000. *The Lexus and the Olive Tree.* New York: Anchor Books.

———. 2005. *The World Is Flat.* New York: Farrow, Straus and Giroux.

Gauntlett, David. 2002. *Media, Gender, and Identity.* London: Routledge.

Gereffi, Gary. 1994. "The Organization of Buyer-Driven Global Commodity Chains: How U.S. Retailers Shape Overseas Production Networks." In Gereffi and Korzeniewicz, eds., *Commodity Chains and Global Capitalism.* Westport, Conn.: Praeger.

———. 2001. "Beyond the Producer-driven / Buyer-driven Dichotomy: The Evolution of Global Value Chains in the Internet Era." *IDS Bulletin* 32, no. 3: 30–40.

Gereffi, Gary, John Humphrey, Raphael Kaplinsky, and Timothy J. Sturgeon. 2001. "Introduction: Globalisation, Value Chains, and Development." *IDS Bulletin* 32, no. 3: 1–8.

Gereffi, Gary, and Miguel Korzeniewicz, eds. 1994a. *Commodity Chains and Global Capitalism.* Westport, Ct.: Praeger.

Gereffi, Gary, and Miguel Korzeniewicz. 1994b. "Introduction: Global Commodity Chains." In Gereffi and Korzeniewicz, eds., *Commodity Chains and Global Capitalism.* Westport, Conn.: Praeger.

Giddens, Anthony. 1991. *Modernity and Self-Identity.* Stanford, Calif.: Stanford University Press.

Gillis, J. R. 1997. *A World of their Own Making: A History of Myth and Ritual in Family Life.* Oxford: Oxford University Press.

Goldfrank, Walter L. 1994. "Fresh Demand: The Consumption of Chilean Produce in the United States." In Gereffi and Korzeniewicz, eds., *Commodity Chains and Global Capitalism.* Westport, Conn.: Praeger.

González, Humberto. 1998. "Sustainability and Global Commodity Chains: Export Agriculture in Mexico." Conference of Latin American Studies Association. Panel AGRO 07. "La intermediación en las cadenas internacionales de mercancías agrícolas." Chicago, Illinois.

Bibliography

Goodrich, Dana C. Jr. 1972. *The Future Role of Terminal Wholesale Markets in the U.S. Floriculture Industry*. Minneapolis: National Colloqium on Marketing Horticultural Crops.

Goody, Jack. 1993. *The Culture of Flowers*. Cambridge: Cambridge University Press.

Gordon, Jean, and Jan McArthur. 1988. "American Women and Domestic Consumption, 1800–1920: Four Interpretive Themes." In *Making the American Home: Middle Class Women and Domestic Material Culture, 1840–1940,* edited by Marilyn Ferris Motz and Pat Browne. Bowling Green, Ohio: Popular Press.

Granovetter, M. 1985. "Economic Action and Social Structure: The Problem of Embeddedness." *American Journal of Sociology* 91, no. 3: 481–510.

Gregory, C. A. 1982. *Gifts and Commodities*. London: Academic Press.

Gudeman, Stephen. 2001. *The Anthropology of Economy: Community, Market, and Culture*. Oxford: Blackwell.

Haley, B. Jr. 1972. *Projected Changes in the Market Functions of Grower Shippers of Floricultural Crops in the United States*. Minneapolis: National Colloqium on Marketing Horticultural Crops.

Harrison, Bennett. 1997. *Lean and Mean: The Changing Landscape of Corporate Power in the Age of Flexibility*. New York: Guilford Press.

Harvey, David. 1989. *The Condition of Postmodernity*. Cambridge, Mass.: Basil Blackwell.

Hasha, Gene. 1999. *The European Union's Common Agricultural Policy: Pressures for Change—An Overview*. Washington: U.S. Department of Agriculture/Economic Research Service.

Haviland-Jones, Jeannette, Holly Hale Rosario, Patricia Wilson, and Terry R. McGuire. 2005. "An Environmental Approach to Positive Emotion: Flowers." *Evolutionary Psychology* 3: 104–32.

Heilbroner, Robert, and William Milberg. 1995. *The Crisis of Vision in Modern Economic Thought*. Cambridge: Cambridge University Press.

Hirst, Paul, and Grahame Thompson. 1999. *Globalization in Question: The International Economy and the Possibilities of Governance*. Cambridge: Polity Press.

Hobsbawm, Eric. [1968]. 1999. *Industry and Empire: The Birth of the Industrial Revolution*. New York: New Press.

Homberger, Eric. 1994. *The Historical Atlas of New York City*. New York: Henry Holt.

Hooker, Mark T. 1999. The History of Holland. Westport, Conn.: Greenwood Press.

Horkheimer, Max, and Theodor W. Adorno. [1944]. 1997. "The Culture Industry: Enlightenment as Mass Deception." *The Dialectic of Enlightenment*. New York: Continuum.

Hughes, Alex. 2000. "Retailers, Knowledges, and Changing Commodity Networks: The Case of the Cut Flower Trade." *Geoforum* 31: 175–90.

——. 2004. "Accounting for Ethical Trade: Global Commodity Networks, Virtualism, and the Audit Economy." In *Geographies of Commodity Chains,* edited by Alex Hughes and Suzanne Reimer. London: Routledge.

Huizinga, W. 1986. *Dutch Agricultural Development, 1600–1880*. The Hague: Landbouw–Economisch Instituut Stafadeling.

Humphery, Kim. 1998. *Shelf Life.* Cambridge: Cambridge University Press.

Humphrey, John, and Hubert Schmitz. 2000. *Governance and Upgrading: Linking Industrial Cluster and Global Value Chain Research.* IDS Working Paper 120. Brighton, U.K.: Institute of Development Studies.

Hyams, Edward. 1966. *The English Garden.* New York: Harry N. Abrams.

Jaffee, Steven M. 1994. "Contract Farming in the Shadow of Competitive Markets: The Experience of Kenyan Horticulture." In *Living under Contract,* edited by Peter Little, D. Watts, and Michael J. Watts. Madison: University of Wisconsin Press.

Jameson, Fredric. 1991. "The Cultural Logic of Late Capitalism." In *Postmodernism, or, The Cultural Logic of Late Capitalism.* Durham, N.C.: Duke University Press.

Jekyll, Gertrude, and Edward Mawley. [1902] 1983. *Roses.* Salem, N.H.: Ayer Company.

Jerardo, Alberto. 2002. *Floriculture and Nursery Crops Situation and Outlook Yearbook.* Washington: U.S. Department of Agriculture / Market and Trade Economics Division, Economic Research Service.

——. 2004. *Floriculture and Nursery Crops Situation and Outlook Yearbook.* Washington: U.S. Department of Agriculture / Market and Trade Economics Division, Economic Research Service.

Johnson, Doyle C. 1990. *Floriculture and Environmental Horticulture Products: A Production and Marketing Statistical Review, 1960–88.* Washington: U.S. Department of Commerce/Economic Research Service and National Technical Information Service.

Klein, Naomi. 1999. *No Logo: Taking Aim at the Brand Bullies.* New York: Picador.

Kopytoff, Igor. 1986. "The Cultural Biography of Things: Commoditization as Process." In *The Social Life of Things: Commodities in Cultural Perspective,* edited by Arjun Appadurai. New York: Cambridge University Press.

Korovkin, Tanya. 2003. "Cut-Flower Exports, Female Labor, and Community Participation in Highland Ecuador." *Latin American Perspectives* 30, no. 131: 18–42.

Korzeniewicz, Miguel. 1994. "Commodity Chains and Marketing Strategies: Nike and the Athletic Footwear Industry." In Gereffi and Korzeniewicz, eds., *Commodity Chains and Global Capitalism.* Westport, Conn.: Praeger.

Korzeniewicz, Roberto P., Walter Frank, and Miguel E. Korzeniewicz. 1995. "Vines and Wines in the World-Economy." In *Food and Agrarian Orders in the World-Economy,* edited by Philip McMichael. Westport, Conn.: Praeger.

Korzeniewicz, Roberto, P. Martin, and William Martin. 1994. "The Global Distribution of Commodity Chains." In Gereffi and Korzeniewicz, eds., *Commodity Chains and Global Capitalism.* Westport, Conn.: Praeger.

Krupa, Chris. 2001. "Producing Neoliberal Rural Spaces: Labor and Community in Ecuador's Cut-Flower Sector." Paper presented at the Latin American Studies Association meeting, September 2001, Washington, D.C.

Lamont, Michele, and Virág Molnár. 2001. "How Blacks Use Consumption to Shape their Collective Identity." *Journal of Consumer Culture* 1: 31–45.

Lash, Scott, and John Urry. 1987. *The End of Organized Capitalism.* Madison: University of Wisconsin Press.

Leach, William. 1993. *Land of Desire: Merchants, Power, and the Rise of a New American Culture*. New York: Vintage.

Lee, Martyn J. 1993. *Consumer Culture Reborn*. London: Routledge.

Lie, John. 1997. "The Sociology of Markets." *Annual Review of Sociology* 23: 341–60.

Little, Peter D. and Michael J. Watts. 1994. *Living under Contract: Contract Farming and Agrarian Transformation in Sub-Saharan Africa*. Madison: University of Wisconsin Press.

Llambi, Luis. 1994. "Opening Economies and Closing Markets: Latin American Agriculture's Difficult Search for a Place in the Emerging Global Order." In *From Columbus to ConAgra: The Globalization of Agriculture and Food*, edited by Alessandro Bonanno, Lawrence Busch, William H. Friedland, Lourdes Gouveia, and Enzo Mingione. Lawrence, Kan.: University Press of Kansas.

Mabberley, D. J. 1993. *The Plant-Book: A Portable Dictionary of the Higher Plants*. Cambridge: Cambridge University Press.

Maharaj, N., and G. Dorren. 1995. *The Game of the Rose*. Utrecht: International Books.

Mann, Susan Archer. 1990. *Agrarian Capitalism in Theory and Practice*. Chapel Hill: University of North Carolina Press.

Marchand, Roland. 1985. *Advertising the American Dream: Making Way for Modernity 1920–1940*. Berkeley: University of California Press.

Marcus, George E. 1995. "Ethnography in/of the World System: The Emergence of Multi-Sited Ethnography." *Annual Review of Anthropology* 24: 95–117.

Mauss, M. 1990. *The Gift*. New York: W. W. Norton.

McConnell, Campbell R., and Stanley L. Brue. 1996. *Macroeconomics: Principles, Problems, and Policies*. New York: McGraw-Hill.

McCracken, Grant. 1988. *Culture and Consumption: New Approaches to the Symbolic Character of Consumer Goods and Activities*. Bloomington: Indiana University Press.

McGuire, Diane Kostial. 1989. *Gardens of America: Three Centuries of Design*. Charlottesville, Va.: Thomasson-Grant.

Meier, V. 1999. "Cut-Flower Production in Colombia—A Major Development Success Story for Women?" *Environment and Planning* 31: 273–89.

Mena, Norma. 1999. *Impacto de la floricultura en los campesinos de Cayambe*. Quito: Instituto de Ecología y Desarrollo de las Comunidades Andinas IEDECA.

Mick, David Glen, and Michelle DeMoss. 1990. "To Me from Me: A Descriptive Phenomenology of Self-Gifts." *Advances in Consumer Research* 17: 677–82.

Miller, Daniel. 1995. *Acknowledging Consumption*. London: Routledge.

———. 1997. *Capitalism: An Ethnographic Approach*. Oxford: Berg.

———. 1998. *A Theory of Shopping*. Ithaca, N.Y.: Cornell University Press.

———. 2001a. *The Dialectics of Shopping*. Chicago: University of Chicago Press.

———, ed. 2001b. *Home Possessions*. Oxford: Berg.

Miller, Michael B. 1981. *The Bon Marché*. Princeton, N.J.: Princeton University Press.

Min, Pyong Gap. 1996. *Caught in the Middle: Korean Merchants in America's Multiethnic Cities*. Berkeley: University of California Press.

———. 1998. *Change and Conflicts: Korean Immigrant Families in New York.* Needham Heights, Mass.: Allyn and Bacon.

Mintz, Sidney W. 1985. *Sweetness and Power.* New York: Viking Penguin.

———. 1996. *Tasting Food, Tasting Freedom: Excursions into Eating, Culture and the Past.* Boston: Beacon Press.

Money-Collins, Holly. 1997. "Weddings." In *A Centennial History of the American Florist,* edited by Frances Porterfield Dudley. Topeka, Kan.: Florists' Review Enterprises.

Naylor, R. T. (1987). *Hot Money and the Politics of Debt.* New York: Simon and Schuster.

Nichols, Rose Standish. [1902]. 2003. *English Pleasure Gardens.* Boston: David R. Godine.

Noland, Dianne. 1997. "Holidays." In *A Centennial History of the American Florist,* edited by Frances Porterfield Dudley. Topeka, Kan.: Florists' Review Enterprises.

Norton, Mary Beth, et al. 2001. *A People and a Nation: A History of the United States.* Sixth Edition. Boston: Houghton Mifflin.

Ohmann, Richard M. 1996. *Selling Culture: Magazines, Markets, and Class at the Turn of the Century.* New York: Verso.

Orlean, Susan. 2000. *The Orchid Thief.* New York: Ballantine Books.

Otnes, Cele, and Elizabeth H. Pleck. 2003. *Cinderella Dreams: The Allure of the Lavish Wedding.* Berkeley: University of California Press.

Palan, Zonia, and Carlos Palan. 1999. "Employment and Working Conditions in the Ecuadorian Flower Industry." Working paper. International Labor Organization Sectoral Activities Program.

Park, Kyeyoung. 1997. *The Korean American Dream: Immigrants and Small Business in New York City.* Ithaca, N.Y.: Cornell University Press.

Peiss, Kathy. 1996. "Making Up, Making Over: Cosmetics, Consumer Culture, and Women's Identity." In *The Sex of Things: Gender and Consumption in Historical Perspective,* edited by Victoria de Grazia and Ellen Furlough. Berkeley: University of California Press.

Perez-Aleman, Paola. 2003. "Decentralised Production, Organisation and Institutional Transformation: Large and Small Firm Networks in Chile and Nicaragua." *Cambridge Journal of Economics* 27, no. 6: 789–805.

Piore, Michael J., and Charles F. Sabel. 1984. *The Second Industrial Divide.* New York: Basic Books.

Plattner, Stuart. 1989a. "Economic Behavior in Markets." *Economic Anthropology.* Stanford, Calif.: Stanford University Press.

———. 1989b. "Markets and Marketplaces." *Economic Anthropology.* Stanford: Stanford University Press.

Plumptre, George. 1993. *The Garden Makers.* London: Pavilion Books.

Pollan, Michael. 2001. *The Botany of Desire.* New York: Random House.

Poole, Deborah. 1997. *Vision, Race, and Modernity: A Visual Economy of the Andean Image World.* Princeton, N.J.: Princeton University Press.

Porter, Michael E. 1990. *The Competitive Advantage of Nations.* New York: Free Press.

Prince, Tom, and Tim Prince. 1998. *California Cut-Flower Production & Industry Trends.* Columbus, Ohio: Self-published marketing research report.

Product Board for Horticulture. 2000. *Strength in the Chain.* Zoetermeer: Product Board for Horticulture.

Raynolds, Laura T. 1994. "Institutionalizing Flexibility: A Comparative Analysis of Fordist and Post-Fordist Models of Third World Agro-Export Production." In Gereffi and Korzeniewicz, eds., *Commodity Chains and Global Capitalism.* Westport, Conn.: Praeger.

Reinikka, Merle A. [1972]. 1995. *A History of the Orchid.* Portland, Ore.: Timber Press.

Roseberry, William. 1996. "The Rise of Yuppie Coffees and the Reimagination of Class in the United States." *American Anthropologist* 98, no. 4: 762–75.

Royer, Kenneth R. 1998. *Retailing Flowers Profitably.* Lebanon, Pa.: Royer Publishing.

Rutz, H., and B. Orlove, eds. 1989. *The Social Economy of Consumption.* Lanham, Md.: University Press of America.

Salamea, Lucia, and William F. Waters. 1995. "La cuestión de género en la reestructuración de la agricultura ecuatoriana." In *El rostro femenino del mercado de trabajo rural en America Latina,* edited by Sara Maria Flores. Caracas: UNRISD-Nueva Sociedad.

Sanjek, Roger. 2001. "Color-Full before Color Blind: The Emergency of Multiracial Neighborhood Politics in Queens, New York City." *American Anthropologist* 102, no. 4: 762–72.

Scammon, Debra L., Roy T. Shaw, and Gary Bamossy. 1982. "Is a Gift Always a Gift?" *Advances in Consumer Research* 9: 531–36.

Schama, Simon. 1987. *The Embarrassment of Riches: An Interpretation of Dutch Culture in the Golden Age.* New York: Vintage Books.

Schneider, Jane. 1999. "In and Out of Polyester: Desire, Disdain, and Global Fibre Competitions." *Anthropology Today* 10, no. 4: 3–10.

Schor, Juliet B. 1999. *The Overspent American: Why We Want What We Don't Need.* New York: Harper Perennial.

Seaton, Beverly. 1988. "Making the Best of Circumstances: The American Woman's Back Yard Garden." In *Making the American Home: Middle Class Women and Domestic Material Culture, 1840–1940,* edited by Marilyn Ferris Motz and Pat Browne. Bowling Green, Ohio: Popular Press.

Shetter, William, Z. 1997. *The Netherlands in Perspective: The Dutch way of Organizing a Society and its Setting.* Utrecht: Centrum Buitenlanders.

Silvergleit, Ira. 2001. *The Changing Floriculture Industry: A Statistical Overview by the Society of American Florists' Business and Economic Trends Committee.* Alexandria, Va.: Society of American Florists.

Slater, Don. 1997. *Consumer Culture and Modernity.* Cambridge: Polity Press.

Slater, Don, and Sam Binkley. 2002. "Existentialism with an Historical Imagination: A Round-Table Discussion with Agnes Heller and Marshall Berman." *Journal of Consumer Culture* 2, no. 1: 119–34.

Smart, Alan. 1997. "Oriental Despotism and Sugar-Coated Bullets: Representations of the Market in China." In Carrier, ed., *Meanings of the Market.*

Smith, Sally, Diane Auret, Stephanie Barrientos, Catherine Dolan, Karin Kleinbooi, Chosani Njobvu, Maggie Opondo and Anne Tallontire. 2004. *Ethical Trade in African Horticulture: Gender Rights and Participation.* Brighton, U.K.: Institute of Development Studies.

Stanford, Lois. 2000a. "The Globalization of Agricultural Commodity Systems: Examining Peasant Resistance to International Agribusiness." In *Commodities and Globalization: Anthropological Perspectives,* edited by Angelique Haugerud, Priscilla M. Stone, and Peter D. Little. Lanham, Md.: Rowman and Littlefield.

——. 2000b. "The Globalization of California's Avocado Industry: Anthropological Perspectives on the Role of Organizations." Paper presented at American Anthropological Association Meeting, San Francisco.

Statistiek, Central Bureau voor de. 1999. CBS-Landbouwtelling. Agricultural Census, 1999. Voorburg, Netherlands: Central Bureau voor de Statistiek.

Stole, Inger L. 2003. "Televised Consumption: Women, Advertisers, and the Early Daytime Television Industry." *Consumption, Markets and Culture* 6, no. 1: 65–80.

Strijker, D. 1986. *Structural Development towards a Modern Agricultural Sector, 1880–1985.* The Hague: Landbouw-Economisch Instituut Stafadeling.

Sturgeon, Timothy J. 2001. "How Do We Define Value Chains and Production Networks?" *IDS Bulletin* 32, no. 3: 9–18.

Talbot, John M. 1995. "The Regulation of the World Coffee Market: Tropical Commodities and the Limits of Globalization." In *Food and Agrarian Orders in the World-Economy,* edited by Philip McMichael. Westport, Ct.: Praeger.

Taplin, Ian M. 1994. "Strategic Reorientation of U.S. Apparel Firms." In Gereffi and Korzeniewicz, eds., *Commodity Chains and Global Capitalism.* Westport, Conn.: Praeger.

Tenenbaum, David. 2002. Would a Rose Not Smell as Sweet? *Environmental Health Perspectives* 110: 240–47.

Tewari, M. 1999. "Successful Adjustment in Indian Industry: The Case of Ludhiana's Woollen Knitwear Cluster." *World Development* 27, no. 9: 1651–52.

Tranberg Hansen, Karen. 2000. *Salaula: The World of Secondhand Clothing and Zambia.* Chicago: University of Chicago Press.

Traube, Elizabeth G. 1996. "'The Popular' in American Culture." *Annual Review of Anthropology* 25: 127–51.

Treadway, Robert L. 1997. "Origins: The Floral Industry before 1897." In *A Centennial History of the American Florist,* edited by Frances Porterfield Dudley. Topeka, Kan.: Florists' Review Enterprises.

Trip, Ger. 2000. *Decision Making and Economic Performance of Flower Producers.* Ph.D. Dissertation. Wageningen: Wageningen University.

van der Horst, Han. 1996. *The Low Sky: Understanding the Dutch.* The Hague: Scriptum Books.

Van Loon, Joost. 2000. "Virtual Risks in an Age of Cybernetic Reproduction." In *The*

Risk Society and Beyond: Critical Issues of Social Theory, edited by Barbara Adam, Ulrich Beck, and Joost Van Loon. London: Sage Publications.

Van Stuijvenberg, J. H., ed., 1961. *De Bloemisterij in Nederland: Uitgave ter gelenheid van het 50 jarig bestaan van de vereniging "de Nederlandse Bloemisterij."* The Hague: Nederlandse Economische Hogeschool.

Veblen, Thorstein. [1899]. 1994. *The Theory of the Leisure Class.* New York: Penguin.

Verdaasdonk, Dorothee. 2002. "Changes in Cultural Repertoires: Choices Made by Movie Goers." Paper presented at American Sociological Association Meeting at Erasmus University Rotterdam.

Vernon, Raymond. 1966. "International Investment and International Trade in the Product Cycle." *Quarterly Journal of Economics* 80, no. 2: 190–207.

———. 1979. "The Product Cycle Hypothesis in a New International Environment." *Oxford Bulletin of Economics and Statistics:* 255–67.

Verrilli, Kay. 1997. *Violet Notes.* Rhinebeck, N.Y.: Museum of Rhinebeck History.

Vogt, George. 1972. *Changes in Retailing Floricultural Crops to meet the Future Demands of U.S. Consumers.* Minneapolis: National Colloqium on Marketing Horticultural Crops.

Wallerstein, Immanuel. 1974. *The Modern World System.* New York: Academic Press.

———. 2004. *World-Systems Analysis.* Durham, N.C.: Duke University Press.

Ward, Ronald W. 1997. "Evaluating PromoFlor: Have the Promotions of Fresh Cut Flowers and Greens Had an Impact?" Gainesville: University of Florida, Food and Resource Economics Dept.

Warde, Alan. 1997. *Consumption, Food and Taste: Cultural Antimonies and Commodity Culture.* London: Sage Publications.

———. 2000. "Eating Globally: Cultural Flows and the Spread of Ethnic Restaurants." In *The Ends of Globalization: Bringing Society Back In,* edited by Don Kalb, Marco van der Land, Richard Staring, Bart van Steenbergen, and Nico Wilterdink. Lanham, Md.: Rowman and Littlefield.

Waters, W. E., and J. W. Prevatt. 1983. "A Description of the Scope, Magnitude and Challenges facing the Florida Floricultural Industry in the 1980s." Bradenton: University of Florida, Agricultural Research and Education Center.

Weekly Florists' Review. 1997. 100th Year Collectors' Edition. Vol. 188.

Wells, Richard. 1999. The "Sensationalist Press." Master's Thesis. New York: New School for Social Research.

Wharton, Edith. 1924. *Old New York New Year's Day (The 'Seventies).* New York: D. Appleton and Company.

White, Harrison, C. 1981. "Where Do Markets Come From?" *American Journal of Sociology* 87, no. 3: 517–47.

White, Roger. 1997. *Cut Flowers: A Study of Major Markets.* Geneva: International Trade Centre UNCTAD/WTO.

Williams, Peter, Phil Hubbard, David Clark, and Nigel Berkeley. 2001. "Consumption, Exclusion, and Emotion: The Social Geographies of Shopping." *Social and Cultural Geography* 2, no. 2: 203–20.

Wilson, Suzanne, and Marta Zambrano. 1994. "Cocaine, Commodity Chains, and Drug Politics: A Transnational Approach." In Gereffi and Korzeniewicz, eds., *Commodity Chains and Global Capitalism*. Westport, Conn.: Praeger.

Wolf, Eric R. 1990. *Europe and the People without History*. Berkeley: University of California Press.

Woloch, Nancy. [1996]. 2002. *Women and the American Experience: A Concise History*. New York: McGraw-Hill.

Wrigley, Neil, and Michelle Lowe. 2002. *Reading Retail: A Geographical Perspective on Retailing and Consumption Spaces*. London: Arnold.

Zobbe, Henrik. 2001. "The Economic and Historical Foundation of the Common Agricultural Policy in Europe." Fourth European Historical Economics Society Conference, Merton College, Oxford.

Zukin, Sharon. 1995. *The Cultures of Cities*. Oxford: Blackwell.

289

Index

Craven, William (4th Earl of Craven), 29–30

cultural significance of flowers, 3–4, 55–56, 228–29, 235n2; among immigrant groups, 131; communication of innovation and change, 189–91; "culture of flowers," 16–18; fragrance of flowers, 197–99, 269nn11–12; markers of group identity and status, 205–7; for middle class consumers, 16–32, 130–31; symbolic production using flowers, 140; for upper class consumers, 22–24, 33–34. *See also* identity and meaning of flowers; media impact; social relationships

Cunningham, Michael, 130, 141–43, 144

Defoe, Daniel, 74

delphiniums, 112, 229, 257n5, 265n7

department stores, 17–18, 236–37n1, 241n12

designers. *See* freelance floral designers

developmental states, 79

development of new flowers. *See* new flower development

Devonshire, 6th Duke of (William George Spencer Cavendish), 22

Diana, Princess of Wales, 30, 210–11

direct sales system, 40–41, 48–49, 118–22, 242n23

distribution. *See* middlemen

diversification, 6, 13

Dole Fresh Flowers, 14, 159–60, 184, 186–89; production in Latin America by, 72, 230, 252n23, 253n38, 267n34; retail website of, 148, 263n36

Donzel, Catherine, 25, 30

double primroses, 26

Douglas, Mary, 212

Downing, Andrew Jackson, 19, 237n6

dry shipping, 250n28

du Gay, Paul, 193

Dunlop, M. H., 32

dwarf flowering cherries, 24

Easter, 45, 202, 270n23

economic factors, 4, 7, 9, 235n2; changing tastes of consumers, 13–14, 236nn7–8; comparative advantage, 93–96, 252–53n29, 255n53; consignment system, 34, 39–40, 47, 241–42n16, 242n21, 242nn23–24; decline of U.S. growers, 44–47; direct sales system, 40–41, 48–49, 242n23; distance from market, 35, 241–42n16; exchange rates, 80–81, 88–89, 94, 169, 253–54n39; global expansion of flower growing, 42–43, 55–56, 72–73, 243n30, 250n31; high order competitive advantage, 94–96; investments of capital, 55, 71–72, 87–88, 89, 96, 250n31, 252n20, 253n36; low order competitive advantage, 94; major cut flowers vs. specialty cut flowers, 54, 62, 242n20; NAFTA's impact, 43, 67; nature-exporting nations, 93–94; political stability, 88, 253n36, 255n55; price of flowers, 33, 37, 38, 62, 246n55, 256n59, 257–58n9; for retail florists, 51, 52, 246nn50–51; state support, 74, 75, 77–79, 86–87, 250n1, 251n9, 251–52nn13–14; trade controls, 9, 65–68; for wholesale florists, 47–50, 49, 50, 245n44, 245n46, 245n48; for working women, 53, 246n54, 269n13. *See also* innovation and change

Ecuador, 81–96, 112–26, 229–30, 252n17; bouquet assembly in, 113, 122, 158, 259n24; commercial flower growing in, 13, 41, 42, 43, 50, 63–65, 82–84; consignment marketing system in, 113–16, 117; currency values and exchange rates in, 88–89; direct marketing system in, 118–19; exports from, 58, 59, 60, 82–85, 96, 116, 248n18, 252n21; farm size in, 112–13; growing conditions in, 97, 256n1;

294

importer-wholesaler firms in Miami, 188, 267nn40–41; innovation and change in, 93, 119–22, 127–28; investment capital in, 82, 87–88, 96, 121, 252n20; knowledge acquisition in, 113, 123–26; labor costs in, 89–90, 93; local grower-shippers in, 113, 258–59n19; low order competitive advantages of, 93–96; marketing relationships in, 85, 113–14, 124–26; new flowers in, 123–26, 259–60n25; pregnant employees in, 91; racial hierarchies in, 92; rose crop of, 1–2, 42, 65, 66, 82, 83, 96, 256n59, 265n7; Russian demand for roses from, 83, 87, 96, 252n25; shipping and middlemen costs in, 116, 117, 259nn20–21; short-cycle crops in, 83–84; state support in, 86–87, 252n19; trade controls in, 65; trade organizations in, 85, 253n30; transportation costs in, 69, 83, 87; transportation infrastructure in, 82, 86–87; U.S. trade policies toward, 65, 66, 67; women laborers in, 90–93; working conditions in, 90–93, 255nn50–51

Elle Decor magazine, 218, 220

English Landscape Gardening School, 19–20, 237n3

ethnographic methodology, 9–12

European Union: Common Agricultural Policy (CAP) of, 78, 251n12; currency values and exchange rates of, 81; farm subsidies in, 252n19; flower markets in, 75, 96, 251n11; impact on Netherlands flower policies of, 77–78; import duties in, 67; phytosanitary inspection requirements of, 67–68

Evans, Peter, 79

Expoflores, 85, 89, 252n21, 253n30

exported flowers, 6, 11, 58, 59, 63–65, 93–96, 247n3; currency values and exchange rates, 80–81, 88–89; marketing challenges of, 85–86; market knowledge, 107–8; repackaging and loss of national origins, 110–11

F. W. Battenfeld and Son, 243n37

Fairbanks, Michael, 87, 93–94, 252–53n29, 253–54n39

Falcon Farms, 267n40

'Fancy Amazon' roses, 125

farms. See growers

farm stands, 46

Farrand, Beatrix Jones, 237–38n9

fashion, 27–28, 239n26

FCFGCC. See Fresh-Cut Flower Global Commodity Chain

field-grown flowers, 63, 112

filières. See global commodity chains

Fine, Ben, 6–7, 228

Fine Gardening magazine, 223

'First Red' rose, 258n13

Florafax International, 245–46n49

Floral Data Standardization Task Force, 266n18

floral designers, 132–34, 139–40, 149, 153, 190, 223–25, 231

floral foam, 31

Floral Trade Council, 44

Flores Colombianas, 42

floriculture education, 78, 126–27, 228, 253n31; in Ecuador, 113, 123–26; in Netherlands, 105–9

Florida, 34–35, 36, 44, 50, 241n14. See also Miami flower market

Florists' Transworld Delivery (FTD), 148, 245–46n49

Flower Council of Holland, 111–12

flower markets, 13, 34, 128–29, 245nn42–43. See also Aalsmeer flower market; Miami flower market; New York wholesale flower market

Flowernet.com, 187–88

Flower Promotion Organization, 213–14

295

297

provising growers, 127; knowledge acquisition in, 78, 97–99, 105–9, 113, 123–27, 163, 253n31, 256n2; symbolic production using flowers, 140. *See also* new flower development; specialty chain

insecticides, 38, 91

inspections, 2, 10, 67–68, 249n22, 261n9

In Style magazine, 216, 218, 220

Inter-American Development Bank, 82

International Cut Flower Growers Association, 62

International Monetary Fund, 82

Internet technology, 71, 250n30, 263n36; flower gift services, 137–38; flower-selling sites, 148

irises, 257n5

Isabell, Robert, 140, 167–68

Isherwood, Baron, 212

Israel, 67, 110, 247n4, 253n36

Italian growers, 43

ixieas, 62, 248n11

Japan, 67

jasmines, 33

Jekyll, Gertrude, 19, 21, 25, 237–38n9, 238n15

journeys of flowers, 1–3

Keeler, Thomas, 243n27

Kenya, 255–56n56, 267n31; contract flower growing in, 121; growing conditions in, 97, 256n1; off-shore auctions, 110

Kew Gardens, 21, 238n13

knowledge. *See* floriculture education; innovation and change; networks of relationships

Kohler faucet advertisements, 214–16

Kopytoff, Igor, 190–91

Korea, 86

Krupa, Chris, 89–90, 255n51

labor: in automated greenhouses, 101–2; bouquet-making assembly lines, 158–59; costs for off-shore growers, 42, 86, 89–90, 93, 243n29; immigrant populations, 261n16; for wedding bouquets, 30; women's labor, 93–96, 254nn45–48; working conditions, 90–93, 254n46, 255nn50–51

Lager and Hurrell orchids, 29

Land of Desire (Leach), 241n12

landscape gardening, 19–20, 237n3

"language of flowers" fads, 18, 29–30, 204–5, 237n2

Latin America. *See names of specific countries*

Leach, William, 241n12

Lee, Martyn, 221

Leopold, Ellen, 7, 228

liatrises, 65

Lie, John, 98

lilies, 12, 20, 100, 229, 265n7; desirability of, 149; diversification of, 58; forbears of, 21; replacement plants for, 105; U.S. consumption of, 257n5; in wedding bouquets, 30

lilies of the valley *(Convallaria),* 30, 62

Lindsay, Stace, 87, 93–94, 252–53n29, 253–54n39

lisianthus, 12, 100, 123–24, 229

literature on gardening, 18–19, 91, 237–38nn7–9; trade organization publications, 62, 245–46n49. *See also* magazines; media impact

local grower-shippers, 40–41, 113, 242n22, 258–59n19

Loudon, John Claudius, 19, 237n4

Luria, Daniel, 256n58

Macy's flower show, 140

magazines, 8–9, 14, 17–18, 192–93, 216–25; advertising in, 213–16, 221–23, 274n61; celebrity portrayals in, 215–16, 273n52, 273n54; circulation of,

new flower development (*cont.*)
231–34, 238n17; breeding and, 69–70,
108–9, 259–60n25; hybridization
and, 69–70, 94; knowledge acquisition in, 105–9, 113, 123–26, 253n31;
profitable characteristics in, 38; role
of middle class consumers in, 21–22,
24
New York Metropolitan Area (NYMA),
130, 228–29, 274n62; consumers in,
7–8, 130–31; convenience stores in,
132–34, 138–39, 141–43, 160; freelance
floral designers in, 139–40, 149, 153;
growers in, 27, 35–38, 143, 236n10;
immigrant populations in, 131, 137,
260nn5–7, 261n16, 262n24; imports
to, 132, 133, 261nn9–10; Korean stores
in, 141–42, 262n24; magazine circulation in, 218, 219, 220, 221, 273–
74n59, 274nn63–64; mass retailers
in, 261n12; mobile wholesalers in,
159–61; Mother's Day flower survey
of, 150–51; retail sales in, 132–52,
263n42; specialty cut flower sales in,
132, 133; supermarket floral services
in, 146; traditional florists in, 134–35;
wholesalers in, 152–61, 260n1
New York wholesale flower market, 2,
42, 152–55, 245n42
New Zealand, 67, 68–69
Nicaragua, 230
Nichols, Rose Standish, 237–38n9

obsolescence of passé flowers, 8
Ohio growers, 44
Ohmann, Richard M., 17, 224
Old New York New Year's Day (Wharton), 15
orange blossoms, 18, 29–31
orchids (*Phalaenopsis*), 12, 147,
238nn16–17; growers of, 247n6,
265n7; hunting of, 20; as markers of
identity and status, 206–7; popu-

larity of, 21–22; tissue-culture propagation method for, 271–72n35
organization of global systems. *See* governance
oriental lilies, 21, 149
Orlean, Susan, 20, 22
Otnes, Cele, 208
out-of-season flowers, 22–34, 130, 232–
33, 242–43n25

pampas grass, 24
pansies, 24
Paxton, Joseph, 19, 22, 237n4
peddlers, 143
peonies, 26, 39, 167–68, 265n6
People magazine, 215
Perez-Aleman, Paola, 230
peripheral regions, 5
Peru, 67, 248n18
Peruvian lilies. *See* alstroemerias
phytosanitary inspections, 67–68,
249n22, 261n9
Pillsbury Company, 267n31
Pinchbeck Nursery, 243n37
Piore, Michael J., 38–39
plant hunting, 18, 20–21, 238nn11–12
Plattner, Stuart, 172
Pleck, Elizabeth H., 208
Pollan, Michael, 97, 124
pompon chrysanthemums, 35–39, 83–
84. *See also* chrysanthemums
Porter, Michael, 94
potted plants, 52, 146, 147, 257n8,
259n23, 261n12
power. *See* governance of global commodity chains
predatory states, 79
primroses, 24
producer-driven systems, 5, 235n2n4
production. *See* growers
professional associations. *See* trade organizations
proms, high school, 150

303

305

306

Catherine Ziegler received her Ph.D. in social and cultural anthropology from the New School for Social Research. She teaches history and anthropology at Parsons: The New School for Design. She is the author of *The Harmonious Garden: Color, Form, and Texture* (1996).

Library of Congress Cataloging-in-Publication Data

Ziegler, Catherine.
Favored flowers: culture and economy in a global system / Catherine Ziegler.
p. cm.
Includes bibliographical references and index.
ISBN 978-0-8223-4007-2 (cloth : alk. paper)
ISBN 978-0-8223-4026-3 (pbk. : alk. paper)
1. Cut flower industry. I. Title.
SB443.Z54 2007
331.892'835966—dc22   2006102944